HUMANITARIAN DISARMAMENT

This book argues that the humanitarian framing of disarmament is not a novel development, but rather represents a re-emergence of a much older and long-standing sensibility of humanitarianism in disarmament. It rejects the 'big bang' theory that presents the Anti-Personnel Landmines Convention 1997, and its successors – the Convention on Cluster Munitions 2008, and the Treaty on the Prohibition of Nuclear Weapons 2017 – as a paradigm shift from an older traditional state-centric approach towards a more progressive humanitarian approach. It shows how humanitarian disarmament has a long and complex history, which includes these treaties.

This book further argues that the attempt to locate the birth of humanitarian disarmament in these treaties is part of the attempt to cleanse humanitarian disarmament of politics, presenting humanitarianism as a morally superior discourse in disarmament. However, humanitarianism carries its own blind spots and has its own hegemonic leanings. It may be silencing other potentially more transformative discourses.

Treasa Dunworth is an Associate Professor at the Faculty of Law, University of Auckland, New Zealand. She has acted as consultant for the New Zealand Ministry of Foreign Affairs and Trade, providing legal advice regarding nuclear weapons disarmament. In 2017, she joined the delegation of United Nations Institute for Disarmament Research (UNIDIR) at the negotiations for the Prohibition of Nuclear Weapons Treaty.

CAMBRIDGE STUDIES IN INTERNATIONAL AND COMPARATIVE LAW: 148

Established in 1946, this series produces high quality, reflective and innovative scholarship in the field of public international law. It publishes works on international law that are of a theoretical, historical, cross-disciplinary or doctrinal nature. The series also welcomes books providing insights from private international law, comparative law and transnational studies which inform international legal thought and practice more generally.

The series seeks to publish views from diverse legal traditions and perspectives, and of any geographical origin. In this respect it invites studies offering regional perspectives on core *problématiques* of international law, and in the same vein, it appreciates contrasts and debates between diverging approaches. Accordingly, books offering new or less orthodox perspectives are very much welcome. Works of a generalist character are greatly valued and the series is also open to studies on specific areas, institutions or problems. Translations of the most outstanding works published in other languages are also considered.

After seventy years, Cambridge Studies in International and Comparative Law sets the standard for international legal scholarship and will continue to define the discipline as it evolves in the years to come.

A list of books in the series can be found at the end of this volume.

HUMANITARIAN DISARMAMENT

An Historical Enquiry

TREASA DUNWORTH
University of Auckland

CAMBRIDGE
UNIVERSITY PRESS

University Printing House, Cambridge CB2 8BS, United Kingdom

One Liberty Plaza, 20th Floor, New York, NY 10006, USA

477 Williamstown Road, Port Melbourne, VIC 3207, Australia

314-321, 3rd Floor, Plot 3, Splendor Forum, Jasola District Centre, New Delhi - 110025, India

103 Penang Road, #05-06/07, Visioncrest Commercial, Singapore 238467

Cambridge University Press is part of the University of Cambridge.

It furthers the University's mission by disseminating knowledge in the pursuit of education, learning and research at the highest international levels of excellence.

www.cambridge.org
Information on this title: www.cambridge.org/9781108462969
DOI: 10.1017/9781108644105

First published 2020
First paperback edition 2022

A catalogue record for this publication is available from the British Library

Library of Congress Cataloging in Publication data
Names: Dunworth, Treasa Moira, author.
Title: Humanitarian disarmament : an historical enquiry / Treasa Dunworth, University of Auckland,
Description: Cambridge, United Kingdom; New York, NY, USA : Cambridge University Press, 2020. | Series: Cambridge studies in international and comparative law | Based on author's thesis (doctoral – University of Melbourne, 2019) issued under title: 'What's past is prologue' : humanitarian disarmament from St Petersburg to New York. | Includes bibliographical references and index.
Identifiers: LCCN 2020004391 | ISBN 9781108473927 (hardback) | ISBN 9781108644105 (epub)
Subjects: LCSH: Humanitarian law. | Arms control. | War (International law)
Classification: LCC KZ6471 .D86 2020 | DDC 341.7/33–dc23
LC record available at https://lccn.loc.gov/2020004391

ISBN 978-1-108-47392-7 Hardback
ISBN 978-1-108-46296-9 Paperback

CONTENTS

ACKNOWLEDGEMENTS

I owe very many thanks stretching back over many years. To my PhD supervision team at Melbourne University: Tim McCormack, Tania Voon and Robert Mathews. In different ways, each was a major source of support and I am grateful to all three. But there were many others who provided me with feedback, sources, ideas, information and challenges over the years as I worked on this project (writing may well be a solitary endeavour, but developing the underlying ideas most certainly is not!): Maartje Abbenhuis, Dylan Asafo, John Borrie, Lyndon Burford, John Burroughs, Tim Caughley, Hilary Charlesworth, Maddy Chiam, Monique Cormier, Kate Dewes, Thomas Gregory, Rob Green, Dell Higgie, Anna Hood, Natalia Jevglevskaja, Dan Joyner, Ken Keith, Frank Kirwan, Dino Kritsiotis, Kobi Leins, Rain Liivoja, Campbell McLachlan, Janet McLean, Andrew Mitchell, Manfred Nowak, Anne Orford, Dianne Otto, Josh Paine, Sundhya Pahuja, Daniel Rietiker, Kevin Riordan, Richard Slade, Lucy Stewart, Lisa Tabassi and Andrew Webster.

I want to especially acknowledge and express heartfelt thanks to all the wonderful librarians who helped me along the way: in particular to Stephanie Carr and Tracey Thomas at Auckland University. Like all of us who work within the academy, I am indebted to our librarians for their expertise, knowledge and professionalism.

My thanks reach back to long before the formal start of this project. In 1995 I started work as a Researcher for the Harvard Sussex Program on Arms Control and Arms Limitation, at the time led by Julian Perry Robinson (at Sussex) and Matthew Meselson (at Harvard). Although I did not realise it at the time, it was here that the seeds of this project were planted. It is fitting therefore that both Julian and Matt appear in the following pages: Matt, then a young academic, led a Commission to enquire into the effects of use of herbicides by the United States during the Vietnam War (Chapter 4); Julian represented the World Health Organization at the series of meetings convened as part of the 'Human Rights in Armed Conflict' initiative through the 1970s which was an important humanitarian campaign responding to the human suffering engendered by the Vietnam War (Chapter 4). Matt and Julian stand as testament to the long history of the quest for disarmament propelled by a humanitarian sensibility – even if neither of them would express it like that. I was privileged to work for them and I am grateful to both of them for the many opportunities they afforded me. From that period of my professional life, I also acknowledge and thank Sergei Batsanov, Daniel Feakes, Walter Krutzsch, Kathleen Lawand, Lisa Tabassi and Anil Wadhwa. Conversations and discussions with all of them raised questions for me that I have only started to explore in this project.

Outside of my professional life, thanks are also due: to Lisa Tremewan who first inspired me to study law and from whom I learnt about the need to acknowledge law's limitations, even as we strive to make real its possibilities; to Dympna, Eilish and Moira who encouraged their little sister every step of the way (and long before I embarked on this project); to Janet and Steven and all of my extended family in New Zealand and elsewhere, for forgiving (I hope!) my absences, silences and neglect. I dedicate this thesis to my mother-in-law, Ngaire Wilkinson, who by virtue of being from a different generation and a different time, did not have my opportunities, but who ensured that I was able to embrace those that came my way.

Finally, I am eternally grateful to Marty for his love and support. He has been my steadfast champion, has accepted and facilitated my absences whether physical or otherwise, and has been waiting patiently for me to return.

TABLE OF CASES

Coenca Brothers *v*. Germany, (Greco-German Mixed Arbitral Tribunal) Annual Digest 1927–8, Case No 389

Greenham Women against Cruise *v*. Ronald Reagan and the Joint Chiefs of Staff 755 F.2d 34; 1985 U.S. App LEXIS 29227

Kiriadolou *v*. Germany, (Greco-German Mixed Arbitral Tribunal) Annual Digest 1929–30, Case No 301

Legality of the Use by a State of Nuclear Weapons in Armed Conflict (Advisory Opinion) (Judgment) [1996] ICJ Rep 66

Legality of the Threat of Use of Nuclear Weapons (Advisory Opinion) (Judgment) [1996] ICJ Rep 226

Military and Paramilitary Activities in and against Nicaragua (Nicaragua *v*. United States) (Merits) [1986] ICJ Rep 14

Nuclear Tests (Australia *v*. France) (Judgment) [1974] ICJ Rep 253

Nuclear Tests (New Zealand *v*. France) (Judgment) [1974] ICJ Rep 457

Pulp Mills on the River Paraguay (Argentina *v*. Paraguay) ICJ Rep [2010] 14

The Case of the SS 'Lotus' (France *v*. Turkey) (Judgment) [1927] PCIJ (ser A) No 10

TABLE OF TREATIES

Agreement for United Nations Relief and Rehabilitation Administration (27 November 1944)

Amended Protocol on Prohibitions or Restrictions on the Use of Mines, Booby-Traps and Other Devices, opened for signature 31 May 1995, 35 ILM 1206 (entered into force 3 December 1998)

Charter of the International Military Tribunal, 82 UNTS 279 (signed and entered into force 8 August 1945)

Charter of the United Nations 1945

Comprehensive Nuclear-Test-Ban Treaty, opened for signature 24 September 1996, 35 ILM 1439 (not yet in force)

Convention on Cluster Munitions, opened for signature 3 December 2008, 2688 UNTS 39 (entered into force 1 August 2010)

Convention on Prohibitions or Restrictions on the Use of Certain Conventional Weapons which may be deemed to be Excessively Injurious or to have Indiscriminate Effects (with Protocols I, II and III), opened for signature 10 April 1981, 1342 UNTS 137 (entered into force 2 December 1983)

Convention on the Prohibition of the Development, Production, Stockpiling and Use of Chemical Weapons and on their Destruction, opened for signature 13 January 1993, 1975 UNTS 45 (entered into force 29 April 1997)

Convention on the Prohibition of the Development, Production and Stockpiling of Bacteriological (Biological) and Toxin Weapons and on their Destruction, opened for signature 10 April 1972, 1015 UNTS 163 (entered into force 26 March 1975)

Convention on the Prohibition of the Use, Stockpiling, Production and Transfer of Anti-Personnel Mines and on their Destruction, opened for signature 3 December 1997, 2056 UNTS 211 (entered into force 1 March 1999)

Convention on the Rights of Persons with Disabilities, opened for signature 30 March 2007, 2515 UNTS 3 (entered into force 3 May 2008)

Declaration Renouncing the Use, in Time of War, of Explosive Projectiles under 400 Grammes Weight, opened for signature 29 November 1868, [1901] ATS 125 (entered into force 11 December 1868)

Geneva Convention for the Amelioration of the Condition of the Wounded and Sick in Armed Forces in the Field, opened for signature 12 August 1949, 75 UNTS 31 (entered into force 21 October 1950)

Geneva Convention for the Amelioration of the Condition of the Wounded in the Field, opened for signature 22 August 1864, 129 Consol TS (entered into force 22 June 1865)

Geneva Convention for the Amelioration of the Condition of the Wounded, Sick and Shipwrecked Members of the Armed Forces at Sea, opened for signature 12 August 1949, 75 UNTS 85 (entered into force 21 October 1950)

Geneva Convention Relative to the Protection of Civilian Persons in Time of War, opened for signature 12 August 1949, 75 UNTS 287 (entered into force 21 October 1950)

Geneva Convention Relative to the Treatment of Prisoners of War, opened for signature 12 August 1949, 75 UNTS 135 (entered into force 21 October 1950)

Protocol Additional to the Geneva Conventions of 12 August 1949, and Relating to the Protection of Victims of International Armed Conflicts, opened for signature 12 December 1977, 1125 UNTS 3 (entered into force 7 December 1978)

Protocol Additional to the Geneva Conventions of 12 August 1949, and Relating to the Protection of Victims of Non-International Armed Conflicts, opened for signature 12 December 1977, 1125 UNTS 609 (entered into force 7 December 1978)

Protocol for the Prohibition of the Use in War of Asphyxiating, Poisonous or Other Gases, and of Bacteriological Methods of Warfare, opened for signature 17 June 1925, (1929) XCIV LNTS 65–74 (entered into force 8 February 1928)

Protocol on Explosive Remnants of War to the Convention on Prohibitions or Restrictions on the Use of Certain Conventional Weapons which may be Deemed to be Excessively Injurious or to Have Indiscriminate Effects (Protocol V), opened for signature 28 November 2003, 2399 UNTS 100 (entered into force 12 November 2003)

Rome Statute of the International Criminal Court, opened for signature 17 July 1998, 2187 UNTS 90 (entered into force 1 July 2002)

The Antarctic Treaty, signed 1 December 1959, 402 UNTS 71 (entered into force 23 June 1961)

Treaty Banning Nuclear Weapon Tests in the Atmosphere, in Outer Space and under Water, opened for signature 5 August 1963, 480 UNTS 43 (entered into force 10 October 1963)

Treaty between the United States of America and the Union of Soviet Socialist Republics on the Elimination of their Intermediate-Range and Shorter-Range Missiles 1987 signed 8 December 1987, 27 ILM 1186 (entered into force 1 June 1988)

Treaty of Peace between the Allied and Associated Powers and Germany, signed 28 June 1919 (entered into force 10 January 1920)

Treaty on the Non-Proliferation of Nuclear Weapons, opened for signature 1 July 1968, 729 UNTS 161 (entered into force 5 March 1970)

Treaty on the Prohibition of Nuclear Weapons, opened for signature 20 September 2017 (not yet in force)

ABBREVIATIONS

AEC	Atomic Energy Commission (United Nations)
Amended Protocol II	Amended Protocol on the Prohibitions or Restrictions on the Use of Mines, Booby-Traps and Other Devices 1995
AP I	Protocol Additional to the Geneva Conventions of 12 August 1949, and Relating to the Protection of Victims of International Armed Conflicts 1977
AP II	Protocol Additional to the Geneva Conventions of 12 August 1949, and Relating to the Protection of Victims of Non International Armed Conflicts 1977
APLM	Anti-personnel landmine
APLM Convention	Convention on the Prohibition of the Use, Stockpiling, Production and Transfer of Anti-Personnel Mines and on their Destruction 1997
CCA	Commission for Conventional Armaments (United Nations)
CCM	Convention on Cluster Munitions 2008
CCW	Convention on the Prohibitions or Restrictions on the Use of Certain Conventional Weapons which may be deemed to be Excessively Injurious or to have Indiscriminate Effects 1980
CD	Conference on Disarmament
Charter	Charter of the United Nations 1945
Covenant	Covenant of the League of Nations 1920
CTBT	Comprehensive Nuclear-Test-Ban Treaty 1996
CWC	Convention on the Prohibition of the Development, Production, Stockpiling and Use of Chemical Weapons and on their Destruction 1993
ECOSOC	Economic and Social Council of the United Nations
ERW	Explosive remnants of war
Geneva Conventions 1949	Geneva Convention for the Amelioration of the Condition of the Wounded and Sick in Armed Forces in the Field 1949, Geneva Convention for the

	Amelioration of the Condition of the Wounded, Sick and Shipwrecked Members of the Armed Forces at Sea 1949, Geneva Convention Relative to the Protection of Civilian Persons in Time of War 1949, Geneva Convention Relative to the Treatment of Prisoners of War 1949
Geneva Protocol	Protocol for the Prohibition of the Use in War of Asphyxiating, Poisonous or Other Gases, and of Bacteriological Methods of Warfare 1925
IAEA	International Atomic Energy Agency
ICBL	International Campaign to Ban Landmines
ICJ	International Court of Justice
ICRC	International Committee of the Red Cross
INF	Intermediate Nuclear Forces Treaty 1987
MTCA	Mixed Temporary Commission on Armaments of the League of Nations
NAC	New Agenda Coalition
NAM	Non-Aligned Movement
NGO	Non-Governmental Organisation
NPT	Treaty on the Non-Proliferation of Nuclear Weapons 1968
OEWG	Open-Ended Working Group
PAC	Permanent Armaments Commission of the League of Nations
Protocol II	Protocol on the Prohibitions or Restrictions on the Use of Mines, Booby-Traps and Other Devices to the Convention on Prohibitions or Restrictions on the Use of Certain Conventional Weapons which may be deemed to be Excessively Injurious or to have Indiscriminate Effects 1980
PTBT	Partial Test Ban Treaty 1963
SIPRI	Stockholm International Peace Research Institute
TPNW	Treaty on the Prohibition of Nuclear Weapons 2017
UN	United Nations
UNDP	United Nations Development Programme
UNESCO	United Nations Educational, Scientific and Cultural Organization
UNIDIR	United Nations Institute for Disarmament Research
UNRRA	United Nations Relief and Rehabilitation Agency
WCP	World Court Project
WHO	World Health Organization
WILPF	Women's International League for Peace and Freedom

1

Introduction

I The Context

In 1997, the International Campaign to Ban Landmines (ICLB) and Jody Williams were awarded the Nobel Peace Prize 'for their work for the banning and clearing of anti-personnel mines'.[1] The Committee explained that: 'The ICBL and Jody Williams started a process which in the space of a few years changed a ban on anti-personnel mines from a vision to a feasible reality. The [Anti-Personnel Landmines] Convention ... is to a considerable extent a result of their important work'.[2] Some commentators heralded a new era of 'humanitarian disarmament' with suggestions that the Anti-Personnel Landmines Convention (APLM Convention) was the first to breathe life into the concept.[3] A commonly held assumption was that a key change was the way in which anti-personnel landmines were 'reframed' as a humanitarian problem and thus able to be approached within the parameters of human security rather than through an arms control lens using the logic of national security.[4]

There seemed to be broad consensus that a shift had occurred away from the orthodox national security paradigms that had calcified disarmament

[1] Nobel Media, 'Nobel Peace Prize 1997' (Press Release, 10 October 1997) www.nobelprize.org.

[2] Ibid.

[3] Convention on the Prohibition of the Use, Stockpiling, Production and Transfer of Anti-Personnel Mines and on their Destruction, opened for signature 3 December 1997, 2056 UNTS 211 (entered into force 1 March 1999). See Denise Garcia, 'Humanitarian Security Regimes' (2015) 91(1) *International Affairs* 55, 57.

[4] Mandy Turner, Neil Cooper and Michael Pugh, 'Institutionalised and Co-opted: Why Human Security Has Lost Its Way' in David Chandler and Nik Hynek (eds.), *Critical Perspectives on Human Security: Rethinking Emancipation and Power in International Relations* (London: Routledge, 2010), pp. 83, 87.

efforts in the preceding decades, towards a humanitarian approach espousing a humanitarian assessment of the impact on weapons.[5]

As Rebecca Johnson put it:

> Disarmament, once regarded as the business of governments and their military experts, is driven now by concepts of international and human security, intersecting with globalist perspectives in which governance is assessed by international standards, with value attached to human rights and humanitarian effects that erode the primacy formerly accorded to national security justifications, military force, and state sovereignty.[6]

II The Argument

My core claim is that this humanitarian framing of weapons and disarmament is not a novel development, but rather represents a re-emergence of a much older and long-standing sensibility of humanitarianism in disarmament discourse.[7] I reject the 'big bang' theory that presents the APLM Convention as a paradigm shift from an older traditional state-centric approach towards a more progressive humanitarian approach to the regulations of weapons. My argument is that humanitarian disarmament, far from being a creation of the campaign against anti-personnel landmines, in fact has a long, complex and intensely politicised history. I see the APLM Convention as part of that history, not as its genesis.

Why does the starting point of 'humanitarian disarmament' matter?[8] First, to view the APLM Convention as a start point in humanitarian

[5] It should be noted however that the decade 1987–97 saw the conclusion of a number of important disarmament-related treaties including the Treaty between the United States of America and the Union of the Soviet Socialist Republics on the Elimination of their Intermediate-Range and Shorter-Range Missiles, signed 8 December 1987, 27 ILM 1186 (entered into force 1 June 1988) (INF Treaty); the Convention on the Prohibition of the Development, Production, Stockpiling and Use of Chemical Weapons and on their Destruction, opened for signature 13 January 1993, 1975 UNTS 45 (entered into force 29 April 1997) (Chemical Weapons Convention) and the Comprehensive Nuclear-Test-Ban Treaty, opened for signature 24 September 1996, 35 ILM 1439 (not yet in force) (CTBT).

[6] Rebecca Johnson, 'Arms Control and Disarmament Diplomacy' in Andrew F. Cooper, Jorge Heine and Ramesh Thakur (eds.), *The Oxford Handbook of Modern Diplomacy* (Online Version, Oxford: Oxford University Press, 2015), p. 597.

[7] And see the work of the United Nations Institute for Disarmament Research (UNIDIR) for an historically aware sensibility: John Borrie and Vanessa Martin Radin (eds.), *Disarmament as Humanitarian Action: From Perspective to Practice* (Geneva: UNIDIR, 2006).

[8] In the following paragraphs I draw on the ideas of Philip Alston writing in the context of the historiography of human rights: Philip Alston, 'Does the Past Matter? On the Origins of Human Rights' (2013) 126 *Harvard Law Review* 2043.

disarmament is to obliterate earlier attempts by states and civil society to draw attention to, and to try to address, the human suffering caused by those particular weapons. It also obliterates a longer history of opposition to many weapons over time on the grounds of their particular cruelty. In this book, I have chosen 1868 as the starting point of my analysis. In that year, the St Petersburg Declaration was adopted banning the use of projectiles that would explode on impact with a human body.[9] While I do not claim this as an alternative single start point in the overall story of humanitarian discourse about weapons, it constituted the first multilateral agreement to ban a weapon and therefore it is my starting point.

Second, the shorter history implies a narrative of progress, which masks a more complex reality. As I will show, there has not been a steady, progressive infusion of humanitarian ideals into the thinking about and practice of disarmament. Rather, there have been periods when humanitarianism seemed to have greater traction, only to be sidelined and, taking a long view, it is clear that there have been failures as well as successes. If any pattern can be discerned, it seems to me that it is a lack of a pattern. Success (and failure) of any disarmament initiative is nearly always contingent on external factors, including, but not limited to the humanitarian sensibilities of the time; technology (existing and anticipated); the people involved – diplomats, civil society campaigners, scientists and health professionals, military and political leaders of the time; as well as world events more generally.

The contingency of humanitarian disarmament leads me to the third reason why this longer history matters. A recurring theme to emerge in this longer history of humanitarian thinking about weapons control is the way in which the champions of humanitarianism often position themselves outside of and apart from the politics of weapons control. As I will show, this is true of humanitarianism generally, but it is especially visible when a humanitarian discourse is brought to bear on the regulation of weapons. While this is a recurring theme throughout the history recounted here, the apolitical positioning is directly addressed in Chapter 8, showing how humanitarian disarmament, like humanitarianism itself, is inherently and inevitably political – it is just that it is politics of a different kind. But it is politics nonetheless.

[9] Declaration Renouncing the Use, in Time of War, of Explosive Projectiles under 400 Grammes Weight, opened for signature 29 November 1868, [1901] ATS 125 (entered into force 11 December 1868).

Thus, in challenging the creation myth of humanitarian disarmament as residing within the APLM Convention, my aim is not just to challenge the 'starting point'. I do not simply want to give an account of a longer, more ambivalent history of humanitarian sensibilities in disarmament. Rather, I also highlight how the attempt to locate the birth of humanitarian disarmament in the APLM Convention is in part an attempt to bring that treaty cleansed of earlier politics in disarmament, into a morally superior world of 'humanitarian disarmament'. In my view, humanitarian disarmament is not necessarily morally superior to any other way of thinking about disarmament – it is simply one particular way of discussing disarmament and one that has had some success in achieving disarmament agreements. That being conceded, and as I will show, humanitarianism carries with it its own blind spots, its own hegemonic leanings, and I will conclude that it may be silencing other potentially more transformative discourses about disarmament.

III Some Terminology

It is necessary at the outset to articulate what is meant by particular terms, which in turn clarifies the scope of this project. In this part, I explain what is meant by the terms 'disarmament', 'humanitarianism' and 'humanitarian disarmament'.[10]

A Disarmament

In a narrow sense, 'disarmament' can mean the total elimination of a particular category of weapons.[11] However, in this book, I use the term in a wider sense to include the limitation or reduction (through negotiated international instruments or otherwise) of the means by which nations (or other entities) wage war. Thus, this book captures not only 'pure disarmament' treaties such as the Chemical Weapons Convention, which requires states parties to eliminate their stockpiles of chemical weapons, but also captures agreements such as the Protocol for the Prohibition of the Use in War of Asphyxiating, Poisonous or Other Gases, and of Bacteriological

[10] There is a rich literature on what is meant by the first two terms, so as will become apparent, I have adopted a working understanding of the terms, without taking a position as to how the terms should be understood more broadly. The third term 'humanitarian disarmament', as we will see, has received relatively little attention in the literature.

[11] Alva Myrdal, *The Game of Disarmament: How the United States and Russia Run the Arms Race* (New York: Pantheon Books, 1976), p. xv.

Methods of Warfare (Geneva Protocol 1925) which simply prohibits the use of such weapons.[12]

Some disarmament treaties include provisions on the use of specific weapons, including prohibiting (not just limiting) use of those weapons. Again, the Chemical Weapons Convention serves as an example.[13] International humanitarian law, sometimes referred to as the law of armed conflict, also includes in its ambit rules about the use (rather than existence or possession) of weapons of war. For example, the use of poison or poisoned weapons is prohibited in this body of law.[14] However, while my approach to 'disarmament' does encapsulate attempts to reduce or limit weapons, it does not reach as far as examining international humanitarian law directly. That being said in this context, the two areas of law – disarmament and international humanitarian law – are closely related in that both are concerned with controlling weapons. Indeed, much of the story of disarmament is best understood in the broader context of earlier attempts to restrict the use of a particular weapon using international humanitarian law.[15] Nevertheless, while I do engage with such attempts, it is only to understand more fully the subsequent disarmament attempts.

Another boundary that is important to identify at the outset is the way in which disarmament relates to 'non-proliferation'. Non-proliferation is understood as measures designed to maintain a status quo by preventing the spread of certain weapons – the Treaty on the Non-Proliferation of Nuclear Weapons (NPT) is the foremost example.[16] As with international humanitarian law, non-proliferation objectives generally, and the NPT specifically, form an important part of the backdrop to disarmament efforts. Because non-proliferation efforts are actions aimed at limiting (the

[12] Chemical Weapons Convention art. 1; Protocol for the Prohibition of the Use in War of Asphyxiating, Poisonous or Other Gases, and of Bacteriological Methods of Warfare, opened for signature 17 June 1925, (1929) XCIV LNTS 65–74 (entered into force 8 February 1928).

[13] Chemical Weapons Convention art. 1.

[14] International Committee of the Red Cross, *Customary International Humanitarian Law Volume 1: Rules* (Cambridge: Cambridge University Press, 2009) rule 72.

[15] See Robert J. Mathews and Tim McCormack, 'The Relationship between International Humanitarian Law and Arms Control' in Helen Durham and Tim McCormack (eds.), *The Changing Face of Conflict and the Efficacy of International Humanitarian Law* (The Hague: Kluwer Law International, 1999), p. 65.

[16] Treaty on the Non-Proliferation of Nuclear Weapons, opened for signature 1 July 1968, 729 UNTS 161 (entered into force 5 March 1970).

possession of) weapons, they can be considered to be part of 'disarmament'. However, I have not done so in this study in that I have not included the NPT as a subject matter in its own right.

A final point of terminology relates to 'arms control'. The term was coined in the 1950s to denote agreements to limit the arms race, in particular the nuclear arms race between the Soviet Union and the United States. Arms control initiatives included attempts to freeze the number of nuclear weapons and related technology at a given level, or to engage in mutual limitation agreements.[17] In recent decades, the terms 'disarmament' and 'arms control' are sometimes used interchangeably.[18] While my enquiry does not specifically address the bilateral arms control initiatives of the 1950s, my broad understanding of the term 'disarmament' means that arms control initiatives are included.

In this book, I will generally use the term 'disarmament' to include not only the complete elimination of a category of weapons, but limitation and reduction efforts, prohibitions on use of weapons and even activities such as attempts to limit or prohibit nuclear weapons testing.[19]

B Humanitarianism

The *Oxford English Dictionary* defines humanitarianism as being a 'concern for human welfare as a primary or pre-eminent moral good'.[20] The modern understanding of international humanitarianism, at least in the period covered here (1868 to the present day), is probably best captured not just as a concern for human welfare, but as a concern for the human welfare of *strangers*. That is, a sense of compassion and concern for those who are neither family members, relatives or indeed, even from our own communities.[21] As Michael

17 Mirko Sossai, 'Disarmament and Non-Proliferation' in Nigel White and Christian Henderson (eds.), *Research Handbook on International Conflict and Security: Jus ad Bellum, Jus in Bello and Jus Post Bellum* (Cheltenham: Edward Elgar, 2013) pp. 41–2.

18 For a critical perspective on the issue of terminology between 'disarmament' and 'arms control', see Neil Cooper, 'Putting Disarmament Back in the Frame' (2006) 32(2) *Review of International Studies* 353.

19 Jozef Goldblat, *Arms Control: The New Guide to Negotiations and Agreements* (London: Sage Publications, 2002), p. 3.

20 *Oxford English Dictionary* (3rd ed., online, Oxford: Oxford University Press, 2009).

21 See Iain Wilkinson, *The Problem of Understanding Modern Humanitarianism and Its Sociological Value* (Oxford; Malden, CA: UNESCO; Wiley & Sons, 2016), p. 3;

Barnett puts it: feelings of compassion for 'strangers in distant lands'.[22]

Closely related to, and emerging from the earlier idea of charity, humanitarianism is presented as altruistic, solely focused on the urge to alleviate human suffering. The anti-slavery movement and the creation of the Red Cross and Red Crescent movement are often identified as the beginnings of modern transnational humanitarianism.[23]

As I will discuss in some detail in Chapter 8, while humanitarianism is often presented as a universal value, it is open to diverse understandings in practice (delivery of 'humanitarian assistance' for example), often in uneasy relationship with local traditions, values and practices. It is also subject to critical scrutiny from historians, philosophers and scholars from critical media studies and security studies. These are all discussed more fully in Chapter 8. Nevertheless, for present purposes, 'humanitarianism' can be understood as a lens which purports to focus on human suffering (often, but not necessarily only, of strangers) and the need to alleviate that suffering.

C *Humanitarian Disarmament*

The meaning of the term 'humanitarian disarmament' has received relatively little attention in the legal literature,[24] although there are a number of considerations of what the term encapsulates from critical security scholars.[25] Sauer and Pretorius attempt to capture the essence of a humanitarian approach as being one which articulates a principle-

Michael Barnett, *Empire of Humanity: A History of Humanitarianism* (Ithaca; London: Cornell University Press, 2011), p. 21; Steven Pinker, *The Better Angels of Our Nature: A History of Violence and Humanity* (London: Penguin Books, 2011), p. 4.

22 Barnett, *Empire of Humanity: A History of Humanitarianism*, above n. 21, p. 20.

23 Barnett, *Empire of Humanity: A History of Humanitarianism*, above n. 21; Didier Fassin, *Humanitarian Reason: A Moral History of the Present* (California: University of California Press, 2012); Bruno Cabanes, *The Great War and the Origins of Humanitarianism 1918–1924* (Cambridge: Cambridge University Press, 2014). But note that some histories reach further back: Jean Guillermand, 'The Historical Foundation of Humanitarian Action' (1994) 298 *International Review of the Red Cross* 42 and 'The Historical Foundation of Humanitarian Action' (1994) 299 *International Review of the Red Cross* 194.

24 But see Bonnie Docherty, 'Ending Civilian Suffering: The Purpose, Provisions, and Promise of Humanitarian Disarmament Law' (2010) 15 *Austrian Review of International and European Law* 7–44 at 16–17; Ritu Mathur, *Red Cross Interventions in Weapons Control* (Maryland: Lexington Books, 2017), pp. 1–22; Borrie and Radin, *Disarmament as Humanitarian Action: From Perspective to Practice*, above n. 7.

25 See for example, Neil Cooper, 'Humanitarian Arms Control and Processes of Securitization: Moving Weapons along the Security Continuum' (2011) 32(1) *Contemporary Security Policy* 134.

based complete ban on a weapon, adopts a fast-track approach to negotiations, starting with NGOs/civil society, moving to like-minded states and has a goal of justice and human rights, rather than state security.[26] Bonnie Docherty suggests that there are three common features of 'humanitarian disarmament' instruments: putting in place an absolute ban on the use, production, transfer and stockpiling of specific weapons, providing for remedial obligations (in this context, demining and assistance to victims) and putting in place a cooperative implementation approach.[27]

For the purposes of this book, and without determining that there can, or should, be a singular understanding of the term, I use 'humanitarian disarmament' to capture two core ideas. First, humanitarian disarmament brings a humanitarian lens to discussions about whether or not a particular class of weapon should be prohibited or subjected to (further) limits on use. That is, disarmament debates become infused with a humanitarian sensibility, rather than conducting those debates and discourses purely in the context of state security. This sensibility has always been present in the related field of international humanitarian law, or law of armed conflict, with its underlying attempt to balance the imperatives of military necessity in warfare with a need to prevent indiscriminate attacks or effects on civilians and as well, to prevent superfluous or unnecessary suffering more generally.[28] Thus, there is a close connection between the international humanitarian law as it relates to the use of weapons in war, and the concept of humanitarian disarmament. However, a key difference between international humanitarian law as it pertains to weapons, and disarmament, whether approached from a humanitarian perspective or not, is that the former deals with only the use of the weapons during armed conflict, while the latter also addresses the existence of those weapons.

The second feature of humanitarian disarmament that distinguishes it from disarmament as traditionally understood is that humanitarian disarmament also involves a question of process, or how disarmament agreements or policies are reached. Broadly, it suggests that entities

[26] Tom Sauer and Joeliem Pretorius, 'Nuclear Weapons and the Humanitarian Approach' (2014) 26(3) *Global Change, Peace and Security* 233, 246.

[27] Docherty, 'Ending Civilian Suffering: The Purpose, Provisions, and Promise of Humanitarian Disarrangement Law', above n. 24, pp. 16–17.

[28] See generally, William H. Boothby, *Weapons and the Law of Armed Conflict* (Oxford: Oxford University Press, 2009).

other than states influence, formally or informally, discussions, debate, formulation of state policy and actual negotiations.[29]

In sum then, humanitarian disarmament is a combination of a humanitarian sensibility in the substance of the debates, and participation by, or presence of, non-state entities in the negotiation processes.

IV Overview of the Book

The first three chapters (2–4) proceed chronologically and weave together the development of ideas of humanitarianism and ideas about disarmament from a starting date of 1868 with the St Petersburg Declaration through to 1980, the year in which the Convention on Conventional Weapons (CCW) was concluded.[30]

Chapter 2 explores the emergence of both transnational humanitarianism and international disarmament as they emerged in the late nineteenth century, particularly from 1868 and how they developed for the next sixty-five years until the breakdown of the League of Nations. Captured within this discussion are the disarmament attempts in the Hague Peace Conferences as well as the work within the League of Nations. As I will show, they were all imbued with a spirit of humanitarianism, in keeping with the times. In terms of disarmament, while there were some important and enduring successes, this period ends with the breakdown of the World Disarmament Conference in 1933 which had been convened by the League of Nations. Humanitarian disarmament may have had important achievements in this period, but it did not prevent the coming World War and its attendant escalation in weapons technology. Indeed, there were many who subsequently argued that it was the humanitarian ethos of the time, particularly as relating to weapons, that was at least part of the cause of the Second World War.

Chapter 3 covers the two decades following the Second World War. The central argument here is that the humanitarian disarmament discourse was marginalised in this period. I explore a number of possible

[29] For thoughtful reflections on this broader engagement, see John Borrie and Ashley Thornton, *The Value of Diversity in Multilateral Disarmament Work* (New York: United Nations Institute for Disarmament Research, 2008).

[30] Convention on Prohibitions or Restrictions on the Use of Certain Conventional Weapons which may be deemed to be Excessively Injurious or to have Indiscriminate Effects (with Protocols I, II and III), opened for signature 10 April 1981, 1342 UNTS 137 (entered into force 2 December 1983).

reasons for this: the mutation of public morality that ensued from the slaughter and violence of the War; the security framework of the new United Nations which radically transformed the approach to disarmament compared to the League before it; and the advent of the 'Atomic Age'. Even though disarmament was sidelined, in some important ways the period can be seen as a period of humanitarianism.[31] As such, I show how ideas of humanitarian disarmament persisted, evidenced in particular by the work of the International Committee of the Red Cross (ICRC) attempting to broker agreement on legal frameworks that would regulate indiscriminate weapons, although as I will show, these efforts had faltered by the mid-1960s.

Chapter 4 takes as its focus the brutality of the Vietnam War and I argue that the War, coupled with the rise of the Non-Aligned Movement, retriggered a humanitarian discourse in the context of weapons and the way in which they were used. I examine two separate but related strands of what I see as humanitarian disarmament discourse in this period (1965–80). The first emerged from within the global Red Cross and Red Crescent movement with attempts to update and improve international humanitarian law. The second came from states of the Non-Aligned Movement working within the United Nations General Assembly in particular through the Human Rights in Armed Conflict initiative with its genesis in the Tehran Conference 1968. The chapter concludes with an analysis of the CCW, a treaty often seen as a disappointing compromise and thus neglected or marginalised in many accounts of humanitarian disarmament, but which I argue was an important moment in humanitarian disarmament.

The next three chapters (5–7) consider three contemporary treaties in turn: the APLM Convention (Chapter 5); the Convention on Cluster Munitions (CCM) (Chapter 6);[32] and the Treaty on the Prohibition of Nuclear Weapons (TPNW) (Chapter 7).[33] Each chapter examines the way in which each treaty is an exercise in 'humanitarian disarmament'. The analysis shows how humanitarian disarmament practice is

[31] See Roger P. Alford, 'The Nobel Effect: Nobel Peace Prize Laureates as International Norm Entrepreneurs' (2008–9) 49 *Virginia Journal of International Law* 61, 92 labelling 1944–59 the 'Humanitarian Period'.

[32] Convention on Cluster Munitions, opened for signature 3 December 2008, 2688 UNTS 39 (entered into force 1 August 2010).

[33] Treaty on the Prohibition of Nuclear Weapons, opened for signature 20 September 2017 (not yet in force).

continuously evolving, and this evolution carries with it its own compromises and complexities.

Chapter 5 examines the evolution and content of the APLM Convention and argues that the Convention was a significant departure from orthodox disarmament practice but not for the two reasons generally posited (that is, a 'new' humanitarian framing and a 'new' engagement by civil society). Instead, I argue that the APLM Convention is a humanitarian disarmament exemplar in four respects: its challenge to the existing disarmament architecture; its contribution to the momentum of increasing transparency of disarmament diplomacy; the way in which it manages verification of compliance with its provisions; and its incorporation of victim assistance provisions. Seen in this light, the APLM Convention is another important milestone in the overall development of humanitarian disarmament, but seen in the context of this longer history, it is clear that the APLM Convention is not its genesis.

I examine the CCM in Chapter 6, showing how in some respects this treaty consolidated the humanitarian disarmament practice of the APLM Convention ten years earlier. However, I also show how the CCM departed from earlier practice in two important respects. First is the way in which the treaty defines 'cluster munitions' and I explain and argue that its reversed burden of proof represents an important, possibly revolutionary development. However, I do not see the CCM as an entirely progressive development because with the further strengthening of victim assistance and environmental remediation provisions, I argue that the treaty is regressive in terms of the way the user states were absolved of responsibility for clearance and destruction. Seen in the light of the efforts of the non-aligned states from the 1960s onwards, I suggest that these provisions were regrettable (but perhaps inevitable) compromises.

Chapter 7 analyses the contours of the campaigns against nuclear weapons over the more than seventy years since the first (and still only) nuclear weapon attacks in war. I explore whether and to what extent these campaigns can be considered to fall under the rubric 'humanitarian disarmament'. I argue that the various campaigns have always been humanitarian in ethos even though for a long period of time the language of humanitarianism was not explicit. I examine the TPNW concluded in 2017 to show how the practice of humanitarian disarmament continues to evolve and I pay particular attention to the victim assistance provisions in the treaty and the way in which this treaty 'came home' to the General Assembly.

Chapter 8 steps away from the detail of particular regimes and eras and examines four critiques made of humanitarianism generally: the politics of humanitarian discourse and practice; humanitarianism's complicity with militarism; humanitarianism's imperative of action; and finally, the way in which humanitarian discourse creates and perpetuates hierarchies of suffering. In each instance, I examine the extent to which those critiques have traction in the context of humanitarian disarmament, thus revealing the shortcomings of a humanitarian disarmament discourse.

My conclusion in Chapter 9 briefly restates my core argument: that the evidence presented here shows that, far from being an invention of the post–Cold War era, humanitarian disarmament has had a long and complex history dating back at least 150 years and that this history reveals failures as well as successes, limitations as well as potential. Without rejecting the value of a humanitarian framing, I end by questioning whether other discourses might be available to us to think about disarmament.

2

The Origins of Humanitarian Disarmament

I Introduction

A core claim of my thesis is that the humanitarian framing of disarmament is not a contemporary phenomenon. The humanitarian discourse did not emerge in the post–Cold War world, epitomised by the Anti-Personnel Landmines Convention (APLM Convention) in 1997, repeated and reinforced by the Convention on Cluster Munitions (CCM) in 2008 and most recently, by the Treaty on the Prohibition of Nuclear Weapons (TPNW) in 2017.[1] Rather, my argument is that the influence of the humanitarian disarmament discourse in recent decades is a re-emergence of a long-standing sensibility about humanitarianism in disarmament.

Where, then, do we find the origins of humanitarian disarmament? If humanitarian disarmament is not a phenomenon of the post–Cold War era, where do its roots lie? And why does it matter? These questions are the focus of this chapter.

Eschewing the idea of a 'big bang' moment of humanitarian disarmament, instead I trace the origins of the sensibility to the late-nineteenth century – a period by which modern transnational humanitarianism had emerged, epitomised by the anti-slavery campaigns and the birth of the Red Cross Movement. By the 1860s, that humanitarian sensibility had started to appear in discussions about the regulation and even prohibition of certain weapons during war. The first treaty expression of this

1 Convention on the Prohibition of the Use, Stockpiling, Production and Transfer of Anti-Personnel Mines and on their Destruction, opened for signature 3 December 1997, 2056 UNTS 211 (entered into force 1 March 1999); Convention on Cluster Munitions, opened for signature 3 December 2008, 2688 UNTS 39 (entered into force 1 August 2010); Treaty on the Prohibition of Nuclear Weapons, opened for signature 20 September 2017 (not yet in force).

sensibility was contained in the St Petersburg Declaration which banned the use of projectiles that would explode on impact with the human body.[2] The ban was agreed due to the perceived unnecessary suffering this would cause to a human target. However, far from being a singular defining moment in humanitarian disarmament, the St Petersburg Declaration was an expression of an evolving humanitarian disarmament discourse, inextricably intertwined with the broader humanitarian impulse of the time. Reflecting the linkages between humanitarianism and humanitarian disarmament, this chapter traces both the emergence of transnational humanitarianism and the efforts towards international disarmament in the late-nineteenth century, and follows their progress together for the next seven decades, through to the outbreak of the Second World War. This narrative traverses the Hague Peace Conferences of 1899 and 1907, the calamity of the First World War, the neglected but significant work of the League of Nations, in particular the ambitious but ultimately doomed Disarmament Conference 1932–4, and, finally, the breakdown and dissolution of the League system.

I do not suggest that in this period there was a simple linear progression away from the pursuit of national security embedded in a single-minded sovereign towards a benign cosmopolitan humanitarianism. Rather, my aim is to show that international humanitarianism and international disarmament emerged in a shared context. The significant point to notice about this shared origin is that both international humanitarianism and international disarmament appealed to an apolitical cosmopolitan sensibility. I will show that an important appeal of the humanitarian sensibility was that it appeared to transcend politics. Humanitarian disarmament was also framed as an apolitical discourse – a discourse that would free disarmament ambitions from the narrow self-interests of states.

The following section (Section II) traces the emergence of modern transnational humanitarianism showing how its roots were exemplified by the anti-slavery movement, the establishment of the International Committee of the Red Cross (ICRC), and the emergence of international 'peace societies'. In Section III, examining the control of weapons more specifically in the period prior to the First World War, I show the way in which humanitarian sensibilities were brought to bear in discussions

[2] Declaration Renouncing the Use, in Time of War, of Explosive Projectiles under 400 Grammes Weight, opened for signature 29 November 1868, [1901] ATS 125 (entered into force 11 December 1868).

about the conduct of war, even to the extent of setting down some rules about which weapons could be used lawfully. What we would describe today as civil society (then 'peace societies') were the conduits of humanitarianism, and were generally pitted against more pragmatic and hard-headed state-centric sensibilities.

In Section IV I explore the work of the League of Nations in disarmament and the fate of humanitarianism more generally in the post–First World War landscape. The League is well known for its work on humanitarian activities, including the campaigns against the trafficking of women and children, slavery and the extensive work involved in the repatriation of prisoners following the War.[3] In comparison, the League's disarmament efforts have been relatively neglected, but here as well there were important developments, not least the convening of the 1932 Disarmament Conference. A significant point which emerges is that both the League's humanitarian activities and its disarmament work were seen as complementary elements of the League's ultimate aim of securing and maintaining peace. Further, within the disarmament work of the League, I will show that while humanitarianism was an important underlying motivation, it was far from universally embraced, particularly in the disarmament sphere.

In summary then, this chapter locates the origins of humanitarian disarmament in the more general humanitarian movement of the nineteenth century and shows that one appeal of humanitarianism was the sense that it might offer a way to transcend politics. But I will also show that even from its inception, it proved impossible to unravel politics from humanitarianism. These are themes which persist throughout the long story of humanitarian disarmament into today's debates.

II The Emergence of Modern Humanitarianism

The idea of acting with compassion or giving charity in response to the needs of others is not a modern notion.[4] This narrow sense of

[3] For a contemporary view, see Dame Rachel Crowdy, 'The League of Nations: Its Social and Humanitarian Work' (1928) 28(4) *American Journal of Nursing* 350.

[4] Michael Barnett, *Empire of Humanity: A History of Humanitarianism* (Ithaca; London: Cornell University Press, 2013), p. 19. See as well, Monika Krause, *The Good Project: Humanitarian Relief NGOs and the Fragmentation of Reason* (Chicago: University of Chicago Press, 2014), ch. 4; Didier Fassin, *Humanitarian Reason: A Moral History of the Present* (California: University of California Press, 2011); Bruce Cabanes, *The Great War and the Origins of Humanitarianism, 1918–1924* (Cambridge: Cambridge University Press, 2014). There are also much older accounts of ideas of what we would call today

humanitarianism – compassion for those who are suffering – is as old as human history itself and is evident in all of the world's religious traditions.[5] That being said, it is generally accepted that the modern understanding of humanitarianism, a concern for the suffering of 'strangers in distant lands', emerged in the context of the European Enlightenment, having grown out of these older ideas of compassion and charity.[6] Peter Stamatov, for example, argues that the practice of what he terms 'long-distance advocacy' emerged from the practice of religious actors, in particular Quakers, from the sixteenth to eighteenth centuries in the context of imperial European expansions of that era responding to the mistreatment and conditions of indigenous communities and enslaved Africans.[7] Michael Barnett explains it this way:

> Humanitarianism is imprinted by modernity, the Enlightenment, and the belief that it is possible to engineer progress. … [T]he humanitarian movements of the nineteenth century, including those that were devoutly religious, frequently articulated a confidence in using modern scientific techniques and public interventions to improve the human condition.[8]

This modern humanitarianism was different from what had come before in two important ways. First, it was different in the way in which it was organised, with a shift away from private acts of charity by the privileged and the pious, towards a form of governance involving 'societies' and

humanitarianism: Jean Guillermand, 'The Historical Foundation of Humanitarian Action' (1994) 298 *International Review of the Red Cross* 42 and 'The Historical Foundation of Humanitarian Action' (1994) 299 *International Review of the Red Cross* 194. The literature on the abolitionist movement is enormous, but for a focused study on the slavery and humanitarianism, see Alanna Sullivan-Vaughan, 'History of Slavery and Humanitarianism', MA Thesis, University of Auckland (2012); And see the collection of essays in (2012) 40(5) *Journal of Imperial and Commonwealth History* exploring humanitarianism in the context of empire.

[5] See Guillermand, 'The Historical Foundation of Humanitarian Action', above n. 4, discussing the humanist tendencies across all religions, as well as in the work of Socrates, Plato and Aristotle through to Grotius and De Vattal. For a discussion of Jewish giving, see Michael Walzer, 'On Humanitarianism: Is Helping Others Charity, or Duty, or Both?' (July/August 2011) 90(4) *Foreign Affairs* 69. For zakat (obligatory giving of alms to the poor) in the Islamic tradition, see Raj Bhala, *Understanding Islamic Law*, 2nd ed. (North Carolina: North Carolina Press, 2016), pp. 329–36.

[6] See Iain Wilkinson, The Problem of Understanding Modern Humanitarianism and its Sociological Value (UNESCO, 2016) 3; Barnett, *Empire of Humanity*, above n. 4, p. 21; Steven Pinker, *The Better Angels of Our Nature: A History of Violence and Humanity* (London: Penguin Books, 2011), p. 4.

[7] Peter Stamatov, *Origins of Global Humanitarianism* (Cambridge: Cambridge University Press, 2013), p. 14.

[8] Ibid., p. 21.

'associations' as well as religious institutions all striving to make a better society.[9] Second, it was no longer confined to the suffering of those 'at home' (meaning, in the West, slavery, child labour, health and hygiene standards for example), but also encompassed the suffering of distant strangers. The era of transnational humanitarianism had dawned.

Thus, modern transnational humanitarianism was very much a movement that originated in the West.[10] With its focus on responding to suffering and need, humanitarianism emerged to provide an 'illusion of a global moral community'.[11] In this way, modern transnational humanitarianism seemed to exist beyond politics, beyond religion. The humanitarian impulse was one of concern for fellow human beings regardless of race, status, religion or geography. This positioning of humanitarianism as outside of, or above, politics is what made it such a powerful force as it emerged, and what explains its power today.

However, despite this apparent distancing from politics, modern transnational humanitarianism has always been embedded in politics, not distinct from it. As Barnett explains:

> Modern humanitarianism's roots are located in the West. Although these values might have universal appeal, or might have become universal as a consequence of interactions and cross-cultural dialogue, the history of humanitarianism reflects many of the tensions that exist between the 'West' and the non-Western world. Indeed, one of humanitarianism's defining traits is the attempt to spread the values and practices of the 'international community' to places where they are either absent or dormant.[12]

The anti-slavery movement and the creation of the Red Cross movement are generally identified as two key starting points of modern transnational humanitarianism.[13] In both cases, this explicit apolitical

[9] Barnett, *Empire of Humanity*, above n. 4, p. 21.

[10] Pinker, *The Better Angels of Our Nature*, above n. 6, explores the possible reasons for this 'humanitarian revolution' as he terms it, suggesting possible causes as increased affluence because people can be more compassionate as their own lives improved: at p. 205; and increased literacy because of the way in which it provides exposure to other people's vantage points: at p. 211.

[11] Didier Fassin, 'The Predicament of Humanitarianism' (2013) 22(1) *Qui Parle: Critical Humanities and Social Sciences* pp. 33, 37.

[12] Michael Barnett, 'Humanitarianism as a Scholarly Vocation' in Michael Barnett and Thomas G. Weiss (eds.), *Humanitarianism in Question: Politics, Power, Ethics* (New York: Cornell University Press, 2008), pp. 235, 241.

[13] Krause, *The Good Project*, above n. 4, pp. 100–3 (discussing the role of the ICRC in the making of modern humanitarianism). On slavery, see: Margaret Abruzzo, *Polemical Pain:*

positioning of humanitarianism is evident. Both appeal to a shared humanity and a sense of global kinship. In this way, both attempt to position themselves outside or above politics. In both cases, we can see that humanitarianism, with its single-minded purpose being to alleviate human suffering unconditionally and without ulterior motive, is presented as being outside or above politics.[14]

The abolitionist movement was quintessentially humanitarian. A key focus of the movement was the call to alleviate human suffering, starting with a movement within what we would today call civil society to campaign against the slave trade, and subsequently to campaign against slavery itself. This appeal to a shared humanity was epitomised by the anti-slavery slogan 'Am I Not a Man and a Brother?' written on a scroll beneath an image of a shackled slave.[15] As part of their campaign strategy, the abolitionists introduced into the public domain facts about the brutality and cruelty in the way slaves were treated (quite apart from the act of slavery itself).[16] So even while the campaign was attempting to achieve political change, it positioned itself as being above, not within, politics.[17] The campaign was presented as moral and humanitarian, rather than itself being a form of politics, even as it challenged existing prevailing attitudes and policies, including powerful economic interests.

Similarly, the entire Red Cross Movement is a story of humanitarianism. The creation story of the Red Cross has at its centre Henri Dunant arriving at the Battle of Solferino in 1859, witnessing appalling cruelty and destruction, and responding to that by elevating that suffering above all other considerations (including the merits of either side's involvement in the war).[18] Dunant subsequently established the International

Slavery, Cruelty, and the Rise of Humanitarianism (Baltimore: John Hopkins University Press, 2011).

14 Miriam Ticktin, 'Transnational Humanitarianism' (2014) 43 *Annual Review of Anthropology* 273, 276.

15 Barnett, *Empire of Humanity*, above n. 4, p. 58.

16 Ibid., p. 59.

17 Barnett, *Empire of Humanity*, above n. 4, acknowledges that other dynamics were at play, noting that some streams of anti-slavery activists were motivated not so much by a concern for the welfare of others, but as a means of expanding evangelicalism: at p. 59. For a more detailed exploration of the issues, see Rob Skinner and Alan Lester, 'Humanitarianism and Empire: New Research Agendas' (2012) 40(5) *Journal of Imperial and Commonwealth History* 729.

18 See Daniel Warner for an account of the early life of Henri Dunant, arguing that his 'humanitarianism' should be seen in the context of his Calvinist upbringing: Daniel Warner, 'Henry Dunant's Imagined Community: Humanitarianism and the Tragic' (2013) 38(1) *Alternatives: Global, Local, Political* 3.

Committee for Relief to the Wounded joined by a group of business men from Geneva, which evolved into the International Committee of the Red Cross and the creation of a network of national Red Cross societies.[19] Five years later, the treaty regime had started to be built, with the adoption, in 1864, of the Geneva Convention for the Amelioration of the Condition of the Wounded in the Field (Geneva Convention 1864).[20] The story epitomises the humanitarian spirit, a human response to human suffering in war. As Daniel Warner says:

> If we assume that war and violence are extensions of the political, then we understand the traditional description of humanitarian space as an area separate from the political, and that this separation is a critical ideological concept that is fundamental to organizations like the International Committee of the Red Cross (ICRC). Impartiality, neutrality and independence are predicated on separating the humanitarian from the political. One acts within the humanitarian space in the midst of, but separate from, the political.[21]

And so we see the birth of modern humanitarianism, with its roots in older religious notions of charity and compassion, being fashioned (in the West at least) from the Enlightenment as a universal appeal to a shared humanity. In doing so, humanitarianism explicitly articulated an apolitical position – a point of view that was beyond politics, beyond religion. The following section explores how those foundations influenced the development of humanitarian sensibilities in the discussion of weapons of war.

III Humanitarian Disarmament Prior to the First World War

There is a long history of discussions around the desirability of disarmament, of attempts to limit or prohibit the use of weapons in war, or for states to reach agreement on reducing their respective levels of armaments.[22] Some commentators suggest that the story of disarmament should start in 1648 with the Peace of Westphalia on the basis that one of

[19] For an account of the development of the International Committee of the Red Cross, see: David P. Forsythe, *The Humanitarians: The International Committee for the Red Cross* (Cambridge: Cambridge University Press, 2005) ch. 1.

[20] Geneva Convention of the Amelioration of the Condition of the Wounded in the Field, opened for signature 22 August 1864, 129 Consol TS (entered into force 22 June 1865).

[21] Daniel Warner, 'The Politics of the Political/Humanitarian Divide' (1999) 81 *International Review of the Red Cross* 109, 110.

[22] See Merze Tate, *The Disarmament Illusion* (New York: Macmillan Group, 1942) looking back to the peace plans of philosophers such as Jean Jacques Rousseau, Immanuel Kant and

the constituent treaties provided that all of the combatants' fortifications were to be demolished and that no new installations were to be erected.[23] Certainly, across history, many peace treaties included provisions limiting weapons and armies.[24] Similarly, within the laws of war, there were limits on the type of weapons which could be used in conflict ranging from crossbows to poisons.[25]

However, the phenomenon of the control of weapons as a matter of international treaty law, rather than as a limitation clause in a particular peace treaty, really only emerged in the nineteenth century.[26] This section traces early disarmament attempts, looking in particular at the St Petersburg Declaration (Section III.A), the Hague Peace Conference 1899 (Section III.B) and finally, the Hague Peace Conference 1907 (Section III.C).

A The St Petersburg Declaration: the First Treaty Prohibition of a Weapon

The first formal international agreement prohibiting the use of a weapon was agreed in 1868 with the St Petersburg Declaration which prohibited the use, in war, of explosive projectiles under 400 grams in weight.[27] Five years earlier, the Russians had developed these projectiles, the primary objective of which was to blow up ammunition wagons because of the way in which the projectile exploded on contact with a hard surface.[28]

Jeremy Bentham: at p. 3; Hans Wehberg, *The Limitation of Armaments: A Collection of the Projects Proposed for the Solution of the Problem, Preceded by an Historical Introduction* (Washington: Carnegie Endowment for International Peace, 1921); Andrew Webster, 'Hague Conventions (1899, 1907)' in Gordon Martel (eds.), *The Encyclopedia of War* (Oxford: Blackwell Publishing, 2012), p. 1; H. A. Smith, 'The Problem of Disarmament in the Light of History' (1931) 10(5) *International Affairs* 600; Scott Keefer, 'Building the Palace of Peace: The Hague Conference of 1899 and Arms Control in the Progressive Era' (2006) 8 *Journal of the History of International Law* 1.

23 Coit D. Blacker and Gloria Duffy, *International Arms Control: Issues and Agreements*, 2nd ed. (Stanford: Stanford University Press, 1984), p. 81.

24 Alexander Gillespie, *A History of the Laws of War: The Customs and Laws of War with Regard to Arms Control* (Oxford: Hart Publishing, 2011), Vol III, pp. 7–13.

25 See for example, Henry Sumner Maine, *International Law: A Series of Lectures Delivered before the University of Cambridge, 1887* (London, 1888) explaining the demise of the crossbow: at p. 13.

26 Frits Kalshoven, 'Disarmament Law' (1985) 191 *Collected Courses of the Hague Academy of International Law* 305, 306.

27 St Petersburg Declaration, operative paragraph 6.

28 Scott Keefer, '"Explosive Missals": International Law, Technology, and Security in Nineteenth-Century Disarmament Conference' (2014) 21(4) *War in History* 445, 450–1 discusses the development of the technology.

While that appeared militarily useful, once the technology was further developed to cause it to explode on contact with soft, rather than hard, substances, concerns started to be voiced about the damage which these exploding bullets could inflict on a human body.[29]

It is easy to see, then, why the St Petersburg Declaration is so often hailed as a humanitarian instrument. This is so particularly because it emerged around the same time as a rise of humanitarian sensibilities in the conduct of war generally, as manifested in the Red Cross movement and the accompanying treaties and proclamations addressing the treatment of the sick and wounded in battle.[30] However, other explanations for the turn to international arms control are offered. Scott Keefer, for example, argues that the agreements are better seen as a manifestation of concerns about the rapidly developing military technology at the time, as well as a quest for military superiority, rather than expressions of humanitarian sentiment.[31] Keefer argues that a key feature of the discussions in the late-nineteenth century was the rising cost of weapons development in the face of a 'dizzying revolution in military technology' and the maintenance of armies.[32]

It is always difficult, if not impossible, to ascertain the true motives of contracting states in situations such as this. What is clear is that, in the context of the Declaration, the call for international regulation of the explosive projectiles was couched in humanitarian terms. The Preamble to the St Petersburg Declaration uses expressions such as 'alleviating as much as possible the calamities of war' and states the object of avoiding the useless aggravation of

[29] Frits Kalshoven, 'Conventional Weaponry: The Law from St. Petersburg to Lucerne and beyond', reprinted in Frits Kalshoven, *Reflections on the Law of War: Collected Essays* (Leiden, Netherlands: Martinus Nijhoff Publishers, 2007) pp. 377, 378–80 discussing the reaction of a Major Fosbery in 1879 to these concerns, essentially taking the position that the more cruel the weapon, the more unlikely it was that states would resort to war and the more effective the weapon, the quicker hostilities would draw to a close.

[30] US War Department, *Instructions for the Government of Armies of the United States in the Field by Order of the Secretary of War* (*Lieber Code*), General Orders No 100 (24 April 1863), as reproduced in Dietrich Schindler and Jirí Toman (eds.), *The Laws of Armed Conflicts: A Collection of Conventions, Resolutions, and Other Documents*, 3rd edn (Dordrecht, Netherlands: Martinus Nijhoff Publishers, 1988), p. 3; Geneva Convention 1864.

[31] Keefer, 'Explosive Missals', above n. 28, p. 450.

[32] Ibid., p. 449. For a detailed discussion of the pace of the evolution of military technology at the time, see Antulio J. Echevarria, 'The Arms Race: Qualitative and Quantitative Aspects' in Roger Chickering, Dennis Showalter and Hans Van De Ven (eds.), *The Cambridge History of War: War and the Modern World Volume IV* (Cambridge: Cambridge University Press, 2012), p. 163.

suffering. A humanitarian sensibility then, while not necessarily the entire explanation, was certainly a key factor in these early attempts at regulating the use of weapons.[33]

B *The Hague Peace Conference 1899: an Exercise of Humanitarian Disarmament?*

Taken together, the two Hague Peace Conferences of 1899 and 1907 are important milestones in the modern era of international disarmament. They are also important events when considering the evolution of humanitarian disarmament. Although today, the Conferences are often presented as being clear instances of humanitarianism, a broader study of the various accounts reveal that there were mixed and complex motives for convening and attending the Hague Conferences.[34] Undoubtedly, the Conferences were influenced at least in part by a humanitarian spirit, but the record also shows a great deal of hard-headed pragmatism at play, with a complex relationship emerging between the two. Section III.B.1 explores the lead-up to the Conference showing these dynamics playing out, while Section III.B.2 analyses the outcomes of the Conference.

The Conferences are significant in the story of humanitarian disarmament in a second important way: that is, in the way in which non-governmental lobbyists were engaged in the Conferences, both in the lead-up to the events and in observing and reporting on the diplomats at work. Here we see very clearly the role of civil society in advancing the cause of disarmament. This is explored in detail in Section III.B.3.

33 One of Keefer's key arguments in rejecting this treaty as a wholly humanitarian initiative is the inclusion of the reciprocity clause (Keefer, 'Explosive Missals', above n. 28, p. 455), but in my view, this argument reveals a misunderstanding of a 'humanitarian' initiative.

34 For a recent exposition, see generally, Maartje M. Abbenhuis, *The Hague Conferences and International Politics, 1898–1915* (London: Bloomsbury, 2018); see also, Tate, *The Disarmament Illusion*, above n. 22; Webster, 'Hague Conventions (1899, 1907)', above n. 22; Detley F. Vagts, 'The Hague Conventions and Arms Control' (2000) 94 *American Journal of International Law* 31. See the overview of the 1899 Conference and its proceedings by Robin Sharwood, 'Princes and Peacemakers: The Story of the Hague Peace Conference of 1899' in Timothy L. H. McCormack, Michael Tilbury and Gillian D. Triggs (eds.), *A Century of War and Peace: Asia-Pacific Perspectives on the Centenary of the 1899 Hague Peace Conference* (The Hague; Boston; London: Kluwer Law International, 2001), p. 3. For the sense of the time from the point of view of people rather than state diplomacy, see Barbara Tuchman, *The Proud Tower: A Portrait of the World before the War 1890–1914* (New York: Macmillan, 1966).

1 The Invitation

The 1899 Conference was convened by Czar Nicholas II. The Czar's Foreign Minister, Count Mouravieff, issued the invitation to attend in the following terms:

> The maintenance of general peace and a possible reduction of the excessive armaments which weigh upon all nations present themselves, in the existing condition of the whole world, as the ideal towards which the endeavors of all Governments should be directed.
>
> The humanitarian and magnanimous views of His Majesty the Emperor, my august master, are in perfect accord with this sentiment.[35]

Thus, the invitation went on, conditions were right to seek: 'the most effective means of ensuring to all peoples the benefits of a real and lasting peace, and above all of limiting the progressive development of existing armaments.'[36] A humanitarian motivation is certainly evident from the terms of the invitation itself, particularly given that this was the first time that a global peace conference had been convened, not with the reactive aim of bringing an existing conflict to an end, but rather as a proactive attempt (at least purported) to bring about a 'lasting peace'.[37] That in itself suggests that the proposed Conference would transcend the politics of war and conflict, and instead work towards what we would term today 'international peace and security'.

The humanitarian framing of the invitation notwithstanding, there is a great deal of debate about the true motives behind the invitation.[38] On the one hand, contemporary peace activists enthusiastically commended the Czar for the move and ascribed to him pure humanitarian ideals.[39] But many commentators, contemporary and subsequently, held the view

[35] *Russian Circulate Note Proposing the First Peace Conference, August 1898*, reproduced in James Brown Scott (ed.), *Hague Conventions and Declarations of 1899 and 1907: Accompanied by Tables of Signatures, Ratifications and Adhesions of the Various Powers, and Texts of Reservations*, 2nd ed. (New York: Oxford University Press, 1915), p. xv.

[36] Ibid.

[37] Webster, 'Hague Conventions (1899, 1907)', above n. 22, p. 1. See generally, Sharwood, 'Princes and Peacemakers', above n. 34; Dan L. Morrill, 'Nicolas II and the Call for the First Hague Peace Conference' (1974) 46(2) *Journal of Modern History* 296; John Mack, 'Nicholas II and the Rescript for Peace of 1898: Apostle of Peace or Shrewd Politician?' (2004) 31(12) *Russian History* 83.

[38] See Morrill, 'Nicolas II and the Call for the First Hague Peace Conference', above n. 37; Vagts, 'Hague Convention and Arms Control', above n. 34, p. 33 (stressing the financial burdens of armaments as a motive).

[39] Tuchman, *The Proud Tower*, above n. 34, pp. 231–3, using Bertha von Suttner's book *Lay Down Your Arms* (1889) as an example. Morrill, 'Nicolas II and the Call for the First

that the humanitarian aim articulated in the original Russian circular was deceitful and hypocritical.[40]

One of the most detailed examinations of accounts of the lead-up to the Russian decision to convene the Conference is by Morrill.[41] Those accounts show that there were a number of different motivations at play. There were concerns (particularly on the part of the Minister of War, Aleksei Kuropatkin, as well as the Czar himself) about committing any further money to armaments at that time, but nevertheless officials and the Czar remained concerned about military security and maintaining Russia's power.[42] One means by which military spending could be reduced while maintaining security was to engineer an 'arms freeze'.[43] Indeed, the seeds of the idea of a peace conference lay in a much less ambitious proposal that Russia agree a ten-year moratorium with Vienna on the deployment of the newly developed rapid-fire field artillery in Germany and Austria-Hungary.[44] It seems from Morrill's account that the initial idea of a moratorium was a response to the financial expense involved in deploying the artillery.[45] However, Morrill goes on to explain that when the proposed moratorium was presented to the Czar, it was presented not as a financial matter, but as a humanitarian gesture.[46] It was a proposal that the Czar adopted with enthusiasm, even though there is evidence that the Czar was also concerned about the financial implications of needing to supply the army with the new artillery.[47] Over time, and with the involvement of the Ministry of Foreign Affairs among others, a number of other motives and concerns were in play, not least the broader relationship with Great Britain and the need to counter British attempts to portray Russia as 'aggressive and bombastic'.[48]While acknowledging the range of different

Hague Peace Conference', above n. 37, at p. 296 suggests that W. T. Stead, a prominent journalist of the time, was also favourably inclined to the Czar.

40 Morrill, 'Nicolas II and the Call for the First Hague Peace Conference', above n. 37 concludes that several factors, some pragmatic and some idealist, probably influenced the Czar.

41 Morrill, 'Nicolas II and the Call for the First Hague Peace Conference', above n. 37.

42 The technical innovation and development of weapons at the time is traced and discussed by Echevarria, 'The Arms Race: Qualitative and Quantitative Aspects', above n. 32.

43 Morrill, 'Nicolas II and the Call for the First Hague Peace Conference', above n. 37, p. 298.

44 Ibid.

45 Ibid. See also discussion by Vagts, 'The Hague Conventions and Arms Control', above n. 34, pp. 31–2 on the relationship between the industrial revolution and the development of weapons technology.

46 Morrill, 'Nicolas II and the Call for the First Hague Peace Conference', above n. 37, p. 298.

47 Ibid., p. 299.

48 Ibid., p. 303.

motives, Morrill concludes that the Russian motives in concluding the peace conference were at least in part sincere.[49] As he says: '[N]either pragmatism nor idealism monopolized the scene. Although the relative weight of the latter lost ground, so to speak, almost immediately from the beginning, both were present throughout'.[50] Arthur Eyffinger as well has written in some detail on the motives behind the invitation, also reaching the conclusion that a mixture of impulses were at play: financial interests; short term political concerns regarding the relative military capabilities of Austria-Hungary; and a sincere pacifist sensibility at least on the part of the Czar.[51]

The twin pragmatic and idealistic tones of the Conference are also visible in its final resolution, which refers both to the economic costs of weapons as well as to the 'moral welfare' of people: 'The restriction of military charges, which are at present a heavy burden on the world, is extremely desirable for the increase of the material and moral welfare of mankind'.[52] The opening paragraph of the Final Act stresses the humanitarian theme: 'The International Peace Conference, convoked in the best interests of humanity by His Majesty the Emperor of All the Russias . . .'.[53]

2 The Outcomes

The results of the Conference itself also evince this blend of pragmatism and idealism. In all, of the fifty-nine states invited, twenty-six attended the Conference, which took place over a ten-week period from 18 May to 29 July 1899. Three treaties were concluded: the Convention for the Pacific Settlement of International Disputes, the Convention with Respect to the Laws and Customs of War by Land and the Convention for the Adaptation to Maritime Warfare of the Principles of the Geneva Convention 1864.[54] In addition, and of particular relevance for the

[49] Ibid., p. 298. Compare to Keefer, 'Explosive Missals', above n. 28, who is much more inclined to view the Russian actions with cynicism.

[50] Morrill, 'Nicolas II and the Call for the First Hague Peace Conference', above n. 37, p. 313.

[51] Arthur Eyffinger, *The 1899 Hague Peace Conference: 'The Parliament of Man, The Federation of the World'* (The Hague; London; Boston: Kluwer Law International, 1999), pp. 15–25.

[52] Final Acts of the First and Second Hague Peace Conferences, Together with the Draft Convention on a Judicial Arbitration Court reproduced in Scott, Hague Conventions and Declarations of 1899 and 1907, above n. 35, p. 28.

[53] Ibid., p. 1.

[54] Convention for the Pacific Settlement of International Disputes 1899, reproduced in Scott, *Hague Conventions and Declarations of 1899 and 1907*, above n. 35, p. 41; Convention with Respect to the Laws and Customs of War by Land 1899, reproduced in Scott, *Hague Conventions and Declarations of 1899 and 1907*, above n. 35, p. 100;

current discussion, agreement was reached on three declarations relating to particular weapons or means of warfare.[55] The first of those was the Declaration Prohibiting the Discharge of Projectiles and Explosives from Balloons.[56] As its name suggests, it prohibited dropping projectiles and explosives from balloons – essentially a regulation of aerial bombardment, a relatively new and untested mode of warfare at the time.[57] The other two declarations were about weapons directly, rather than a means of delivery of a weapon: Declaration (IV, 2) Concerning Asphyxiating Gases (an agreement to abstain from the use of projectiles the sole object of which was the diffusion of asphyxiating or deleterious gases) and Declaration (IV, 3) Concerning Expanding Bullets (an agreement to abstain from the use of bullets which expand or flatten easily in the human body).[58] There was no agreement on the question of rapid-fire artillery – the technology at the heart of the original proposal for the Conference.

Considering these outcomes through the lens of the debate on the humanitarian credentials of the Conference, the results point in both directions. On the one hand, the starting (at least stated) ambition of the Conference – to bring about a general and lasting peace – was not realised. Therefore, retreating to the more modest aim of achieving agreement on a series of prohibitions of various weapons types or means of delivery could be characterised as humanitarian progress. On the other hand, by retreating from the more fundamental aim of a lasting peace, and by agreeing to a compromise of a ban on a few categories of weapons, it could be said that the use of all other weapons types is

Convention for the Adaptation to Maritime Warfare of the Principles of the Geneva Convention 1864, reproduced in Scott, *Hague Conventions and Declarations of 1899 and 1907*, above n. 35, p. 163.

55 For an overview, see Vagts, 'The Hague Convention and Arms Control', above n. 34.

56 Hague Declaration of 1899 (IV, 1) Prohibiting the Discharge of Projectiles and Explosives from Balloons, reproduced in Scott, *Hague Conventions and Declarations of 1899 and 1907*, above n. 35, p. 220.

57 According to its first operative paragraph, the Declaration was only to remain in force for five years and, as per operative paragraph two, it was binding only as between the parties to the treaty in times of war. It was extended at the 1907 Conference until the close of the Third Peace Conference, which never eventuated.

58 Declaration (IV, 2) Concerning Asphyxiating Gases 1899, reproduced in Scott, *Hague Conventions and Declarations of 1899 and 1907*, above n. 35, p. 225; and Declaration (IV, 3) Concerning Expanding Bullets 1899, reproduced in Scott, *Hague Conventions and Declarations of 1899 and 1907*, above n. 35, p. 227. See also Robert J. Mathews, 'Chemical and Biological Weapons' in Rain Liivoja and Tim McCormack (eds.), *Handbook on the Law of Armed Conflict* (London: Routledge, 2016), pp. 212, 214.

implicitly accepted. Thus, the partiality of humanitarianism was revealed – the weapons that were banned ostensibly purely on humanitarian grounds are actually the weapons on which political agreement could be reached. That is not to say that the agreements did not represent a humanitarian advance, but rather that it is over-simplistic to view the agreements as being arrived at in an apolitical manner dictated only by a humanitarian impulse.

The same divergence is evident when the agreements themselves are considered in more detail. The two Declarations on weapons (on Asphyxiating Gases and on Expanding Bullets) can be seen as instances of both humanitarian idealism and political pragmatism. Both contained reciprocity clauses: that is, as with the St Petersburg Declaration before them, these Declarations were applicable only in wars between two or more contracting Powers and furthermore, would cease to be binding if one of the belligerents were to be joined by a non-contracting power. The Declaration Prohibiting the Discharge of Projectiles and Explosives from Balloons had a similar limitation and further, it was to remain in force for only five years. In his analysis of the outcomes of the Conference, Keefer relies on the reciprocity clauses and the five-year limitation to the aerial bombardment declaration to support his rejection of the humanitarian framing of the Conference and its outcomes. He correctly points out that the Geneva Convention of the Amelioration of the Condition of the Wounded in the Field 1864 did not contain a reciprocity clause.[59] He further argues, based on a detailed examination of the British papers and attitudes to the Conference, that the British were antagonistic to the idea of arms control.[60] In addition, during the Conference, there was a particular objection to the ban on expanding bullets, as this was perceived by the British as a challenge to them in particular.

In my view, Keefer takes his argument too far. While it is true that a reciprocity clause does suggest something other than a pure humanitarian impulse, it does not absolutely preclude the humanitarian motives of at least some of the negotiators. It is already clear from the examination of the Russian preparation for the Conference, as discussed by Morrill, that the motives for convening the Conference were varied, as were the motives of the different participants in choosing to accept the invitation.

[59] Keefer, 'Explosive Missals', above n. 28, p. 455.

[60] Ibid., pp. 458–9. He explains that because the United Kingdom was a relatively small power, the technology was very important in order to maintain its position as a Great Power. There were also real concerns about the need to conduct (unlimited) warfare with the 'savage races'.

But to suggest from this that there was no humanitarian impulse is to take the argument too far. Indeed, Keefer even acknowledges in his conclusion that there were two major rationales – strategic interest and humanitarian concern.[61] Further, Keefer himself explains that the five-year limit on aerial bombardment is explained by the delegates' uncertainty about the way in which the technology was developing.[62]

Another significant outcome of the Conference in terms of control of weapons was what came to be known as the 'Martens Clause' appearing as a preambular paragraph to the Hague Convention (II) With Respect to the Laws and Customs of War on Land. That paragraph provided:

> Until a more complete code of the laws of war has been issued, the High Contracting parties deem it expedient to declare that, in cases not included in the Regulations adopted by them, the inhabitants and the belligerents remain under the protection and the rule of the principles of the law of nations, as they result from the usages established among civilized peoples from the laws of humanity, and the dictates of the public conscience.[63]

The clause is considered to be the first time that humanitarian considerations were embodied within legal rules.[64] As Cassese points out, whatever the merits of the debate around its normative value at the time, or the motivations behind it, it is unquestionable that the provision has had a significant impact in the development of both international humanitarian law and disarmament law.[65]

Whatever the debates regarding the true motivations behind the Conference, the significance of its outcomes show that public opinion can and did influence the negotiating positions at the time and subsequently. While the Declarations all contained reciprocity clauses, in fact, the ban on the weapons did go on to form the basis of more generally applicable rules.[66] This was despite the fact that, as discussed above, the

61 Ibid., p. 463.

62 Ibid., p. 462.

63 Preambular paragraph 9.

64 Antonio Cassese, 'The Martens Clause: Half a Loaf or Simply Pie in the Sky?' (2000) 11(1) *European Journal of International Law* 187, 188.

65 The literature on the Martens Clause is vast. For an overview, see Cassese, 'The Martens Clause', ibid. and citations therein. See also the more recent critical reflection by Rotem Giladi, 'The Enactment of Irony' (2014) 25(3) *European Journal of International Law* 847 referring to the 'Martens cult'; and Ticktin, 'Transnational Humanitarianism', above n. 14.

66 See International Committee of the Red Cross, *Customary International Humanitarian Law* (New York: Cambridge University Press, 2005), rules 72 and 77.

instruments were formally applicable only if all belligerents in a conflict were party to the Declarations. While Britain refused to ratify any of the three Declarations in 1899, that position changed and Britain acceded to the two weapons Declarations in 1907 and to the Declaration on aerial bombardment in 1909.[67] Why was this the case? One powerful answer lies in the second important feature of humanitarian disarmament, namely, the role of public opinion and civil society. In this respect, the First Hague Peace Conference was an important milestone in the story of humanitarian disarmament and it is to that we now turn.

3 Civil Society and Public Opinion

The nineteenth-century peace movement was 'highly organised, international in scale, very high profile and at times brilliantly led' and it played a significant role in persuading world powers that the Czar's invitation had to be accepted.[68] This reflected the fact that, as explained above, the period was one of a developing humanitarian sensibility and a 'public sensitivity to suffering'.[69] Within arms limitation particularly, peace societies were among the first international NGOs referred to in this era as 'private international associations'.[70] Charnovitz calculates that by 1900 there were 425 peace societies in existence.[71] At that time, the peace societies had a particular interest in issues of arms limitation and disarmament – issues that were seen as essential components of peace. Thus, the International Peace Bureau, created in 1891 with the aim of

[67] Scott Andrew Keefer, 'Building the Palace of Peace: The Hague Conference of 1899 and Arms Control in the Progressive Era' (2006) 8 *Journal of the History of International Law* 1, 13.

[68] Sharwood, above n. 34, p. 7. Steve Charnovitz, 'Two Centuries of Participation: NGOs and International Governance' (1996–7) 18 *Michigan Journal of International Law* 183. Both Sharwood and Charnovitz bemoan the neglect in the literature of the power, scale and force of these early peace movements. Charnovitz especially chides scholars for ignoring pre-1945 developments. He traces NGO participation back to 1775 and work on the opposition to the slave trade, although he notes that there was NGO engagement with international law prior to that. See also Steve Charnovitz, 'Nongovernmental Organizations and International Law' (2006) 100 *American Journal of International Law* 348, 349.

[69] Vagts, 'The Hague Convention and Arms Control', above n. 34, p. 32 and Charnovitz, 'Two Centuries of Participation', above n. 68, pp. 191–2.

[70] Charnovitz, 'Two Centuries of Participation', above n. 68, p. 192. And see the discussion of the emergence of peace activism by Thomas Richard Davies, *The Possibilities of Transnational Activism: The Campaign for Disarmament between the Two World Wars* (Leiden; Boston: Martinus Nijhoff Publishers, 2007), ch. 3.

[71] Charnovitz, 'Two Centuries of Participation', above n. 68, p. 192.

coordinating annual peace congresses, passed resolutions on disarmament at all of its congresses.[72]

The first major opportunity for a concerted civil society disarmament campaign, however, came with the 1899 Peace Conference. A key aim of civil society was to inform and influence public opinion, but also to lobby participating government delegations in the lead-up to the Conference, as well as during the Conference itself. Thus, civil society activities included extensive information campaigns including public demonstrations as well as specific petitions to delegations.[73] Many peace activists attended the Conference itself (it was the first such event to permit public access to diplomatic discussions),[74] and in doing so, they did not just report on the discussions over the weeks of the Conference, but also persistently lobbied delegates to adopt positions favourable to disarmament. The journalist William T Stead wrote the chronicles of the proceedings in what can be seen as a nineteenth-century 'blog'.[75] A petition was presented to the President of the Conference with over a million signatures from women worldwide.[76]

In a pattern that was to repeat, there was not a direct correlation between the lofty disarmament ambitions of the peace movement and the more modest outcomes of the Conference. Nonetheless, the involvement of civil society within the Conference itself, and as a conduit to the public, marks the Conference as an important example of humanitarian disarmament.

C *The Second Hague Peace Conference 1907: Disarmament Waning*

The Final Resolution of the 1899 Conference stated that it would be 'highly desirable' to 'further study' the disarmament question.[77]

[72] Davies, 'Campaign for Disarmament between the Two World Wars', above n. 70, p. 32.
[73] Ibid., p. 33; Charnovitz, 'Two Centuries of Participation', above n. 68, p. 196. And see Eyffinger, 'The 1899 Hague Peace Conference', above n. 51, ch. 9, especially pp. 351–2.
[74] Tuchman, *The Proud Tower*, above n. 34, pp. 257–8.
[75] For a short overview of the colourful life of William T. Stead, see Tuchman, *The Proud Tower*, above n. 34, pp. 245–8. Interestingly, the Conference is not mentioned in his biography: W. Sydney Robinson, *Muckraker: The Scandalous Life and Times of W.T. Stead* (London: Robson Press, 2012).
[76] Davies, 'Campaign for Disarmament between the Two World Wars', above n. 70, p. 34.
[77] Tuchman, *The Proud Tower*, above n. 34 explains that 'limitation of armaments rather than disarmament was the question at issue, but the single word, being less awkward, was generally used at the time' to mean disarmament: at p. 276. She characterises the sentiment in the Final Resolution as 'pious dirge': at p. 267.

However, events in the intervening years had not enhanced the conditions for fruitful (or indeed, any) disarmament discussions given the Russian defeat in the Russo-Japanese War (1904–5)[78] and the massive increase in military expenditure by Britain triggered by the Boer War (1899–1902).[79] Thus, by 1907, there was little, if any, enthusiasm for disarmament on the part of the major powers.[80] Even among the contemporary scholarly commentators, there was a debate as to whether disarmament was useful or dangerous.[81]

In fact, while the Russians formally convened the Conference as they had done for the 1899 Conference, this time the invitation came about due to American insistence. By now the Russians were more reluctant. As regards disarmament issues being included in the agenda of the Conference, there was some hostility, with the Russian Foreign Minister at the time, Izvolsky, saying that disarmament was 'a craze of Jews, Socialists and hysterical women'.[82] Germany, too, was resistant with the Kaiser stating that if disarmament was raised in any form, his delegates would leave the Conference.[83] Thus, by the time the Russians issued the draft agenda for the Conference in April 1907, all reference to armaments had been dropped.[84]

78 Arthur Eyffinger, 'A Highly Critical Moment: Role and Record of the 1907 Hague Peace Conference' (2007) 54(2) *Netherlands International Law Review* 197, 203. See also the short discussion by Francis Anthony Boyle, *Foundations of World Order: The Legalist Approach to International Relations (1898–1922)* (Durham: Duke University Press, 1999), pp. 72–3.

79 A. J. A. Morris, 'The English Radicals' Campaign for Disarmament and the Hague Peace Conference of 1907' (1971) 43(3) *The Journal of Modern History* 367, 369–70.

80 Webster, 'Hague Conventions (1899, 1907)', above n. 22, p. 3. See also the discussion by Andre T. Sidorowicz, 'The British Government, the Hague Peace Conference of 1907, and the Armaments Question' in B. J. C. McKercher (ed.), *Arms Limitation and Disarmament: Restraints on War, 1899-1939* (Westport: Praeger Publishers, 1992), p. 1, in which he suggests that the British attempt to get disarmament on the table was due to the newly elected Liberal Party trying to make good on its election promise to reduce expenditure on armaments, while remaining safe in the knowledge that their naval strength would be maintained. See the full discussion by Tuchman, *The Proud Tower*, above n. 34, explaining how the Britain and the United States agreed to put disarmament on the table for discussion, on the shared understanding that it would not result in any actual outcomes: at pp. 267–88.

81 Compare Richmond Pearson Hobson, 'Disarmament' (2008) 2 *American Journal of International Law* 743 and Benjamin F. Trueblood, 'The Case for Limitation of Armaments' (1908) 2 *American Journal of International Law* 758.

82 Tuchman, *The Proud Tower*, above n. 34, p. 277.

83 Ibid.

84 Morris, 'The English Radicals' Campaign for Disarmament', above n. 79, p. 374.

However, while there was resistance to even discussing disarmament among diplomats, in particular among the Great Powers, public pressure could not so easily be dismissed.[85] The peace movement would have been outraged if there had not been some efforts to reach a truce on armaments.[86] This is why the 1907 Conference can be classified under the rubric 'humanitarian disarmament' – not so much in terms of outcomes (as we will see, they were disappointing), but in terms of the engagement by civil society.

In disarmament terms, the Conference was an almost absolute failure. Over a four-month conference, only twenty-five minutes were devoted to disarmament. Tuchman observes that this only happened due to the British delegation being concerned about the strength of public opinion and so, Sir Edward Grey (UK) moved a resolution calling for further serious study of the issue.[87] The Final Act said:

> The Second Conference of Peace confirms the Resolution adopted by the Conference of 1899 in regard to the limitation of military expenditure; and inasmuch as military expenditure has considerably increased in almost every country since that time, the Conference declares that it is eminently desirable that the Governments should resume the serious examination of this question.[88]

While the lack of progress in disarmament was disappointing, and would seem to point to a conclusion that the humanitarian impulse had been wholly ineffective, more broadly the Conferences had brought about a fundamental change. Andrew Webster concludes that the Conferences are significant because, while they achieved little in the way of actual reduction of armaments, they planted the idea among disarmament advocates that there could be, and even should be, an international authority involved in disarmament.[89] Indeed, this was an idea that resurfaced within the League of Nations. Looking at the question of humanitarian disarmament more specifically, the Conferences showed the importance of lobbying by civil society. And while that did succeed in bringing state delegations to a negotiation, and even getting disarmament on the agenda, it did not dictate actual outcomes.

85 Tuchman, *The Proud Tower*, above n. 34, p. 280.
86 Ibid. See also, Webster, 'Hague Conventions (1899, 1907)', above n. 22, pp. 3–4.
87 Tuchman, *The Proud Tower*, above n. 34, records that this only proceeded because of the need to be responsive to some degree to English public opinion: at p. 280.
88 Final Act of the Second International Peace Conference 1907, reproduced in Scott, *Hague Conventions and Declarations of 1899 and 1907*, above n. 35, p. 28.
89 Webster, 'Hague Conventions (1899, 1907)', above n. 22, p. 5.

The Conference ended with a call for a Third Conference to be convened in 1915, but of course, by then the First World War had engulfed the Powers and obliterated any possibilities for reconvening a third time.

IV Interwar Humanitarian Disarmament: The League of Nations

However distant the goal of disarmament may have seemed in 1907, with the outbreak of the First World War it became a lost cause. All over Europe and even further afield, there was a massive weapons development and corresponding resources expended on arms build-up. The period saw the further development and large-scale use of machine guns, the Zeppelin, submarine U-boats and perhaps most notoriously, the development and use of chemical weapons ('gas warfare'). The War unleashed an unprecedented humanitarian catastrophe in terms of the scale and manner of the slaughter. Taken together, these changes resulted in a radically altered landscape in terms of both humanitarian action and the challenge of disarmament. While the League is often remembered for the failure of the World Disarmament Conference which convened between 1932 and 1934, as I will show in this section, there were a number of significant instances of humanitarian disarmament during the interwar years.

Section A canvasses the way in which the League institutionalised and professionalised humanitarianism, while Section B shows how disarmament was an important feature of the League of Nations. In particular, I discuss three aspects of the League's disarmament work: the engagement between the League and civil society (Section IV.B.1); the work of the Temporary Mixed Commission on Armaments (Section IV.B.2); and the negotiations for the Geneva Protocol (Section IV.B.3). Section IV.C then provides some concluding reflections on the League's legacy of humanitarian disarmament.

A *The Evolution of Humanitarianism in the Interwar Years*

The First World War was a humanitarian catastrophe in terms of the severity and scale of the destruction wrought by the War, the numbers of sick and wounded (including civilians), and especially the unprecedented numbers of displaced persons in Europe as the War came to an end.[90]

[90] Barnett, *Empire of Humanity*, above n. 4, p. 82.

The scale of the humanitarian crisis meant the immediate post-War years saw a dramatic expansion of humanitarian relief work.[91] Unprecedented numbers of civil society organisations concerned with different aspects of welfare were created in the 1920s – in fact, twice the number created during the entire nineteenth century.[92] In the United States, a number of relief societies started to consolidate their activities in order to more effectively organise and deliver aid across the Atlantic to a war-stricken Europe. In this way, humanitarianism started to institutionalise and professionalise.[93] At the same time, and as a consequence, humanitarianism moved further away from its explicitly religious roots. As Barnett explains, 'humanitarianism's once-explicit religious discourse was losing ground to the discourse of humanity and international community'.[94] Thus, in comparison to pre-War practices, in the years after 1918 humanitarianism evolved to become a more secular, professional enterprise and, with the involvement of international agencies such as the International Labour Organization (ILO), it became an international project.[95]

In this context, the newly created League of Nations filled an important role.[96] The League epitomised the humanitarian sensibilities of the post-War world and provided an international institutional framework to advance humanitarian aims. Indeed, even as the Covenant of the League of Nations (the Covenant)[97] was being negotiated, there was extensive NGO engagement. Peace groups such as the Women's International League for Peace and Freedom (WILPF), which had been formed in 1915, came to Paris to lobby the negotiators, along with many other groups lobbying for diverse issues such as minority rights, public health, education issues, trafficking in women and children, narcotics, refugee issues, child welfare and labour issues.[98]

[91] Ibid., p. 86.

[92] Charnovitz, 'Two Centuries of Participation', above n. 68, pp. 212–46.

[93] Barnett, *Empire of Humanity*, above n. 4, p. 82. See also discussion by Cabanes, *The Great War and the Origins of Humanitarianism*, above n. 4, p. 4.

[94] Barnett, *Empire of Humanity*, above n. 4, p. 94.

[95] Cabanes, *The Great War and the Origins of Humanitarianism*, above n. 4, p. 105.

[96] For overview of the humanitarian programme of the League, see Zara Steiner, *The Lights That Failed: European International History 1919–1933* (New York: Oxford University Press, 2005), pp. 367–71.

[97] Treaty of Peace between the Allied and Associated Powers and Germany, signed 28 June 1919 (entered into force 10 January 1920) pt I.

[98] See Charnovitz, 'Two Centuries of Participation', above n. 68, pp. 213–46 for a detailed account of this period.

Despite the level of engagement, only one provision in the Covenant referred to NGOs, and that was article 25 in which member states agreed: 'to encourage and promote the establishment and co-operation of duly authorized voluntary national Red Cross organizations having as purposes the improvement of health, the prevention of disease, and the mitigation of suffering throughout the world'.[99] Despite this unpromising starting point in terms of Covenant provisions, the actual practice of the League was relatively open to NGOs, going beyond the strict letter of the Covenant (although this did not remain constant over its life). NGOs were invited to participate in meetings, and they played a significant role in the work of the League including not only immediate relief work, but also longer-term projects such as protection of national minorities, resettlement of refugees following the war, work on health standards as well as the considerable work of the ILO in the area of workers' protection.[100]

The League institutionalised, professionalised and internationalised humanitarian action and facilitated the emergence of a secular network of expert humanitarians.[101] In doing so, it created an 'illusion of a global moral community'.[102] That community included not just states, but an active civil society, concerned about humanitarian issues. The ILO illustrates the receptivity to the idea of a broader community – with its tripartite structure whereby each delegation included a state official, a union official and a representative from industry.[103]

B *The Rise of Disarmament in the League*[104]

This sense of a transnational community with a shared commitment to humanitarian action infused the disarmament agenda of the League.[105]

[99] Treaty of Peace between the Allied and Associated Powers and Germany, signed 28 June 1919 (entered into force 10 January 1920) (Treaty of Versailles) Article 25 which encouraged cooperation with the Red Cross and its work on health, alleviation of disease and mitigation of suffering. For discussion, see Charnovitz, 'Two Centuries of Participation', above n. 68, p. 220.

[100] Charnovitz, 'Two Centuries of Participation', above n. 68, pp. 212–46. See also Steiner, *The Lights That Failed*, above n. 96, ch. 7.

[101] Cabanes, *The Great War and the Origins of Humanitarianism*, above n. 4, p. 303.

[102] Fassin, 'The Predicament of Humanitarianism', above n. 11, p. 37.

[103] Charnovitz, 'Two Centuries of Participation', above n. 68, pp. 216–17.

[104] For an official record of the disarmament work of the League, see United Nations Secretariat, *Historical Survey of the Activities of the League of Nations Regarding the Question of Disarmament 1920–1937*, UN Doc A/AC50/2 (18 June 1951).

[105] Andrew Webster points out that the Covenant itself does not itself use the expression 'disarmament', instead referring to the 'regulation', 'reduction' or 'limitation' of

The very first article of the Covenant required members of the League to accept 'such regulations as may be prescribed by the League in regard to its military, naval, and air forces and armament'. Complementing this, Article 8 of the Covenant began with a general statement about the relationship between peace and disarmament. It provided:

> The Members of the League recognise that the maintenance of peace requires the reduction of national armaments to the lowest point consistent with national safety and the enforcement by common action of international obligations.[106]

Before the War, the relationship between peace and disarmament had been the subject of a lively debate. While the peace activists held firmly to the view that disarmament was an important aspect of achieving international peace, others saw the relationship differently.[107] In a precursor to deterrence theory of the twentieth century, many subscribed to the view that the key to peace lay in military strength.[108] American naval strategist of the time, Alfred Thayer Mahan went so far as to argue that disarmament would bring about the destruction of western civilisation.[109]

Thus, in Article 8, it seemed as though the Covenant had articulated a major shift away from the peace-first-disarmament-later paradigm, which had dominated in the pre-War era. Following the War,

armaments: Andrew Webster, 'Making Disarmament Work: The Implementation of the International Disarmament Provisions in the League of Nations Covenant, 1919–1925' 16 (3) *Diplomacy and Statecraft* (2005) 551, 552. Webster points out that issue of terminology reflected and perpetuated the significant differences in understanding what the League was to do. See as well the discussion by Steiner, *The Lights That Failed*, above n. 96, pp. 372–82, ch. 11, ch. 14.

[106] Discussed by Steiner, *The Lights That Failed*, above n. 96, p. 372.

[107] But see the statement by Christine Lange, the Norwegian delegate to the League in 1921: 'I wonder whether it is not the very armaments of the nations which create conflicts. In any case they create distrust, and perpetuate the atmosphere of mutual fear among the nations, which is the most profound and fruitful cause of international crises. So far from providing a guarantee of security, armaments constitute an element of insecurity.' Cited by Andrew Webster, 'The League of Nations and Grand Strategy: A Contradiction in Terms?' in J. W. Taliaferro, N. M. Ripsman and S. E. Lobell (eds.), *The Challenge of Grand Strategy: The Great Powers and the Broken Balance between the World Wars* (New York: Cambridge University Press, 2012) p. 93, n. 37.

[108] See John Lambelet, 'Do Arms Races Lead to War?' (1975) 12 *Journal Peace Research* 123. See also David Cortright, *Peace: A History of Movements and Ideas* (New York: Cambridge University Press, 2008), ch. 5.

[109] Alfred Thayer Mahan, *Armaments and Arbitration or the Place of Force in the International Relations of States* (New York and London: Harper & Brothers, 1912), p. 120.

a common, even dominant, view was that the War had been caused, at least in part, by the build-up of arms.[110] That, coupled with the scale and manner of the slaughter during the War, particularly with the new technology (the Zeppelins and chemical weapons for example), explains Article 8 and the League's emphasis on disarmament. Disarmament was seen as part of the overall humanitarian objectives of the League.

However, despite this important shift in thinking, there was by no means an uncontested move towards disarmament as a route to peace, whether couched in humanitarian terms or otherwise. For example, in the aftermath of the War, both Great Britain and France were of the view that there was 'no substitute for military power in underwriting the safety of the state',[111] despite their public (rhetorical) commitment to the cause of disarmament. That being said, there was strong public feeling about the need to limit, if not eliminate stockpiles of armaments. There were also powerful financial reasons to curb arms in the wake of the devastation in Europe. However, there remained a strong belief at state level, particularly France, which was most vulnerable to Germany, in the need to maintain armaments for defensive purposes.[112]

Nonetheless, Article 8 went on to elaborate how these general statements about disarmament were to be translated into action. The League Council was to formulate implementation plans, which would be revised at least every ten years.[113] The Council was also to advise on the problem of the private arms trade, and member states undertook to exchange information on their armaments, military programmes and war-industries. Article 9 anticipated the creation of a Commission to advise the Council on disarmament matters. Articles 22 and 23 addressed the regulation of the global arms trade. Taken as a whole, the Covenant was the most ambitious and far-reaching attempt at international

110 Steiner, *The Lights That Failed*, above n. 96, p. 372. The literature on the causes of the First World War is vast. For an accessible, relatively recent discussion, see Niall Ferguson, *The Pity of War* (New York: Basic Books, 1999), especially chs. 1–4. Sir Edward Grey, the British Foreign Secretary wrote that the 'enormous growth of armaments in Europe, the sense of insecurity and fear caused by them – it was these that made war inevitable.' Cited in Webster, 'Making Disarmament Work', above n. 105, p. 551.

111 Steiner, *The Lights That Failed*, above n. 96, p. 373.

112 Ibid.

113 With a similar arrangement as with today's Security Council there were a mixture of permanent and non-permanent members, with two year rotating terms for the latter group. The United Kingdom and France were permanent members for the entire life of the League; Japan held permanent membership until 1933 and Italy until 1937. Germany was a permanent member from 1926 to 1933 and the USSR between 1934 and 1939.

disarmament at the time, and indeed remains so today. Inserted at the insistence of United States President Woodrow Wilson these disarmament provisions, and the thinking that lay behind them, epitomised the humanitarian sensibilities and the internationalist spirit of the League in the context of disarmament.[114] But they did not entirely eclipse the standard armaments-for-security paradigm.

However, in the present context, my specific argument is that the League was not only important in the history of attempts at international disarmament, but also a significant chapter in the development of ideas about humanitarian disarmament. Three aspects of the League's work on disarmament are discussed in the following sections to support this argument. The first is the way in which the League engaged with civil society on disarmament matters. The second instance of humanitarian disarmament was the creation of the Mixed Temporary Commission on Armaments (MTCA). The third, and most well-known example, was the Geneva Protocol 1925 which prohibited the use of chemical and biological weapons in war.[115] In all three examples, as I will show, there was an ever-present struggle against the armaments-for-security paradigm.

1 Civil Society, the League and Disarmament

A key element of the definition of 'humanitarian disarmament' is engagement with and by civil society.[116] In other words, humanitarian disarmament means that discussions and negotiations around disarmament are in some way open to engagement with, and possibly even influence by, civil society. This has been an important part of humanitarian initiatives in the disarmament sphere because it allows a space for issues to be considered outside of the context of direct national (security) interests.

Civil society played an active role in the League even before its formal creation. The humanitarian consequences of the War added to the impetus of the peace movement and those within the movement who were particularly concerned with disarmament. The WILPF was created

[114] Andrew Webster, 'Piecing Together the Inter-war Disarmament Puzzle: Trends and Possibilities' (2003–4) 59 *International Journal* 187; See also Leonard V. Smith, 'The Wilsonian Challenge to International Law' (2011) 13 *Journal of the History of International Law* 179; Webster points out that there are important differences between the early and later League eras when discussing disarmament: Webster, 'Making Disarmament Work', above n. 105, p. 564.

[115] Protocol for the Prohibition of the Use in War of Asphyxiating, Poisonous or Other Gases, and of Bacteriological Methods of Warfare, opened for signature 17 June 1925, (1929) XCIV LNTS 65–74 (entered into force 8 February 1928).

[116] Chapter 1, Section IV.C.

in 1915 and it would become an enduring voice for disarmament, adopting strategies and processes still used in today's humanitarian disarmament campaigns.[117] It was not alone in planning for the creation of an intergovernmental institution to be created following the war to maintain peace.[118] Organisations such as the Inter-Parliamentary Union were also in preparation mode. Thus, by Paris in 1919, when the Covenant of the League came to be drafted, there was strong civil society activity and high public expectations that disarmament was to be an important part of the post-War settlement.[119] The perception: '[I]n the broad public imagination was that armaments should be reduced in a coordinated and binding international format, as member states renounced their right to unrestricted control of their own armaments'.[120] In terms of the actual functioning of the League, as discussed above, there was unprecedented engagement by civil society in the early years across all sectors of its work (slavery, labour, refugees, minority rights and so on), and the League's disarmament agenda was no exception. In the early years of the League's work, the Secretariat provided considerable information to the public, and NGOs had considerable access to the workings of the League bodies, including the Council and the Assembly.[121] Particular projects attracted greater attention from the public. For example, as Zara Steiner explains, the Kellogg-Briand Pact negotiations in the late 1920s had caught the public imagination and there was a flood of petitions demanding progress and that a date be set for a world disarmament conference.[122] Similarly, as discussed below, the shocking impact of the use of chemical weapons during the War was the subject of wide concern, with scientists as well as peace activists closely following the discussions about a possible ban.

Looking at the disarmament agenda specifically, Davies explains:

> The scale of transnational mobilization that became achievable after the First World War is particularly well illustrated by the campaign for

117 The meeting which established WILPF is described by A. C. F. Beales, *The History of Peace: A Short Account of the Organised Movements for International Peace* (London: G. Bell & Sons Ltd, 1931), pp. 281–2.

118 Charnovitz, 'Two Centuries of Participation', above n. 68, p. 213.

119 Ibid., pp. 213–16.

120 Webster, 'The League of Nations and Grand Strategy', above n. 107, p. 108.

121 See generally Charnovitz, 'Two Centuries of Participation', above n. 68, pp. 213–46.

122 Steiner, *The Lights That Failed*, above n. 96, pp. 575–7. And see the detailed account of the background to the Pact and its influence in the international order in Oona A. Hathaway and Scott J. Shapiro, *The Internationalists: How a Radical Plan to Outlaw War Remade the World* (New York: Simon and Schuster, 2017).

> disarmament that took place in the 1920s and early 1930s. This campaign mobilized a uniquely broad spectrum of civil society groups (from Rotary International to the Communist International!), including the world's principal labour, humanitarian, religious, students,' women's and peace organizations of the period. The campaign peaked during the World Disarmament Conference convened by the League of Nations in 1932–3, at which INGOs [international non-governmental organisations] with a combined membership estimated to have been between two hundred million and a billion people lobbied delegates for a general disarmament convention. The scale of the activities that these organizations undertook is illustrated by the disarmament petition circulated by women's international organizations from 1930 to 1932, which remains the world's largest international petition in terms of the proportion of the world's population that signed it.[123]

As the years progressed, from the optimistic 1920s, to the unfolding tragedy of the 1930s, both the desire for disarmament and the humanitarian sensibility within many of the member states of the League waned, but popular opinion remained strongly in favour of disarmament. Indeed, during this period, it seems that civil society lobbying for disarmament was at an all-time high. Even as member states were no longer sure of the disarmament cause, and the League Secretariat had started being less open to civil society, the force of civil society in the form of peace groups maintained forward momentum. As Webster argues: 'The progress to a draft disarmament convention in 1930 did not spring from the common cause of a transnational community of experts, but rather came through the intercession of national governments responding to the external pressure of public demands for progress'.[124] The Disarmament Conference ended in abject failure as the League itself collapsed. Despite the years of preparatory work, and the months of work of the Conference, it ended without any agreement at all.

But while public opinion could not stop the collapse of the Conference (or indeed the League), public opinion and lobbying by NGOs repeatedly forced (some) member states to remain at the table and keep discussions going for as long as they did. Time and time again during the League years, states found themselves in situations where they could not publicly reject disarmament initiatives. This was the case particularly for Britain

[123] Davies, 'Campaign for Disarmament between the Two World Wars', above n. 70, pp. 9–10; See as well Charnovitz, 'Two Centuries of Participation', above n. 69, p. 231.

[124] Andrew Webster, 'The Transnational Dream: Politicians, Diplomats and Soldiers in the League of Nations' Pursuit of International Disarmament, 1920–1938' (2005) 14(4) *Contemporary European History* 493, 517.

and France in the context of naval disarmament. Webster concludes that 'domestic political pressures in each of the main naval powers, arising from common fears of a naval arms race, independently moved their policy makers to seek an agreement'[125]

As such, civil society played an active and important role in the disarmament work of the League. It is therefore a significant example of humanitarian disarmament in action.

2 The Temporary Mixed Commission on Armaments: Institutionalised Engagement with Civil Society

The creation of the Temporary Mixed Commission on Armaments (TMCA) stands as an extraordinary example of engagement with civil society in disarmament matters. It came about as a counterweight to the state-led structures of the League. As outlined above, under the Covenant, the Council had ultimate responsibility for disarmament. As required by Article 9, it duly established the Permanent Armaments Commission (the PAC or Commission) in May 1920, which was tasked with advising 'the Council on the execution of the provisions of Articles 1 and 8 and on military, naval and air questions generally'. However, the Commission was composed entirely of military officials from Council members (one each from the respective wings of their armed forces – land, naval and air).[126] Inevitably then, with this composition, the focus was not on the broad disarmament aims set out in the Covenant, but on national security interests and, in particular, the disarmament of Germany.[127] Indeed, the Commission was so adverse to the broader disarmament progress, it reported to the Council in December 1920 that it would be 'premature and dangerous' to attempt to draft an international scheme for the general reduction of armaments.[128] Almost immediately, then, it became clear that the grand visions of (some of the) Covenant drafters were to be subsumed under the security concerns of the Great Powers, at least where the PAC was concerned.

In response to the lack of progress in the Council and the PAC by the end of 1920, at the instigation of the Norwegian delegation and the Inter-Parliamentary Union, the Assembly recommended the creation of

[125] Webster, 'Piecing Together the Inter-War Disarmament Puzzle', above n. 114, p. 192.

[126] Webster, 'Making Disarmament Work', above n. 105, p. 553.

[127] Ibid., p. 554. See as well, Andrew Webster, '"Absolutely Irresponsible Amateurs": The Mixed Temporary Arms Commission on Armaments 1921–1924' (2008) 54(3) *Australian Journal of Politics and History* 373, 375.

[128] Webster, 'Transnational Dream', above n. 124, p. 510.

another disarmament body – the TMCA.[129] Unlike the PAC, the TMCA was to be 'composed of persons possessing the requisite competence in matters of a political, social and economic nature' to prepare proposals 'for the reduction of armaments'.[130] The aim was to have a broader sense of the problem of disarmament, rather than being confined to the technical military approach, which was dominant in the PAC.[131]

Not surprisingly, from the beginning, the idea of such an independent body met with quite some resistance from the Council. The first concern was membership and so, instead of a purely civilian membership, the Council was only prepared to agree to a membership that also included six military experts drawn from the PAC membership. This diluted, but did not destroy, the TMCA's independence.[132] Other compromises were that the Commission was to be temporary, needing to be renewed each year. Thus, the body emerged in slightly more modest form than had been envisaged in the Assembly among the smaller powers. That being said, it was still an extraordinary advance.

The work of the TMCA was wide-ranging, considering at different times proposals to limit land-based armaments,[133] a draft treaty on general disarmament,[134] a draft treaty on Mutual Assistance and a series of reports on means to control the private manufacture of armaments.[135] The TMCA also reported on the known effects of chemical warfare and possible effects of bacteriological warfare (which was to form the basis of the work on the Geneva Protocol 1925 as discussed more fully below),[136] engaged in surveys of national armaments, and elaborated the League's 'right of investigation' within the ex-enemy powers.[137]

Ultimately, however, national interest won out and the TMCA was discontinued in 1924 as the Preparatory Commission started work in anticipation of the World Disarmament Conference.

129 Webster, 'Absolutely Irresponsible Amateurs', above n. 127, p. 376.

130 Ibid., p. 375.

131 Ibid.

132 Ibid.

133 Ibid., p. 379 discussing Lord Esher's proposal to apply a system of ratios to the land and air forces of the major powers, so that for example, the French army in Europe would be reduced from around 334,000 men to 180,000.

134 The product of the work of Lord Robert Cecil, for discussion see Webster, 'Absolutely Irresponsible Amateurs', above n. 127, pp. 381–4.

135 Webster, 'Making Disarmament Work', above n 105, pp. 557–8.

136 Ibid., p. 561.

137 See Webster, 'Absolutely Irresponsible Amateurs', above n. 127, for a detailed consideration of the work of the TMCA.

Even in today's terms, it was an extraordinary innovation, and a great example of humanitarian disarmament, in terms of both process (a formal mechanism to bring in non-state based expertise) and substance. As Andrew Webster concludes, the TMCA can be seen as a:

> [F]ascinating experiment in the possibilities of transnationalism within an international organization. The hope was that eminent private individuals, unbound by the directives of governments who naturally viewed disarmament from the view point of their own strategic interests, might transcend the narrow national self-interests of individual governments and work to achieve a goal of common interest to all humanity. In the realm of national security, no other League committee would ever be given such freedom and such latitude, or possess such moral authority.[138]

Ultimately, the TMCA did not succeed in its disarmament goals, but it nonetheless remains an important part of the story of humanitarian disarmament.

3 Geneva Protocol 1925: Humanitarian Response to the War

The third example of humanitarian disarmament in the work of the League is the Geneva Protocol 1925, which was negotiated as part of the Conference for the Supervision of the International Trade in Arms and Ammunition and in Implements of War. The Protocol outlawed the 'use in war of asphyxiating, poisonous or other gases, and of all analogous liquids, materials or devices'[139] and extended that ban to 'bacteriological methods of warfare'.[140]

The Protocol serves as an example of humanitarian disarmament in that it was a response to the concerns raised about the use of chemical weapons in the War and also because of the way that civil society engaged in lobbying for the ban. The 1899 Peace Conference had reached agreement on a Declaration banning 'asphyxiating gases'[141] and, following the First World War, Germany had been prohibited from possessing 'asphyxiating, poisonous or other gases and all analogous liquids, materials or devices'.[142] With the widespread use of chemical weapons in the

[138] Ibid., p. 387. Footnotes omitted.

[139] The quoted language is taken from the Preamble. The operative clause goes on to say that the High Contracting Parties accept the prohibition.

[140] 1925 Geneva Protocol first operative paragraph.

[141] Declaration (IV, 2) Concerning Asphyxiating Gases 1899, reproduced in Scott, Hague Conventions and Declarations of 1899 and 1907, above n. 35, p. 225, discussed above at Section III.B.2.

[142] Treaty of Versailles art. 171.

First World War, humanitarian concerns deepened. Unsurprisingly then, the issue of chemical warfare was one of the first to be considered by the PAC. It was unable to advance the issue, however, mostly it seems due to an inability to envisage how to constrain the production and use of a weapon that was 'dual use', in that while the chemicals could be, and were, weaponised, they also had legitimate peaceful purposes. In 1922, the TMCA took up the project, and having consulted with scientific experts, a report was prepared on the effects of those weapons. In this way, a 'dialogue of dread' was developed around them – that is, concerns were highlighted about the humanitarian impact of the weapons.[143] In part because of this scientific and factual data, the ground was ready for the United States proposal at a Conference convened in 1925 to consider the problem of traffic in arms, to agree to a separate Protocol prohibiting the use in war of biological or chemical weapons.[144]

The humanitarian aspect of the weapons was also crucial during the US debate on ratification of the Geneva Protocol 1925.[145] There was widespread public support for a ban. An informal poll cited by Slotten shows that 380,000 people were in favour of a ban with only 169 against. For those in favour of the USA joining the ban, it was because chemical weapons were seen as a 'major symbol of the inhumanity of war'.[146]

C The League's Legacy of Humanitarian Disarmament

The League is remembered as a failure in terms of its disarmament aspirations. However, a closer study of the work in that era shows that, not only was disarmament an important and pervasive feature of the League's work, but in that work, there are remarkable exercises of what we would call humanitarian disarmament initiatives today.

143 The term is from Richard Price, *The Chemical Weapons Taboo* (New York: Cornell University Press, 1997), p. 93.

144 Ibid., pp. 88–92 (discussing the negotiations); Webster, 'Making Disarmament Work', above n. 105, p. 562. And see the discussion by Mathews explaining that ultimately because the major military powers did not want to give up their option to use chemical weapons, the Protocol ended up being a 'no first use' compromise: Mathews, 'Chemical and Biological Weapons', above n. 58, p. 216.

145 Price, *The Chemical Weapons Taboo*, above n. 143, pp. 92–6; Hugh R. Slotten 'Humane Chemistry or Scientific Barbarism? American Responses to World War I Poison Gas, 1915–1930' (1990) 77(2) *Journal of American History* 476, 488.

146 Slotten, 'American Responses to World War I Poison Gas', above n. 145, p. 488. Interestingly the other side (opposing the ban) also drew on humanitarian arguments. See Price, *The Chemical Weapons Taboo*, pp. 98–9. See also discussion in Chapter 7 below.

That is not to say that the League was uncomplicatedly humanitarian in approach. From the beginning, there was a strong push back against the humanitarians. There were radically different views among peace activists and states, smaller and more powerful states, and even the public and private positions of states. It rapidly became clear that there was a serious disjuncture between those in the League Secretariat,[147] idealistic drafters such as Lord Robert Cecil on the British delegation,[148] President Woodrow Wilson on the American delegation,[149] and more hard-headed realists, such as France.[150]

The hard-headed realist approach to disarmament in this era is evident in the disarmament of Germany, which has received most of the attention in the scholarly work, in particular in linking the harshness of both the disarmament requirements and the extent of reparations to the subsequent rise of Hitler and ultimately, to the outbreak of the Second World War. The Treaty of Versailles provided that the German army should be limited to 100,000 men, and denied all tanks and heavy artillery.[151] The navy was severely restricted.[152] An air force was not permitted at all. The manufacture of arms and munitions was severely restricted.[153] The disarmament of the defeated states was separated from any broader discussion of disarmament. Further, unlike other disarmament work of the League, the disarmament of the defeated states was an entirely state-centred affair with no input from civil society whatsoever.[154] This demonstrates that even at the first full flush of humanitarian sensibilities at Versailles about a new world order, there were 'no go' areas where hard power dictated processes and outcomes.[155]

147 See Salvador de Madariaga, *Disarmament* (New York: Coward McCann, 1929) and *Morning without Noon: Memoirs* (Farnborough, Saxon House, 1973). He was chief of the Disarmament Section in the League's Secretariat.

148 See Lord Robert Cecil, *A Great Experiment* (London: Jonathan Cape, 1941) and discussion by Webster, 'Absolutely Irresponsible Amateurs', above n. 127, p. 380.

149 See generally Smith, 'The Wilsonian Challenge to International Law', above n. 114.

150 Noting the note of caution sounded by Smith as to the way in which the 'fixation on the personal' can obscure more important issues: Ibid., p. 180.

151 Treaty of Versailles part V.

152 Ibid.

153 Ibid.

154 For a general account of the process (and a notable absence of reference to civil society), see Lorna S. Jaffe, 'Abolishing War? Military Disarmament at the Paris Peace Conference, 1919' in B. J. C. McKercher (ed.), *Arms Limitation and Disarmament: Restraints on War, 1899–1939* (Connecticut: Praeger Publishers, 1992), p. 43.

155 The lack of engagement by civil society in the disarmament aspects of the negotiations is also evident from the overview in Steve Charnovitz, 'The Emergence of Democratic Participation in Global Governance (Paris, 1919)' (2003) 10(1) *Indiana Journal of Global*

A key aspect of the League's work in disarmament is that even at a state level, or to a certain extent at a state level, there was a sense of a humanitarian imperative in operation. This is usually referred to as the 'idealist' sensibilities in the League of Nations. The role of the individual delegate does seem to have been very important.[156] The Stanford Study Group also identifies the lesson from the League as being the role of public opinion. They say that the lesson is that public opinion can compel leaders to work towards disarmament – or to appear to do so. Over the long run, however, they caution that the subtle interplay of new events and the frustrations of negotiation may deflect the public's attention or even alter its perceptions.[157]

By the mid-1930s, the impacts of the Great Depression, the rise of isolationist tendencies and the rapid rearming of Germany and Japan combined to erode much of the force of humanitarianism and disarmament.[158]

V Conclusion

This chapter has located the origins of humanitarian disarmament within the broader transnational humanitarian movement that emerged from the mid- to late-nineteenth century (bearing in mind that this movement in turn originated in earlier iterations of humanitarianism). Locating the origins of humanitarian disarmament in this era is important at a purely descriptive level. First, this is because it situates the early bans on some weapons within the humanitarian disarmament frame. While they all fall short of actual disarmament in the sense of obligatory elimination of a category of weapon, the St Petersburg Declaration banning some explosive projectiles, the weapons regulations imposed as a result of the Hague Peace Conference 1899, and the Geneva Protocol 1925 banning

Legal Studies 45, pp. 60–72 in which he discusses four categories of NGO participation at Versailles: labour unions, Jewish organisations, women's groups and the American Red Cross. Disarmament is not mentioned. Similarly, disarmament is not mentioned in the discussion by Thomas Davies, *NGOs: A New History of Transnational Civil Society* (Oxford: Oxford University Press, 2014). Further, the primary sources seem not to mention civil society in the context of disarmament discussions at the Peace Conference: see Joseph V. Fuller (ed.), *Papers Relating to the Foreign Relations of the United States, The Paris Peace Conference, 1919* (Vols I–XIII) (US Government Printing Office, 1942) available at www.history.state.gov. My thanks to Dr Anna Hood on this point.

156 Discussed by Blacker and Duffy, *International Arms Control*, above n. 23, pp. 92–3.

157 Ibid., p. 93.

158 Krause, *The Good Project*, above n. 4, p. 103.

chemical and biological weapons, are all important steps in the history of humanitarian disarmament because of the way in which each of those weapons were stigmatised on the basis of their capacity to inflict human suffering, and the way they set the seeds for future further developments. Including this era in the story of humanitarian disarmament is also important because it reveals the way in which early civil society (the peace associations) organised and lobbied in the cause of peace and disarmament, something that would become, and remains, an enduring feature of contemporary humanitarian disarmament efforts.

However, there is a more fundamental point in capturing this earlier history. It demonstrates that humanitarian disarmament is not, and has not been, an ideal which had steadily and inevitably progressed and evolved. In fact, the opposite is true: by the time the League disintegrated, the idealistic humanitarian impulses of the late 1800s had been well and truly left behind. As we will see in subsequent chapters, humanitarianism would have its place again in disarmament discourse but as the world edged closer to the Second World War, it seemed consigned to history.

This chapter has also illustrated the way in which humanitarian claims in the context of opposition to particular weapons were always positioned as a way to avoid hard security claims and the politics of sovereign states. That is, from this early period, humanitarianism and humanitarian disarmament were presented in opposition to politics, as a counter to the national interest. As will be evident from the discussion to come, this has remained a constant in humanitarian disarmament discourse. But as I have shown in this chapter, humanitarianism is not so much apolitical, or above politics, it is just a politics of a particular kind. This too will be a constant in the coming decades.

Finally, situating the origins of humanitarian disarmament in this era allows us to see the apparent dilemma at the heart of disarmament discourse. Does disarmament lead to peace, or ought we strive for peace and then in security, work towards disarmament? It was a dilemma very much alive in the minds of the delegates attending the Hague Peace Conference in 1899, the Versailles Conference in 1919 as the League was created and the Disarmament Conference in the 1930s. Pleas for disarmament based on humanitarian consideration attempt to avoid that dilemma but in fact, the dilemma is unavoidable and the humanitarian pleas are, by necessity, selective and so privilege some forms of suffering over others; and some theatres of suffering over others.

In the chapters that follow, we will see these dynamics playing out again and again.

3

The Manhattan Project to 'Operation Rolling Thunder'[1]

Humanitarian Disarmament Sidelined

I Introduction

With the demise of the League of Nations and the outbreak of the Second World War the landscapes for both disarmament and humanitarianism underwent a paradigm shift. In a dynamic repeated from the First World War, the conflict triggered a massive renewal of development and acquisition of weapons and weapons technology, with the most profound shift being the development of the atomic bomb in the Manhattan Project and the subsequent attacks on Hiroshima and Nagasaki in what turned out to be the final days of the war.[2] The nuclear age had dawned with the United States emerging from the war as the world's only nuclear-weapon possessor state.

The war experience also transformed humanitarianism.[3] The destruction wrought by the war necessitated humanitarian assistance on a scale never before seen. The estimated death toll (battlefield and civilians) is fifty-five million people, although some estimates go as high as sixty-two to seventy-eight million.[4] Most of Europe's infrastructure had been destroyed, and large parts of Asia and North Africa had been badly

[1] Operation Rolling Thunder was part of the strategic bombing campaign carried out by US military aircraft throughout North Vietnam from March 1965 to October 1968.

[2] As Albert Einstein expressed it: 'The unleashed power of the atom has changed everything save our modes of thinking and we thus drift toward unparalleled catastrophe.' Telegram (24 May 1946) sent to prominent Americans, reproduced in Robert Andrews (ed.), *Famous Lines: A Columbia Dictionary of Familiar Quotations* (New York: Columbia University Press, 1997), p. 340.

[3] Michael Barnett, *Empire of Humanity: A History of Humanitarianism* (London: Cornell University Press, 2011), p. 97.

[4] The fifty-five million figure is used by Steven Pinker, *The Better Angels of Our Nature: A History of Violence and Humanity* (London: Penguin, 2011), p. 235; the higher figures are stated by Kesternich et al., 'The Effects of World War II on Economic and Health Outcomes across Europe' (2014) 96(1) *Rev Econ Stat* 103, 106.

affected. In part due to the resulting massive scale of the post-War relief efforts and in part reflecting contemporary bipolar politics embodied by the Cold War, humanitarian assistance and its underlying ideals of humanitarianism became a tool to advance the national security interests of the major donor states.

With this transformed landscape as context, my central argument in this chapter is that the humanitarian discourse relating to disarmament was seriously marginalised in the first two decades following the end of the Second World War. Indeed, disarmament itself (whether couched in the language of humanitarianism or otherwise) struggled: despite sustained attempts from a number of quarters there was little, if any, normative development in disarmament law during these years. Nevertheless, I argue that the attempts during this period had two important long-term consequences. First, the work of the International Committee of the Red Cross (ICRC) in these decades laid the basis for subsequent (and more successful) attempts to develop the law as I will show in Chapter 4. Thus, by the time of the Vietnam War it would become apparent that a great deal of the groundwork had been laid for the humanitarian campaigns that would respond to the waging of that war. Second, an explicit contest between humanitarianism and disarmament emerged and crystallised in these decades. This manifested initially as an institutional tug of war between the ICRC and the United Nations, but this was more a fundamental conceptual rift, not simply a reflection of institutional ambitions.

To begin, in Section II, I provide a brief overview of the way in which weapons technology developed in advance of and during the Second World War, examining in particular anti-personnel landmines, incendiary weapons, major developments in aerial warfare and of course nuclear weapons. This provides a sense of the period's impetus towards weapons development and rearmament and away from ideas of disarmament. Section III then explores three further factors that, in my view, resulted in an environment resistant to humanitarian disarmament following the war. First, I elaborate on what Alva Myrdal described as 'the mutation of public morality' during the war and I suggest that this may explain the slow reaction to the escalation of weapons technology and its humanitarian impact (Section III.A).[5] Second, I explore the way in which humanitarianism itself was institutionalised in the years following the war, as this

[5] Alva Myrdal, *The Game of Disarmament: How the United States and Russia Run the Arms Race* (New York: Pantheon Books, 1976), p. 250.

paints the backdrop for the fate of its subspecies 'humanitarian disarmament' in these years (Section III.B). Third, I show how the security framework of the Charter of the United Nations (the Charter) radically transformed the approach to disarmament from the League era, shifting from an ideal of peace through disarmament, to one of peace preceding disarmament (Section III.C).

In the remainder of the chapter (Sections IV and V), I explore the attempts within the UN system and the ICRC to regulate (or indeed eliminate) certain categories of weapons in this period. Neither succeeded. While the new multilateral architecture of the United Nations generated considerable institutional noise about weapons, little was actually achieved. In fact, as the Cold War deepened, the 'arms race' (as it came to be called), resulted in levels of armaments escalating to hitherto incomprehensible levels. Similarly, attempts by the ICRC to regulate, if not eliminate, some indiscriminate weapons were unsuccessful.

One further introductory point: while this chapter considers the years 1945–65 in examining the fate of disarmament and humanitarian discourse, it does not canvass the important developments that took place in this period relating to the campaigns against nuclear weapons. These are discussed in Chapter 7.

II Weapons Development in the Second World War

If the First World War had been notable for its weapons technology, it paled into insignificance compared to the technological advances in weapons technology in the years preceding and during the Second World War. Indeed, the arms race had gotten underway even as the League was still convening the World Disarmament Conference.[6] This section considers four types of weapons or weapons technology which stand out in terms of their humanitarian impact on civilian populations: the advent of large-scale aerial bombing, the rapid development of landmines technology, 'improved' incendiary weapons and finally, the atomic bomb. An understanding of the scale of the technological development provides a sense of the period's impetus towards weapons development and rearmament and away from ideas of disarmament.

[6] For details of the interwar arms race, see Joseph Maiolo, *Cry Havoc: How the Arms Race Drove the World to War, 1931–1941* (New York: Basic Books, 2010).

A Advent of Large-Scale Aerial Bombing

The era of modern aerial bombing began several decades before the Second World War, on 16 October 1912, when a number of grenades were dropped on a railway station in Turkey from a biplane, as part of the Balkan War of 1912.[7] During the First World War, aerial bombing had been in its infancy and overall the resulting deaths and infrastructure damage were relatively light.[8] However, the 1930s saw a number of air-bombing atrocities, including in the course of the Second Sino-Japanese War, in the Italian Abyssinian Campaign in Ethiopia and during the Spanish Civil War.[9] These were not the only atrocities: British and French aircraft regularly carried out aerial bombing raids in 'campaigns of colonial pacification' during this period.[10]

With the escalation of aerial warfare during the Second World War civilian society became the new front line.[11] Aerial bombing was a feature of the war from the–beginning: German bombings of Warsaw in 1939, the Blitz in Britain in 1940–1 and the decimation of Rotterdam in 1940. It was not only Germany that engaged in aerial bombardment. As the war wore on, the initial 'precision' bombing very quickly disintegrated into area bombing. As Haulman explains: 'The United States Army Air Corps entered World War II confident that it could destroy key strategic enemy targets with precision daylight raids. Over the course of the war, however, the United States largely abandoned the attempt and resorted to wholesale bombing of enemy cities, often with incendiaries at night.'[12] This was also a calculated approach of the Allies.[13] Thus, by the end of the war, cities such as Hamburg, Dresden and Tokyo were laid waste.[14] Hamburg was bombed repeatedly but the most infamous of the raids took place in

[7] Richard Overy, *The Bombing War: Europe 1939–1945* (New York: Penguin Books, 2013), p. 1.

[8] Ibid., pp. 20–1. See the discussion by Isabel V. Hull, *A Scrap of Paper: Breaking and Making International Law during the Great War* (Ithaca, New York: Cornell University Press, 2014), pp. 282–3.

[9] Overy, *The Bombing War*, above n. 7, pp. 32–3.

[10] Ibid., p. 32.

[11] Ibid, p. 127.

[12] Daniel L. Haulman, 'Precision Aerial Bombardment of Strategic Targets: Its Rise, Fall, and Resurrection' (2008) 55(4) *Air Power History* 25, 26.

[13] See generally, Richard Overy, 'Making and Breaking Morale: British Political Warfare and Bomber Command in the Second World War' (2015) 26(3) *Twentieth Century British History* 370.

[14] Stockholm International Peace Research Institute (SIPRI), *Incendiary Weapons* (Cambridge: MIT Press, 1975), p. 34. See also the detail provided by Kenneth Hewitt, 'Place Annihilation: Area Bombing and the Fate of Urban Places' (1983) 73(2) *Annals of the Association of American Geographers* 257, 262–70.

July and August 1943, which destroyed more than 50 per cent of the city, killed between 60,000–100,000 people and rendered around 750,000 people homeless.[15] The firebombing attack on Dresden in February 1945 devastated this cultural centre, leaving between 25,000–35,000 people dead.[16] The American attack on Tokyo in March 1945, just five months before the atomic bomb was unleashed, resulted in sixteen square miles of the city being incinerated, with more than 100,000 people killed. Over a million people were left homeless.[17]

B Development of Landmines Technology

The second category of weapons technology to undergo massive development during this period was landmines. Landmines were not a new feature of war.[18] For example, so-called 'torpedoes' had been used in the American Civil War: kegs of explosives kept just below the water's surface, designed to detonate on contact. Similar devices were used on land.[19] During the First World War, landmines took the form of buried artillery shells with exposed fuses, so that the risk of explosion blocked enemy advances.[20]

However, the Second World War brought the development and use of the technology to a new level. The development, particularly of anti-personnel, rather than anti-tank, landmines was in large part a response

[15] SIPRI, *Incendiary Weapons*, above n. 13, p. 34.

[16] Tami Davis Biddle, 'Dresden 1945: Reality, History, and Memory' (2008) 72(2) *The Journal of Military History* 413, 423–4. Earlier estimates were much higher, but these numbers have now been discredited.

[17] Conrad C. Crane, *American Airpower Strategy in World War II: Bombs, Cities, Civilians and Oil* (Lawrence: University Press of Kansas, 2016), p. 175.

[18] See for example, Frank Faulkner, *Moral Entrepreneurs and the Campaign to Ban Landmines* (Amsterdam: Brill, 2007), p. 58 discussing the caltrop – a weapon used in Roman times which was a wooden block with metal spikes protruding to deter the approach of the enemy. Stuart Maslen provides a concise overview of the different views on the origins of the anti-personnel mines: Stuart Maslen, *Commentaries on Arms Control Treaties: The Convention on the Prohibition of the Use, Stockpiling, Production, and Transfer of Anti-Personnel Mines and on their Destruction* (Oxford, New York: Oxford University Press, 2004), pp. 2–3 and citations therein.

[19] See Jack H. McCall Jr, 'Infernal Machines and Hidden Death' (1994) 24 *Georgia Journal of International and Comparative Law* 229, 232.

[20] Alex Vines, 'The Crisis of Anti-Personnel Mines', in Maxwell A. Cameron, Robert J. Lawson and Brian W. Tomlin (eds.), *To Walk without Fear: The Global Movement to Ban Landmines* (Toronto: Oxford University Press, 1998), p. 118. See as well, Human Rights Watch and Physicians for Human Rights, *Landmines: A Deadly Legacy* (United States of America: Human Rights Watch, 1993), p. 16.

to the development of the tank.[21] Tanks were immune to small arms fire, and so an anti-tank device was developed whereby a container of high explosive was buried under the earth, which would detonate in response to the pressure of a tank passing.[22] As opposing forces would clear those mines to allow tanks to advance, it became necessary to use mines to deter access by mine-clearing soldiers. Thus, smaller, but extremely destructive anti-personnel mines (basically small glass or metallic containers holding less than a half-kilogram of explosive) were developed to deter anti-tank mine clearance.[23] Inevitably, anti-personnel mines started to be developed and used in their own right, not simply as a device to protect tanks by preventing demining.[24]

It was these anti-personnel mines that wreaked such havoc during and after the war on civilians. More than 300 million mines were used during the Second World War.[25] In North Africa, 1,000 mines were laid daily by Axis forces before the British offensive at El Alamein.[26] The Soviet Union laid approximately 40,000 mines in preparation for the German 1943 offensive.[27] German troops laid more than four million mines in coastal France.[28] As such, by the end of the Second World War, there had been massive use of both anti-vehicle and anti-personnel mines, particularly in North Africa.[29]

[21] Asia Watch and Physicians for Human Rights, *Landmines in Cambodia: The Coward's War* (United States of America: Human Rights Watch, 1991), p. 5. See also Vines, 'The Crisis of Anti-Personnel Mines', above n. 19.

[22] Rae McGrath, *Landmines and Unexploded Ordnance: A Resource Book* (London: Pluto Press, 2000), p. 1. For a clear technical explanation of the different type of mines and the historical development of the technology, see Malvern Lumsden, *Anti-personnel Weapons* (London: Taylor & Francis, 1978), pp. 180–90.

[23] Vines, 'The Crisis of Anti-Personnel Mines', above n. 19, p. 119.

[24] Asia Watch and Physicians for Human Rights, *Landmines in Cambodia*, above n. 20, p. 6.

[25] Vines, 'The Crisis of Anti-Personnel Mines', above n. 19, p. 118. He estimates that 220 million mines were deployed by the Soviet Union, 80 million by Germany and 17 million by the United States. He cites to a US Defense Intelligence Agency report obtained by Human Rights Watch under the Freedom of Information Act.

[26] McCall, 'Infernal Machines and Hidden Death', above n. 18, p. 234.

[27] Ibid.

[28] Ibid., p. 235.

[29] Stuart Casey-Maslen, *Anti-personnel Mines under Humanitarian Law: A View from the Vanishing Point* (New York: Transnational Publishers, 2001), p. 6. See also Khairi Sgaier, 'Explosive Remnants of World War II in Libya: Impact on Agricultural Development', in Arthur H. Westing (ed.), *Explosive Remnants of War: Mitigating the Environmental Effects* (London: Taylor and Francis, 1985), p. 33 explaining the devastating effects of uncleared landmines in Libya. See Vines, 'The Crisis of Anti-Personnel Mines', above n. 19, p. 119 for a discussion on the impact in Egypt. See also International Committee of

C Incendiary Weapons

Incendiary weapons – designed to set fire to objects or persons, as opposed to incidentally causing burning – also caused unprecedented human destruction and suffering during the Second World War. As with landmines, flamethrowers and fire had long been part of warfare.[30] During the First World War, some of the Zeppelin attacks included incendiary bombs, but the technology available at the time did not make them particularly effective. Many of the weapons did not ignite at all and firefighters were able to extinguish many fires that did start.[31]

With the advent of air power, incendiary weapons became increasingly militarily effective. In Ethiopia in 1935, Italy used incendiary weapons initially from tanks and later from aircraft, as a means of terrorising civilians.[32] In August that year, Japan firebombed Shanghai, killing tens of thousands of civilians.[33] Prior to the Second World War, the fearsome power of incendiaries is perhaps epitomised by the German and Italian attack on Guernica in 1937, which involved the deployment of twenty-four tonnes of bombs, including approximately eight tonnes of thermite incendiaries.[34]

Despite attempts prior to the Second World War to control or even ban the use of incendiary weapons, their use escalated during the war.[35] However, the development of napalm in 1943 (a form of incendiary weapon consisting of gelled petroleum and thus able to stick to its target and burn at an extremely high temperature) brought about a fundamental change in the nature and effectiveness of incendiary warfare.[36]

Incendiaries other than napalm were also developed and used including thermite, magnesium powder, chlorine trifluoride and white

the Red Cross (ICRC), *Anti-Personnel Landmines: Friend or Foe? A Study of the Military Use and Effectiveness of Anti-Personnel Mines* (Geneva: ICRC, 1996), p. 27.

30 See W. Hays Parks, 'The Protocol on Incendiary Weapons' (1990) 30 *International Review of the Red Cross* 535, 535–6. For an early history of incendiary warfare, see SIPRI, *Incendiary Weapons*, above n. 13, pp. 1–30.

31 Hays Parks, 'The Protocol on Incendiary Weapons', above n. 29, explains that the first aerially delivered incendiary devices were used in May 1915 when German Zeppelins bombed London and estimates that in 1915 more than 70 per cent of the munitions dropped on London by Zeppelins were incendiaries: at p. 535.

32 SIPRI, *Incendiary Weapons*, above n. 13, p. 27.

33 Robert M. Neer, *Napalm: An American Biography* (Cambridge: Harvard University Press, 2013), p. 24, ch. 11.

34 Ibid., p. 24.

35 SIPRI, *Incendiary Weapons*, above n. 13, pp. 30–40.

36 Neer, *Napalm*, above n. 32, p. 16.

phosphorus. With this development in technology, incendiary weapons were transformed from 'unreliable devices of World War I to major weapons of tactical and strategic warfare'.[37] The most notorious instances include the use of incendiary bombs by Germany against Coventry and London in 1940, the use of incendiaries in the Allied bombing of Dresden and Hamburg and the United States firebombing of Japanese cities, in particular Tokyo, in 1945.[38]

Initially, the use of incendiaries were justified on the basis that the attacks were 'precision bombing', but as the war progressed, and as area bombing became acceptable in the name of undermining civilian morale and support for the war effort, incendiary weapons were seen as a means of making aerial bombardment more efficient and effective.[39] Thus, the attacks on cities including Dresden, London, Hamburg, Rotterdam and Tokyo caused more catastrophic devastation than would have been the case had a comparable number of high-explosive, but non-incendiary bombs been used.

D Nuclear Weapons

In what turned out to be the final days of the Second World War, the United States dropped two atomic bombs on the Japanese cities of Hiroshima and Nagasaki. Although estimates vary, it seems that either immediately or within three months, 140,000 people died in the Hiroshima blast with 70,000 fatalities in the attack on Nagasaki.[40] City infrastructure in both cases was utterly destroyed. The scale of the destruction became apparent in the following weeks and the first

[37] SIPRI, *Incendiary Weapons*, above n. 13, p. 30.

[38] Mark Seldon, 'Bombs Bursting in Air: State and Citizen Responses to the US Firebombing and Atomic Bombing of Japan' in Kinnia Yau Shuk-ting (ed.), *Natural Disaster and Reconstruction in Asian Economies: A Global Synthesis of Shared Experiences* (New York: Palgrave Macmillan, 2013), pp. 81–4. Seldon cites to the US Strategic Bombing Survey calculating that 87,793 people died in the raid of 9–10 March; and that 40,918 people were injured. Over a million people were rendered homeless. See United States Strategic Bombing Survey, *The Effects of the Atomic Bombings of Hiroshima and Nagasaki* (19 June 1946), available at www.trumanlibrary.org.

[39] SIPRI, *Incendiary Weapons*, above n. 13, p. 32.

[40] These figures are from Lawrence S. Wittner, *One World or None: A History of the World Nuclear Disarmament Movement Through 1953* (Stanford: Stanford University Press, 1993), p. 35. Wittner cites various sources for his estimates, including the United States Strategic Bombing Survey, above, n. 38. The death toll would ultimately rise taking into account deaths from related cancers in the months, years and decades following.

ominous signs of radiation sickness appeared. On 30 August 1945, a few weeks after the bombing, Red Cross delegates arrived in Hiroshima, and reported by telegram:

> Visited Hiroshima thirtieth conditions appalling. City wiped out eighty per cent all hospitals destroyed or seriously damaged inspected two emergency hospitals conditions beyond description. Effect of bomb mysteriously serious. Many victims apparently recovering suddenly suffer fatal relapse due to decomposition of white bloodcells and other internal injuries now dying in great numbers. Estimated still over one hundred thousand wounded in emergency hospitals located surroundings sadly lacking bandaging materials medicines. Please solemnly appeal to Allied High Command consider immediate airdrop relief action over centre city. Required substantial quantities bandages surgical pads ointments for burns sulfamides also bloodplasma and transfusion equipment. Immediate action highly desirable also dispatch medical investigating commission. Report follows confirm receipt.[41]

The atomic age had begun.

III Resistance to Humanitarian Disarmament

Despite the rapidly escalating weapons technology in the lead-up to and during the war and the resulting catastrophe in terms of the human impact and the destruction of infrastructure, there was a much less visible humanitarian outrage than had been evident in the aftermath of the First World War. In this section, I identify three possible factors that may explain this. The first was the 'mutation of public morality' or a desensitisation to human suffering, induced by the scale of the suffering during the war. A second possible factor was the institutionalisation of humanitarianism in the way that humanitarian relief was delivered after the war. A third factor was the turning away in the Charter from disarmament and towards 'security'. I argue that these factors resulted in an environment resistant to humanitarian disarmament.

A Mutation of Public Morality

On 26 April 1937, the Basque town of Guernica was bombed from the air by the German Luftwaffe and the Italian Aviazione Legionaria in

[41] Fritz Bilfinger, ICRC, telegram dated 30 August 1945, reproduced in Vincent Bernard, 'A Price Too High: Rethinking Nuclear Weapons in Light of their Human Cost' (2015) 97 (899) *International Review of the Red Cross* 499, 499.

support of General Franco in the Spanish Civil War. The attack took place over several hours one market-day and, as a result, the town was almost completely destroyed. Several hundred civilians were killed.[42] It was not just that this attack came from the air and seemed directed at the town itself, rather than at a military target (although there was a military base just outside the town): an added horror was the use of incendiary weapons. The attack became a symbol of wanton attacks on civilians, and evidence (to the Allies) that the Germans had abandoned any pretence of civilised behaviour.[43] As Overy put it '[n]o single event played as large a part in confirming for the European public that the bombing of civilians was now to be an established part of modern warfare'.[44]

George Steer, a reporter for *The Times* newspaper, reported on the bombing the following day and commented:

> In the form of its execution and the scale of the destruction it wrought, no less than in the selection of its objective, the raid on Guernica is unparalleled in military history. Guernica was not a military objective. A factory producing war material was untouched. So were two barracks some distance from the town. The town lay far behind the lines. The object was seemingly the demoralisation of the civil population and the destruction of the cradle of the Basque race.[45]

Beevor explains:

> Eyewitnesses described the resulting scenes in terms of hell and the apocalypse. Whole families were buried in the ruins of their houses, or crushed in the *refugios* [essentially air-raid shelters]; cattle and sheep, blazing with white phosphorus, ran crazily between the burning buildings until they died. Blackened humans staggered blindly through the flames, smoke and dust, while others scrabbled in the rubble, hoping to dig out friends and relatives. . . . Guernica was a burned skeleton.[46]

[42] At the time, it was reported that around 1700 people had died in the aerial attacks that day, but more recent historical work suggests 170–300. See Antony Beevor, *The Battle for Spain: The Spanish Civil War 1936–1939* (London: Penguin Books, 2006), p. 232. See also Overy, *The Bombing War*, above n. 7, p. 34 pointing out that reports at the time suggested that 1400 of a population of 6000 were reported to be dead although today, it is understood to be around 240.

[43] Richard Overy, *The Bombers and the Bombed: Allied Airwar over Europe 1940–1945* (New York: Penguin Press 2015), p. 45.

[44] Overy, *The Bombing War*, above n. 7, p. 33.

[45] George Steer, 'Slowly, systematically pounded to pieces' *Times* [London, England] (reprinted) 5 May 2015.

[46] Beevor, *The Battle for Spain*, above n. 41, p. 232.

Within eight years, terror bombing, which had seemed so exceptional and appalling in 1937, had morphed into a routine mode of warfare. If not quite acceptable, then terror bombing was certainly not considered inherently atrocious: there was a sense among military and political leaders, as well as in the public, that it was justified in certain circumstances. In this way, the scale of the destruction of the Second World War, and in particular the escalation of aerial bombardment, led to what Alva Myrdal has termed 'the mutation of public morality'.[47] Each overwhelming attack – London, Rotterdam, Hamburg, Dresden, Berlin, Tokyo, Yokohama, Darwin – and ultimately the atomic bomb attacks against Hiroshima and Nagasaki, served to create and to exemplify a sense of total war.[48] Examining the way in which terror bombing of civilians was normalised in this period, Ronald Kramer suggests a number of contributing factors, including the social construction of a 'moral war', technological fanaticism and ideological dehumanisation.[49]

In this way, the atomic attacks against Japan in August 1945 did not raise moral concerns among most of the decision-makers.[50] Initially at least, the bombs in Nagasaki and Hiroshima were simply a continuation of what had come before. As Nina Tannenwald says: 'Use of the bomb did not at the time raise a profound moral issue for most of the decision-makers, for two reasons: the continuity between nuclear and conventional bombing, and the general erosion of moral restraints over the course of the war, much of it due to strategic bombing practices'.[51] The degradation of moral concerns came about not only because of aerial bombardment, but also due to other large-scale atrocities such as the

[47] Myrdal, *The Game of Disarmament*, above n. 5, p.250.

[48] See Geoffrey Best, *Humanity in Warfare* (New York: Columbia University Press, 1980), pp. 262–85 discussing the development of aerial bombardment and in particular the shift during the Second World War from precision targeting to strategic bombing, which he says played its share in 'lowering the moral sensibility of Allied war-leaders so that, in 1945, it was not unnatural for them to think of dropping the atomic bomb on cities as it surely would have been even three or four years earlier': p. 284.

[49] See generally, Ronald Kramer, 'From Guernica to Hiroshima to Baghdad: The Normalization of the Terror Bombing of Civilians' in William J. Chambliss, Raymond J. Michalowski and Ronald C. Kramer (eds.), *State Crime in a Global Age* (Cullompton; Portland: Willan Publishing, 2010), p. 118.

[50] See the detailed discussion by Barton J. Bernstein, 'The Atomic Bombings Reconsidered' (1995) 74(1) *Foreign Affairs* 135.

[51] Nina Tannenwald, *The Nuclear Taboo: The United States and the Non-Use of Nuclear Weapons since 1945* (Cambridge: Cambridge University Press, 2007), p. 79. It should be noted that many of the scientists involved in the development of the atomic bomb did express serious misgivings about the developing technology – see the discussion in Chapter 7.

Japanese 'Rape of Nanking', the Holocaust perpetuated by Germany and the routine internment of enemy aliens, all of which perpetuated a 'redefinition of morality'.[52] As Barton Bernstein explains: 'While the worst atrocities were perpetrated by the Axis, all the major nation-states sliced away at the moral code — often to the applause of their leaders and citizens alike. By 1945 there were few moral restraints left in what had become virtually a total war'.[53] This shift in morality is evidenced in the results of the opinion polls taken in the United States following the Nagasaki and Hiroshima bombings. On 8 August 1945 (two days after Hiroshima and the day before Nagasaki), 85 per cent of respondents in a Gallup poll approved of using the bomb on Japanese cities.[54] Later polls showed that only 5 per cent of those polled opposed the use of nuclear weapons under any circumstances.[55] 54 per cent favoured the way in which the bombings took place; 14 per cent would have preferred a test demonstration before the use of the weapons on a city target; but 23 per cent wanted the United States to use many more weapons before Japan had a chance to surrender.[56]

In my view, then, unlike the reaction to the First World War which led to various humanitarian campaigns, the catastrophic destruction of the Second World War, and its immediate precursors, led to a numbing of moral outrage. Just eight years had passed since Guernica, but in moral terms, the discourse around means and methods of war was unrecognisable.

B *Institutionalised Humanitarianism*

The second feature of the post-War landscape to militate against a humanitarian disarmament campaign was the way in which humanitarianism itself changed in this period. As discussed in Chapter 2, the first phase of modern humanitarianism in the wake of the First World War had featured increased formal institutionalisation of the humanitarian relief efforts in response to the scale of the relief efforts required at the time, and a corresponding move away from a charity/welfare lens.[57] That

52 Bernstein, 'The Atomic Bombings Reconsidered', above n. 49, p. 151.

53 Ibid.

54 Wittner, *One World or None*, above n. 39, pp. 55–6.

55 Tannenwald, *The Nuclear Taboo*, above n. 50, p. 89.

56 Ibid.

57 Bruno Cabanes, *The Great War and the Origins of Humanitarianism 1918–1924* (New York: Cambridge University Press, 2014), p. 4. In recognising the shift between the two 'phases' of humanitarianism, it is important not to overstate the rupture and in particular not to present the first phase as some golden age of humanitarianism: a point

trend accelerated and deepened in light of the scale of the destruction following the Second World War: Europe lay in ruins, millions of people had been killed, whole cities were devastated, infrastructure was destroyed and economies had been laid waste. Further millions of people had been displaced.[58] Private philanthropy and charity, no matter how generous, could not constitute an adequate response. What was needed was a coordinated international relief operation.[59]

That came in the form of the United Nations Relief and Rehabilitation Agency (UNRRA) established in 1943 even before the war ended to provide 'measures of relief of victims of war in any area under the control of any of the United Nations'.[60] Led by the United States, forty-four states were involved in UNRRA's establishment and operation – thus, it really was an international institutionalised response.[61] The stated aim was for UNRRA to be 'as politically neutral as nearly as possible'.[62] Its mandate was to provide emergency relief, and to assist with rehabilitation. Thus, UNRRA epitomised the transition from passive charity (relief) to active welfare (rehabilitation).[63]

It was a small step from an institutionalised programme of rehabilitation to the idea of aid as a form of development, which in turn linked to the idea that more attention needed to be paid to the root causes of crises, rather than simply responding to humanitarian emergencies.[64]

recognised by Michael Barnett himself, even as he draws a distinction between the two phases. Barnett, *Empire of Humanity*, above n. 3, p. 5. See also Rob Skinner and Alan Lester, 'Humanitarianism and Empire: New Research Agendas' (2012) 40(5) *The Journal of Imperial and Commonwealth History* 729; and Matthew Hilton, 'Ken Loach and Save the Children' (2015) 87(2) *Journal of Modern History* 354.

58 In Occupied West Germany alone, there were six million displaced persons, and a further six to seven million displaced in the Soviet Occupied Zone: See G. Daniel Cohen, 'Between Relief and Politics: Refugee Humanitarianism in Occupied Germany 1945–1946' (2008) 43(3) *Journal of Contemporary History* 437, 440.

59 Gerard Daniel Cohen, *In War's Wake: Europe's Displaced Persons in the Postwar Order* (Oxford: Oxford Scholarship Online, 2012), p. 59.

60 *Agreement for United Nations Relief and Rehabilitation Administration* (27 November 1944), art. I (2)(a). Despite its name, it actually preceded the creation of the United Nations. At this point, the term 'united nations' referred to the united nations of the Allied forces.

61 Cohen, *In War's Wake*, above n. 58, pp. 59–62.

62 Philipp Weintraub, 'UNRRA: An Experiment in International Welfare Planning' (1945) 7 (1) *The Journal of Politics* 1, 14.

63 Cohen, 'Between Relief and Politics', above n. 57, p. 438. Barnett, *Empire of Humanity*, above n. 3, p. 122.

64 Barnett, *Empire of Humanity*, above n. 3, p. 122. Oxfam serves as an example. Created initially as a famine relief agency in 1942, it evolved into a development agency. By the end of the 1970s, Oxfam spent less than 10 per cent of its budget on emergency relief and over 50 per cent on development issues. See David Chandler, 'The Road to Military

The shift from relief to development was explicitly linked to the need to ensure security. It was 'humane and charitable' to provide assistance, United States President Roosevelt explained, but it was also 'a clear matter of enlightened self-interest – and of military strategic necessity'.[65]

The source of the funding also had an impact. Being relatively untouched by the war in terms of its infrastructure and economy, the United States was now experiencing a booming post-War economy. As such, it was uniquely placed to fund the relief effort and as a result, the United States became the major source of funds.[66]

With these changes, it was increasingly difficult for humanitarian agencies to maintain their impartiality and neutrality.[67] Fairly or not, humanitarianism had become suspect and this in turn made claims of humanitarianism in the context of disarmament debates politically suspect.

C *Marginalising Disarmament in the United Nations Charter*

The third way in which humanitarian disarmament was marginalised in the wake of the Second World War was the way in which the new international legal regime sidelined disarmament as a feature of post-War governance. Whatever its ultimate disappointments, disarmament had been an important feature of the work and ambitions of the League of Nations. In stark contrast, in the United Nations, the Charter turned firmly towards an ideal of collective security and in doing so, decoupled peace from disarmament. Whereas the League's approach was peace through disarmament, in the Charter the idea was to pursue peace through a robust collective security system, and in time create the necessary conditions to discuss disarmament.[68]

Humanitarianism: How the Human Rights NGOs Shaped a New Humanitarian Agenda' (2001) 23 *Human Rights Quarterly* 678, pp. 686–7.

65 *President Roosevelt's Radio Address*, 9 November 1943, cited by Weintraub, 'UNRRA: An Experiment in International Welfare Planning', above n. 61, p. 17.

66 Jessica Reinisch, 'Internationalism in Relief: The Birth (and Death) of UNRRA' (2011) Supplement 6 *Past and Present* 261, 285.

67 Barnett, *Empire of Humanity*, above n. 3, p. 104.

68 Daniel Cheever, 'The UN and Disarmament' (1965) 19(3) *International Organization* 463, 467. See also James Fry, 'Early Security Council Efforts at Nuclear Non-Proliferation Law and Policy: Cooperation Forgotten' (2012) 21 *Transnational Law and Contemporary Problems* 337.

This shift in focus is clear when the texts of the Covenant of the League of Nations ('the Covenant')[69] and the Charter are compared. The 'peace through disarmament' language of the Covenant was replaced by a more equivocal attitude to the peace/disarmament dynamic in the Charter. In Article 8 of the Covenant, the League's members had recognised that 'the maintenance of peace requires the reduction of national armaments to the lowest point consistent with national safety and the enforcement by common action of international obligations'. In contrast, Articles 1 and 2 of the Charter, setting out the principles and purposes of the United Nations, make no reference whatsoever to disarmament.

Indeed, the Charter as a whole contains only three references to disarmament. First, the General Assembly is allotted a specific role in dealing with the arms question. Article 11 provides:

> The General Assembly may consider the general principles of cooperation in the maintenance of international peace and security, including the principles governing disarmament and the regulation of armaments, and may make recommendations with regard to such principles to the Members or to the Security Council or to both.

This is notably weaker in formulation than the language of Article 8 of the Covenant, and even that was included at the suggestion of the Soviet Union with Britain and the United States opposed to its inclusion.[70] Article 24 of the Charter, dealing with the Security Council's responsibilities for maintaining international peace and security, makes no mention of disarmament.[71] There is a passing reference in Article 26:

> In order to promote the establishment and maintenance of international peace and security with the least diversion of armaments of the world's human and economic resources, the Security Council shall be responsible for formulating with the assistance of the Military Staff Committee referred to in Article 47, plans to be submitted to the Members of the United Nations for the establishment of a system for the regulation of armaments.

[69] Treaty of Peace between the Allied and Associated Powers and Germany, signed 28 June 1919 (entered into force 10 January 1920) pt I.

[70] Leland M. Goodrich, *Charter of the United Nations: Commentary and Documents*, 3rd ed. (New York: Columbia University Press, 1969), p. 118.

[71] See generally, Jane Boulden, Ramesh Thakur and Thomas G. Weiss, 'Context, Foundations, Actors, Tools, Prospects' in Jane Boulden, Ramesh Thakur and Thomas G. Weiss (eds.), *The United Nations and Nuclear Orders* (United States of America: United Nations University Press, 2009), p. 6.

The third reference to disarmament is in Article 47, dealing with the Military Staff Committee.[72] Article 47(1) provides:

> There shall be established a Military Staff Committee to advise and assist the Security Council on all questions relating to the Security Council's military requirements for the maintenance of international peace and security, the employment and command of forces placed at its disposal, the regulation of armaments, and possible disarmament.

Thus, the provisions taken together are much weaker than the sweeping nature of Articles 8 and 9 of the Covenant.

The differences between the two systems are also revealed by considering the League's references to 'security' rather than to 'peace'. The word security appears only once in the Covenant (in the preamble), but even then it is linked to peace. The relevant provision says that the purpose of the League is 'to promise international cooperation and to achieve international peace and security'. Instead, the Covenant uses terms such as peace, peace of nations and peace of the world.[73] In contrast, security is the epicentre of the Charter, with the term 'international peace and security' used thirty-two times.[74] Indeed, the 'inherent' right of self-defence in Article 51 of the Charter is meaningless without the corresponding right to possess weapons.

One of the reasons behind the absolute shift in approach to disarmament from the Covenant to the Charter was the prevailing feeling that the Second World War might have been avoided if, for example, the Allied nations had also rearmed so that Germany and Japan did not have such a military advantage, in contrast to the idea that one of the causes of the First World War had been a build-up of arms.[75]

It is important to note that the Charter was drafted during, not following, the war and so, in that context, disarmament was inconceivable.[76] The atomic bombing of Hiroshima and Nagasaki took

[72] The Military Staff Committee was never created.

[73] Avi Beker, *Disarmament without Order: The Politics of Disarmament at the United Nations* (Westport: Greenwood Press, 1985), p. 8.

[74] Ibid., p. 9.

[75] Jozef Goldblat, 'The Role of the United Nations in Arms Control: An Assessment' (1986) 7 *Arms Control* 115; Inis L. Claude, *Swords into Plowshares: The Problems and Progress of International Organization* (New York: Random House, 1971), p. 292; Harold K. Jacobson, 'International Law: The Crisis in Arms Control' (1984) 82 *Michigan Law Review* 1588, 1590. See the general discussion of the contemporary debates on German 'war guilt' in Hull, *A Scrap of Paper*, above n. 8, pp. 7–12.

[76] Bruno Simma, *The Charter of the United Nations: A Commentary* (Oxford; New York: Oxford University Press, 1994), p. 423. See also Goldblat, 'The Role of the United Nations

place only six weeks after the Charter was signed.[77] While the Manhattan Project had been underway at the time the United Nations Charter negotiations were being conducted, the Project had not been public knowledge and most of the states involved in the negotiations were unaware of the extent of the progress in developing a nuclear weapon by the United States.[78] With the Hiroshima and Nagasaki bombings, the atomic age began and the peace-security-disarmament dynamic fundamentally and irrevocably shifted. Whereas previously, relative military power had waxed and waned across states and across particular armament types and capabilities, with the advent of atomic weapons, a clear trump card had emerged and it was in the hands of only one state – for the time being. In this framework, with its plea to humanitarian sensibilities and its call for broader engagement on security issues, humanitarian disarmament was resolutely pushed to the margins.

The marginalisation of humanitarian disarmament was also inevitable in light of the way in which civil society in the disarmament sphere was squeezed out in the new framework. More broadly, civil society was given a formal role in the United Nations by virtue of Article 71 of the Charter, which provided that the Economic and Social Council (ECOSOC) consult with certain accredited non-governmental organisations on matters within the ECOSOC's competence.[79] This formalised what had been the informal arrangement within the League of Nations and so was a progressive step. However, in the disarmament context, it was regressive because it excluded disarmament NGOs as that was not within the competence of ECOSOC.[80] That exclusion is consistent with the more cautious approach to disarmament generally in the Charter.

It was also consistent with the more cautious approach that had emerged in Geneva towards the end of the League period. As discussed

in Arms Control', above n. 74, p. 117; Beker, *Disarmament without Order*, above n. 72, p. 13.

77 In fact, the treaty was not yet in force, and so the United Nations did not yet exist in formal legal terms.

78 Cheever, 'The UN and Disarmament', above n. 67, p. 466.

79 Steve Charnovitz, 'Two Centuries of Participation: NGOs and International Governance' (1996–7) 18 *Michigan Journal of International Law* 183, 249–53. See also Nicolas Hachez, 'The Relations between the United Nations and Civil Society: Past, Present, and Future' (2008) 5 *International Organizations Law Review* 49, 50–71; A critical perspective of the relationship is offered in Dianne Otto, 'Nongovernmental Organizations in the United Nations System: The Emerging Role of International Civil Society' (1996) 18 *Human Rights Quarterly* 107.

80 Charnovitz, 'Two Centuries of Participation', above n. 78, pp. 249–53.

in Chapter 2, while the League was initially very open to engagement with civil society in a wide variety of activities including disarmament, that engagement had started to stagnate. From 1935, there had been what Charnovitz characterises as a period of disengagement.[81] This was more widespread than just the issue of disarmament and was in part due to a changing attitude of the League itself, which had been very open to NGO activity initially, but was less so as time advanced.

As the United Nations came into being then, prospects for humanitarian disarmament were not good. The humanitarian ethos of many of those involved in the League had given way to a realist contractual model of international engagement. Internationalist idealism had given way to an ideology of collective security. In this process, disarmament had been discredited as a strategy for peace and security and participation by non-state actors had been much more tightly constrained.

IV Disarmament in the Early United Nations

In light of these forces, the prospects were not good for a UN-led disarmament strategy. However, modestly drawn as they were, it was still possible that the Charter provisions could have been the basis of some meaningful progress on disarmament. Indeed, the experience in the human rights sphere attests to the fact that even in the case of limited reference in the Charter itself, it is possible to make meaningful progress. This was not to be the case with disarmament in the first two decades of the United Nations.

That being said, when considering the early years of the United Nations, there was considerable activity in terms of developing institutional structures to discuss and work on disarmament issues.[82] One such institutional structure was the Atomic Energy Commission (AEC), created in 1946 with the stated aim of controlling atomic energy to ensure its use for peaceful purposes only and to work towards 'the elimination from national armaments of atomic weapons and all other major weapons adaptable to mass destruction'.[83] The AEC comprised all members of the Security Council plus Canada (when it was not a member of the Council), and reported to the Security Council. It achieved very little, however, as it

[81] Ibid., pp. 246–9.

[82] See detailed discussion by Myrdal, *The Game of Disarmament*, above n. 5, pp. 69–84.

[83] *Establishment of a Commission to Deal with the Problems Raised by the Discovery of Atomic Energy*, GA Res 1/1, UN GAOR, 1st sess, 17th plen mtg, UN Doc A/Res/1/1 (24 January 1946).

was deadlocked almost immediately due to disagreements about whether there should be an international system of control, with the United States (as the only nuclear weapon possessor state at this point) arguing strongly for such a system,[84] and the USSR firmly opposed, claiming it wanted instead the elimination of all atomic weapons before considering an international control system.[85] There were also uncertainties about the decision-making process to be followed in the AEC, namely, whether being a subsidiary body of the Security Council, the veto privileges continued to apply. The difference in views is unsurprising when one considers that at this point, the United States was the sole nuclear weapon possessor state, and the USSR was still three years away from a successful detonation of an atomic weapon.[86]

The following year, the Security Council created a second institution: the Commission for Conventional Armaments (CCA), the aim of which was to achieve 'general regulation and reduction of armaments and armed forces'.[87] The membership was the same as for the AEC – all members of the Security Council plus Canada. Like its sister Commission dealing with atomic issues, it was unable to make any real progress, constrained by seemingly intractable differences between states on the appropriate relationship between limits on conventional weaponry and forces and atomic weapons, and continuing questions regarding the decision-making process.[88]

Both Commissions became inactive and were formally dissolved in 1952.[89] Replacing them, and attempting to address the artificial split between discussions around atomic issues and conventional weapons, the General Assembly then established the United Nations Disarmament Commission in 1952.[90] Initially with the same membership of the earlier Commissions, this was expanded to twenty-five members in 1957 and then to the full UN membership in 1958. The Commission in turn established a five-Power Sub-Committee

[84] This proposal for an International Authority came to be known as the Baruch Plan.

[85] Myrdal, *The Game of Disarmament*, above n. 5, pp. 73–7.

[86] In fact, the United States conducted its first post-War nuclear test ('Test Able') in the Marshall Islands on 1 July 1946, a mere seventeen days after the Baruch Plan was presented to the Commission.

[87] SC Res 18 (1947), UN Doc S/268/Rev.1/Corr.1 (13 February 1947).

[88] Fry, 'Early Security Council Efforts', above n. 67, pp. 347–8.

[89] Myrdal, *The Game of Disarmament*, above n. 5, pp. 78–80.

[90] *Regulation, Limitation and Balanced Reduction of All Armed Forces and All Armaments; International Control of Atomic Energy*, GA Res 502 (VI), UN GOAR, 6th sess, 358th plen mtg, UN Doc A/RES/502(VI) (11 January 1952).

(consisting of Canada, France, the Soviet Union, United Kingdom and the United States).[91] This body too failed to make any progress and it stopped meeting after 1965.[92] The core difficulty remained: a seemingly unbridgeable gap between the United States, insisting that an international verification mechanism had to be the first step in the process of disarmament, and the Soviet Union, insisting that an absolute and unconditional prohibition on the use of atomic weapons was a non-negotiable first step.[93]

Thus, while the United Nations did not make much progress in disarmament in its early history, it is nonetheless clear that there was a great deal of institutional activity. In addition to that, the General Assembly maintained an impressive output in terms of resolutions on disarmament-related issues, starting from the very first session.[94] As the years went on, the General Assembly took an active role in disarmament matters, passing increasing numbers of resolutions each year dealing with a broad range of disarmament matters.[95] Still, little was actually achieved. As Alva Myrdal expressed it, the activity reflected 'propaganda gaming' on both sides.[96]

In 1960, there was an important attempt to consider disarmament from something other than a state-security paradigm. The General Assembly requested the Secretary-General to appoint a group of experts to assist him in a study of the national, social and economic consequences of disarmament. They produced an extensive and unanimous report in

[91] United Nations, *The United Nations and Disarmament 1945–1970* (New York: United Nations, 1970), p. 3.

[92] It was reconstituted at the General Assembly's First Special Session on Disarmament in 1978.

[93] Myrdal, *The Game of Disarmament*, above n. 5, pp. 72–8.

[94] *Establishment of a Commission to Deal with the Problems Raised by the Discovery of Atomic Energy*, above n. 82; *Principles Governing the General Regulation and reduction of Armaments*, GA Res 41(1), UN GAOR, 1st sess, 63rd plen mtg, UN Doc A/RES/41/1 (14 December 1946).

[95] All the General Assembly resolutions dealing with disarmament related matters from 1946 to 1969 are listed in United Nations, *The United Nations and Disarmament 1945–1970*, above n. 90, pp. 385–91; All resolutions from 1970 to 1975 are listed in United Nations, *The United Nations and Disarmament 1970–1975* (New York: United Nations, 1976), pp. 23–742. Subsequent resolutions are listed in the *Disarmament Yearbooks* published by the United Nations since 1976.

[96] Myrdal, *The Game of Disarmament*, above n. 5, p. 80. Writing in an early collection of essays edited by Louis Henkin, William Frye described it as 'diplomatic shadow-boxing, thoroughly overladen with propaganda': William R. Frye, 'The Quest for Disarmament since World War II' in Louis Henkin (ed.), *Arms Control Issues for the Public* (New York: Prentice Hall, 1961), pp. 18, 19.

1962.[97] The report concluded that global military expenditure was US$120 billion, equating to 8–9 per cent of the annual global output of goods and services. The report also noted that 85 per cent of the spending was accounted for by seven countries: Canada, West Germany, France, China, the Soviet Union, the United Kingdom and the United States. Despite the report being made widely available and despite being discussed and endorsed by the General Assembly later that year, and subsequently, no tangible outcomes ever eventuated from this work.[98]

The Ten-Nation Committee on Disarmament was established in 1959 by a decision of the foreign ministers of France, the Soviet Union, the United Kingdom and the United States.[99] Created outside the United Nations in an attempt to sidestep the veto deadlock of the Security Council, it was envisaged initially as operating as an expert technical body, rather than a political body. In 1962, it became the Eighteen-Nation Committee on Disarmament to allow participation by some non-aligned states.[100] Progress here was better than within the United Nations proper: following the Cuban Missile Crisis in October 1962, the Committee Member States endorsed the Partial Test Ban Treaty in 1963,[101] as well as the agreement to install a hotline between Washington and Moscow.[102] Discussions were initiated on a number of other issues.

The lack of substantive progress in disarmament in the first two decades of the UN was consistent with lack of progress in two other related areas. First, despite the widespread and shocking use of particular weapons and means of warfare during the war, none of the post–Second World War criminal trials attempted any prosecutions involving the use of weapons. No charges were laid regarding either bombardment or the use of any other weapons, possibly due to the fact that the Allies had

[97] Report of the Secretary-General Transmitting the Report of his Consultative Group, *Economic and Social Consequences of Disarmament*, E/3593/Rev.1 (28 February 1962).

[98] United Nations, *The United Nations and Disarmament: 1945–1985* (New York: United Nations, 1985), pp. 147–8.

[99] Evenly balanced between East-West, the original ten members were: Bulgaria, Canada, Czechoslovakia, France, Italy, Poland, Romania, the Soviet Union, the United Kingdom and the United States.

[100] Being Brazil, Burma, Ethiopia, India, Mexico, Nigeria, Sweden and the United Arab Republic. The body then became the Conference of the Committee on Disarmament from 1969 to 1978.

[101] Treaty Banning Nuclear Weapon Tests in the Atmosphere, in Outer Space and under Water, opened for signature 5 August 1963, 480 UNTS 43 (entered into force 10 October 1963).

[102] Albert Legault and Michel Fortmann, *A Diplomacy of Hope: Canada and Disarmament* (Quebec: McGill-Queen's University Press, 1992), pp. 197–201.

behaved in exactly the same manner, particularly where aerial bombardment was concerned.[103]

The Nuremberg Charter in fact would have allowed for such prosecutions. One of the war crimes listed was 'wanton destruction of cities, towns, or villages, or devastation not justified by military necessity'.[104] Under crimes against humanity was included 'inhumane acts committed against any civilian population'.[105] Thus, it is clear that the failure to prosecute was due to lack of political will, rather than legal incompetence.

A second area of comparable silence was in the avoidance in the United Nations of revisions of the law of armed conflict. In 1947, the United Nations created the International Law Commission to work on the 'progressive development and codification of international law'.[106] But it chose not to engage in a codification of the laws of war, on the basis that this might signal a lack of confidence in the ability of the new United Nations to keep the peace.[107]

Looking at the lack of any real progress in disarmament in the United Nations and related structures in the first twenty years following the war, a number of reflections can be made. First, the advent of atomic weapons, initially only possessed by the United States, dramatically changed views about the efficacy of the Charter, even before the Charter could be implemented. Second, the General Assembly took a more active role in disarmament-related matters as the Security Council repeatedly failed to overcome Cold War-induced stalemate.[108] As the number of member states increased, the political balance in the General Assembly changed with the voices of what would become the Non-Aligned Movement becoming more influential. These voices were to become stronger in the coming years, challenging the bipolar dominance of the discussion.

Finally, humanitarian sensibility in disarmament discourses was very much sidelined in all of the discussions, with one exception being the

[103] Telford Taylor, *Nuremberg and Vietnam: an American Tragedy* (Chicago: Quadrangle Books, 1970), p. 89.

[104] Charter of the International Military Tribunal, 82 UNTS 279 (signed and entered into force 8 August 1945) art. 6(b).

[105] Nuremberg Charter art. 6(c).

[106] *Establishment of an International Law Commission*, GA Res 174 (II), UN GAOR, 2nd sess, 133rd plen mtg, UN Doc A/RES/174 (21 November 1947).

[107] Frits Kalshoven, 'Reaffirmation and Development of International Humanitarian Law Applicable in Armed Conflict: The Conference of Government Experts, 24 May–12 June, 1971', reprinted in Frits Kalshoven, *Reflections on the Law of War* (Leiden: Martinus Nijhoff, 2007), pp. 33, 68.

[108] Cheever, 'The UN and Disarmament', above n. 67, p. 478.

attempt by the General Assembly to discuss the economic and social implications of disarmament.[109] On the whole, discussions were dominated by the United States and the USSR and security was very much conceived in state-centric sensibilities. This was the era when deterrence theory came to dominate and a state-centric security discourse dominated the global political landscape.[110] Thus, despite the institutional noise, there were few tangible outcomes on disarmament. The Antarctic Treaty in 1959 did make Antarctica a demilitarised zone and the Partial Test Ban Treaty in 1963 helped to bring about the cessation of atmospheric nuclear tests.[111] But neither of these were 'pure' disarmament treaties in the sense that they did not put in place any obligation to eliminate nuclear weapons altogether. And neither of these two treaties did anything to stop the escalation of military expenditure and development.

On the horizon though, with the emergence of the Non-Aligned Movement, the landscape started to change.

V Humanitarian Discourse in the Law of Armed Conflict

Within the humanitarian world of the ICRC, the discourse was rather different. In fact, within one month of the Hiroshima bombing, the ICRC started to address the challenge of nuclear weapons and, in keeping with its mandate, its statements expressing concern about the technology were couched in humanitarian terms. Thus, on 5 September 1945, the ICRC wrote to the Red Cross National Societies expressing concerns about the 'latest developments of the technique of warfare', an expression presumably meaning the combination of aerial warfare, incendiary weapons and the atomic bomb.[112] In 1948, the International Committee presented a report to the 17th International Conference held in Stockholm which in turn adopted Resolution XXIV:

[109] Report of the Secretary-General, *Economic and Social Consequences of Disarmament*, above n. 96.

[110] See for example, Henry Kissinger, *Nuclear Weapons and Foreign Policy* (New York: Harper, 1957); see also Julius Stone, *Law and Policy in the Quest for Survival: Six Lectures Broadcast by the ABC in November and December 1960* (Redfern: Hogbin Poole Press, 1960).

[111] The Antarctic Treaty, signed 1 December 1959, 402 UNTS 71 (entered into force 23 June 1961).

[112] The circular is reproduced in Francois Bugnion, 'The International Committee of the Red Cross and Nuclear Weapons: From Hiroshima to the Dawn of the 21st Century' (2005) 87 (859) *International Review of the Red Cross* 511, 514.

> [N]oting that the use of non-directed weapons, which cannot be aimed with precision or which devastate large areas indiscriminately, would involve the destruction of persons and the annihilation of the human values which it is the mission of the Red Cross to defend, and that use of these methods would imperil the very future of civilisation.[113]

On that basis, the meeting went on to 'earnestly request[s] the Powers solemnly to undertake to prohibit absolutely all recourse to such weapons and to the use of atomic energy or any similar force for purposes of warfare'.[114]

The discourse, with its emphasis on the humanitarian consequences of the use of the weapons, could not have been in greater contrast with the state-centric security discourse prevailing in the United Nations. However, as we will see, the humanitarian framing would not be enough to make any meaningful difference in the course of the negotiation and agreement on what would become the four Geneva Conventions 1949, or indeed in the efforts in the 1950s to develop the law on indiscriminate weapons.

A *The 1949 Geneva Conventions*

The law of armed conflict had always addressed weapons to a certain extent. In the nineteenth and early-twentieth centuries, this body of law had developed as two distinct legal threads. The first was the so-called Hague Law which imposed restrictions on weapons and on methods and means of warfare.[115] Key agreements emanating from this part of the law have been discussed in Chapter 2, including bans on exploding bullets, expanding bullets and the use of chemical weapons. The second thread of the law of armed conflict was the so-called Geneva Law which regulated the *conduct* of war rather than the weapons of war with the aim of ensuring respect for and humane treatment of war casualties and non-combatants.[116]

In light of the catastrophic impact wrought on civilians in the course of the Second World War, it was clear that there was an immediate need to revise and update the existing legal framework – not just about weapons,

113 Non-directed Weapons, Resolution XXIV, *Report of the 17th International Conference of the Red Cross, Stockholm, 20–30 August 1948* (Stockholm, August 1948) 94.

114 Ibid.

115 See generally, William H. Boothby, *Weapons and the Law of Armed Conflict* (New York: Oxford University Press, 2009).

116 This distinction is considered by many to be no longer valid. See for example, Boothby, ibid., p. 2 ('the distinction is now more of historical and academic interest than of any practical significance').

but also for those parts of the law that dealt with the protection of civilians and the humane treatment of war casualties, including prisoners of war and persons under occupation. Earlier treaties had assumed hostilities in which armed forces faced each other in battlefields and thus, while there were some rules aimed at protecting civilians (for example, the prohibition on bombardment of undefended towns),[117] generally, the needs of civilians were not addressed, because the law rested on the (increasingly outdated) assumption that civilians were not usually present in the theatre of war.[118]

The law on weapons use and deployment was clearly lagging behind the pace of technology. The most recent update on weapons law had been in 1925, with the conclusion of the Geneva Protocol, prohibiting the use of chemical and biological weapons in warfare.[119] Aerial bombardment had been addressed at the 1899 Hague Peace Conference, with an agreement to prohibit, for five years, 'the launching of projectiles and explosives from balloons, or by other new methods of a similar nature'.[120] In 1907, that Declaration was readopted so that the prohibition would remain in place until the convening of a Third Peace Conference, which never took place.[121] In 1923, the Hague Rules on Air Warfare were drafted at the Washington Conference on the Limitation of Armaments, Article 22 of which prohibited any 'air bombardment for the purpose of terrorizing the civil population, of destroying or damaging private property not of military character, or of injuring non-combatants'.[122] Complementing that, Article

[117] Regulations Respecting the Laws and Customs of War on Land 1907 (annex to the Convention (IV) Respecting the Laws and Customs of War on Land, opened for signature 18 October 1907, 36 Stat. 2227, T.S. No. 539) (entered into force 26 January 1910) art. 25.

[118] Waldemar A. Solf, 'Protection of Civilians against the Effects of Hostilities under Customary International Law and under Protocol I' (1986) 1(1) *American University International Law Review* 117, 127.

[119] Protocol for the Prohibition of the Use in War of Asphyxiating, Poisonous or Other Gases, and of Bacteriological Methods of Warfare, opened for signature 17 June 1925, (1929) XCIV LNTS 65–74 (entered into force 8 February 1928). See Chapter 2, Section IV.C.

[120] Hague Declaration of 1899 (IV, 1) Prohibiting the Discharge of Projectiles and Explosives from Balloons, reproduced in James Brown Scott (ed.), *Hague Conventions and Declarations of 1899 and 1907: Accompanied by Tables of Signatures, Ratifications and Adhesions of the Various Powers, and Texts of Reservations*, 2nd ed. (Oxford: Oxford University Press, 1915), p. 220. See Chapter 2, Section III.B.

[121] Hague Declaration of 1907 (XIV) Prohibiting the Discharge of Projectiles and Explosives from Balloons, reproduced in Scott (ed.), ibid., p. 220.

[122] Hague Rules of Aerial Warfare 1923, reprinted in Adam Roberts and Richard Guelff (eds.), *Documents on the Laws of War*, 3rd ed. (Oxford: Oxford University Press, 2003), p. 141.

24(1) of the Rules provided that air bombardment would only be legitimate when 'directed at a military objective, that is to say, an object of which the destruction or injury would constitute a distinct military advantage to the belligerent'. However, these Rules had never been adopted as treaty rules.[123]

Regarding anti-personnel landmines, there were no specific legal prohibitions against their use. Used against combatants, it would seem at this point that their use was entirely legal. The question was whether they breached the prohibition against indiscriminate warfare on the basis that many anti-personnel landmines lay dormant and subsequently posed a deadly danger to civilians for years, possibly decades, after the conflict. Incendiary weapons came under the same legal analysis: no specific prohibition was in place against their use, but they were to be assessed in light of the prohibition against indiscriminate warfare.

Despite this disjuncture between the rapid development of weapons technology and the absence of legal adaptation, the post-War revision of the law of armed conflict that took form in the four Geneva Conventions 1949 was silent on the issue of weapons.[124] The revision process was started by the ICRC even as the war continued and the protection of civilians was a key concern for the ICRC.[125] As it transpired, two categories of harm to civilians were addressed in the resulting treaties – the treatment of civilian enemy aliens and the treatment of civilians in occupied territories. In fact, for the first time, there was an entire treaty devoted to the protection of civilians in war: the Fourth Geneva Convention.[126] However, there were no provisions on weapons, notwithstanding that the leading cause of civilian deaths in the war was aerial bombardment.[127] Indeed, the only reference to weapons of any kind in the treaties is a provision in the Third Geneva Convention providing that

[123] Despite this, Kalshoven states that the Rules 'were widely regarded as an authoritative statement of the law on air warfare': Frits Kalshoven, 'Bombardment: From "Brussels 1874" to "Sarajevo 2003"' reproduced in Frits Kalshoven (ed.), *Reflections on the Law of War: Collected Essays* (Boston: Martinus Nijhoff Publishers 2007), pp. 431, 438.

[124] Geoffrey Best, *War and Law since 1945* (Oxford: Oxford University Press, 1994), pp. 103–15. The USSR tabled a proposal in the course of the negotiations to ban the use of atomic weapons, which failed (35:9 with five abstentions).

[125] For a full discussion of the lead-up to the diplomatic conference in August 1949, as well as the negotiations during the Conference itself, see Best, ibid., ch. 4 and Best, *Humanity in Warfare*, above n. 47, ch. V.

[126] Geneva Convention Relative to the Protection of Civilian Persons in Time of War, opened for signature 12 August 1949, 75 UNTS 287 (entered into force 21 October 1950).

[127] R. R. Baxter, 'Humanitarian Law or Humanitarian Politics?' (1975) 16 *Harvard Journal of International Law* 1, 2.

prisoners of war may not be employed on labour that is 'unhealthy or dangerous' and that the removal of mines is considered dangerous labour.[128] Thus, while the 1949 treaties attempted to respond to the realities of the civilian casualties of the Second World War, it failed to protect civilians against the realities of modern weaponry.[129]

Geoffrey Best explains this silence by pointing out that the Allies too had been engaged in indiscriminate warfare and so, just as the post-War criminal prosecutions failed to engage with use of prohibited weapons or modes of attack, so too would it have been politically difficult to draw up prohibitions on the use of certain weapons. Pleas on the basis of humanitarianism were insufficient to shift militarily significant states from their position that they had a sovereign right to develop and use weapons technology to defend themselves against aggressive states.

Another explanation for the exclusion of weapons from the revised treaties lies in the distinction between prohibiting the use of weapons and eliminating them, that is, the banning of the use of weapons compared to the prohibition on possession. Writing in 1948, for example, Professor Bourquin explained that with the vast destructive power of the atomic bomb and other massively destructive means of warfare, it was naïve to think that a prohibition on use alone would suffice. History teaches us otherwise, he claimed.[130] Thus, he argued that a prohibition on use (the scope of the law of armed conflict) would be ineffective, and it would also be necessary to institute a system of international control and verification (along the lines being discussed by the United Nations Atomic Energy Commission at the time). By this line of reasoning, he concluded the problem was one beyond the remit of the ICRC.

The interconnection between prohibition of use and prohibition of possession is revealed in the attempt by the USSR to address atomic weapons in the negotiations for what would become the Geneva Conventions 1949. The USSR tabled a draft resolution in Committee III, as well as in the plenary session, which would have inserted into the treaties a ban on the use of atomic, chemical and

[128] Geneva Convention Relative to the Treatment of Prisoners of War, opened for signature 12 August 1949, 75 UNTS 135 (entered into force 21 October 1950).

[129] Solf, 'Protection of Civilians against the Effects of Hostilities', above n. 117, at p. 127; Kalshoven, 'Conference of Government Experts 1971', above n. 106, p. 69; Casey-Maslen, *View from the Vanishing Point*, above n. 28, p. 13.

[130] Maurice Bourquin, 'The Red Cross and Treaty Protection of Civilians in Wartime' (1948) Supplement No. 1 *International Review of the Red Cross* 11, 19.

biological weapons.[131] The resolution failed to even reach a point at which it could be formally considered, ostensibly on the basis that questions of atomic energy were properly considered by the United Nations in the context of the Atomic Energy Commission.[132] It was thus dropped from the negotiations, but the diplomatic dance reveals that even in this humanitarian space, the power politics of military superiority were at play.[133]

Whatever the motivations of those opposing the inclusion of weapons-related provisions, the result was that in a treaty revision exercise specifically designed to ameliorate the humanitarian impacts on civilians in war, the treaties failed to address a key humanitarian danger – that of weapons technology. The treaties opened for signature on 12 August 1949. Seventeen days later, the Soviet Union completed its first successful nuclear weapon test and joined the United States as a nuclear power.

B The ICRC's Indiscriminate Warfare Framework

Even with the failure to include questions of weapons in the 1949 treaties, and despite the growing entrenchment within the United Nations itself, the ICRC persisted with its campaign against indiscriminate weapons for several more years – efforts that would not bear fruit for several more decades.[134]

On 5 April 1950, the ICRC issued a plea to states, setting out the objection to nuclear weapons and aerial bombardment, that is, that the weapons were inherently indiscriminate and they caused suffering much greater than the military advantage, particularly in light of resulting burns and the inability of victims to access adequate medical

[131] Frits Kalshoven, 'The Netherlands and International Humanitarian Law Applicable in Armed Conflicts' in Frits Kalshoven, *Reflections on the Law of War: Collected Essays* (Leiden: Martinus Nijhoff Publishers 2007), pp. 275, 300.

[132] Discussed by Best, *War and Law since 1945*, above n. 123, pp. 109–14. See also Kalshoven, ibid., pp. 299–300.

[133] And see Bugnion, 'The International Committee of the Red Cross and Nuclear Weapons', above n. 111, pp. 515–17.

[134] See Kalshoven, 'Conference of Government Experts 1971', above n. 106, p. 69; Louis Maresca and Stuart Maslen (eds.), *The Banning of Anti-Personnel Landmines: The Legal Contribution of the International Committee of the Red Cross 1955–1999* (Cambridge: Cambridge University Press, 2000), pp. 15–18; Robert J. Mathews, 'The 1980 Convention on Certain Conventional Weapons: A Useful Framework Despite Earlier Disappointments' (2001) 83 (844) *International Review of the Red Cross* 991, 992–3.

treatment.[135] The ICRC went on to convene a meeting of experts in early 1954 to consider and discuss the 'dangers of war from the air and the use of blind weapons'.[136] In May 1954, the Board of Governors of the Red Cross at its 23rd session in Oslo requested the ICRC to examine the issue further.[137] Accordingly, in mid-1955, the ICRC distributed to National Societies Draft Rules for the Protection of the Civil Population from the Dangers of Indiscriminate Warfare which it had prepared, calling for comments from states.[138]

Detailed reaction was received from a number of National Societies, and the ICRC subsequently convened a working party of experts on an informal basis to discuss those reactions. The outcome of that meeting was, the ICRC reported, that while all participants were opposed to the idea of total war, it was generally felt that the Red Cross could make a more 'valuable contribution by keeping to its own purely humanitarian and general aims'.[139] Despite this less than supportive reaction, the Rules were further revised and resubmitted to states for additional comment.[140] Taking into account the concerns expressed by states and experts, the ICRC had by this time changed the name of the Rules from Draft Rules for the Protection of the Civil Population from the Dangers of Indiscriminate Warfare to the less confrontational Rules for the Limitation of the Dangers Incurred by the Civilian Population in Time of War, thus dropping reference to 'indiscriminate warfare', and it was this version that was presented to the International Red Cross Conference in New Delhi in 1957.[141]

135 The Appeal is reproduced in Bugnion, 'The International Committee of the Red Cross and Nuclear Weapons', above n. 111, pp. 516–17.

136 International Committee of the Red Cross, 'The Protection of the Civilian Population in Atomic, Chemical and Bacteriological Warfare' (November 1954) *Revue Internationale de la Croix-Rouge et Bulletin Internationale Des Sociétés de la Croix-Rouge* 213, 213.

137 Ibid., pp. 213–14.

138 Draft Rules for the Limitation of the Dangers Incurred by the Civilian Population in Time of War (International Committee of the Red Cross, Geneva, April 1958), reprinted in part in Maresca and Maslen (eds.), *The Banning of Anti-Personnel Landmines*, above n. 133, pp. 15–18.

139 Advisory Working Party of Experts delegated by National Red Cross Societies, 'Legal Protection of the Civilian Population' (June 1956) *Revue Internationale de la Croix-Rouge et Bulletin Internationale Des Sociétés de la Croix-Rouge* 93, 97.

140 Draft Rules for the Limitation of the Dangers Incurred by the Civilian Population in Time of War (October 1956) *Revue Internationale de la Croix-Rouge et Bulletin Internationale Des Sociétés de la Croix-Rouge* 163.

141 Kalshoven, 'Conference of Government Experts 1971', above n. 106, p. 69. The revised Draft Rules are reproduced in Dietrich Schindler and Jiri Toman (eds.), *The Laws of*

The 1957 Conference resolved that the objectives of the Rules were in line with the Red Cross ideals of the 'requirements of humanity' in warfare, and that the Rules should be forwarded to governments for further consideration. Although the ICRC circulated the revised Draft Rules to all National Societies following the 1957 Conference, they were not well received so that the ICRC itself concluded that the Rules 'could hardly longer serve as a basis for its future studies given the absence of favourable reactions from governments'.[142] Thus, the project ended.[143]

The conditions had been utterly unfavourable. First, with the USSR, and then the United Kingdom, France and China having successfully developed nuclear weapons, the atomic bomb genie was well and truly out of the bottle, and positions had hardened within the United Nations discussions as the decade progressed. Although it was perfectly clear by the early- to mid-1950s that the United Nations was not going to make much progress on 'arms control' much less on disarmament in the foreseeable future, there was still no way for the ICRC to step into the breach. Time and time again, it was warned away from the project. It was clear that the major military powers were not prepared to commit themselves to any restrictions on their choice of weapons, or how they would deploy them in conflict. With the advent of the Korean War, there was an even greater reluctance on the part of states to even consider having their choice of weapons curtailed.

Relying on the 'indiscriminate weapon' route was also problematic because at this point in time, debate continued about the precise status of the prohibition against indiscriminate weapons. For example, Boothby expresses the view that the prohibition of indiscriminate attacks was not a binding rule before 1977, although he concedes that the principle was taking shape at this point.[144] While there did seem to be broad agreement that a total war concept should be rejected, which would seem to accept that there should be some limits on the choice of weapons, nonetheless,

Armed Conflicts: A Collection of Conventions, Resolutions, and Other Documents (Leiden: Martinus Nijhoff Publishers, 2004), p. 339.

142 'The Lot of the Civilian Population in War-Time' (February 1966) *International Review of the Red Cross* 79, 82–3.

143 Kalshoven, 'Conference of Government Experts 1971', above n. 106, p. 69. See also comment by Mathews, '1980 Convention on Certain Conventional Weapons', above n. 132, p. 992 that 'there was insufficient support by governments' to transform the Draft Rules to treaty form; see also, Baxter, 'Humanitarian Law or Humanitarian Politics?', above n. 125, p. 3.

144 Boothby, *Weapons and the Law of Armed Conflict*, above n. 114, p. 75.

the international community was still some time away from a clear treaty rule expressly prohibiting indiscriminate attacks.

In the end, it seems as though the fatal objection to the project turned on the humanitarian/disarmament divide. The major military powers argued that it was inappropriate for the question of weapons to be discussed in the context of the Geneva Law. Rather, weapons were a matter for the Hague Law and probably a matter for the United Nations, not the ICRC. The handwritten comment by an unknown reader on the (scanned) text of the Draft Rules held by US Army's Judge Advocate General's School Library is telling. Alongside Article 14 is a hand-written comment: 'this is disarmament without effective international control'.

VI Conclusion

It would be too blunt a conclusion to suggest there was no humanitarian impulse at all in disarmament in the two decades following the Second World War. But the foregoing discussion has certainly shown that disarmament was sidelined and humanitarianism eclipsed.

Nevertheless, in October 1958, Mr Masutero Inoué, the then Director of Foreign Affairs of the Japanese Red Cross, published an article entitled 'National preparatory measures by the Red Cross against the dangers of atomic warfare' in the *International Review of the Red Cross*. The piece (prefaced by what seems like an unusually cautious note from the editor to the effect that the article is published on the author's sole responsibility) explains the impact of the atomic bombing on Hiroshima and goes on to explain some proposals for preparedness for nuclear war including establishing and training a corps of specialised medical personnel; developing individualised protective procedures (on the basis that it would not be possible to rely on any centralised assistance); planning for coordinating refugee relief subsequent to any attack; and working on medical research for radiation sickness.[145] Thus, discussions about the human impact of a nuclear attack may have been side-lined in the United Nations, and even in the ICRC, but they were not entirely extinguished. As well, as we will see in Chapter 7, the human (and environmental) impacts of ongoing nuclear testing would continue to be matters of grave concern in civil society, even if some governments steadfastly refused to engage.

[145] M. Inoué, 'National Preparatory Measures by the Red Cross against the Dangers of Atomic Warfare' (October 1958) *International Review of the Red Cross* 219.

And on the horizon, there was another growing light – what would become known as the Non-Aligned Movement. In 1955, delegations of twenty-nine countries from Africa and Asia met in Bandung, Indonesia to promote decolonisation and to give voice to African and Asian states. Their final communiqué at that meeting addressed the question of disarmament and particularly nuclear weapons and in doing so, the states present chose to use the language of humanity:

> The Conference considered that disarmament and the prohibition of the production, experimentation and use of nuclear and thermo-nuclear weapons of war are imperative to save mankind and civilisation from the fear and prospect of wholesale destruction. It considered that the nations of Asia and Africa assembled here have a duty towards humanity and civilisation to proclaim their support for disarmament and for the prohibition of these weapons and to appeal to nations principally concerned and to world opinion, to bring about such disarmament and prohibition.[146]

As time passed, a key position for the non-aligned states was that disarmament discussions should take place in a multilateral forum, rather than through bilateral arrangements dictated by superpower agendas and perceptions of security.[147] This was at least in part due to a sensibility that the possession (and use) of weapons – particularly weapons of mass destruction – were matters of concern to the entire international community of states, not simply the superpowers of the time.[148]

So, as the world moved inexorably towards the Vietnam War, the humanitarian discourse in the context of weapons control had been seriously marginalised, but it was not completely silenced.

[146] *Final Communiqué of the Asian-African conference of Bandung* (24 April 1955), para. F(2).

[147] Hennie Strydom, 'The Non-Aligned Movement and the Reform of International Relations' (2007) 11 *Max Planck Yearbook of United Nations Law* 1.

[148] Plesch surmises that the approach (in these early days at least) of the states from the South to the question of weaponry lay in part that many of these states had felt the brunt of the weaponry both as colonies and in the course of their wars of independence: Dan Plesch, 'The South and Disarmament at the UN' (2016) 37(7) *Third World Quarterly* 1203.

4

Humanitarian Disarmament Rising

The Vietnam War and the Campaigns against Indiscriminate Weapons

I Introduction

In the previous chapter I argued that, in the early decades of the United Nations, the humanitarian discourse in disarmament was marginalised, although not completely silenced. The core argument of this chapter is that the Vietnam War reignited that discourse. Numbers and data cannot adequately convey the scale of the destruction wrought in that war, or the catastrophic human suffering and ecological disaster which ensued. However to give some context, during Operation Rolling Thunder (a three-year aerial bombing campaign conducted by the US Air Force in Vietnam from February 1965–October 1968) more bombs were dropped on Vietnam than had been dropped in all of Europe during the Second World War.[1] Combined with the ferocity of the campaign was the fact that the weapons being used were different in scale and degree. Now, aerial bombardment combined with a new generation of landmines, being able to be deployed over ever-greater areas, more advanced incendiary weapons some of which were also delivered by air, along with widespread use of herbicides.

Vietnam, then, became the new springboard for the humanitarian disarmament push.[2] Within the United States, particularly from the late 1960s, there was increasing popular opposition to the war and a key feature of that opposition was to the use of particular weapons: anti-personnel

[1] Robert S. McNamara (with Brian VanDeMark), *In Retrospect: The Tragedy and Lessons of Vietnam* (New York and Toronto: Random House, 1995), p. 174.

[2] Robert J. Mathews, 'The 1980 Convention on Certain Conventional Weapons: A Useful Framework Despite Earlier Disappointments' (2001) 83(844) *International Review of the Red Cross* 991, 992–3. See also, R. R. Baxter, 'Conventional Weapons under Legal Prohibitions' (1977) 1(3) *International Security* 42, 45.

landmines, herbicides and napalm. Much of this opposition was couched in the language of humanitarianism – a focus on the human suffering (and ecological destruction) inflicted by those weapons.

There was not only popular opposition to the war and its weapons. Many of the non-aligned states voiced increasing opposition to and concern about the scale of the destruction and the level of civilian casualties.[3] The Non-Aligned Movement (NAM) was taking form, with increasing demands that certain weapons should be prohibited entirely, or at the very least, their use should be subject to further and more stringent regulation. As I will show, the NAM fought this battle along two front lines: the first within the ICRC movement attempting to use international humanitarian law and the second within the rapidly expanding United Nations General Assembly. Although little of substance was achieved in either of these initiatives, combined, they kept the question of indiscriminate weapons squarely on the international agenda and, I argue, they are important, if not completely successful, humanitarian disarmament campaigns.

However, at the same time, and as discussed in the previous chapter, humanitarianism as an ideal had become politically suspect since the Second World War. In the context of the Vietnam War, it became clear that the protests against the weapons being deployed were inextricably linked to protests about the war itself. Thus, as the war became increasingly perceived as being unjust, the humanitarian nature of the weapons concerns became inextricably linked to opposition to the war itself.[4] Indeed, humanitarian arguments were frequently dismissed as being pro-communist. Bertrand Russell, writing to the *New York Times* in 1963 challenging the use of napalm in Vietnam, was criticised for his 'unthinking receptivity to the most transparent communist propaganda'.[5] In 1967 Martin Luther King, who had denounced the use of napalm ('this business of burning human beings with napalm . . . cannot be reconciled with wisdom,

[3] For a discussion on the rising levels of civilian casualties across different conflicts, see Gerd Oberleitner, *Human Rights in Armed Conflict: Law, Practice, Policy* (Cambridge: Cambridge University Press, 2015), p. 53.

[4] See for example, J. Ashley Roach, 'Certain Conventional Weapons Convention: Arms Control or Humanitarian Law?' (1984) 105 *Military Law Review* 3, in which he comments that views 'purported to be humanitarian, but actual involved political views regarding Vietnam': p. 6.

[5] Robert M. Neer, *Napalm: An American Biography* (Cambridge: Harvard University Press, 2013), p. 131.

justice and love'), was himself denounced by 168 American newspapers.[6] Thus, while the war was the impetus for a revived humanitarianism, that humanitarianism was portrayed as politically suspect and was often publicly chastised.

Setting the scene then, in Section II I give an account of the catastrophic weaponry deployed in the war, along with an account of the public protests, including the increasing alarm within the scientific community about the effects and impact of the weapons. Combined, these sources of discontent show the 'grass roots' humanitarian disarmament discourse (re)emerging in this period.[7]

In Section III I go on to consider the two campaigns against the weapons being used. First, there was an attempt to include discussions about weapons in the context of developing the law of armed conflict, in particular aiming to reach agreement on prohibiting the use of certain indiscriminate weapons in war. Second, the 'human rights in armed conflict' initiative spearheaded at the 1968 Tehran Conference, and maintained by the states of the NAM, started to work in the United Nations General Assembly to challenge the use of those same weapons. My argument is that while neither of these campaigns could be described as 'successful' in that neither brought about the elimination (or even outright prohibition) of any category of weapons, both stand as important instances of attempts to use humanitarian arguments to constrain the development and use of weapons. Perhaps because of their very modest success, they have been neglected in the literature and accounts of humanitarian disarmament. One of my aims in this chapter is to recover them.

In the final section of the chapter (Section IV) I analyse the Convention on Conventional Weapons 1980 (CCW), arguing that it is the first 'humanitarian disarmament' instrument of the post–Second World War era. Undoubtedly a compromise text, falling far short of the ambitions of many states, nevertheless, I show how it is a testament to the humanitarian disarmament work of the preceding decades and in fact can be seen at least in part as a result of the opposition to the Vietnam War. Perhaps more importantly, it also set the stage for future breakthroughs, including the Anti-Personnel Landmines Convention 1997, which I consider in the next chapter.

[6] Ibid., p. 114.

[7] In the same period, there were rising concerns within civil society and states about the dangers posed by nuclear weapons as well. These are discussed in Chapter 7.

II The Humanitarian Catastrophe in Vietnam

Humanitarian concerns were reignited by aerial bombardment and the widespread use of three weapons in particular in Vietnam: incendiary weapons; herbicides; and anti-personnel landmines. The human and environmental impact of these weapons, combined with intense print and televised media attention given to the war more generally, gave impetus to a massive humanitarian public response including rising opposition among many in the scientific and medical communities.[8] This section gives an account of each of those categories of weapons and traces how a humanitarian discourse emerged in response.

A Incendiary Weapons, Especially Napalm

Incendiary weapons have been a feature of warfare from earliest times, but it was really only from the First World War and beyond (with the advent of aerial warfare) that incendiaries became genuinely effective as weapons.[9] As discussed in Chapter 3, with the development of advanced incendiary weapons including napalm during the Second World War, incendiary weapons became much more reliable and effective, due to the way napalm adheres to its target, and due to its ability to burn at extremely high temperatures.[10] Following the Second World War, napalm continued to be used in a number of colonial wars,[11] but it was unleashed to an unprecedented extent in the Korean War. According to Neer, Washington ordered a 'scorched earth' approach in Korea, with 32,357 tons of napalm – twice that used against Japan during the

[8] For a discussion of the television and broader media coverage on Vietnam and survey of the related literature, see Matthias Bandtel and Jens Tenscher, 'Front Cover Imagery and the Social Construction of the Vietnam War: A Case Study of LIFE Magazine's Iconology and its Impact on Visual Discourse' (2014) 7(2) *Journal of War and Culture Studies* 100. On scientists, see: Kelly Moore, *Disrupting Science: Social Movements, American Scientists, and the Politics of the Military, 1945–1975* (Princeton: Princeton University Press, 2008).

[9] Broadly speaking, incendiary weapons are weapons designed to injure or damage through fire (as opposed to causing incidental fire damage) although as will become evident, this is not a clear-cut distinction. For an overview of different types of incendiary weapons, see *Napalm and Other Incendiary Weapons and all Aspects of their Possible Use Report of the Secretary-General*, 27th sess, Agenda Item 30(c), A/8803 and Corr. 1 (9 October 1972).

[10] See Chapter 3.

[11] For example, the French and Vietnamese in Indochina (1946–54), the French in Algeria, the British in Malay. For discussion, see Stockholm International Peace Research Institute (SIPRI), *Incendiary Weapons* (Cambridge: MIT Press, 1975) pp. 40–69.

Second World War – being used to 'make it a wilderness'.[12] While concerns were voiced about this, even in the House of Commons in the United Kingdom,[13] the scale and manner of destruction did not initially capture the popular imagination in the United States.

By 1966 in Vietnam, napalm had become an integral weapon in the arsenal of the United States.[14] The Stockholm International Peace Research Institute (SIPRI) calculated that the likely total tonnage of air-dropped napalm, phosphorus and other incendiary munitions had exceeded 400,000 tons by August 1973 – more than a tenfold increase from the Korean War.[15] Neer estimates that 4,500 tons of napalm per month was being dropped, with the bombing peaking by 1968 at 5,900 tons per month.[16]

The figures by themselves do not convey the humanitarian impact of the weapon and while it took some time for information to become available, that started to emerge by 1967 with a series of magazine and newspaper reports in the United States.[17] Medical practitioners began to express concern about the effects of the weapon, in particular the serious burns, suffocation and the extremely painful nature of the injuries.[18] The increasing publicity led to a broad-based campaign in the United States against the leading manufacturer of napalm: The Dow Chemical Company.[19]

With the passage of time, the enduring image of napalm in the Vietnam War has become that of its most famous victim, Kim Phúc – a young Vietnamese girl, burning and terrified, fleeing an incendiary attack along with her brother and cousins in Trang Bang in 1972.[20] The image came to epitomise the devastating human impact of the war. And

[12] Discussed by Neer, *Napalm*, above n. 5, pp. 91–104; p. 98 (for the quote on wilderness). See also SIPRI, *Incendiary Weapons*, ibid., pp. 43–7; Bruce Cumings, *The Korean War: A History* (United States: Modern Library, 2010), pp. 149–54.

[13] United Kingdom, *Parliamentary Debates*, House of Commons, 12 May 1952, vol. 500, col. 848.

[14] Neer, *Napalm*, above n. 5, p. 111.

[15] SIPRI, *Incendiary Weapons*, above n. 11, p. 49–52. Drawing on data about use of general munitions in Vietnam along with US procurement of napalm bombs. This figure captures only napalm delivered by air and does not include ground weapons.

[16] Neer, *Napalm*, above n. 5, p. 111.

[17] Peter Reich and Victor Sidel, 'Napalm' (1967) 277(2) *The New England Journal of Medicine* 86–8; William F. Pepper, 'The Children of Vietnam' (January 1967) 5(7) *Ramparts* 53; Martha Gellhorn, 'Suffer the Little Children' (January 1967) *Ladies' Home Journal* 108; Perry and Levin, 'Where the Innocent Die' (January 1967) *Redbook* 103. These and other publications are discussed by Neer, *Napalm*, above n. 5, p. 113.

[18] Reich and Sidel, 'Napalm', above n. 17, p. 87.

[19] Neer, *Napalm*, above n. 5, pp. 109–25.

[20] *New York Times*, 9 June 1972. The photograph is reproduced in Neer, *Napalm*, above n. 5, p. 3.

yet, perhaps like many iconic humanitarian images, it masks a more complex reality.[21] In fact, that particular attack was not launched by American troops. Rather, it was a South Vietnamese aircraft which deployed the incendiaries that day.[22]

Thus, despite its iconic status, the photograph was not the trigger for the campaigns against the use of incendiary weapons. Rather, the 'trigger' was the persistent efforts stretching back to the mid-1960s by war correspondents and medical doctors to make the public and government officials aware of the devastation. These efforts in turn led to public campaigns against The Dow Chemical Company, the leading manufacturer of napalm.[23] But regardless of precisely when, or by what trigger, popular opinion shifted, there is no doubt that incendiary weapons did come to epitomise the new face of warfare and was part of the impetus in the coming years to limit the use of indiscriminate weapons.

B Herbicides

A second category of weapons raising humanitarian concerns was herbicides, particularly the most infamous of them, so-called 'Agent Orange'. As with incendiary weapons, ecological destruction, including crop destruction, has been a feature of warfare for millennia.[24] However, the use of herbicides as a weapon on a large scale was a feature of the post–Second World War era, again facilitated by aerial warfare. Britain was the first to use modern herbicides during its war in what was then Malaya in the early 1950s. From 1951–3, the British sprayed STCA, 2,4-D and 2,4,5-T initially as defoliants to reduce the risk of ambush, and then subsequently for the destruction of crops aimed at food denial against the Malay insurgents.[25]

[21] There is a considerable literature on the photograph, some of it in the broader context of media portrayals of conflict: Denise Chong, *The Girl in the Picture: The Story of Kim Phuc, the Photograph, and the Vietnam War* (New York: Penguin Books, 1999); Bandtel and Tenscher, 'Front Cover Imagery and the Social Construction of the Vietnam War' above n. 8; Guy Westwell, 'Accidental Napalm Attack and Hegemonic Visions of America's War in Vietnam' (2011) 28(5) *Critical Studies in Media Communication* 407. For contemporary reaction, see Pepper, 'The Children of Vietnam', above n. 17.

[22] Neer, *Napalm*, above n. 5, p. 3.

[23] Ibid., pp. 109–25.

[24] Arthur H. Westing, 'Herbicides in War: Past and Present' in Arthur H. Westing (ed.), *Herbicides in War: The Long-Term Ecological and Human Consequences* (London: Taylor and Francis, 1984), p. 3.

[25] Ibid.; S. Connor and A. Thomas, 'How Britain Sprayed Malaya with Dioxin' (1984) 101 (1393) *New Scientist* 67.

The United States had been conducting trials with various herbicides since the 1940s but they had not been deployed in military operations until the Vietnam War. Starting in 1961 and continuing for a decade, seventy-three million litres of herbicide were sprayed over Vietnam.[26] The operation – Operation Ranch Hand – resulted in 1.7 million hectares being sprayed (sometimes repeatedly in the same area).[27] Around 86 per cent of the spraying was aimed at forest defoliation in order to destroy the highly effective cover for Viet Cong forces, with the remaining 14 per cent aimed at crop denial.[28] The saturation spraying denuded over two million hectares of forest and destroyed 200,000 hectares of farmland.[29] Extensive records were kept of each spraying campaign and, from that data, it is estimated that up to 17.6 million people were exposed to the chemicals.[30] Around 62 per cent of the herbicide was Agent Orange, a mixture of herbicides 2,4-D and 2,4,5-T: the latter contaminated with dioxin TCDD.[31] Although the peak years of the spraying were 1967–9, overall the campaign lasted for ten years from September 1961–June 1970.

From the publication of Rachel Carson's *Silent Spring* in 1962, concerns had started to be expressed about the widespread use of pesticides and insecticides for general use in domestic agriculture.[32] Nevertheless, the human impact of the spraying campaign in Vietnam was not understood immediately, as there was a lack of clarity about the precise formulation and toxicity of the chemicals. As such, public and scientific reactions against herbicides initially were based on concerns about the resulting defoliation. In January 1966, a group of twenty-nine scientists

26 The spraying was largely conducted over South Vietnam, although there were forays into Cambodia, Laos and North Vietnam as well. See Westing, 'Herbicides in War: Past and Present', above n. 24, p. 4.

27 Ibid., p. 5. For details of the spraying campaigns, see Tables 1.1, 1.2 and 1.3, pp. 6–7. See as well the detailed discussion by John Constable and Matthew Meselson, 'The Ecological Impact of Large Scale Defoliation in Vietnam' (1971) *Sierra Club Bulletin* 4.

28 Arthur Westing (SIPRI), *Ecological Consequences of the Second Indochina War* (Stockholm: Almqvist & Wiksell International, 1976), p. 27.

29 Edwin Martini, *Agent Orange: History, Science and the Politics of Uncertainty* (Amherst: University of Mass Press, 2012), p. 2.

30 Susan Hammond and Arnold Schecter, 'Agent Orange: Health and Environmental Issues in Vietnam, Cambodia, and Laos' in Arnold Schecter (ed.), *Dioxins and Health: Including Other Persistent Organic Pollutants and Endocrine Disruptors* 3rd ed. (New Jersey; Canada: John Wiley and Sons, 2012), p. 469.

31 Jeanne Mager Stellman et al., 'The Extent and Patterns of Usage of Agent Orange and Other Herbicides in Vietnam' (2003) 422 (6933) *Nature* 6817.

32 Rachel Carson, *Silent Spring* (London: Hamish Hamilton, 1962).

from the Boston area (mostly Harvard University and Massachusetts Institute of Technology) took out a full page advertisement in the *New York Times*, to oppose the use of 'chemical agents for the destruction of crops', saying that the practice was 'barbarous and indiscriminate' and a 'shocking deterioration of our moral standards'.[33] One of the scientists involved in that publication, Professor Matthew Meselson, was appointed to head the Herbicide Assessment Commission of the American Association for Advancement of Science (AAAS).[34] The Commission reported to the AAAS in December 1970, finding that around half of South Vietnam's coastal mangrove forests had been sprayed,[35] 20 per cent of mature hardwood forest had been targeted as well as a considerable portion of cropland. With the release of the Commission's report, the White House announced a phasing out of the herbicide operations.[36]

It took longer for the human impact of the herbicide programme to be quantified and properly understood.[37] The Commission had also stated that it found some evidence of a link to stillbirths, but could not make a conclusive finding. Writing in 1971, Constable and Meselson noted the continuing uncertainty of both the human impact and the long-term ecological impacts of the herbicide programme.[38] Congress ordered a further study but that was not released until 1974. When the Congressional Report was released, it confirmed the extent of the human illnesses and deaths caused by exposure to and ingestion of herbicides.[39]

[33] Kelly Moore, *Disrupting Science: Social Movements, American Scientists, and the Politics of the Military, 1945–1975* (New Jersey: Princeton University Press, 2008), p. 134. See also, David Zierler, *Invention of Ecocide* (Athens: University of Georgia Press, 2011), p. 101.

[34] Joel Primack and Frank von Hippel, *Advice and Dissent: Scientists in the Political Arena* (New York: Basic Books Inc., 1974), ch. 11(exploring the work of Matthew Meselson and the United States Policy on Chemical and Biological Warfare), pp. 143, 153–61.

[35] Ibid., p. 159.

[36] Ibid., p. 160.

[37] Peter Sills, *Toxic War: The Story of Agent Orange* (Tennessee: Vanderbilt University Press, 2014), esp. ch. 21 (writing in the context of the impact on US veterans who had been deployed to Vietnam).

[38] Constable and Meselson, 'Ecological Impact of Large Scale Defoliation', above n. 27, p. 9.

[39] Committee on the Effects of Herbicides in South Vietnam, National Academy of Sciences, *The Effects of Herbicides in South Vietnam: Part A Summary and Conclusions* (Washington DC, 1974). For discussion see, Bruce F. Meyers, 'Soldier of Orange: The Administrative, Diplomatic, Legislative and Litigatory Impact of Herbicide Agent Orange in South Vietnam' (1979) 8(2) *Boston College Environmental Affairs Law Review* 159, 171; Zierler, *Invention of Ecocide*, above n. 33, p. 154; Primack and von Hippel, *Advice and Dissent: Scientists in the Political Arena*, above n. 34, p. 161.

Thus, it was members of the scientific community that led the charge against the use of herbicides in Vietnam. It is clear now that herbicides caused crop destruction and thus human dislocation on a massive scale, catastrophic and long-term environmental harm, as well as intergenerational birth defects and deaths. However, the harm was 'slow moving', sometimes not immediately apparent (illness and intergenerational harm), and often private (stillbirths and miscarriages). This lack of sensationalism made it more difficult to capture the public imagination – compared to, for example, the shocking and immediately traumatic reports of napalm use. Nevertheless, the campaign against herbicides including by members of the scientific community did eventually succeed in a change of policy, and thus stands as an illustration of the importance of evidence-based research in supporting any humanitarian disarmament campaign.

C *Anti-Personnel Landmines*

The third category of weapon raising humanitarian concerns was anti-personnel landmines and while all parties involved in the Vietnam War were users, the scale of the use by the United States was unprecedented.[40] Between 1966 and 1968, the United States is reported to have procured 114 million anti-personnel landmines.[41] Looking at civilian impact, by 1973 there were over 80,000 amputees in South Vietnam, with perhaps 50 per cent of those injuries being caused by landmines.[42]

It was not just the scale of use that caused such a humanitarian crisis: novel modes of deployment also facilitated massively increased numbers of anti-personnel landmines to be laid. Although some mines had been delivered by air during the Second World War, most mines (both anti-vehicle and anti-personnel) had been hand-placed. A major advance in mine technology came in the 1960s with the development of 'scatterable' landmines which were mines designed to be delivered by aircraft, missile, artillery or ground dispenser, and which would be activated

[40] International Committee of the Red Cross (ICRC), *Anti-personnel Landmines: Friend or Foe? A Study of the Military Use and Effectiveness of Anti-personnel Mines* (Geneva: ICRC, 1997) 29.

[41] Stuart Casey Maslen, *The Convention on the Prohibition on the Use, Stockpiling, Production and Transfer of Anti-Personnel Mines and on their Destruction* (Oxford: Oxford University Press, 2004), p. 5. See the detailed discussion by Rae McGrath, *Landmines and Unexploded Ordnance: A Resource Book* (London: Pluto Press, 2000), pp. 7–8.

[42] Malvern Lumsden, *Anti-personnel Weapons* (London: Taylor and Francis, 1978), p. 35.

automatically (that is, become 'live') as they hit the ground. The scatterable technology allowed deployment of large numbers of anti-personnel landmines over a much larger area than was previously possible and was thus more 'efficient'. However, as a consequence, it became impossible to reliably record the placement of the mines, leading to a dramatic escalation in civilian deaths and injury, even after the cessation of hostilities.[43] Further, the technology triggered a shift in the purpose of mine-laying. In the Second World War, mines had been predominately defensive (protection from land invasions), but now, with scatterable technology, their use became more offensive: including preventing the flow of troops and supplies from North to South Vietnam through Laos and Cambodia.[44] Mines were also used for area denial and consequently vast areas of farmland and village communities became unsafe for civilian use.[45]

In these ways, anti-personnel landmines became a particularly important tool for the United States in terms of the broader Indo–China War. In Laos, for example, the United States carried out 580,000 bombing missions, which is equivalent to one mission every eight minutes for nine years.[46] In Cambodia, starting from 1967, when North Vietnamese troops mined their military camps that they had established inside the Cambodian border, there was extensive use of anti-personnel landmines by all parties to the conflict.[47] The scale of the use is apparent from reports of mine clearance teams to the effect that in one kilometre stretch, they cleared 6,000 anti-personnel mines.[48]

As with incendiary weapons and herbicides, scientists and medical doctors played an important part in providing information on, and

43 IRIN, *Laying Landmines to Rest? IRIN Web Special on Humanitarian Mine Action* (November 2004).

44 Don Hubert, *The Landmine Ban: A Case Study in Humanitarian Advocacy* (Providence: Thomas J. Watson Jr. Institute for International Studies, 2000), p. 4; Lumsden, *Anti-Personnel Weapons*, above n. 42, explains that the USA placed emphasis on 'area denial' from the earliest phases of the war, citing to US Department of Defense: p. 35. See also Alex Vines, 'The Crisis of Anti-Personnel Mines' in Maxwell A. Cameron, Robert J. Lawson and Brian W. Tomlin (eds.), *To Walk Without Fear: The Global Movement to Ban Landmines* (Toronto; New York: Oxford University Press, 1998), pp. 118, 120; McGrath, *Landmines and Unexploded Ordnance*, above n. 41, p. 5.

45 Hubert, *The Landmine Ban*, above n. 44, p. 5.

46 Statement of Titus Peachey on behalf of the Mennonite Central Committee to Congressional Hearing available in *The Global Landmine Crisis* S. Hrg. 103-666 (1994), 124 citing to 121 Congressional Record 14266 (1975).

47 See generally, Asia Watch and Physicians for Human Rights, *Landmines in Cambodia: The Coward's War* (United States of America: Human Rights Watch, 1991).

48 Ibid., p. 35.

attempting to raise public awareness about, the use of landmines during the war itself.[49] Even within the military, questions were raised with some discussion emerging about the deleterious humanitarian impact of anti-personnel landmines and cluster munitions.[50] That being said, it was not until the Afghanistan and Cambodian conflicts that concerns about widespread use of anti-personnel landmines were expressed by less technically specialised NGOs and the deleterious humanitarian impacts of those weapons gained more traction in terms of popular concern.

III Two Humanitarian Campaigns against Weapons in Vietnam

The catastrophic impact of these weapons and more generally, the scale of the Vietnam war gave rise to a number of campaigns to limit, or even prohibit outright these and other weapons. In this section I explore two of those campaigns: first, the renewed attempt to bring weapons into the scope of the law of armed conflict; second, the 'human rights in armed conflict' initiative attempting to bring a human rights discourse to the use of weapons. Both campaigns arose as specific responses to the way in which the Vietnam War was being waged and my argument is that they can be viewed as humanitarian disarmament campaigns in that they were motivated by, and consistently drew attention to, the human suffering engendered by the weapons in question.

Before turning to examine these two campaigns, it is worth noting an overarching dynamic in the international system during the period under review (approximately 1965–80). With the process of decolonisation now in play, there was a changing balance of power within the UN General Assembly, and rising demands of the NAM against the dominance of the West and East within the UN multilateral system. Disarmament was a core value of the NAM.[51] Indeed, at the first meeting of the non-aligned states in Bandung in 1955, the closing declaration addressed disarmament and particularly nuclear weapons. In doing so, the participating states used the language of humanity:

> The Conference considered that disarmament and the prohibition of the production, experimentation and use of nuclear and thermo-nuclear weapons of war are imperative to save mankind and civilization from

[49] See for example, K. F. King, 'Orthopedic Aspects of War Wounds in South Vietnam' (1969) 51(1) *The Journal of Bone and Joint Surgery* 112.

[50] Michael Krepon, 'Weapons Potentially Inhumane: The Case of Cluster Bombs' (1973–5) 52 *Foreign Affairs* 595.

[51] Dan Plesch, 'The South and Disarmament' (2016) 37(7) *Third World Quarterly* 1203.

> the fear and prospect of wholesale destruction. It considered that the nations of Asia and Africa assembled here have a duty towards humanity and civilization to proclaim their support for disarmament and for the prohibition of these weapons and to appeal to nations principally concerned and to world opinion, to bring about such disarmament and prohibition.[52]

Over time, the positions of the newly independent states evolved. In the earlier part of the period being considered in this chapter (1965 onwards), there was considerable concern in the Third World about the use of weapons by Western colonial powers against the peoples of the Third World since the end of the Second World War – by the British on the Malayan Peninsula; by the French and then also the USA in Indo-China, by the Portuguese in Angola and so on. But with the passage of time, as military dictators replaced some of the governments of early independence in several of the former colonies, the dynamic changed.[53] Thus, by the late 1970s, some of those same governments previously advocating for prohibitions on certain categories of weapons, now resisted attempts to ban weapons – particularly inexpensive but militarily effective weapons such as anti-personnel landmines. However, in the period under consideration in this chapter, Third World policy was dominated by consolidated opposition to the US use of force against the North Vietnamese.

A The First Campaign: Attempting to Bring Weapons into the Scope of the Geneva Law of Armed Conflict

As discussed in Chapter 3, immediately following the Second World War, the ICRC had attempted to generate some agreement within the international community on restrictions or prohibitions on particular categories of weapons.[54] However, that project, in the form of Draft Rules on Indiscriminate Weapons, had ground to a halt due to a reluctance by a number of militarily significant states to participate in the project. The war in Vietnam, increasing numbers of newly decolonised states joining the ranks of the global Red Cross and Red Crescent Movement, and the

[52] *Final Communiqué of the Asian-African Conference of Bandung* (24 April 1955) at para. F(2).

[53] See Michael E. Lathan, 'The Cold War in the Third World, 1963–1975', in Melvyn P. Leffler and Odd Arne Westad (eds.), *Cambridge History of the Cold War* (Cambridge: Cambridge University Press, 2010), p. 258.

[54] See Chapter 3.

rapid advances in weapons technology, combined to bring the question of increasing international legal regulation of indiscriminate weapons back on the international agenda.

For states concerned about the use of indiscriminate weapons, drawing on the law of armed conflict was an obvious approach. It could be seen as an attempt to build on the perceived gap in the so-called Hague Law, that part of the law of armed conflict that regulated the conduct of hostilities, including the use of weapons in armed conflict.[55] As Séan McBride stated, it was incongruous to ban the dropping of bombs from balloons, as stipulated in the Hague Declaration XIV 1907, but for the same body of law to remain silent on the use of modern weapons.[56] It was also incongruous to be concerned about the treatment of victims of a bombing, while leaving unchallenged the nature of the bomb itself.

As I will show, this campaign to bring weapons more directly into the scope of the law of armed conflict only partially succeeded. Ultimately, the 1977 revisions to existing treaty law (the four Geneva Conventions 1949) did not ban any particular weapons outright. However, the revisions did incorporate much more detailed provisions about targeting rules and put in place generally applicable prohibitions against indiscriminate weapons. As such, a fair conclusion would be that this particular humanitarian disarmament campaign met with only mixed success.

1 The 1965 Resolution of the International Conference of the Red Cross and Red Crescent Movement

The campaign had its seeds in 1965 when the International Conference of the Red Cross and Red Crescent Movement adopted a Resolution entitled 'Protection of the Civilian Populations Against the Dangers of Indiscriminate Warfare'. Operative paragraph XX provided:

> that the right of the parties to a conflict to adopt means of injuring the enemy is not unlimited;
>
> that it is prohibited to launch attacks against the civilian populations as such;

55 The law of armed conflict was traditionally seen as developing in two separate branches: the Hague Law, dealing with the conduct of war (weapons and means of warfare); and the Geneva Law, which focused on protection of victims of war.

56 Séan McBride, 'Human Rights in Armed Conflicts: The Inter-Relationship between the Humanitarian Laws and the Law of Human Rights' (1970) 9 *Military Law and Law of War Review* 373, 385.

> that distinction must be made at all times between persons taking part in the hostilities and members of the civilian population to the effect that the latter be spared as much as possible;
>
> that the general principles of the Law of War apply to nuclear and similar weapons.[57]

The Resolution went on to request the ICRC to continue to develop international humanitarian law in order to address the problem of 'indiscriminate warfare'. The impetus behind the Resolution was the growing concerns within the emerging NAM about the way in which indiscriminate weapons were being used in conflicts, particularly wars of independence as well as concerns about the increasing intransigence of the nuclear weapons states to work substantively towards agreement on the prohibition of nuclear weapons.

Unsurprisingly, there was an immediate pushback by a number of militarily significant states against this humanitarian framing and the attempt to directly address the use of indiscriminate weapons. In part those objections turned on whether the ICRC was the appropriate locus for such discussions given the existence of the UN Disarmament Commission. On that basis, many states considered that the ICRC should confine itself to consolidating existing rules for the protection of civilians, the sick and the wounded and in that way the mandate of the ICRC and the Disarmament Commission would be clearly delineated.[58] This 'jurisdictional issue' can be seen as the start of a decade-long tug of war between the United Nations and the ICRC as to where the question of weapons should be discussed.[59]

Contentious it may have been, nevertheless after a hiatus of more than a decade since the failed Draft Rules on Indiscriminate Weapons,

[57] International Conference of the Red Cross, *Protection of the Civilian Populations Against the Dangers of Indiscriminate Warfare* (Resolution XXVIII, 1965). See Frits Kalshoven, 'The Conference of Government Experts on the Reaffirmation and Development of International Humanitarian Law Applicable in Armed Conflicts, 24 May–12 June 1971' reprinted in Frits Kalshoven, *Reflections on the Law of War* (Leiden; Boston: Martinus Nijhoff Publishers, 2007), pp. 33, 34–5. See also Keith Suter, *An International Law of Guerrilla Warfare: The Global Politics of Law-Making* (New York: St Martin's Press, 1984), p. 99.

[58] See generally, R. R. Baxter, 'The Evolving Laws of Armed Conflicts' (1973) *Military Law Review* 99 and Suter, *An International Law of Guerrilla Warfare*, above n. 57, p. 97. For views opposing engagement by the ICRC, see W. Hays Parks, 'Means and Methods of Warfare' (2006) 38 *George Washington International Law Review* 511, 515; Roach, 'Certain Conventional Weapons Convention', above n. 4, p. 9.

[59] Baxter, 'Evolving Laws of Armed Conflict', above n. 58, p. 100.

increased international legal regulation of conventional weapons was back on the international agenda.

2 The Work of the Conference of Government Experts 1971–3

The ICRC began its work as directed and, in consultation with experts, prepared a report entitled 'Reaffirmation and Development of the Laws and Customs Applicable in Armed Conflicts', which was then presented and discussed at the next international conference held in Istanbul in 1969.[60] From there, it was agreed that a Conference of Government Experts should be convened to continue the work.

The Conference of Government Experts held two sessions – in 1971 and 1972 – but the question of weapons was immediately sidelined due to the unwillingness of the major military powers to engage with it.[61] By now, the ICRC itself was showing a decided reluctance to deal with the issue, conceding ground at the first session by expressing the view that while it was appropriate to discuss general principles applicable to the use of weapons (noting that it had been asked at the Istanbul international conference to do so), any more concrete proposals would be more appropriately dealt with by other agencies dealing with weapons: namely, the Committee for the Conference on Disarmament.[62] However, the ICRC had not entirely abandoned the project. Its statement concluded with a mild warning that 'if the Conference's work is not completed within the near future, the ICRC will take up its position again, if its collaboration can help towards finding a solution to the problems'.[63]

[60] Kalshoven, 'Conference of Government Experts 1971', above n. 57, p. 35.

[61] ICRC, *Conference of Government Experts on the Reaffirmation and Development of International Humanitarian Law Applicable in Armed Conflicts: Report of the Work of the Conference* (Geneva, August 1971); ICRC, *Conference of Government Experts on the Reaffirmation and Development of International Humanitarian Law Applicable in Armed Conflicts: Report of the Work of the Conference*, Vols 1 & 2 (Geneva, August 1972). For commentary: see Kalshoven, 'Conference of Government Experts 1971', above n. 57; Frits Kalshoven, 'The Conference of Government Experts on the Reaffirmation and Development of International Humanitarian Law Applicable in Armed Conflicts (Second Session), 3 May–2 June 1972' reprinted in Kalshoven, *Reflections on the Law of War*, above n. 57, p. 57.

[62] Suter, *An International Law of Guerrilla Warfare*, above n. 57, p. 96.

[63] ICRC, *Conference of Government Experts 1971*, above n. 61, p. 117. Discussed by Frits Kalshoven, 'The Conference of Government Experts on the Use of Certain Conventional Weapons, Lucerne, 24 September–18 October, 1974' reprinted in Kalshoven, *Reflections on the Law of War*, above n. 57, p. 150.

By the time the second session of the Conference of Experts convened (3 May–2 June 1972), draft texts for what would become the two Additional Protocols to the Geneva Conventions had been prepared by the ICRC and were presented to participants. Weapons were only addressed in a general way in the drafts, and only in proposed draft Protocol I, dealing with international armed conflict.[64] Entitled 'Means of Combat', draft Article 30 provided:

> 1. Combatants' choice of means of combat is not unlimited.
> 2. It is forbidden to use weapons, projectiles of substances calculated to cause unnecessary suffering, or particularly cruel methods and means.
> 3. In cases for which no provision is made in the present Protocol, the principle of humanity and the dictates of the public conscience shall continue to safeguard populations and combatants pending the adoption of fuller regulations.

Draft Article 30 did not advance the law in any meaningful way because in essence, it was a simply a reaffirmation of the Hague Regulations (Articles 22 and 23(e)) and the Martens Clause, both from 1899.[65] Unsurprisingly then, it was insufficient to address the concerns of those states that wished to achieve more specific and rigorous regulations of weapons use.[66] Egypt, Finland, Mexico, Norway, Sweden, Switzerland and Yugoslavia proposed that in addition to setting out general rules on prohibiting indiscriminate attacks, there should also be explicit prohibitions on incendiary weapons containing napalm or phosphorus; delayed-action weapons (including anti-personnel landmines); and fragmentation weapons.[67] The proposal was endorsed by a further seven states – Algeria, Austria, Kuwait, Libya, Mali, Saudi Arabia and Syria.[68]

The proposal did not succeed, reflecting in part at least, the relative lack of resources and expertise by those prohibitionist states.[69] The working structure of the session also conspired against the prohibitionist

[64] For an explanation about this scant attention, see ICRC, *Conference of Government Experts 1972,* above n. 61, para. 3.14.

[65] Kalshoven, 'Conference of Government Experts 1972 (Second Session)', above n. 61, p. 67.

[66] ICRC, *Conference of Government Experts 1972,* above n. 61, paras 3.8–3.10.

[67] Proposal Submitted by the Experts of Egypt, Finland, Mexico, Norway, Sweden, Switzerland and Yugoslavia, Draft Article 30 (CE/COM III/C33) reproduced in ICRC, *Conference of Government Experts 1972,* Vol. 2, above n. 61, p. 57.

[68] Ibid.

[69] Helen M. Kinsella, 'Superfluous Injury and Unnecessary Suffering: National Liberation and the Laws of War' (2017) *International Origins of Social and Political Theory* 205, especially pp. 218–19.

states. Throughout the sessions, work had been divided into four Commissions, but none of them had been specifically assigned the weapons question. Ultimately, that task fell to Commission III, the mandate of which was to consider combatants and civilian populations, including journalists. This was less than ideal both in terms of time and expertise available to discuss the weapons issues.[70]

In an attempt not to entirely abandon attempts to include regulation of weapons in the Protocols, at the closing session of 1972 meeting, nineteen states joined in a statement requesting that there be a more comprehensive discussion of express prohibitions on specific categories of weapons.[71]

3 Government Experts on the Use of Certain Conventional Weapons 1973–6

That request led to a further round of meetings – and this time the participants were to focus on weapons issues only, being explicitly directed to study 'the question of conventional weapons that might be deemed to cause unnecessary suffering or have indiscriminate effects'.[72] In all, three expert meetings were convened: in 1973 (Geneva); in 1974 (Lucerne); and in 1976 (Lugano).[73]

The first meeting of experts in 1973 considered in some detail issues arising from a range of conventional weapons: small-calibre projectiles, blast and fragmentation weapons, time-delay weapons, incendiary weapons and more briefly, laser weapons.[74] While it was encouraging that there was now a forum dedicated to discussing weapons issues, overall the report emanating from the meeting prepared by the ICRC was a cautious document. As the ICRC explained, it was only 'documentary

[70] Kalshoven, 'Conference of Government Experts 1972 (Second Session)', above n. 61, p. 61.

[71] Proposal Submitted by the Experts of Argentina, Austria, Brazil, Denmark, Egypt, Finland, the Federal Republic of Germany, Iraq, Kuweit (sic), Lebanon, Lybia (sic), Mexico, the Netherlands, Norway, Spain, Sweden, Switzerland, Syria and Yugoslavia, CE/SPF/2, reproduced in ICRC, *Conference of Government Experts 1972*, Vol. 2, above n. 61, pp. 115, 203.

[72] Resolution XIV, *Prohibition or Restriction of Use of Certain Weapons* (XXIInd International Conference of the Red Cross, Teheran 1973).

[73] ICRC, Report of the Work of the Experts, *Weapons that May Cause Unnecessary Suffering or Have Indiscriminate Effects* (1973); ICRC, *Conference of Government Experts on the Use of Certain Conventional Weapons (Lucerne, 24 Sept.–18 Oct. 1974)* (1975); ICRC, *Conference of Government Experts on the Use of Certain Conventional Weapons (Second Session – Lugano, 28.1–26.2.1976)* (1976).

[74] ICRC, Report of the Work of the Experts (1973), above n. 73. For discussion, see SIPRI, *Incendiary Weapons*, above n. 11, p. 71.

in character' in that it simply set out information on the effects of the various weapons, but it did not advance any concrete proposals as to how (or even whether) those weapons should be regulated.[75]

The report was considered and discussed at the Lucerne and Lugano expert meetings in 1974 and 1976 respectively.[76] However, both meetings were marked by deep disagreement among the experts as to the nature and impact of particular categories of weapons, as well as the appropriate balance between what was necessary for effective military campaigns compared to the risks to civilians from indiscriminate use of particular weapons. The split fell into two camps: the 'Swedish group'[77] on the one hand (calling for generic bans on the weapons) with the 'Western group'[78] and Warsaw Pact states on the other (insisting on retaining their right to use all weapons, subject only to the general principles of the law of armed conflict).

While it is difficult to decipher the diplomatic language of the official reports of the meetings, the level of disagreement and indeed, animosity, between states is much more apparent from the records of a panel discussion which took place in Washington in 1973 as part of the Annual Meeting of the American Society of International Law.[79] The panel entitled 'Human Rights in Armed Conflict' was actually devoted to the question of the regulation of weapons. The speakers were George Aldrich, the Deputy Legal Adviser of the United States Department of State; Dr Hans Blix, Legal Adviser of the Swedish Ministry of Foreign Affairs; and Frits Kalshoven, Adviser to the Dutch Government and Rapporteur of the Expert Conferences. Aldrich was prepared to concede that the law of war had not kept up with weapons technology, but was nonetheless adamant that it was 'completely unrealistic' to think about changes in weapons law.[80] Dr Blix, at the other end of the spectrum, was critical even of the ICRC, which he claimed had adopted such a 'quiet diplomacy' that world opinion could not be properly informed.[81]

[75] ICRC, *Weapons that May Cause Unnecessary Suffering or Have Indiscriminate Effects*, above n. 73, para. 11.

[76] ICRC, *Conference of Government Experts* (Lucerne, 1974) and ICRC, *Conference of Government Experts* (Lugano, 1976), above n. 73.

[77] Egypt, Mexico, Norway, Sudan, Sweden, Switzerland and Yugoslavia.

[78] Australia, Belgium, Canada, Denmark, Federal Republic of Germany, France, Ireland, Italy, Japan, the Philippines and the United States.

[79] 'Human Rights and Armed Conflict: Conflicting Views' (1973) 67 *American Society of International Law Proceedings* 141.

[80] Ibid., p. 148.

[81] But see Mathews, 'The 1980 Convention on Certain Conventional Weapons', above n. 2, on the cautious approach of the ICRC: p. 994.

In any event, the series of expert meetings came to an end without any agreement on weapons restrictions and without even agreement on a way forward. Nonetheless, in my view, these three expert sessions are an important part of the history of humanitarian disarmament campaigns despite the inability to take the issues any further at that point. First, they serve as examples of the abolitionist states attempting to advance disarmament and doing so in large part on the basis of a concern for the human suffering caused by those weapons. Second, while there was no real advance in the law at this point, the work of the experts in these three meetings started to lay the foundation for the negotiations for what would, in time, become the Convention on Certain Conventional Weapons 1980.

4 The Diplomatic Conference for the 1977 Protocols

Despite the specific disagreements between states on how (or indeed, whether) weapons should be further regulated, it had been clear from the earlier meetings in 1971 and 1972 that states were agreed that it was time for an overall revision of the law of armed conflict. That process evolved into full diplomatic negotiations, which took place from 1974–7. Those negotiations provided the next avenue for the prohibitionist states (broadly speaking, the neutral European states and developing states) to advance their cause and they did so by attempting to introduce discussions about restrictions on the use of particular weapons into the overall discussions about the law of armed conflict.

Once again, however, those attempts met with only limited success. For example, Austria, Egypt, Mexico, Norway, Sweden, Switzerland and Yugoslavia issued a working paper calling for a ban on certain weapons, listing in particular: incendiary weapons; anti-personnel fragmentation weapons; flechettes; especially injurious small calibre weapons; and anti-personnel landmines.[82] However, all such ban proposals were rebuffed by the major military states (the USA, many NATO states, the USSR and other Warsaw Pact states).[83]

Some limited success was achieved in strengthening the original draft Article 30 which had been introduced by the ICRC in 1972. That text eventually evolved into Article 35 of the finally agreed text of Additional Protocol I, which provided:

[82] *Official Records of the Diplomatic Conference on the Reaffirmation and Development of International Humanitarian Law Applicable in Armed Conflicts, Geneva (1974–1977)* vol XVI, Working Paper CDDH/IV/201 (7 February 1975) 556.

[83] Mathews, 'The 1980 Convention on Certain Conventional Weapons', above n. 2, p. 994.

1. In any armed conflict, the right of the Parties to the conflict to choose methods or means of warfare is not unlimited.
2. It is prohibited to employ weapons, projectiles and material and methods of warfare of a nature to cause superfluous injury or unnecessary suffering.
3. It is prohibited to employ methods or means of warfare which are intended, or may be expected, to cause widespread, long-term and severe damage to the natural environment.[84]

In addition, there were new and much more detailed provisions on targeting and indiscriminate warfare, including a rearticulation of the 'basic rule' on distinction.[85] A further advance was the inclusion of Article 36 requiring states to undertake a review of new and modified weapons systems to ensure that all new proposed development and/or acquisition of weapons would comply with existing international legal obligations.[86]

The outcome fell far short of the original ambitions of the abolitionist states. And even these general provisions were further weakened by reservations and declarations of understanding made by the major military powers, all of which made it clear, for example, that they did not accept that these general principles applied to nuclear weapons, a position they had adopted from the start of the negotiations.[87]

However, the flame was kept alive with Resolution 22, adopted in closing the Conference, which recommended that a Conference of Governments should convene 'with a view to reaching: (a) agreements on prohibitions or restrictions on the use of specific conventional weapons'.[88] It was a small victory for the humanitarian disarmament

[84] Protocol Additional to the Geneva Conventions of 12 August 1949, and Relating to the Protection of Victims of International Armed Conflicts (Protocol I), opened for signature 8 June 1977, 1125 UNTS 3 (entered into force 7 December 1978 ('Additional Protocol I') art. 35.

[85] Additional Protocol 1 arts 51–7.

[86] See generally Natalia Jevglevskaja, *States Weapons Review Obligations under Article 36 of the 1977 Additional Protocol I to the Geneva Conventions and Beyond* (PhD, University of Melbourne, 2018).

[87] *Official Records of the Diplomatic Conference*, above n. 82, vol. VIII, France (p. 193), USA (p. 295) and UK (p. 303). See for example, statements made on ratification by the United Kingdom to the effect that the 'rules introduced by the Protocol apply exclusively to conventional weapons ... [and] do not have any effect on and do not regulate or prohibit the use of nuclear weapons', reproduced in Adam Roberts and Richard Guelff (eds.), *Documents on the Laws of War*, 3rd ed. (Oxford; New York: Oxford University Press, 2003), p. 510.

[88] *Official Records of the Diplomatic Conference*, above n. 82, vol I, Resolution 22 (IV) Follow up Regarding Prohibition or Restriction of Use of Certain Conventional Weapons 215.

discourse when measured against the original ambitions of the prohibitionist states.

On one view, this first campaign against specific weapons arising from their widespread use in the Vietnam War in the form of strengthening the law of armed conflict was a failure: no outright prohibition of any weapon was achieved and only a very modest advance of the generally stated rules on means and methods of warfare was achieved. However, the work across the decade of the 1970s, particularly when considered alongside the 'human rights in armed conflict' initiative discussed in the next part of the chapter, meant that a humanitarian discourse did survive in the context of weapons, even if very little gain was made in terms of development of the positive law. A particularly important development was the 're-merging' of the so-called Hague and Geneva strands of the law.[89] Weapons law, for so long excluded entirely from the ambit of international humanitarian law, had made some kind of re-entrance. And the stage had been set for what would become the Convention on Certain Conventional Weapons 1980.

But before we turn to discuss the negotiations for that particular treaty, we need to return to what I argue is the second humanitarian disarmament campaign of this era.

B The Second Campaign: the 'Human Rights in Armed Conflict' Initiative

The second humanitarian disarmament campaign of this period had its seeds in the World Conference on Human Rights convened in 1968 to commemorate the twentieth anniversary of the adoption of the Universal Declaration of Human Rights.[90] The Conference adopted Resolution XXIII on Human Rights in Armed Conflicts, which requested the Secretary-General of the United Nations to study:

> (a) [the] steps which could be taken to secure the better application of existing humanitarian international conventions and rules in all armed conflicts;
>
> (b) the need for additional humanitarian international conventions or of possible revision of existing conventions to ensure the better

[89] The expression is from Richard John Erickson, 'Protocol I: A Merging of the Hague and Geneva Law of Armed Conflict' (1978–9) 19(3) *Virginia Journal of International Law* 557.

[90] See generally, Ronald Burke, 'From Individual Rights to National Development: The First UN International Conference on Human Rights, Tehran, 1968' (2008) 19(3) *Journal of World History* 275.

> protection of civilians, prisoners and combatants in all armed conflict, and the prohibition and elimination of the use of certain methods and means of warfare.[91]

It was the final clause of paragraph (b) of the Resolution, addressing the prohibition and elimination of the use of certain methods and means of warfare, which in my view allows the project to be characterised as a humanitarian disarmament campaign. However, as we will see, the actual content of the resulting studies of weapons or means and methods of war was sparse. That being said, overall, the exercise did mean that the question of weapons remained on the agenda of the General Assembly under the rubric of human rights. More concretely, as I will explain, the exercise led to a specific report on napalm and its effects, which in turn fed back into the ICRC-hosted discussions on the question of indiscriminate weapons.

1 Background to Resolution XXIII

Convened in Tehran, the Conference was contentious from the start, serving as a flashpoint for the increasing divisions between the newly decolonised states and the 'old' colonial empires.[92] In particular, the newly decolonised states were focused on their opposition to apartheid and to colonisation and these issues dominated the Conference. There were forceful challenges to the Western conceptions of civil and political individualistic human rights, with many of the newer states arguing for a focus on development instead of human rights, and for a conception of collective rights.[93]

These broader concerns and divisions were reflected in discussions about the law of armed conflict. A key concern for many of the newly-independent states, and lying behind the terms of Resolution XXIII, was that the law of armed conflict ought to be more comprehensively applicable to wars of national liberation, and indeed to non-international armed conflict generally: the aim here was to complement and reinforce the discussions starting to take place in the context of the preparatory work for the revision of the Geneva Conventions 1949.[94]

91 World Conference on Human Rights, 'Res XXIII on Human Rights in Armed Conflict', UN Doc. A/CONF/32/41 (12 May 1968) 18. See *Respect for Human Rights in Armed Conflicts – Report of the Secretary-General*, UN Doc A/8052 (18 September 1970) para. 1. For discussion of the project generally, see Gerd Oberleitner, *Human Rights in Armed Conflict: Law, Practice, Policy* (Cambridge: Cambridge University Press, 2015), ch. 4.

92 Burke, 'From Individual Rights to National Development', above n. 90, p. 277.

93 Ibid., pp. 294–6.

94 See generally Kinsella, 'Superfluous Injury and Unnecessary Suffering', above n. 69.

More specifically, a major concern of the newly independent states was the ongoing Vietnam War with its extensive use of napalm, anti-personnel landmines and herbicides, as well as escalating civilian casualties. Thus, the 'human rights in arms conflict' initiative, as it came to be known, was seized by many states as another avenue of resistance and insistence that there be some international regulation (if not prohibition) of specific weapons.

2 The Reports of the UN Secretary-General

Resolution XXIII led to a total of five reports on 'human rights in armed conflict' between 1969 and 1973, all prepared by the office of the UN Secretary-General,[95] each of which was considered and endorsed by the General Assembly.[96]

The first report, published in 1969, explored the ways in which the law of armed conflict could be strengthened, ostensibly using the promotion of human rights as the justification. Much of the report dealt with the relationship between human rights and armed conflict in a general way. However, there was an important acknowledgement of the gaps in the law of armed conflict dealing with means and methods of warfare,

[95] *Respect for Human Rights in Armed Conflicts – Report of the Secretary-General*, 24th sess, Agenda Item 61, UN Doc A/7720 (20 November 1969); *Respect for Human Rights in Armed Conflicts – Report of the Secretary-General*, 25th sess, Agenda Item 47, UN Doc A/8052 (18 December 1970); *Respect for Human Rights in Armed Conflicts – Report of the Secretary-General*, 26th sess, Agenda Item 52(a), UN Doc A/8370 (2 September 1971); *Respect for Human Rights in Armed Conflicts – Report of the Secretary-General*, 27th sess, Agenda Item 49(a), UN Doc A/8781 (20 September 1972); *Respect for Human Rights in Armed Conflicts – Report of the Secretary-General*, 28th sess, Agenda Item 96, UN Doc A/9123 (19 September 1973). See the detailed discussion by Warren E. Hewitt, 'Respect for Human Rights in Armed Conflict' (1971) 4 *New York University Journal of International Law and Policy* 43.

[96] *Respect for Human Rights in Armed Conflicts*, GA Res 2852 (XXVI), UN GOAR, 26th sess, 2027th plen mtg, UN Doc A/RES/2852(XXVI) (20 December 1971); *Respect for Human Rights in Armed Conflicts*, GA Res 2853 (XXVI), UN GOAR, 26th sess, 2027th plen mtg, UN Doc A/RES/2853(XXVI) (20 December 1971); *Respect for Human Rights in Armed Conflicts*, GA Res 3032 (XXVII), UN GOAR, 27th sess, 2114th plen mtg, UN Doc A/RES/3032(XXVII) (18 December 1972); *Respect for Human Rights in Armed Conflicts*, GA Res 3102 (XXVIII), UN GOAR, 28th sess, 2197th plen mtg, UN Doc A/RES/3102(XXVIII) (12 December 1973); *Respect for Human Rights in Armed Conflicts*, GA Res 3319 (XXIX), UN GOAR, 29th sess, 2319th plen mtg, UN Doc A/RES/3319(XXIX) (14 December 1977); *Respect for Human Rights in Armed Conflicts*, GA Res 3500 (XXX), UN GOAR, 30th sess, 2441st plen mtg, UN Doc A/RES/3500(XXX) (15 December 1975); *Respect for Human Rights in Armed Conflicts*, GA Res 31/19, UN GOAR, 31st sess, 77th plen mtg, UN Doc A/RES/31/19 (24 November 1976); *Respect for Human Rights in Armed Conflicts*, GA Res 32/44, UN GOAR, 32nd sess, 97th plen mtg, UN Doc A/RES/32/44 (8 December 1977).

pointing out that the earlier treaties were only ever meant to be a first step in prohibiting or limiting methods of warfare.[97]

That being said, there was relatively little in this first report about specific regulation of the methods and means of warfare. The paragraphs that did address means and methods were mostly a litany of all the 'work' of the UN General Assembly, meaning resolutions calling for disarmament or expressing concerns about the use of 'non-directed' (that is, indiscriminate) weapons.[98] Napalm was singled out for attention, with the report suggesting that a separate study on the legality of napalm be undertaken.[99] The report concluded by indicating further areas of study, but in its indicative list, there was no mention of the question of 'means and methods' of warfare.[100] In terms of weapons regulation then, the first report was a very modest beginning, but a beginning nonetheless.

The second report was issued in 1970, and aimed to build on the first report and elaborate the issues raised there.[101] Section VII, entitled 'Prohibition and Limitation of Certain Means and Methods of Warfare', recounted the United Nations resolutions passed since the earlier report relating to weapons, mentioning in particular the work of the twenty-fourth session of the United Nations General Assembly in designating the 1970s the Decade of Disarmament,[102] dealing with chemical and biological weapons,[103] and calling on all states to suspend nuclear testing.[104] The demarcation between the 'means and methods' question in the context of international humanitarian law and the disarmament work of the United Nations, particularly within the Conference on Disarmament, was again acknowledged.[105] The report addressed napalm specifically, but only fleetingly, simply noting that the Secretary-General had consulted experts and that there had been wide agreement that a study should be undertaken on the effects of the use of napalm.[106]

97 *Respect for Human Rights in Armed Conflicts – Report of the Secretary-General* (1969), above n. 95, para. 131. See also discussion at para. 4.

98 Ibid., paras 183, 199.

99 Ibid., paras 196–201.

100 Ibid., para. 230.

101 *Respect for Human Rights in Armed Conflicts – Report of the Secretary-General* (1970), above n. 95.

102 Ibid., para. 123.

103 Ibid.

104 Ibid.

105 Ibid., Part VII.

106 Ibid., paras 125–6, para. 265.

The next three reports also touched on weapons regulation, but only as a small section of each overall report and, in fact, the reports evolved into a reporting exercise on the work of the ICRC expert process which had just begun, rather than engaging in any original substantive work. Thus, in September 1971, the third report was essentially a recap of resolutions of the General Assembly from its previous session, and a report on the Conference of Experts meeting that the ICRC had hosted earlier that year.[107] Similarly, the fourth report, issued in September 1972, was essentially a report on the further work of the ICRC with its Conference of Experts.[108] Once again, weapons were canvassed as were the discussions about the (then) draft Article 30. Once again, the Secretary-General reported on the reticence of the ICRC to deal with the issue of particular weapons. The fifth report, presented in 1973, continued the trend of simply reporting on the work of the ICRC Conference of Experts.[109]

Despite the modest reach of the project as a whole as it relates to weapons, seen in a broader context, the Human Rights in Armed Conflict project was an important development in a number of respects. First, for all their brevity on the question, each report did consider weapons and this became a means of keeping humanitarian disarmament issues alive in the forum of the UN General Assembly which in turn played a part in keeping pressure on the ICRC process discussed above in Section III.A.

A second achievement was the preparation of a specific report on napalm and other incendiary weapons in 1972.[110] The Report – *Napalm and Other Incendiary Weapons and All Aspects of their Possible Use: Report of the Secretary-General* – was prepared by seven governmental experts from Nigeria, Peru, Mexico, Romania, Czechoslovakia, Sweden and the USSR, in conjunction with the ICRC, the WHO and the United Nations.[111] It set out detailed information about different types of incendiary weapons, their military utility, their impact in terms of human suffering, as well as the difficulties involved in providing medical care. It concluded that incendiary weapons are cruel weapons that cause great suffering; that their use was often indiscriminate and it was therefore

107 *Respect for Human Rights in Armed Conflicts – Report of the Secretary-General* (1971), above n. 95.

108 *Respect for Human Rights in Armed Conflicts – Report of the Secretary-General* (1972), above n. 95.

109 *Respect for Human Rights in Armed Conflicts – Report of the Secretary-General* (1973), above n. 95.

110 *Napalm and Other Incendiary Weapons and All Aspects of their Possible Use – Report of the Secretary-General*, A/8803/Rev.1, 22 September 1972.

111 Ibid., p. 2.

necessary to consider a clear cut prohibition against their use.[112] States were invited to respond to the Report and twenty-one states did so.[113] Positions were predictable: those states resisting a prohibition couched opposition in the language of the issue needing further study. Other states were clearly in favour of a ban. Several states raised the question of an appropriate forum for discussion, some expressing a view as to the appropriate forum. While the scope of the Report was such that it could not take the issue any further, it was an important achievement nevertheless, being the first formal multilateral consideration of the impact and consequences of the use of napalm. Again, this work eventually fed into the work of the ICRC on the humanitarian issue and laid much of the groundwork for the 1980 treaty to come.

Third, the project gave voice to the non-aligned states on disarmament issues. At this point in time (and still today), the Conference on Disarmament was far from being representative, even with its increase in 1962 to eighteen members to accommodate eight non-aligned states, and a further increase again to twenty-six members in 1969.[114] As such, it was important to non-aligned states to maintain the discussion in the more representative UN General Assembly, not to mention the need to avoid the consensus decision-making processes of the Conference on Disarmament. As the General Assembly grew in size and the western states lost their majority there, the reports and ensuing discussion provided a space for the non-aligned states to protest the use of indiscriminate weapons, particularly in the context of the ongoing conflict in Vietnam. Naturally, this met with strong and sustained resistance from the military powers on the basis of the now familiar argument that any weapons issues were more properly discussed in the Conference on Disarmament.[115]

Thus, this second humanitarian disarmament campaign can be told as a story of failure – a failed attempt from the Tehran Conference onwards to gain some traction within the UN on the question of the use of indiscriminate weapons in armed conflict including in the ongoing

[112] Ibid., pp. 6, 50–2.

[113] *Napalm and Other Incendiary Weapons and All Aspects of their Possible Use – Report of the Secretary-General*, A/9207, 11 October 1973.

[114] It was also renamed in 1969 from the Eighteen Member Committee on Disarmament to the Conference of the Committee on Disarmament. In 1975, there was a further expansion to thirty-one members.

[115] Séan McBride, 'Human Rights in Armed Conflicts The Inter-Relationship between Humanitarian Laws and the Law of Human Rights' (1970) 9 *Military Law and Law of War Review* 373, 386.

conflict in Vietnam. However, my argument here has been that it was an important part of the humanitarian disarmament discourse of the time and it did contribute, along with the work of the ICRC, to the momentum that would materialise in the form of negotiations for the 1980 Convention.

IV The 1980 Convention on Certain Conventional Weapons: Humanitarian Disarmament Realised (in Part)

Although the prohibitionist states had failed in their attempts to include specific weapons regulations in the Additional Protocols themselves, the Diplomatic Conference did agree to a further process with a view to reaching agreement on 'prohibitions or restrictions on the use of specific conventional weapons which may be deemed to be excessively injurious or have indiscriminate effects, taking into account humanitarian and military considerations'.[116] Thus, the stage was set for what would become the Convention on Certain Conventional Weapons (CCW 1980).[117]

In the immediate lead up to negotiations of that treaty, two preparatory meetings were held: in August 1978 and in March/April 1979. The formal negotiations were then convened in two sessions: the first in September 1979, and the second in September 1980.[118] Ultimately, states adopted the laboriously titled Convention on Prohibitions or Restrictions on the Use of Certain Conventional Weapons Which May be Deemed to be Excessively Injurious or to Have Indiscriminate Effects. It was an umbrella treaty, with three protocols: Non Detectable Fragments (Protocol I); Prohibitions or Restrictions on the Use of Mines, Booby-Traps and Other Devices (Protocol II); and Incendiary Weapons (Protocol III). States parties to the treaty had to adopt at least two of the three Protocols for their instrument of ratification or accession to the Treaty to be effective.[119] The Treaty opened for signature on 10 April 1981 and entered into force on 2 December 1983.

[116] Resolution 22 (IV) Follow up Regarding Prohibition or Restriction of Use of Certain Conventional Weapons, above n. 88.

[117] Convention on Prohibitions or Restrictions on the Use of Certain Conventional Weapons which may be deemed to be Excessively Injurious or to have Indiscriminate Effects (with Protocols I, II and III), opened for signature 10 April 1981, 1342 UNTS 137 (entered into force 2 December 1983).

[118] For discussion about the lead up to the negotiations of the *CCW 1980*, see Paul C. Szasz, 'The Conference on Excessively Injurious or Indiscriminate Weapons' (1980) 74 *American Journal of International Law* 212.

[119] CCW 1980 art. 4.3.

Even at the time, assessments of the treaty were not encouraging. At best, it was considered a modest success. Frits Kalshoven (who had served as Rapporteur for the ICRC expert meetings through the 1970s) concluded that while the overall result was not 'overly impressive' neither was it negligible.[120] Robert Mathews called it a 'useful framework', while noting its narrow scope and limited provisions.[121] Others were concerned about its lack of any oversight mechanisms and its weak review mechanism.[122] A more recent commentator labelled it 'unloved' by humanitarians and disarmament advocates alike.[123] Broadly speaking, the Convention and its Protocols were dismissed as too weak to make a real impact on state practice; too full of loopholes and exceptions to genuinely address the problems they purported to address; and containing only the most rudimentary enforcement provisions.[124]

It is undeniable that on paper the CCW 1980 did not go as far as some of its supporters had hoped. First, it entirely excluded chemical, biological and nuclear weapons. Further, as initially adopted, the treaty extended only to international armed conflict,[125] including armed conflicts caught within article 1(4) of Additional Protocol I.[126] Third, of all of the categories of weapons that the prohibitionist states had attempted to regulate, only three made it into an actual Protocol. As such, there were initially no provisions for fuel-air explosives, anti-personnel fragmentation weapons or flechettes. A fourth limitation of the CCW 1980 was that its Protocols fell far short of being outright prohibitions on the use of those weapons, much less a true 'disarmament' treaty. The only outright prohibition in the treaty was Protocol I, which prohibited use of 'any weapon the

[120] Frits Kalshoven, 'Conventional Weaponry: The Law from St. Petersburg to Lucerne and Beyond' in Michael A. Meyer (ed.), *Armed Conflict and the New Law* (London: British Institute of International and Comparative Law, 2003), pp. 251, 268.

[121] Mathews, 'The 1980 Convention on Certain Conventional Weapons', above n. 2, p. 996.

[122] Ibid. For a contemporary account by an international lawyer, see Malcolm Shaw, 'The United Nations Convention on the Prohibitions or Restrictions on the Use of Certain Conventional Weapons, 1981' (1983) 9(2) *Review of International Studies* 110.

[123] Stephanie Carvin, 'Conventional Thinking?: The 1980 Convention on Certain Conventional Weapons and the Politics of Legal Restraints on Weapons During the Cold War' (2017) 19(1) *Journal of Cold War Studies* 38, 38.

[124] Yvette Politis, 'The Regulation of an Invisible Enemy: The International Community's Response to Land Mine Proliferation' (1999) 22 *Boston College International and Comparative Law Review* 465, 473.

[125] CCW 1980 art. 1 (amended in 2001 to extend to all forms of armed conflict).

[126] CCW 1980 art. 7.

primary effect of which is to injure by fragments which in the human body escape detection by X-rays'.[127]

Perhaps the most serious limitation of the treaty was that the categories of weapons which prohibitionist states had fought so long to curtail – anti-personnel landmines and incendiary weapons – ended up being only modest advances on the existing general principles articulated in API 1977. They each limited the circumstances in which mines or incendiary weapons could be used, but those limits fell far short of outright prohibition and even the limits contained serious loopholes and exceptions. In the case of anti-personnel landmines, for example, the rules in Protocol II to the CCW 1980 split between remotely delivered anti-personnel landmines and other landmines.[128] For remotely delivered mines, there had been a strong push to prohibit them outright but instead they were still permitted against military targets, provided they were accurately recorded and contained a neutralising device.[129] Warning needed to be given in the event that the attack might impact on the civilian population.[130] For manually placed mines, Protocol II stipulated that such mines could be used when conflict was imminent or actually taking place. It imposed an obligation to take precautions such as warning signs.[131] Thus, it fell far short of the protections that the prohibitionist states had argued were necessary.

Restrictions on incendiary weapons were similarly compromised. An earlier working group had recommended that an outright prohibition on the use of incendiary weapons be agreed.[132] Further, it was clear from the first preparatory meeting that the many states were in favour of a comprehensive ban.[133] Still, the resulting Protocol (Protocol III) ended up being a significant compromise.[134] It started by restating the prohibition against making the civilian population the target of an attack.[135] It went on to impose an absolute prohibition against using air-delivered

[127] Protocol on Non-Detectable Fragments (Protocol I).

[128] Protocol on Prohibitions or Restrictions on the Use of Mines, Booby-Traps and Other Devices (Protocol II) arts 4 and 5.

[129] Ibid., art. 5(1).

[130] Ibid., art. 5(2).

[131] Ibid., art. 4.

[132] Howard S. Levie, 'Prohibitions and Restrictions on the Use of Conventional Weapons' (1994) 68 *St John's Law Review* 643, 662.

[133] United Nations, *The United Nations Disarmament Yearbook* (New York: United Nations, 1978), p. 356.

[134] Protocol on Prohibitions or Restrictions on the Use of Incendiary Weapons (Protocol III).

[135] Ibid., art. 2(1).

incendiaries against a military target when that target was located within a civilian population.[136] However, the major compromise relating to incendiary weapons was for those weapons delivered other than by air: in such a situation, it remained permissible to attack a military objective with incendiary weapons even within a concentration of civilians provided that the military objective was 'clearly separated' from the civilians and 'all feasible precautions' were taken to avoid or at least minimise incidental loss of life and injury to civilians.[137] Attacks on forests and plant cover were prohibited (a direct reference to the experience of the Vietnam War), except when they were being used to conceal or camouflage military targets.[138]

Still, for all its weaknesses and underlying compromises, overall the CCW 1980 was an important expression of humanitarian disarmament.[139] For the first time, compromised though they were, treaty restrictions on the use of landmines and incendiary weapons had been agreed. This in itself was a major achievement, particularly in light of the opposition that there was even to the idea that weapons ought to be regulated any further.

A second way in which the treaty was an important expression of humanitarian disarmament was that the weapons regulations that were included were in large part *because of* persistent claims about their humanitarian impact. The work of the negotiators was based in large part on the earlier work of the expert groups that had been convened by the ICRC in the early 1970s. The resulting reports, along with the reports being prepared by the ICRC[140] and SIPRI[141] formed the basis of the push by the prohibitionist states.

Finally, the 1980 treaty was an important humanitarian disarmament achievement because of the way in which it straddled disarmament law and the regulation of armed conflict. As discussed earlier, for much of the 1970s, there had been strong resistance by major military powers to discussing issues of weapons at all under the auspices of the ICRC and many delegations (particularly the military developed nations) argued that questions of means of warfare were more properly discussed only

[136] Ibid., art. 2(2).
[137] Ibid., art. 2(3).
[138] Ibid., art. 2(4).
[139] Mathews, 'The 1980 Convention on Certain Conventional Weapons', above n. 2, p. 996.
[140] ICRC, Report of the Work of the Experts 1973, above n. 73.
[141] SIPRI, *Incendiary Weapons*, above n. 11; Westing, *Ecological Consequences of the Second Indochina War*, above n. 28; Lumsden, *Anti-personnel Weapons*, above n. 42.

in the Conference on Disarmament. Even Aldrich, then the Deputy Legal Adviser at the US Department of State, conceded that the law had not kept up with technological developments in weaponry, but nevertheless continued to insist that it was entirely unrealistic to attempt to introduce weapons provisions into international humanitarian law.[142] The negotiating framework of the CCW 1980 then, being a conference convened by the United Nations and open to all member states, was a middle ground between the law of armed conflict paradigm, which fell more squarely within the mandate of the ICRC, and a security/disarmament paradigm which fell within the scope of the less accessible Conference on Disarmament.[143]

V Conclusion

This chapter has shown how a humanitarian disarmament discourse reemerged at least in part as a response to the brutality of the Vietnam War. That in turn led to two important, but neglected, campaigns: the first an attempt to include weapons prohibitions and restrictions within the revisions of the law of armed conflict and the second, a long-standing struggle led by the states of the NAM to keep disarmament on the agenda at the General Assembly through the 'human rights in armed conflict' initiative. Although neither was entirely successful, in combination they did provide the impetus for the negotiations which ultimately led to the Convention on Certain Conventional Weapons 1980 – a modest enough achievement when compared to the initial ambitions of the prohibitionist states and civil society including many within the scientific community.

In contemporary and subsequent commentary, the modest success has perhaps eclipsed the significance of these campaigns and their place in the overall story of humanitarian disarmament. It has also led to an underappreciation of the humanitarian impulse behind the CCW 1980 and a failure to acknowledge the agency and persistence of its proponents, including members of the NAM, particularly the states of the Third World, whose peoples were overwhelmingly the victims of the weapons the treaty sought to limit.

[142] 'Human Rights and Armed Conflict: Conflicting Views', above n. 79, especially p. 148.

[143] Yves Sandoz, 'A New Step Forward in International Law: Prohibitions or Restrictions on the Use of Certain Conventional Weapons' (1981) 220 *International Review of the Red Cross* 3.

The chapter has shown a direct causal connection between the savagery of the Vietnam War and the conclusion of the CCW 1980. As I will show in the next chapter, that treaty became the foundation stone on which the prohibitionists stood to move forward with their attempts to further strengthen the prohibitions against anti-personnel landmines – and, ultimately to conclude a treaty to ban them.

5

Humanitarian Disarmament Triumphant?

The Anti-Personnel Landmines Convention 1997

I Introduction

Adopted in Ottawa in December 1997, the Convention on the Prohibition of the Use, Stockpiling, Production and Transfer of Anti-Personnel Mines and on their Destruction (APLM Convention) is widely hailed among states and civil society alike as a triumph of humanitarian disarmament.[1] The assessment rests on two core claims. The first is the way in which anti-personnel landmines (APLMs) came to be framed as a 'humanitarian problem' rather than as a security issue.[2] The second is the way in which civil society partnered with 'like-minded' states and enjoyed unprecedented access and influence in the lead-up to the treaty negotiations and in the actual negotiations themselves. Indeed, some have gone so far as to say that the APLM Convention only came about because of civil society, a view that would seem to be widely held given the award of the Nobel Peace Prize in 1997 to the umbrella

[1] The Convention on the Prohibition of the Use, Stockpiling, Production, and Transfer of Anti-Personnel Mines and on their Destruction, opened for signature 3 December 1997, 2056 UNTS 211, entered into force 1 March 1999. For some examples of the triumphant discourse, see Bonnie Docherty, 'Ending Civilian Suffering: The Purpose, Provisions, and Promise of Humanitarian Disarmament Law' (2010) 15 *Austrian Review of International and European Law* 7; Jody Williams and Stephen Goose, 'The International Campaign to Ban Landmines' in Maxwell A. Cameron, Robert J. Lawson and Brian W. Tomlin (eds.), *To Walk Without Fear: The Global Movement to Ban Landmines* (Toronto; New York: Oxford University Press, 1998), ch. 2.

[2] See generally the collection of essays in Cameron, Lawson and Tomlin, *To Walk Without Fear*, above n. 1. These views do not just come from the advocates involved, but also are expressed by more academic commentators: for example, see Richard Price, 'Reversing the Gun Sights: Transnational Civil Society Targets Land Mines' (1998) 52(3) *International Organization*, 613, 627–31 discussing the way in which the APLM Convention was 'grafted' onto the earlier taboos regarding indiscriminate weapons.

civil society campaign, the International Campaign to Ban Landmines.[3]

However, in my view, the treaty's credentials as an exercise in humanitarian disarmament do not (only) lie in the way in which anti-personnel landmines were framed as a humanitarian issue, nor in the way in which civil society was involved in the norm development. Both of those features are undoubtedly present in the story of the treaty's evolution, but as I have aimed to demonstrate in earlier chapters, neither the humanitarian framing of the effects of weapons, nor engagement by civil society were novel dynamics in disarmament, and in fact, in some respects, their presence in this context can be seen as a return to a pre–Second World War sensibility.[4]

Nevertheless, undoubtedly, the APLM Convention, and the so-called 'Ottawa Process' in which the treaty was negotiated, significantly departed from orthodox disarmament diplomacy and practice in important respects. In this chapter, I elaborate the four features of the treaty's evolution and content that, in my view, render it as an important humanitarian disarmament instrument: first, the way the treaty negotiations challenged existing disarmament architecture by stepping away from the United Nations; second, the increasing transparency of disarmament diplomacy as a consequence of civil society access; third, the way in which the treaty was implemented post-entry into force and, in particular, the key role civil society played, and is playing, in that process; and finally, the provisions in the treaty relating to victim assistance. Analysis of these features form the core of this chapter and are discussed in Section IV.

Before turning to that discussion, Sections II and III set the scene. The dynamics at play that provided a space for the APLM Convention to

3 'The Nobel Peace Prize 1997'. *Nobelprize.org.* Nobel Media AB 2014. Web. 21 Jun 2018. www.nobelprize.org/nobel_prizes/peace/laureates/1997/index.html. See for example, the suggestion from Ken Anderson that 'the international campaign to ban landmines began entirely – one hesitates to use so strong a word, but in this case it is applicable – as an effort of international NGOs.': Ken Anderson, 'The Ottawa Convention Banning Landmines, the Role of International Non-governmental Organizations and the Idea of International Civil Society' (2000) 11(1) *European Journal of International Law* 91, 104. Compare: M. Patrick Cottrell, 'Legitimacy and Institutional Replacement: The Convention on Certain Conventional Weapons and the Emergence of the Mine Ban Treaty' (2009) 63(2) *International Organization* 217, 219: 'it is difficult to imagine the emergence of the Ottawa Convention without the CCW'.

4 For an argument that the claim that the campaign represented an unprecedented break with the past 'needs to be tempered', see Don Hubert, *The Landmine Ban: A Case Study in Humanitarian Advocacy* (Providence: Thomas J. Watson Jr Institute for International Studies, 2000), p. 40.

emerge are examined in Section II. Three dynamics stand out. First, the existing treaty law in the form of Protocol II to the CCW 1980 (Protocol II) was proving to be ineffective.[5] As the years went on, it was clear that it was an inadequate response to the humanitarian concerns about APLMs. The second dynamic was that while many of the prohibitionist states which had called for a complete ban in negotiating the CCW 1980 remained consistent in their opposition to any use of APLMs, the line-up of concerned states started to change. In large part, this transition was a move from a Non-Aligned Movement (NAM)-dominated discourse to a broader partnership between the NAM states and some European middle powers. Finally, with the end of the Cold War, the next wave of humanitarianism emerged, forming a fortuitous backdrop for the strengthening campaign against APLMs.

With that broader context as background, Section III traces the lead up to the APLM Convention, explaining first the attempts to amend and strengthen Protocol II, and then the subsequent engagement in the so-called 'Ottawa Process' that culminated in the APLM Convention itself. Following a detailed analysis of the humanitarian credentials of the treaty in Section IV, I set out some broader reflections about whether the APLM Convention might be seen as 'humanitarian disarmament perfected' (Section V). While acknowledging the treaty's significance for the reasons elaborated in Section IV, I suggest some complexities and risks to the treaty regime. First, the close partnership between prohibitionist states and civil society may risk civil society being co-opted by the states parties. Second, there are financial vulnerabilities created by having civil society-led compliance oversight mechanisms.

Section VI concludes that while the APLM Convention is indeed an exemplar of humanitarian disarmament in important respects, it bears deeper and more critical engagement particularly as it has formed the basis for subsequent disarmament campaigns.

II The Backdrop to the APLM Convention

The international relations and security studies literature is replete with theories and discussions of precisely how and why the APLM Convention

[5] Protocol on Prohibitions or Restrictions on the Use of Mines, Booby-Traps and Other Devices (Protocol II) to the Convention on Prohibitions or Restrictions on the Use of Certain Conventional Weapons which may be deemed to be Excessively Injurious or to have Indiscriminate Effects, opened for signature 10 April 1981, 1342 UNTS 137 (entered into force 2 December 1983).

emerged when it did.[6] It is not the aim of this section to engage in that debate: rather, my aim is to identify and discuss what I see as three important dynamics at play in the lead up to the Ottawa Process and the resulting treaty negotiations. In my view, appreciating these dynamics allows the APLM Convention to be seen in a broader context and as a part, rather than the source, of a longer, richer story of humanitarian disarmament.

A *The Failure of Protocol II, CCW 1980*

Compromise though it was, if all states – particularly the militarily significant states – had fully complied with Protocol II, CCW 1980 it may well have gone a long way in addressing the growing APLM problem. However, little changed in the years following the adoption of the Protocol and in fact, the problem was intensifying.[7] In Cambodia, the scale of the destruction from landmine use over three decades was just beginning to be comprehended. With the Soviet invasion of Afghanistan in 1979, that country was to become the third most mined country in the world after Cambodia and Angola.[8] Central America and Africa joined the tragic statistics being drawn into the Cold War proxy wars.[9] In Africa, the scale of landmine use was

[6] An early account from many of the NGOs involved in the campaign is in Cameron, Lawson and Tomlin, *To Walk Without Fear*, above n. 1. A more nuanced account is provided by Andrew A. Latham, 'Theorizing the Landmine Campaign: Ethics, Global Cultural Scripts, and the Laws of War' in Rosalind Irwin (ed.), *Ethics and Security in Canadian Foreign Policy* (Vancouver; Toronto: University of British Columbia Press, 2001), p. 160 who calls for commentary on the treaty to move 'beyond the shibboleths of the pro-ban community towards a deeper understanding of the way in which "ethical" foreign policy discourses can develop out of a haphazard and historically contingent combination of geo-political transformation, global cultural change, national identity politics, and the lobbying efforts of moral entrepreneurs': p. 162; see also the accounts by Hubert, *The Landmine Ban*, above n. 4, ch. 3; Leon Sigal, *Negotiating Minefields: The Landmines Ban in American Politics* (New York: Taylor and Francis, 2006); and a ten year retrospective by Jody Williams, Stephen Goose and Mary Wareham (eds.), *Banning Landmines: Disarmament, Citizen Diplomacy, and Human Security* (Lanham: Rowman and Littlefield, 2008). A very detailed account of the lead-up to the treaty and the text as ultimately agreed is in Stuart Casey-Maslen, *The Convention on the Prohibition of the Use, Stockpiling, Production, and Transfer of Anti-Personnel Mines and on their Destruction* (Oxford: Oxford University Press, 2005).

[7] See Stephanie Carvin, 'Conventional Thinking?: The 1980 Convention on Certain Conventional Weapons and the Politics of Legal Restraints on Weapons During the Cold War' (2017) 19(1) *Journal of Cold War Studies* 38.

[8] Human Rights Watch and Physicians for Human Rights, *Landmines: A Deadly Legacy* (United States of America: Human Rights Watch, 1993) 50.

[9] Jack H. McCall Jr, 'Infernal Machines and Hidden Death: International Law and Limits on the Indiscriminate Use of Land Mine Warfare' (1994–5) 24 *Georgia Journal of*

staggering.[10] By independence, 1.5 million landmines remained in Zimbabwe.[11] All sides to the conflict used landmines in Angola, which became Africa's most mine-infested nation.[12] In Mozambique's nationalist struggle against Portugal, both Portugal and the Liberation Army (Frelimo) used mines as part of the armed struggle.[13] In El Salvador, in the wake of the civil war, it was estimated that there were 20,000 landmines remaining in 425 mine fields, covering 436 square kilometres.[14]

Nor had Protocol II prevented the use of new 'improved' technology, which included 'scatterable mines' (that is, remotely delivered) and plastic mines.[15] As discussed in the previous chapter, there had been attempts to put in place an outright prohibition on the use of remotely delivered mines, but this view had not prevailed.[16] While Protocol II had imposed restrictions on their use,[17] they were permitted when an area was designated a military objective but the broad understanding adopted about what 'a military objective' meant in practical terms rendered Protocol II particularly weak.[18] Further, the increasing use of plastic anti-

International and Comparative Law 229. See also Casey-Maslen, *The Convention on the Prohibition of Anti-Personnel Mines*, above n. 6, p. 17.

10 See generally, Human Rights Watch, *Still Killing: Landmines in Southern Africa* (United States of America: Human Rights Watch, 1997); Arms Project Africa Watch, *Landmines in Mozambique* (United States of America: Human Rights Watch, 1994) and Human Rights Watch, *Landmines in Angola* (United States of America: Human Rights Watch, 1993).

11 International Committee of the Red Cross (ICRC), *Anti-personnel Landmines: Friend or Foe? A Study of the Military Use and Effectiveness of Anti-personnel Mines* (Geneva: ICRC, 1997), p. 30.

12 Ibid. See also the discussion by Alex Vines, 'The Crisis of Anti-Personnel Mines' in Cameron, Lawson and Tomlin, *To Walk Without Fear*, above n. 1, pp. 126–7 explaining how insurgent groups were supplied in contravention of UN sanctions.

13 ICRC, *Anti-personnel Landmines: Friend or Foe?*, above n. 11, p. 34 and Vines, 'The Crisis of Anti-Personnel Mines', above n. 12, p. 127.

14 International Campaign to Ban Landmines (ICBL), *Landmine Monitor 2003* (Geneva: ICBL, 2003).

15 McCall, 'Infernal Machines and Hidden Death', above n. 9, p. 240. See also Burris M. Carnahan, 'The Law of Land Mine Warfare: Protocol II to the United Nations Convention on Certain Conventional Weapons' (1984) 105 *Military Law Review* 73, 79.

16 Carnahan, 'Law of Land Mine Warfare', above n. 15, p. 80 : 'a few delegations wanted to ban their use entirely, purportedly on humanitarian grounds, but also in the belief that such a ban would work to the advantage of the technologically less advanced nations'. See above Chapter 4, Section II.C.

17 Protocol II arts 4 and 5. Essentially, they were required to have a neutralising mechanism, the placement of the mines had to be recorded and civilians were to be given advance warning of an attack 'unless the circumstances did not permit'.

18 A number of states made reservations on ratification as to their understanding of 'military objective'.

personnel landmines meant that emplaced mines were more difficult to detect (making them more dangerous in terms of clearance activities or being able to avoid them), and they were also significantly cheaper to produce and therefore more readily accessible.[19]

Thus, APLM use not only continued to escalate in terms of absolute numbers but, due to their low cost and relative accessibility, by the 1990s they had shifted from being a weapon of the leading militaries in the world – during the Second World War; by the United States in Indochina; and by the Soviet Union in Afghanistan – to being a weapon of the Third World nations.

B The Persistence of Prohibitionist States, Albeit a Changing Line-Up

In the 1960s and 1970s, the states of the NAM had persisted in campaigns against the use of indiscriminate weapons including anti-personnel landmines – efforts that had culminated in the admittedly compromised CCW 1980.[20] However, from the 1980s onwards, a significant expansion occurred in the composition of the prohibitionist states, that is, states that sought an outright ban on the use of APLMs, rather than further restrictions on their use.

First, the political changes in the South, and within the NAM itself, as military dictatorships took hold in many of what had been emerging democracies in the early phase of independence, meant that there was less support in the South for prohibition (or even further restrictions) on APLMs.[21] Second, at the same time, there were rising concerns, particularly in some liberal democracies, about the impact of APLMs due to the persistent work of organisations such as the ICRC and Physicians for Human Rights, and these reports were finally gaining

[19] McCall, 'Infernal Machines and Hidden Death', above n. 9, pp. 240–1. He cites US$6.75 for a Pakistani-made P4, and notes that the cost of other common anti-personnel landmines being as low as US$3.00 per unit.

[20] As discussed in Chapter 4, Section IV.

[21] Dan Plesch, 'The South and Disarmament at the UN' (2016) 37(3) *Third World Quarterly* 1203. There was still strong and steady support from within the NAM. For example, speaking at the United Nations on the signing of the Cambodian peace agreement, Prince Norodom Sihanouk of Cambodia (one of the NAM's founding members) called for a ban on the use of landmines: see, Bryan McDonald, 'The Global Landmines Crisis in the 1990s' in Richard A. Matthew, Bryan McDonald and Kenneth R. Rutherford (eds.), *Landmines and Human Security: International Politics and War's Hidden Legacy* (Albany: State University of New York Press, 2004), pp.21, 24. It is, however, notable that Cambodia at that time was not a state party to the CCW 1980, only acceding to that treaty in 1997.

some traction.[22] These changes meant that the campaign against APLMs that reemerged in the 1990s expanded to include more so-called middle powers.[23]

Not only was the line-up of states changing but by the early 1990s, there was a discernible shift in states' positions in that increasing numbers of states were moving away from being prepared to compromise and continue discussing stronger restrictions on use, to making ever more serious calls for an outright ban on APLMs.[24] In 1995, Belgium became the first state to legislate an outright ban on APLMs.[25] In 1996, the ICRC reported that thirty-five states supported an immediate global ban, sixteen had renounced their use by their own armed forces, four had suspended use and at least five states were destroying their stockpiles.[26]

The non-governmental community was also becoming more vocal in its insistence that there should be a complete ban. In 1992, the founding members of what would become the International Campaign to Ban Landmines (ICBL) issued a 'Joint Call to Ban Anti-Personnel Landmines'.[27] In 1993, the President of the ICRC called for a total ban, effectively reversing the ICRC position in the previous decades that it was more realistic to work on restrictions on use rather than an outright ban.[28] In 1994, the Secretary-General of the United Nations reported that the best and most effective way to deal with the APLMs crisis would be a complete ban.[29]

[22] See the discussion by Stuart Maslen, *Anti-Personnel Mines Under Humanitarian Law: A View from the Vanishing Point* (New York: Intersentia–Transnational Publishers, 2001), pp. 14–15. In 1991, Sweden proposed in the UN General Assembly that the CCW 1980 should be strengthened: United Nations, *United Nations Disarmament Yearbook* (New York: United Nations, 1991), pp. 360–2.

[23] On middle powers, see: Ronald M. Behringer, 'Middle Power Leadership on the Human Security Agenda' (2005) 40(3) *Cooperation and Conflict: Journal of the Nordic International Studies Association* 305.

[24] Lou Maresca and Stuart Maslen (eds.), *The Banning of Anti-Personnel Landmines: The Legal Contribution of the International Committee of the Red Cross 1955–1999* (Cambridge: Cambridge University Press, 2000), p. 128.

[25] Casey-Maslen, *The Convention on the Prohibition of Anti-Personnel Mines*, above n. 6, p. 23.

[26] Maresca and Maslen, *The Banning of Anti-Personnel Landmines*, above n. 24, p. 449.

[27] Maslen, *Anti-Personnel Mines Under Humanitarian Law*, above n. 22, p. 17.

[28] John Borrie, *Unacceptable Harm: A History of How the Treaty to Ban Cluster Munitions Was Won* (Geneva: United Nations, 2009), p. 28.

[29] *Statement of Boutros Boutros-Ghali, UN Secretary General*, in United States Senate, Subcommittee on Foreign Operations, Committee on Appropriations, *The Global Landmine* Crisis, S Hrg 103–666, (13 May 1994) 94, 97.

C Humanitarianism Re-emerges

All of this activity was taking place against a rapidly shifting humanitarian landscape.[30] With the end of the Cold War, it seemed for a time as though humanitarianism's time had come. Not only was there a rise in concern about 'suffering strangers',[31] epitomised by international reaction to the famine and war in Somalia from 1992, but there was a growing understanding of the need to deal with the root causes of what came to be known as 'complex humanitarian emergencies'.[32] Thus, in a shift from earlier decades during which there had been a decided reluctance and denial of politics in humanitarian action, there was an 'emerging consensus that [the humanitarian community] can and should engage in politics'.[33]

In the context of landmines, this shift in humanitarianism was also evident. First, while attention by civil society had focused primarily on the risk of catastrophic nuclear war during the Cold War,[34] with the easing of a sense of danger of global destruction from the early 1990s, attention shifted to the *actual* destruction caused by APLMs.[35] Second, for many years medical professionals had been dealing with the consequences of injuries from APLMs. Thus, a significant body of technical and medical information had become available. In the same way as with humanitarian crises more generally, now in the context of APLMs, civil society was increasingly providing important technical expertise. Third, this expertise started to pay dividends when the shift was made from providing apolitical medical assistance in the field to adopting a consciously political position in lobbying for legal change.[36] Humanitarian disarmament, too, was embracing politics.

30 See Samuel Moyn, 'Empathy in History, Empathizing with Humanity' (2006) 45 *History and Theory* 397, 402 referring to the different 'waves' of humanitarianism over time; Michael Barnett, *Empire of Humanity: A History of Humanitarianism* (London: Cornell University Press, 2013), p. 167. While arguing that there was a post–Cold War shift in approaches to humanitarianism, Barnett cautions against seeing this shift in absolute terms, explaining that humanitarianism has had a long history of evolution, phases and changes over time.

31 See Chapter 2, Section II.

32 Barnett, *Empire of Humanity*, above n. 30, pp. 162–3.

33 Ibid., p. 195.

34 See Chapter 7, Sections II and III.

35 Price, 'Reversing the Gun Sights', above n. 2, p. 619.

36 Maslen reports that the ICRC field surgeons, 'sick of amputating the limbs of young children and other civilians', asked the Organisation's headquarters to push for legal change: Maslen, *Anti-Personnel Mines Under Humanitarian Law*, above n. 22, p. 15. Handicap International was influential in French politics: Philippe Chabasse, 'The French

III Towards Legal Change: from Restrictions to Prohibition

These then were the dynamics at play: an ever-escalating, very real, landmines crisis; a growing middle power group of states joining the earlier NAM campaigns against indiscriminate weapons; and a renewed humanitarian sensibility that embraced, not sidestepped, politics. The scene was set for legal change, starting within the framework of the CCW 1980.

A The First CCW Review Conference: Too Little, Too Late

Article 8(3) of the CCW 1980 provided that, ten years after its entry into force, any state party could request that a conference be convened to review its scope and operation and to consider any proposals for amendments to the Convention or any of its protocols. Relying on this provision, France presented its request to the Depositary, the Secretary General of the United Nations.[37] The aim was to discuss a strengthening of the treaty, and in particular its Protocol II. A series of preparatory meetings were convened in response to the request, and the Review Conference itself convened over a three-week period September–October 1995, reconvening for a further session in 1996.[38]

The Review Conference resulted in Protocol II being strengthened in a number of respects.[39] A significant improvement was that it was extended to cover non-international armed conflicts.[40] Further, the amended Protocol (Amended Protocol II) banned outright all use of non-detectable anti-personnel mines.[41] Remotely delivered mines were

Campaign' in Cameron, Lawson and Tomlin, *To Walk Without Fear*, above n. 1, pp. 60, 60–6.

[37] *Convention on Prohibitions or Restrictions on the Use of Certain Conventional Weapons Which May be Deemed to be Excessively Injurious or to Have Indiscriminate Effects*, GA Res 48/79, UN GOAR, 48th sess, 81st plen mtg, UN Doc A/RES/48/79 (16 December 1993), paras 5–7; discussed in Maresca and Maslen, *The Banning of Anti-Personnel Landmines*, above n. 24, p. 127. See as well, Philipe Chabasse, 'The French Campaign', above n. 36, p. 62; although note the suggestion that the idea for the Review Conference came from the United States: Sigal, *Negotiating Minefields*, above n. 6, p. 13.

[38] Final Report, *Review Conference of the States Parties to the Convention on Prohibitions or Restrictions on the Use of Certain Conventional Weapons Which May be Deemed to be Excessively Injurious or to Have Indiscriminate Effect* (CCW/CONF.1/16 (Parts I and II), Geneva, 1996).

[39] Amended Protocol on Prohibitions or Restrictions on the Use of Mines, Booby-Traps and Other Devices, opened for signature 31 May 1995, 35 ILM 1206 (entered into force 3 December 1998).

[40] Ibid., art. 1.2.

[41] Ibid., art. 4, and art. 2(a) of the Technical Annex.

required to have self-deactivation features.[42] There were more clearly defined obligations to map and record minefields that had not been not remotely laid. There was improved protection for humanitarian workers and clearer assignment of responsibility for mine clearance.[43]

However, these improvements fell far short of expectations of the still-growing group of prohibitionist states, and were regarded by them as entirely inadequate to properly address the continuing APLM crisis. Two core failures stood out. First, remotely delivered mines were still not banned outright – there was only the added requirement that they had to have a self-destruct mechanism. That was inadequate, the argument went, because of the unreliability of self-destruct mechanisms and because the definition of 'remotely delivered mines' excluded mines delivered from a land-based missile at 500 metres (in other words, mines delivered in this manner were not required to have the self-destruct mechanism).[44] The second failure lay in the way Amended Protocol II addressed long-lived mines (as opposed to those with a self-destruct mechanism). Again, there was no outright ban agreed, only further restrictions: such mines could still be used if manually emplaced in clearly marked fenced areas, but this restriction only applied 'to the extent feasible'.[45]

In any event, by now the tide had turned away from restrictions and a growing number of states, the ICRC and an increasingly effective and vocal group of NGOs were calling for an outright ban on all APLMs.[46] By the end of the 1995 session of the Review Conference, sixteen states had publicly adopted a pro-ban position.[47] By 1996, fifty states favoured an outright ban. Thus, the Review Conference, working in a paradigm of strengthened restrictions, was increasingly perceived as being fundamentally off-key.[48]

[42] Ibid., art. 5.

[43] Ibid., art. 12 and art. 10 respectively.

[44] Ibid., art. 2(2).

[45] Ibid., art. 6(3).

[46] See Casey-Maslen, *The Convention on the Prohibition of Anti-Personnel Mines*, above n. 6, p. 22; Alicia H. Petrarca, 'An Impetus of Human Wreckage?: The 1996 Amended Landmine Protocol' (1996–7) 27 *California Western International Law Journal* 205, 228; Yvette Politis, 'The Regulation of an Invisible Enemy: The International Community's Response to Land Mine Proliferation' (1999) 22 *Boston College International and Comparative Law Review* 465, 478.

[47] Maresca and Maslen, *The Banning of Anti-Personnel Landmines*, above n. 24, p. 352.

[48] Peter Herby, 'Landmine Negotiations Conclude with Modest Results' (May/June 1996) 312 *International Review of the Red Cross* 361, 365. Even the normally cautious ICRC characterised the situation as 'woefully inadequate': ICRC, Press Release, 'ICRC Views

Responding to this changed dynamic, on 3 May 1996, at the closing plenary of the Review Conference, Canada announced that it would convene a meeting of pro-ban states to discuss ways to maintain the international momentum that had been building towards an outright ban on APLMs.

The Ottawa Process had been born.

B The Ottawa Process

It would be difficult to overstate the significance of this move. It was the first time that a state had chosen to pursue a more ambitious agenda in disarmament outside of an existing multilateral process. It deftly sidestepped both the Conference on Disarmament and the CCW Review Conference process and, in doing so, it avoided the constraints of consensus-based decision-making – a feature of both bodies, and a large part of the explanation for the failure to agree on a stronger Amended Protocol.[49]

Responding to Canada's invitation, fifty pro-ban states met in Ottawa from 3–5 October 1996, starting what came to be known as the Ottawa Process.[50] A Final Declaration was adopted at that meeting, a draft of which had been circulated in advance by Canada and which committed states to seeking the 'earliest possible conclusion of a legally-binding agreement to ban … anti-personnel mines'.[51] A Plan of Action was also adopted, and an early draft treaty which had been prepared by Austria was circulated.[52] On the last day of the meeting, without advance

Amended Landmines Protocol as "Woefully Inadequate"', 3 May 1996, reprinted in Maresca and Maslen, *The Banning of Anti-Personnel Landmines*, above n. 24, pp. 448–9.

49 Casey-Maslen, *The Convention on the Prohibition of Anti-Personnel Mines*, above n. 6, pp. 20–1, 23. See also, Kenneth R. Rutherford, *Disarming States: The International Movement to Ban Landmines* (California: Praeger Security International, 2011), pp. 78–82. On consensus: see John Borrie, 'Tackling Disarmament Challenges' in Williams, Goose and Wareham, *Banning Landmines*, above n. 6, pp. 263, 275.

50 Maslen, *Anti-Personnel Mines Under Humanitarian Law*, above n. 22, p. 78, sets out the fifty states (footnote 546) and lists the further twenty-four states that attended as observers.

51 *Declaration of the Ottawa Conference*, Canada, 3–5 October 1996, reproduced in Casey-Maslen, *The Convention on the Prohibition of Anti-Personnel Mines*, above n. 6, Appendix 3, pp. 360, 361.

52 Hubert, *The Landmine Ban*, above n. 4, p. 21. It was this draft that formed the seed of an international draft treaty that would eventually become the APLM Convention. See Thomas Hajnoczi, Thomas Desch and Deborah Chatsis, 'The Ban Treaty' in Cameron, Lawson and Tomlin, *To Walk Without Fear*, above n. 1, p. 292. Maslen suggests that the very first 'draft' (or possible version) of the eventual treaty was drafted by Werner Ehrlich

consultation with other states, and much to their chagrin,[53] Lloyd Axworthy, then the Canadian Foreign Minister, announced stand-alone negotiations for a ban treaty and invited all states to return to Ottawa in fourteen months to sign the resulting treaty.[54]

Despite that potentially destabilising unilateral move, momentum towards a ban treaty continued to gather. The ensuing twelve months saw a series of follow-up meetings. States met again in Vienna in February 1997 to discuss the (now revised) Austrian draft text.[55] In April, there was a meeting on verification in Germany attended by 121 states.[56] In June, 155 states attended a meeting in Brussels – presented as an official follow-up to the original Ottawa meeting. Ninety-seven states signed the 'Brussels Declaration' supporting (in principle) a comprehensive ban on anti-personnel mines and forwarding the Austrian draft to the formal negotiating conference scheduled for September in Oslo.[57]

The Oslo Conference opened on 1 September 1997 and the ensuing treaty was adopted on 18 September, and opened for signature in Ottawa in December – well within Axworthy's self-imposed deadline.[58] It was signed immediately by 121 states, and entered into force on 1 March 1999.

C *The Anti-Personnel Landmines Convention*

Legal change had arrived. Gone was the restrictions-on-use approach – this treaty banned APLMs.[59] However, it went further than simply addressing their use: it also required states parties to destroy stockpiled

of the Austrian Ministry of Foreign Affairs in his hotel room during the Review Conference: Casey-Maslen, *The Convention on the Prohibition of Anti-Personnel Mines*, above n. 6, p. 24. The text of that 'draft' is reproduced in Casey-Maslen, *The Convention on the Prohibition of Anti-Personnel Mines*, above n. 6, Appendix 4, pp. 396–7.

53 Brian Tomlin, 'On a Fast Track to a Ban: The Canadian Policy Process' in Cameron, Lawson and Tomlin, *To Walk Without Fear*, above n. 1, pp. 185, 205–6.

54 See Rutherford, *Disarming States*, above n. 49, pp. 85–8.

55 See Hajnoczi, Desch and Chatsis, 'The Ban Treaty', above n. 52, pp. 293–6 for an account of how the text evolved; and Maslen, *Anti-Personnel Mines Under Humanitarian Law*, above n. 22, pp. 79–83.

56 Casey-Maslen, *The Convention on the Prohibition of Anti-Personnel Mines*, above n. 6, at para. 8.9.

57 *Declaration of the Brussels Conference on Anti-Personnel Landmines (24–27 June 1997)* reproduced in Casey-Maslen, *The Convention on the Prohibition of Anti-Personnel Mines*, above n. 6, pp. 376–80.

58 Casey-Maslen, *The Convention on the Prohibition of Anti-Personnel Mines*, above n. 6, paras 0.85–0.90.

59 APLM Convention art. 1. Of course, Protocol II remained in force for its ratifying states, leaving in place the restrictions-on-use approach.

APLMs and to clear mined areas under their jurisdiction and control.[60] Reflecting the humanitarian concerns motivating the ban movement, there were quite detailed provisions dealing with cooperation and assistance between states parties in order to implement the treaty's provisions.[61] Despite deep differences between states on the point, the treaty provided only for a very light-touch verification process.[62] Finally, states were required to submit initial and annual reports on holdings of APLMs, and information on progress in clearance and destruction. States were required to enact penal legislation in their domestic law, including criminalising the use of APLMs.[63]

It was an extraordinary achievement in what was an extraordinary decade for international law. The treaty is hailed as a triumph of humanitarian disarmament. While acknowledging its significance in the overall story of humanitarian disarmament, I reject the claim that it marks the beginning of 'humanitarian disarmament'. However, instead of debating starting points, I think that the significant question is whether and to what extent the APLM Convention can be viewed as an exemplar for humanitarian disarmament practice.

It is to that question I now turn.

IV The APLM Convention as Humanitarian Exemplar?

The (widespread) view that the APLM Convention ushered in a new era in humanitarian disarmament rests on two core claims. The first is the way in which the issue of APLMs were framed as a humanitarian issue, rather than as a security issue.[64] The second claim is the unprecedented extent of engagement by civil society and the way in which civil society partnered with like-minded states during the actual negotiations of the treaty. However, neither of these claims support the argument that the APLM Convention was something new. The humanitarian framing of a particular weapon or weapons-type was not a new phenomenon. As is evident from earlier chapters, concerns about weapons have consistently been presented as humanitarian issues, framed as concerns about either

[60] APLM Convention arts 1.2, 4 and 5 respectively. Four years were allowed for destruction of stockpiles, with ten years for clearance.

[61] Ibid., art. 6.

[62] Ibid., art. 8.

[63] Ibid., arts 7 and 9 respectively.

[64] For example, see the collection of essays in Cameron, Lawson and Tomlin, *To Walk Without Fear*, above n. 1.

the indiscriminate nature of the weapon in question or the fact that the weapon wounded or killed in an unnecessarily cruel manner. Further, while civil society engagement with APLMs in the 1990s was unprecedented in its scale (and possibly due to the contemporary revolution of internet communications), this level of activity alone is insufficient to support the claim that the APLM Convention was a humanitarian exemplar.

Yet the APLM Convention did usher in a new paradigm of humanitarian disarmament. In this section, I identify four aspects of the treaty that in my view mark it out as a new and important shift in humanitarian disarmament. First, led by Canada and supported by many states, there was an explicit rejection of the existing negotiating paradigms – essentially a 'walk out' from the CCW process to what was termed at the time a 'new multilateralism'.[65] The second important shift was a direct consequence of the extent of the engagement by civil society, exemplified by the way in which there was increased transparency in terms of the positions of states and the progress (or otherwise) of negotiations and discussions. Long obscured in the shadowy corridors of New York and Geneva, and out-of-sight in closed meetings, the noise and clamour of civil society forced disarmament diplomacy into the light. States were expected to, and did, publicly state, explain and defend their positions. The third novel development, and perhaps the most profound, lay in the way in which civil society, and in particular, the International Campaign to Ban Landmines (ICBL) has monitored implementation of the APLM Convention since its entry into force. Finally, its provision on victim assistance marked out new ground and this came about directly as a result of the humanitarian framing of the issue. In other words, the victim assistance provisions are the tangible result of the humanitarian framing.

These four features of the APLM Convention are now discussed more fully.

A *Challenging Existing Negotiating Paradigms*

In announcing that it would host discussions for a ban treaty at the close of the Review Conference, and thus triggering the so-called Ottawa

[65] Michael Dolan and Chris Hunt, 'Negotiating in the Ottawa Process: The New Multilateralism' in Cameron, Lawson and Tomlin, *To Walk Without Fear*, above n. 1, p. 392.

Process, Canada radically, and possibly irreversibly, altered disarmament diplomacy. Since its creation, the Conference on Disarmament (CD) had been the key forum to discuss matters of disarmament, and while the negotiation of the CCW 1980 under the aegis of the United Nations rather than the CD had been contentious, in part, this reflected that treaty's dual nature – addressing the prohibition and/or regulation of the use of weapons, but firmly grounded in international humanitarian law.[66] In shifting away from the CD, the CCW and the UN, Canada had opened up a further possibility: a 'new multilateralism'.[67] Rather like the grand diplomatic conferences of a previous century, the negotiating forum was a multilateral event, but operated on its own terms. With this step, the CD in Geneva was further marginalised,[68] and the UN's claim to be the fallback forum for multilateral weapons-related negotiations came under challenge.[69]

The question of the locus of negotiations was crucial for two reasons. First, in stark contrast to the limited membership of the Conference on Disarmament (by now sixty-one states), participation in the Ottawa Process was on the basis of self-selection: states were welcome to participate in the subsequent meetings if they committed to the ideal behind the Final Declaration at Ottawa, that is, if they committed to working towards the earliest possible conclusion of a legally binding ban on APLMs. Otherwise, states were welcome to attend as observers.[70] Thus, although stepping outside established frameworks, the Ottawa Process was an inclusive multilateral process, in the sense that any state that signed the Pledge could participate, and even then, all other states could observe.

The second significant consequence of the change in forum was the vexed question of decision-making rules. The CD resolutely

[66] See Chapter 4, Sections III and IV.

[67] Dolan and Hunt, 'Negotiating in the Ottawa Process', above n. 65, p. 392.

[68] This was dramatically illustrated by developments with the Comprehensive Nuclear-Test-Ban Treaty, opened for signature 24 September 1996, 35 ILM 1439 (not yet in force) (CTBT). Substantive negotiations had been ongoing in the CD for the treaty since 1993 but with no prospect of adoption due to the consensus rule. Thus, Australia brought the treaty text to the floor of the UN General Assembly which voted to adopt the treaty thus neatly sidestepping the consensus block in Geneva.

[69] Admittedly, many other treaties had been negotiated in non-UN fora covering a variety of issues, including international humanitarian law, the law of the sea and trade law. However, the point here is that the triggering of the Ottawa Process was a conscious and deliberate rejection of the existing architecture as being inadequate to advance the will of the majority of states.

[70] Hubert, *The Landmine Ban*, above n. 4, p. 18.

works on the basis of consensus-based decision-making, including even on the seemingly innocuous detail of what items are placed on the Agenda of the Conference.[71] While the General Assembly itself provides for voting in its decision-making, oftentimes negotiation mandates stipulate for consensus-based decision making. So, for example, the CCW 1980 was adopted by consensus and, despite some debate on the issue, in practice the Review Conference had been conducted on the basis of consensus.[72] Consensus, over time, had led to stagnation whereby agreement could be, and is, derailed by a few hold-out states and it was a large part of the explanation why neither the CD nor the Review Conference mechanism had been able to progress towards more effective and stringent restrictions on APLMs. The shift to Ottawa allowed for a break with the 'tyranny of consensus'.[73] And break it did. The rules of procedure adopted by the participating states for the actual negotiating conference in Oslo provided for decisions on matters of substance to be taken by a two-thirds majority of the representatives present and voting.[74] The stranglehold of consensus had been broken.[75]

As it happens, the treaty was adopted by consensus and, in the years since, there has never been a recorded vote in the Meetings of the Parties. However, the significant point is that the formal rules of procedure are an important vehicle by which the straitjacket of consensus can be broken. That being said, it is important that the option of calling for a vote remains politically possible and realistic. The practice of the implementing body for the Chemical Weapons Convention (CWC), the Organization for the Prohibition of Chemical Weapons, stands as a caution.[76] There, the rules of procedure for the membership body, the Conference of the States Parties and the executive body, the

[71] Conference on Disarmament, *Rules of Procedure of the Conference on Disarmament*, (CD/8/Rev.9, 19 December 2003) rule 18.

[72] Casey-Maslen, *The Convention on the Prohibition of Anti-Personnel Mines*, above n. 6, p. 20.

[73] The expression is from Borrie, 'Tackling Disarmament Challenges', above n. 49, p. 273.

[74] Diplomatic Conference on a Convention on the Prohibition of the Use, Stockpiling, Production and Transfer of Anti-Personnel Mines and on Their Destruction, *Draft Rules of Procedure* (APL/CRP.2, 1 September 1997), rule 35.

[75] See Casey-Maslen, *The Convention on the Prohibition of Anti-Personnel Mines*, above n. 6, p. 42.

[76] Convention on the Prohibition of the Development, Production, Stockpiling and Use of Chemical Weapons and on their Destruction, opened for signature 13 January 1993, 1975 UNTS 45 (entered into force 29 April 1997).

Executive Council, both provide for majority voting in decision making.[77] Despite this, in over twenty years, decisions are rarely taken by voting despite many contentious issues before the various organs.[78]

B *Increasing Transparency of Disarmament Diplomacy*

The second novel feature of the APLM Convention is the extent to which civil society played a part, not only in building political will among states for a ban, but also in attending, reporting and participating in the Ottawa Process up to and including the Oslo treaty negotiations. For example, at the first meeting in Ottawa in October 1996, the ICBL had full participation rights and NGO campaigners were actively involved in drafting the language of the Final Declaration and the Action Plan.[79] NGOs attended every meeting and conference in the overall process: Vienna, Bonn and Brussels. In Oslo, the formal negotiating event, the ICBL had the status of 'official observer', and was thus permitted to attend all sessions and to make oral interventions at any point.[80] In all, there was an unprecedented level of access.[81]

Over several decades, opportunities for formal engagement by civil society focusing on disarmament and security issues within the United Nations framework had been severely limited as a matter of law, and of practice.[82] NGOs had been able to attend Review Conferences of the CCW 1980, but only public meetings, and without the ability to intervene.[83] The CD was even more resistant to civil society.[84] Thus,

[77] Chemical Weapons Convention arts VIII.18 and VIII.29 (although the Conference of States Parties is exhorted to take decisions by consensus 'as far as possible').

[78] For discussion on the encroachment of consensus in the context of the Chemical Weapons Convention, see Walter Krutzsch and Treasa Dunworth, 'Article VIII: The Organization' in Walter Krutzsch, Eric Myjer and Ralf Trapp (eds.), *The Chemical Weapons Convention: A Commentary* (New York: Oxford University Press, 2014), pp. 256, 258–60. A notable exception was the Fourth Special Session of the Conference of the States Parties to the OPCW which convened in June 2018, responding in large part to the use of chemical weapons in Syria. See: Conference of the States Parties, *Addressing the Threat from Chemical Weapons Use* (C-SS-4/DEC.3, 27 June 2018).

[79] Williams and Goose, 'The International Campaign to Ban Landmines', above n. 1, p. 35.

[80] Casey-Maslen, *The Convention on the Prohibition of Anti-Personnel Mines*, above n. 6, p. 39.

[81] Williams and Goose, 'The International Campaign to Ban Landmines', above n. 1, p. 43; Hubert, *The Landmine Ban*, above n. 4, p. 25.

[82] See Chapter 3, Section III.C.

[83] Hubert, *The Landmine Ban*, above n. 4, p. 12.

[84] See Rebecca Johnson, *Experts, Advocates and Partners: Civil Society and the Conference on Disarmament* (Geneva: UNIDIR, 2011).

the Ottawa Process, while not always completely open to civil society, was nonetheless radically open compared to the practice of previous decades.[85]

The level of access afforded NGOs, the resulting scale of attendance by NGOs, along with rapidly changing methods of internet-based communication, meant that there was an unprecedented level and quality of information being made publicly available on the negotiations. A particular innovation was the way in which the accounts by NGOs of conference proceedings were communicated in accessible, jargon-free language to explain the issues and avoid the technical and diplomatic language that can make it difficult for outsiders to follow debates. In this way, transparency was very much enhanced.

In many ways, this shift to a greater openness reflected what was happening more generally in the international system in this first decade of the post–Cold War era. However, in the context of disarmament diplomacy, this was a profound shift. There has been some debate about whether this unprecedented level of access and engagement should be described as a democratisation of disarmament diplomacy.[86] Without taking a position on the democratisation point,[87] in my view the Ottawa Process was a clear break with the past in terms of transparency and greater accountability of states in formulating and acting upon their disarmament-related foreign policy goals.

C *Verification*

The third aspect of the APLM Convention that marks it out as a humanitarian disarmament exemplar lies within its verification provisions. The treaty was heralded as introducing a new 'cooperative' approach to verification, in contrast to the more orthodox 'intrusive'

[85] Keith Krause, 'Transnational Civil Society Activism and International Security Politics: From Landmines to Global Zero' (2014) 5(2) *Global Policy* 229.

[86] Strongly resisting this idea is Kenneth Anderson, 'The Ottawa Convention Banning Landmines, the Role of International Non-governmental Organizations and the Idea of International Civil Society' (2000) 11(1) *European Journal of International Law* 91, 112. Compare the more measured reflections of Maxwell A. Cameron, 'Democratization of Foreign Policy: The Ottawa Process as a Model' in Cameron, Lawson and Tomlin (eds.), *To Walk Without Fear*, above n. 1, p. 424.

[87] But see Treasa Dunworth, 'Accountability of International Organisations: The Potential Role of NGOs in the Work of Disarmament Bodies' (2016) 14(1) *New Zealand Journal of Public and International Law* 47.

processes.[88] However, while its verification provisions are indeed an important feature of the treaty's humanitarian disarmament credentials, this is not because they are 'cooperative'. Indeed, I question the asserted binary distinction between 'cooperative' and 'intrusive' verification and instead agree with those commentators who suggest that the framework as ultimately agreed was essentially a pragmatic compromise.[89] Rather, in my view, the treaty's contribution to humanitarian disarmament in this context was the way in which civil society, notably the ICBL, led the way on post-EIF verification of compliance.

1 Rejecting the Distinction between Cooperative and Intrusive Verification

Two provisions in the APLM Convention address verification and implementation: Article 7 entitled 'Transparency Measures' requires states parties to report to the UN Secretary-General on the measures being taken to implement their obligations including those related to mine destruction and clearance.[90] The Secretary-General in turn circulates these reports to all other states parties.[91] Article 8 then goes on to specify the mechanisms by which states parties can deal with concerns about alleged non-compliance. Following a general exhortation in Article 8(1) for states 'to work together in the spirit of co-operation to facilitate compliance', the remaining subparagraphs (nineteen in all – the article is by far the longest in the treaty) set out a series of steps for dealing with non-compliance concerns. First, states can make a Request for Clarification through the Secretary-General,[92] before moving to the possibility of discussions in the Meeting of the States Parties, or a Special Meeting of the States Parties.[93] From there, a fact-finding mission can be deployed to investigate the concerns, made up of independent experts and appointed by the Secretary-General, after consultation with the requested state.[94]

88 Docherty, 'Ending Civilian Suffering', above n. 1, pp. 30–6; Stephen D. Goose, 'Goodwill Yields Good Results: Cooperative Compliance and the Mine Ban Treaty' in Williams, Goose and Wareham (eds.), *Banning Landmines*, above n. 6, ch. 7, p. 106.

89 For example, Casey-Maslen, *The Convention on the Prohibition of Anti-Personnel Mines*, above n. 6, pp. 214–15. The language of compromise is also used by Hajnoczi, Desch and Chatsis, 'The Ban Treaty', above n. 52, p. 303. Stephen Goose, writing ten years after the negotiations, also refers to this: Goose, 'Goodwill Yields Good Results', above n. 88, p. 107.

90 APLM Convention art. 7(1)(b)–(i).

91 Ibid., art. 7(3).

92 Ibid., art. 8.2.

93 Ibid., art. 8(3) and 8(5).

94 Ibid., arts 8.8–8.18.

A broad range of positions on verification had emerged during the Ottawa Process. At one end of the spectrum lay those states that considered detailed verification provisions to be an essential element of any meaningful treaty.[95] The then recently concluded Chemical Weapons Convention and the Comprehensive Test Ban Treaty were mentioned as possible models, both of which contained extensive detailed verification provisions and both of which created permanent secretariats to conduct those verification activities. At the other end of the spectrum were the states that argued that the key aim of the APLM Convention ought to be to embed a clear strong norm against APLMs, that time did not permit the crafting of a detailed verification regime and that, in any event, the focus should remain on achieving an outright ban.[96] There were concerns that the states arguing for a robust arms-control type of verification system might be using the debate as a pretext to avoid or delay agreement on a ban.[97]

It was clear from early in the process that the issue of whether and if so, how, compliance would be verified was going to be difficult and contentious. The announcement by Canada as the Ottawa meeting came to a close that the aim was to have a treaty ready for signature in less than fourteen months meant that in reality there would be insufficient time to deal in a detailed manner with difficult technical issues of verification and implementation.

At the Bonn meeting in April 1997, convened to discuss verification measures specifically, Canada proposed a 'Cooperative Implementation Commission'.[98] While this proposal did not receive support, it signalled the emergence of what came to be termed 'cooperative compliance'. As ultimately agreed in Oslo, the text did contain elements of a cooperative approach to verification but in fact, it is more correctly seen as a hybrid of sorts – straddling approaches from international humanitarian law as well as elements from arms control and disarmament treaties.[99] The idea of a fact-finding mission, for example, can be seen to have its roots

[95] Casey-Maslen, *The Convention on the Prohibition of Anti-Personnel Mines*, above n. 6, p. 218 lists in this camp: Australia, France, Germany, Italy, the United Kingdom and the United States, noting that Germany took a particularly strong approach on this point: p. 214.

[96] Ibid., listing in this camp: Austria, Belgium, Canada, Ireland, Mexico, Norway, Netherlands, South Africa and Switzerland.

[97] Ibid., p. 217.

[98] Ibid.

[99] Those final talks were led by Germany and Mexico, representing each end of the spectrum, under the chairmanship of Canada. See ibid., p. 222.

in the International Fact Finding Committee created by the Additional Protocol I to the Geneva Conventions (Additional Protocol I),[100] while the reporting requirements in Article 7 and the Request for Clarification procedure in Article 8 are reminiscent of the dispute resolution provisions of the Chemical Weapons Convention.[101]

The Chemical Weapons Convention, said to exemplify the disarmament-intrusive-model, does contain an intrusive verification system, including the possibility of short-notice challenge inspections.[102] However, a careful reading of that treaty as a whole reveals that all efforts are made to encourage compliance and facilitate clarifications through cooperative measures. Bearing that out, the challenge inspection procedures have never been used in over twenty years of operation. Further, it is not evident that the dominant paradigm in international humanitarian law is cooperative compliance. In fact, for several decades now, we have witnessed a shift to criminal accountability for serious breaches (through the grave breaches regime of the Geneva Conventions 1949 and Additional Protocol I) and then through the Rome Statute for the International Criminal Court.[103] With the emphasis on individual criminal accountability, there is no trace of 'cooperative compliance'.

Thus, there is not such a stark distinction between cooperative and intrusive approaches to verification and the way in which the APLM Convention straddles both spheres was clearly the result of pragmatic diplomatic compromise – the need to get the job done within a very limited timeframe – rather than any coherent aim to devise a new model of cooperative compliance.[104] That compromise, combined with unprecedented access and engagement by civil society in the implementation phase, and an absence of a permanent secretariat responsible for implementation, created the conditions for this novel, and to a great extent, effective and transparent verification system to emerge. This, in my view, is what marks the treaty out as a humanitarian exemplar.

[100] Protocol Additional to the Geneva Conventions of 12 August 1949, and Relating to the Protection of Victims of International Armed Conflicts (Protocol I), opened for signature 8 June 1977, 1125 UNTS 3 (entered into force 7 December 1978) art 90.

[101] Chemical Weapons Convention arts III, IV (declarations) and IX (dispute resolution).

[102] Chemical Weapons Convention art. IX.

[103] Rome Statute of the International Criminal Court, opened for signature 17 July 1998, 2187 UNTS 90 (entered into force 1 July 2002).

[104] Casey-Maslen, *The Convention on the Prohibition of Anti-Personnel Mines*, above n. 6, pp. 214–15; Hajnoczi, Desch and Chatsis, 'The Treaty Ban', above n. 52, p. 303; and Goose, 'Goodwill Yields Good Results', above n. 88, p. 107.

2 Post-EIF Implementation and Verification as Humanitarian Exemplar

Because of an initial lack of a permanent secretariat, states were to submit their Article 7 reports to the Depositary – the Secretary-General of the United Nations, and in turn, those reports would be circulated to all states parties. But other than circulation of the reports, and providing support for the meetings of the states parties, there was no institutional support for monitoring compliance, such as had been built into the chemical weapons disarmament regime.[105] This lack of a dedicated institutional structure opened up a space for civil society to engage with implementation.

In the campaign leading up to the treaty, several civil society organisations reported in detail, over a long period of time, on the existence and continuing use of APLMs and on their consequences, and this information had formed a solid, factual basis for the humanitarian campaigns.[106] Thus, there was a long track record within civil society in information gathering and dissemination. However, it was a major shift to move from victim-oriented reporting in order to support the political campaign for a ban treaty, to data gathering and analysis of mine clearance, destruction and in some cases, use, for the purposes of monitoring compliance with the treaty. Nevertheless, despite some apprehension, the ICBL decided to move forward into this implementation and monitoring phase of the treaty. And so, the *Landmine Monitor* – an annual report on progress with treaty ratification and implementation prepared by the ICBL – was born.[107]

The first report, running to over 1000 pages, was prepared for the first Meeting of the States Parties in Maputo in 1999. Stephen Goose, a member of the core editorial team, recalls the reaction as the report was distributed to delegations:

> It stunned people. I don't think they had any notion that we were going to be able to pull together something that had so much information. The length itself shocked everybody and there was no 'filler' in it; it was very

105 Later an Implementation Support Unit would be created.

106 See for example the sources listed above at n. 10 and n. 11.

107 A detailed discussion can be found in Mary Wareham, 'Evidence-Based Advocacy: Civil Society Monitoring of the Mine Ban Treaty' in Williams, Goose and Wareham, *Banning Landmines*, above n. 6, pp. 49–67. For a theoretical discussion of the role of NGO monitoring and international cooperation in a number of different areas, see Christopher L. Pallas and Johannes Urpelainen, 'NGO Monitoring and the Legitimacy of International Cooperation: A Strategic Analysis' (2012) 7(1) *The Review of International Organizations* 1 and Oliver Meier and Clare Tanner, 'Non-governmental Monitoring of International Agreements' in *Verification Yearbook* (London: VERTIC, 2001), p. 207.

> dense and filled with facts. People began to realize right away too that it wasn't a 'polemic'. It was in fact a very factually based approach to gathering information, a baseline for information from which to gauge progress.[108]

The *Monitor* has been published each year since 1999, is circulated to states parties, and is also publicly available on the ICBL's website.[109] It does not purport to be a formal verification report.[110] Rather, is it an attempt to hold governments accountable for their compliance (or otherwise) with the APLM Convention and it does so by means of publicly available information, including the reports which states themselves provide under Article 7. Without access to that information, the *Monitor* could never have functioned effectively.

It was by no means obvious during the negotiations that the Article 7 reports would be available beyond the states parties. Confidentiality and secrecy had been the hallmarks of earlier arms control treaties. For example, in the Chemical Weapons Convention, state party declarations remain confidential unless the reporting state choses to waive confidentiality.[111] On entry into force, nine states parties to the treaty declared holdings of chemical weapons, and while eight of these were listed in publicly available documents, the final one could not be due to a refusal on the part of that particular state to waive confidentiality.[112] Confidentiality was an important feature of the Chemical Weapons Convention due to the fact that while the treaty permitted the possession, use and transfer of chemicals for peaceful purposes, it still caught those activities within its verification system. To ensure chemical industry support, confidentiality of that information was critical. But that confidentiality ethos also permeated the chemical weapons sphere. Even within the international humanitarian law community, confidentiality or at least discretion, was often considered the most appropriate way in which to encourage states to comply with their obligations. Thus, transparency and openness were unsettling and novel approaches. Interestingly, the suggestion by the ICBL in its early draft treaty that

108 Wareham, 'Evidence Based Advocacy', above n. 107, p. 52 citing to an interview with Stephen Goose. Wareham herself was a member of the team.

109 See www.the-monitor.org/en-gb/home.aspx.

110 See the introduction to any of the issues of the *Landmine Monitor Report*.

111 Chemical Weapons Convention, Annex on the Protection of Confidential Information, para. 2(c)(ii).

112 This state is widely reported as being the Republic of Korea. See for example, the fact sheets by Arms Control Association: www.armscontrol.org/factsheets/cbwprolif.

reports by all states would be made public had failed to get any traction in the negotiations.[113]

Despite these unpromising signs in the negotiations, at the first Meeting of the States Parties, it was agreed that the Article 7 reports should be made public.[114] This decision was explained on the basis that the reports would be of direct relevance to supporting mine clearance:

> Easy access to Article 7 reports would improve the information flow and hence the coordination and effectiveness of global mine-clearance. Indeed, it would run counter to the humanitarian purpose of the Convention to prevent non-States and NGOs from having access to what will be current and accurate information which could be used for mine action purposes. . . . Further, as States Parties will have already given up the option of using anti-personnel mines, questions of national security and confidentiality of information for these purposes become largely irrelevant.[115]

The significance of this step cannot be overstated. It broke with all previous arms control practice, and even marked a shift from the practice within international humanitarian law. In my view, the shift was not only significant in and of itself in terms of permitting civil society to have access to the information, but it also marked a profound change in philosophy from military-secrecy to more transparent engagement more broadly, raising expectations of transparency and openness in future regimes.

D Victim Assistance[116]

The fourth way in which the APLM Convention is an exemplar of humanitarian disarmament lies in its two provisions on victim assistance.

[113] Proposed Draft Convention by the ICBL (20 December 1996) art. 7(2), reproduced in Casey-Maslen, *The Convention on the Prohibition of Anti-Personnel Mines*, above n. 6, p. 398.

[114] First Meeting of the States Parties to the APLM Convention, *Final Report* (APLC/MSP.1/1999/1, 20 May 1999), Annex III ('Circulation of Article 7 Reports').

[115] Ibid., p. 24.

[116] The term is contentious, and over time it has evolved into 'survivor assistance' so as to imbue those affected directly by APLMs with agency, rather than being 'passive victims'. I have used the term 'victim assistance' here as it was the expression used at the time. On victim assistance in the treaty generally, see Robert Eaton, 'An Indispensable Tool: The Mine Ban Treaty and Mine Action' in Williams, Goose and Wareham, *Banning Landmines*, above n. 6, ch. 8; Sheree Bailey and Tun Channareth, 'Beyond the Rhetoric: The Mine Ban Treaty and Victim Assistance' in Williams, Goose and Wareham, *Banning Landmines*, above n. 6, ch. 9.

In the preamble, states parties declare that they wish 'to do their utmost in providing assistance for the care and rehabilitation, including the social and economic reintegration of mine victims'. Article 6(3), the substantive provision, then exhorts State Parties 'in a position to do so' to 'provide assistance for the care and rehabilitation, and social and economic reintegration, of mine victims and for mine awareness programs'.

This was the first time that a disarmament treaty had ever addressed victims so directly. Thus these provisions, modest though they are, represent a radical departure from previous treaty practice and manifest an important development in humanitarian disarmament. But, in my view, it is not simply their presence in the treaty, but the story behind their inclusion as well as their implementation, that marks the treaty out as a humanitarian disarmament exemplar.

1 The Inclusion of the Victim Assistance Provisions

The inclusion of the provisions in the treaty was surprisingly circuitous, given that concern about the suffering of mine victims had been a core platform of pro-ban states. That being said, it was hardly surprising that states were slow on the uptake – it is one thing to espouse humanitarian ideals, quite another to agree to treaty language that might lead to actual rights to survivors of mine warfare.

The reticence among states is illustrated by the silence on the issue in the various drafts as the treaty text evolved. The First Austrian Draft, circulated in November 1996 following the Ottawa meeting, contained no reference to victim assistance.[117] The Second Austrian Draft contained some important assistance provisions but, reflecting the discussions in Vienna, these all addressed assistance in the context of mine clearance and mine destruction – not assistance to actual human victims.[118] A third Austrian draft circulated in May 1997 made no further change.[119]

With the exception of the Landmine Survivors Network (LSN), even civil society was slow to take up the question of victim assistance.[120] In its

[117] Casey-Maslen, *The Convention on the Prohibition of Anti-Personnel Mines*, above n. 6, p. 28. The Draft is reproduced in his Appendix 4, p. 407.

[118] Ibid., pp. 32 and 106. Draft Article 7 is reproduced at p. 177.

[119] Ibid., pp. 34 and 177. The Draft is reproduced in Appendix 4, p. 416.

[120] Jerry White of Landmine Survivors Network (LSN) challenged states at the Ottawa meeting to move beyond rhetorical support for victims and to reframe the discussion from charity to empowerment by considering victim assistance. An extract of his speech is at Gerry White and Ken Rutherford, 'The Role of the Landmine Survivors Network' in Cameron, Lawson and Tomlin (eds.), *To Walk Without Fear*, above n. 1, pp. 106–7.

draft treaty circulated in late 1996 after the Ottawa meeting, the ICBL had included assistance for mine clearance, but made no mention of victim assistance.[121] Leon Sigal's account from interviews with Stephen Goose of ICBL and Jerry White of LSN reveals that the ICBL took the view that a focus on victim assistance might act as a disincentive to some states concerned about how much assistance would cost.[122] There were also concerns that the USA and other ban-opponent states would argue that what was really needed was support for victims, not a ban, and so a focus on assistance might threaten the ban movement.[123] Whatever the reasons, while LSN worked on the issue from the start, the ICBL was slow to champion victim assistance provisions.[124]

Ultimately, the push for inclusion emerged from Africa. In February 1997, the Mozambican Campaign Against Landmines hosted a Conference in Maputo, Mozambique.[125] The Conference, in its Final Declaration, stressing the need for victim assistance, called on 'all governments' to 'increase greatly resources for victim assistance for all mine-contaminated countries' and for those 'who have produced and supplied mines to accept their responsibility and to assist with clearance and victim assistance programs'.[126] In May 1997, the First Continental Conference of African Experts on Landmines was convened in South Africa and attended by more than forty African states.[127] The Plan of Action which emerged included a section entitled 'On Landmine Survivors Assistance', in which governments were urged to work towards establishing 'national Mine Information systems' and to establish 'national Support Funds' for landmines survivors to which international donors could contribute. The Plan of Action also called for the 'active participation' of landmine survivors in the formulation, decision-making and execution of decisions that affect them.[128]

121 The draft is reproduced in Casey-Maslen, *The Convention on the Prohibition of Anti-Personnel Mines*, above n. 6, Appendix 4, p. 398.

122 Sigal, *Negotiating Minefields*, above n. 6, p. 184.

123 Ibid.

124 In a 2002 interview, Stephen Goose commented that the ICBL 'probably hadn't done as much politically on victim assistance as we should have done from the early days' cited in ibid., p. 183.

125 Casey-Maslen, *The Convention on the Prohibition of Anti-Personnel Mines*, above n. 6, p. 32.

126 Africa Policy Information Center, *Landmines: Africa's Stake, Global Initiatives* (Background Paper 009, April 1997) reproduces the final declaration. See: http://kora.matrix.msu.edu/files/50/304/32-130-17BE-84-APIC_Background009_opt.pdf.

127 White and Rutherford, 'The Role of the Landmine Survivors Network', above n. 120, p. 109.

128 *Plan of Action of the First Continental Conference of African Experts on Landmines*, Kempton Park, South Africa, 19–21 May 1997: www.acronym.org.uk/old/archive/textonly/dd/dd15/15afric.htm (Part III).

Despite these developments, by the time of the Brussels meeting in June 1997, no further progress had been made on the evolving draft in terms of the victim assistance provisions (or lack thereof). The aim of the Brussels Conference was to adopt a Declaration which affirmed the goal of reaching agreement on a ban treaty by the end of 1997.[129] However, the draft Declaration prepared prior to the meeting was silent on the question of victim assistance, despite specifically referring to cooperation and assistance in the context of mine clearance. This was to prove a major point of contention, as it was unacceptable to many of the African delegations.[130] Consequently, South Africa initially refused to associate with the Declaration although it did ultimately do so, along with twenty-six other African states.[131]

Going into the actual negotiations then in Oslo, the draft text remained silent on victim assistance, and there remained opposition to any such provision from many states.[132] However, there was support for inclusion particularly from African states,[133] as well as growing pressure from the ICBL,[134] the LNS[135] and the ICRC.[136] The dynamic was further complicated by the fact that those who favoured inclusion, were now taking the view that victim assistance ought to encompass not just rehabilitation as it was originally conceived, but should also include reintegration efforts.

Ultimately, Article 6(3) was agreed as follows:

> Each State Party in a position to do so shall provide assistance for the care and rehabilitation, and social and economic reintegration, of mine victims and for mine awareness programs. Such assistance may be provided, inter alia, through the United Nations system, international, regional or

[129] The Declaration is reproduced in Casey-Maslen, *The Convention on the Prohibition of Anti-Personnel Mines*, above n. 6, p. 376.

[130] Ibid., pp. 38 and 177.

[131] Ibid., pp. 377–8 lists the states that associated themselves with the Declaration.

[132] White and Rutherford, 'The Role of the Landmine Survivors Network', above n. 120, pp. 112–19 contains a detailed account of the Oslo negotiations on victim assistance.

[133] It was not only African states taking this position. For example, Switzerland had suggested language on care and rehabilitation of victims in response to the Third Austrian Draft; Philippines had suggested mentioning assistance in Article 1; and Norway and El Salvador were also supportive. For discussion, see Casey-Maslen, *The Convention on the Prohibition of Anti-Personnel Mines*, above n. 6, pp. 177 and 179.

[134] The ICBL had convened the Maputo meeting in early 1997.

[135] The LNS had obtained legal advice on the issue: see White and Rutherford, 'The Role of the Landmines Survivors Network', above n. 120, p. 112.

[136] The ICRC circulated comments on the Third Austrian Draft, suggesting provisions on care and rehabilitation of landmine victims. See Maresca and Maslen, *The Banning of Anti-Personnel Landmines*, above n. 24, p. 550.

> national organizations or institutions, the International Committee of the Red Cross, national Red Cross and Red Crescent societies and their International Federation, non-governmental organizations, or on a bilateral basis.

With the qualifier 'in a position to do so', the language was not as strong as some would have liked. However, victim assistance, not only for rehabilitation but also for reintegration, had been included in the treaty and that in itself was quite a breakthrough.

It is ironic that, with the passage of time, the provision is lauded as a central feature of the APLM Convention's humanitarian disarmament credentials given that it was so hard-fought at the time. However, it was an important development, not only in and of itself for support for landmines survivors, but also because this advance in the recognition of victims/survivors became an important blueprint for future treaties.

2 The Implementation of the Victim Assistance Provisions Post-EIF

The treaty's standing as a humanitarian disarmament exemplar is also evidenced by the way in which the victim assistance provisions were implemented. As it entered into force, at least seventy-seven states in the world were mine-contaminated, and fifty-three of those states were states parties.[137] As a consequence, even with the immediate ban on use, the numbers of victims continued to rise for many years because there remained the continuing danger from mine contamination pending progress with mine clearance.[138] Victim assistance, then, was central to the humanitarian ethos of the APLM Convention.

There was considerable activity. A first step was the need to gather information. Although Article 7 required states to report on implementation of their obligations under the treaty, it did not specifically require a report on progress with implementing the victim assistance provision (yet another instance of the inferior status of victim assistance in the original treaty scheme). Nevertheless, states parties agreed to a voluntary reporting system, and so, from 2001 some states started to report on their victim assistance activities in so-called 'Article 7 J' reports.

137 Alexander Kmentt, 'A Beacon of Light: The Mine Ban Treaty since 1997' in Williams, Goose and Wareham (eds.), *Banning Landmines*, above n. 6, pp. 17 and 20.

138 Ibid., p. 22, citing to the *Landmine Monitor Report*, explaining that even as late as 2006, still as many as 15,000–20,000 people per year were being killed or injured by mines. By 2014, the *Monitor* was reporting reducing numbers of casualties.

Another important step in implementation was the creation of an Intersessional Standing Committee of Experts on Victim Assistance, Socio-Economic Integration and Mine Awareness (SC-VA).[139] In this way, there was now a process by which victim assistance remained on the agenda of the Meetings of the States Parties. The work of the SC-VA in turn fed into the Meetings of the States Parties and the five-yearly Review Conferences setting out concrete actions to be taken in order to promote victim assistance and thus were further ways in which victim assistance progressed in implementation.

In addition to these more general steps, work also progressed in identifying the most specially affected states. At the First Review Conference in December 2004, states with significant numbers of survivors accepted that they had the 'greatest responsibility to act, but also the greatest needs and expectations for assistance' in providing victim assistance.[140] At times, special funds were devoted to the needs of victims. For example, Switzerland funded a Victim Assistance Specialist to assist with implementation measures.[141]

Despite all of this activity, in a ten-year review in 2009, the *Landmine Monitor* reported that the provisions on victim assistance had made little progress in terms of actual implementation.[142] Still, it should be noted that progress up to that point would likely have been more limited had it not been for the input and work of civil society, particularly those groups working under the banner of the ICBL. As with verification of compliance generally, civil society took the lead in gathering, collating and disseminating the information. The *Landmine Monitor Report* rapidly became the central source of information, both in terms of the ongoing casualty rates and all victim assistance projects.[143] Although the assertion cannot be proven, it seems plausible that this level of close scrutiny must have had a substantial impact on the political momentum within the states parties on

[139] Second Meeting of the States Parties to the APLM Convention, *Final Report* (APLC/MSP.2/2000/1, 19 September 2000), Annex II ('President's Paper on Revisions to the Intersessional Work Programme').

[140] First Review Conference of the States Parties to the APLM Convention, *Final Report*, APLC/CONF/2004/5, 9 February 2005, p. 3.

[141] ICBL, *Landmine Monitor Report 2006*, p. 53.

[142] ICBL, *Landmine Monitor 2009*, p. 1. This is consistent with the tenor of a commentary published in 2008 outside of the narrow context of treaty implementation, but in terms of landmine victim assistance generally: Michael Lundquist, 'Landmine Victim Assistance Progress, Challenges and Best Practices' (2008) 12(1) *Journal of Mine Action*, article 5.

[143] See the discussion by Wareham, 'Evidence-Based Advocacy' above n. 107, pp. 50–2.

implementing victim assistance programmes, particularly given the misgivings of at least some states about the inclusion of victim assistance obligations in the treaty at all.[144] The close engagement by ICBL and the wide dissemination of information was valuable as well because it allowed a better appreciation of the actual (as opposed to assumed) needs of landmines survivors, their families and their communities. Indeed, even the evolution of the term from 'victim assistance' to 'survivor assistance' is illustrative of this appreciation. At the First Review Conference, states agreed on a broader definition of 'victim', away from simple physical impairment, towards a more holistic understanding so that victims would now: 'include those who either individually or collectively have suffered physical or psychological injury, economic loss or substantial impairment of their fundamental rights through acts or omissions related to mine utilization'.[145] Another important development was the shift to a 'rights-based' approach, which migrated across from the Convention on the Rights of Persons with Disabilities (CRPD) and has subsequently infused the Convention on Cluster Munitions.[146] This started to permeate the implementation work on the APLM Convention because landmine survivors often became people with subsequent disabilities and there was a consequent shift in thinking about such people as rights-holders under the CRPD, rather than simply being 'victims', or even 'survivors', under the APLM Convention. Once again, with the ICBL so closely involved in reporting and dissemination, it was easier for the disabilities discourse to permeate the APLM Convention context than it may have been in a state-centric system.

In these ways then, the victim assistance provisions – their existence and their implementation – are an important facet of the APLM Convention's humanitarian disarmament credentials.

V Humanitarian Disarmament Perfected?

The APLM Convention is an overwhelming success: in normative terms, it has made a major contribution to the taboo against anti-personnel

[144] Ibid., pp. 55–7.

[145] *Final Report of the First Review Conference*, above n. 140, para. 64. For discussion, see Kerry Brinkert, 'Understanding Obligations to Victims' (2006) 10(1) *Journal of ERW and Mine Action* 88.

[146] United Nations Convention on the Rights of Persons with Disabilities, opened for signature 30 Mar 2007, (2008) 2515 UNTS 3 (entered into force 3 May 2008); Convention on Cluster Munitions, opened for signature 3 December 2008, 2688 UNTS 39 (entered into force 1 August 2010).

mines;[147] there is a de facto moratorium on transfer of APLMs in place;[148] and since its entry into force, there are fewer producers of mines.[149]

But perhaps most importantly for the present discussion, the APLM Convention also provided an important blueprint for future campaigns against other weapons. The discussion in the previous part elaborated a number of important features that bring it within 'humanitarian disarmament'.

It is not, however, a perfect treaty. There were inevitable compromises within the text, some of which have been discussed earlier, including verification of compliance and the provisions on victim assistance, and other compromises that had to be made such as regarding the precise scope of the prohibitions and questions of interoperability.[150] Implementation, although impressive and far beyond the expectations of many at the time the treaty was concluded, has not been perfect. Some destruction deadlines have not been met, instances of alleged use of landmines have gone uninvestigated and mine clearance remains an overwhelming burden.[151] Most worryingly, in recent years, the numbers of casualties seem to be rising again.[152] Without dismissing any of these imperfections, it should be acknowledged that many other treaties in disarmament and in other spheres suffer from less-than-perfect implementation, so these challenges in themselves are not reason to dismiss the treaty as an important example of humanitarian disarmament.

However, in my view, two concerns arise with the way in which the APLM Convention is championed as an exemplar and how it is used as a blueprint for other regimes. The first relates to the way in which the treaty seems to have escaped scrutiny and critique. This seems to be

147 Price, 'Reversing the Gun Sights', above n. 2.

148 The ICBL reports that nine states which remain outside the treaty regime have enacted formal moratorium on the export of APLMs: ICBL, *Landmine Monitor Report 2018*, p. 15.

149 Adam Bower, 'Norms Without the Great Powers: International Law, Nested Social Structures, and the Ban on Antipersonnel Mines' (2015) 17 *International Studies Review* 347.

150 See for example, the discussion of whether anti-vehicle mines with anti-handling devices were excluded: Stephen Goose, 'The Ottawa Process and the 1997 Mine Ban Treaty' (1998) 1 *Yearbook of International Humanitarian Law* 269, 281; and Hajnoczi, Desch and Chatsis, 'The Treaty Ban', above n. 52, p. 297. On the question of interoperability and the word 'assist' (another contentious scope issue), see Wareham, 'Evidence-Based Advocacy', above n. 107, pp. 57–8.

151 Goose, 'Goodwill Yields Results', above n. 88, pp. 105–12.

152 ICBL, *Landmine Monitor Report 2018*, p. 2.

partly due to a lack of sustained rigorous academic commentary (not least from international lawyers), and partly because the close involvement of civil society in its creation and implementation may have had a co-opting effect, such that civil society has become a partner in treaty implementation processes rather than an external observer and critic.

The second concern relates to the reliance on the ICBL and the *Landmine Monitor Report* in particular as the core of the compliance monitoring for the treaty. The difficulty with this is the consequent financial vulnerability given that the *Monitor* is funded by a relatively small group of states.[153] Without funding, the system simply would not function as there is no obligation on states parties to support the system. The danger of co-option and the financial vulnerability may be pushing the ICBL from its critical advocacy position to a volunteer force supplementing the states parties. That would be to lose an important function of civil society.

VI Conclusion

The APLM Convention is indeed an exemplar of humanitarian disarmament and it has changed the nature of the disarmament discourse in significant ways. This chapter has shown four instances of these changes. First, how the APLM Convention was novel because of the forum in which it was negotiated: outside the traditional multilateral fora, but remaining in a multilateral, inclusive sphere. Second, the engagement by civil society led to a much greater level of transparency in the negotiations and in subsequent implementation. A third way in which the disarmament practice and discourse changed is evident from the victim assistance provisions in the APLM Convention. Finally, the civil society-led oversight of treaty implementation marked a significant shift from previous regimes.

Given its significance in the evolution of disarmament, I suggest that the APLM Convention would bear deeper, more extensive and more critical engagement from scholars and from practitioners in disarmament. This is particularly the case because, as we will see in the following chapter, it has formed the basis of several other campaigns against weapons, two of which are discussed in subsequent chapters: cluster munitions and nuclear weapons.

153 These are listed in every issue of the Monitor.

6

Humanitarian Disarmament Consolidated?

The Convention on Cluster Munitions

I Introduction

Just over a decade after the Convention on the Prohibition of the Use, Stockpiling, Production and Transfer of Anti-Personnel Mines and on their Destruction (APLM Convention)[1] was concluded, 107 states adopted the Convention on Cluster Munitions (CCM).[2] That treaty turned its focus on another weapon widely considered to be indiscriminate – cluster munitions – banning them from use, and requiring states parties to destroy their existing stockpiles and to clear unexploded cluster submunitions in areas under their jurisdiction and control. The CCM is widely perceived as being a natural progression from the APLM Convention.[3] In fact, the two treaties are often coupled together lending an air of inexorable consolidation around the idea of 'humanitarian disarmament'.[4] This is unsurprising given the strong parallels between the two regimes, not least their common roots in the campaign against indiscriminate weapons stretching back to the

[1] The Convention on the Prohibition of the Use, Stockpiling, Production, and Transfer of Anti-Personnel Mines and on their Destruction, opened for signature 3 December 1997, 2056 UNTS 211, entered into force 1 March 1999.

[2] Convention on Cluster Munitions, opened for signature 3 December 2008, 2688 UNTS 39 (entered into force 1 August 2010).

[3] Bonnie Docherty, 'Breaking New Ground: The Convention on Cluster Munitions and the Evolution of International Humanitarian Law' (2009) 31 *Human Rights Quarterly* 934, 941; see generally, Stephen Goose, 'Cluster Munitions in the Crosshairs: In Pursuit of a Prohibition' in Jody Williams, Mary Wareham and Stephen Goose (eds.), *Banning Landmines: Disarmament, Citizen Diplomacy, and Human Security* (Lanham: Rowman and Littlefield, 2008), p. 217 noting similarities and differences.

[4] See for example, Bonnie Docherty, 'Ending Civilian Suffering: The Purpose, Provisions, and Promise of Humanitarian Disarmament Law' (2010) 15 *Austrian Review of International and European Law* 7 referring to the idea of an 'established legal practice' (p. 9).

1960s; the way the weapon in question was reframed as a humanitarian issue challenging the security calculus; the manner in which the negotiations for each treaty took place outside the established diplomatic architecture; and the similarities between the two texts reflecting the way in which the CCM drafters used parts of the APLM Convention as the basis of negotiations.

While acknowledging all of that, the central claim of this chapter is that while the CCM is a consolidation of humanitarian disarmament in some important respects, its negotiation, formulation and implementation reveal some emerging complexities in the theory and practice of humanitarian disarmament which warrant examination. I argue that the CCM represents both an advance in the practice of humanitarian disarmament and a troubling regressive stance. Further, it is not clear, at least so far, that the treaty has been a resounding success, judged by results on the ground in terms of ongoing instances of use of cluster munitions and the slow rate of clearance of unexploded munitions.

I start the chapter, in Section II, by explaining the humanitarian concerns about cluster munitions which lay behind the calls for better regulation, and in the end prohibition, of the weapons, and as I will show, much of this early phase was closely linked with the concerns being raised about anti-personnel landmines (APLMs). In Section III, I provide an overview of the background and lead-up to the CCM, as well as an overview of the treaty's key provisions. In doing so, the parallels between the CCM and the APLM Convention become evident, as well as the way in which the CCM can be seen as a consolidation of humanitarian disarmament. This discussion also reveals how the CCM brought with it significant advances in the practice of humanitarian disarmament.

I turn then to explore in detail the ways in which I see the treaty revealing a more complex picture of humanitarian practice, not simply a repeat performance of the APLM Convention in the context of a different weapon. The first complexity is the way in which the core prohibition in the treaty is structured (Section IV). As I will show, the starting point of the definition is a broad-based prohibition, but allowing for certain types of cluster munitions to be excluded from prohibition if that particular subcategory of munitions can be shown not to pose an unacceptable risk to civilians. This approach – whereby a munition is banned unless exempted – effectively means that there has been a shift in the burden of proof as to what constitutes an acceptable (or humanitarian) weapon.[5] Such an approach is significant for humanitarian disarmament for two reasons. First, at a pragmatic level, the approach shifts the burden of argument onto the militarily powerful, generally better resourced, states. That is, rather than the prohibitionist states having to challenge the permissive status quo, the user states have to justify why they should be allowed to continue to use the weapon. Second, the shifting burden of proof suggests the possibility of quite a profound shift in weapons law. Instead of a landscape where disarmament campaigns move from weapon to weapon and in each case mount an argument as to why that weapon or means of delivery is unacceptable in humanitarian terms, we might imagine an approach emerging where no weapons are acceptable unless proven otherwise. The implications of this shift are potentially far-reaching and as yet unexplored.

In Section V, I examine the second complexity arising from the treaty. This focuses on the 'user state responsibility' debate which lay behind the clearance and victim assistance provisions in the treaty. Here I argue that this aspect of the treaty is a regressive step for humanitarian disarmament. While clearance and assistance provisions were included in the APLM Convention, the CCM went far beyond those provisions.[6] Generally this has been seen as an instance of how innovative the treaty is in terms of humanitarian disarmament practice. However, my argument is that a close examination of the way the relevant provisions evolved reveals the way in which claims of 'humanitarianism' effectively silenced the concerns of states which had themselves been victims of the use of cluster munitions.

Section VI briefly concludes the chapter by suggesting that, more than a decade on, it is not possible to definitively conclude that the treaty is an overwhelming success, despite its very real advances and important contributions to the evolution of humanitarian disarmament.

[5] John Borrie, *Unacceptable Harm: A History of How the Treaty to Ban Cluster Munitions Was Won* (Geneva: United Nations Institute for Disarmament Research, 2009), ch. 6; John Borrie et al., 'Learn, Adapt, Succeed: Potential Lessons from the Ottawa and Oslo Processes for Other Disarmament and Arms Control Challenges' (2009) 2 *Disarmament Forum* 19, 34; Brian Rappert and Richard Moyes, 'The Prohibition of Cluster Munitions: Setting International Precedents for Defining Inhumanity' (2009) 16(2) *Nonproliferation Review* 237.

[6] Bonnie Docherty, 'Ending Civilian Suffering', above n. 4.

II Humanitarian Concerns about Cluster Munitions

A cluster munition is a 'parent munition' that contains within it multiple (sometimes hundreds of) submunitions, and the term includes the parent munition, as well as the submunitions.[7] Delivered by ground artillery, rocket or released from aircraft, the cluster munition disperses the submunitions, which are designed to detonate on impact.[8] Thus, a cluster munition is an 'area weapon' in that it disperses its submunitions over a large area referred to as the weapon 'footprint'.[9] The military justification for this design is that they can attack area targets such as military airfields, concentrations of military personnel, vehicles or armour. They are also useful in attacking moving targets because it is not necessary that all the submunitions strike the target.[10]

The modern use of cluster munitions in conflict dates back to the Second World War.[11] Cluster munitions technology developed rapidly in the aftermath of the war and, by the 1960s, they were in extensive use, particularly by the United States in Indochina.[12] Laos is said to be the most cluster-contaminated country in the world.[13] Mines Action Canada

[7] The term 'cluster weapon' includes the artillery shells and rockets.

[8] William H Boothby, *Weapons and The Law of Armed Conflict* (Oxford: Oxford University Press, 2009) p. 251. The point is significant as it distinguishes them from anti-personnel landmines (APLMs) which are not designed to detonate on impact, but rather are designed to 'lie in wait'.

[9] Alexander Breitegger, *Cluster Munitions and International Law: Disarmament with a Human Face?* (Abingdon; New York: Routledge, 2012), p. 13. See also Virgil Wiebe, 'Footprints of Death: Cluster Bombs as Indiscriminate Weapons under International Humanitarian Law' (2000) 22 *Michigan Journal of International Law* 85, 89.

[10] Boothby, *Weapons and Law of Armed Conflict*, above n. 8, pp. 251, 254–5.

[11] Ibid., p. 253. For a brief discussion about much earlier types of cluster munitions, see Virgil Wiebe, John Borrie and Declan Smyth, 'Introduction' in Gro Nystuen and Stuart Casey-Maslen (eds.), *The Convention on Cluster Munitions: A Commentary* (New York: Oxford University Press, 2010).

[12] Colin King, 'The Evolution of Cluster Munitions' in International Committee of the Red Cross (ICRC) (ed), *Humanitarian, Military, Technical and Legal Challenges of Cluster Munitions* (Montreux, Switzerland, 18–20 April 2007), p. 11; Wiebe, 'Cluster Bombs as Indiscriminate Weapons', above n. 9, pp. 91–2; Breitegger, *Cluster Munitions and International Law*, above n. 9, p. 19; Channapha Khamvongsa and Elaine Russell, 'Legacies of War' (2009) 41(2) *Critical Asian Studies* 281.

[13] Richard Kidd, Director, Office of Weapons Removal and Abatement, US Department of State 'U.S. Intervention on Humanitarian Impacts of Cluster Munitions', Remarks to the CCW Group of Governmental Experts, Geneva, Switzerland, 20 June 2007. See as well, King, 'Evolution of Cluster Munitions', above n. 12, at p. 11 noting that it is believed that after the war, nine million unexploded submunitions remained; Borrie, *Unacceptable Harm*, above n. 5, p. 18; Khamvongsa and Russell, 'Legacies of War', above n. 12; Carmel Capati, 'The Tragedy of Cluster Bombs in Laos' (1997) 16 *Wisconsin International Law Journal* 227, 229–31.

reports that between the end of the Second World War and 2009, cluster munitions were used in thirty-three conflicts.[14] Notable instances include the 1991 Gulf War,[15] in NATO's air campaign over Yugoslavia in 1999,[16] in Afghanistan, first by the Soviet Union in the 1980s and then by the United States since 2001,[17] and in the 2003 invasion of Iraq.[18] Although their use was not as extensive as in some of the previous conflicts, the use of cluster munitions in the Lebanon War 2006, and the resulting contamination through unexploded submunitions, is considered by some commentators to be one of the immediate catalysts for the negotiation of the CCM.[19]

The humanitarian objections to clusters munitions are twofold. First, because the submunitions are dispersed over such a large area, they are generally more prone than 'unitary' munitions to cause civilian harm at the time of the attack and thus they are susceptible to having indiscriminate effects. Indeed, in conditions of contemporary warfare in populated areas, given the large footprint, it is almost inevitable that the weapons will have an indiscriminate effect in that they will strike both military and civilian objects and personnel. Although user states frequently assert that

[14] Mines Action Canada, *Banning Cluster Munitions: Government Policy and Practice* (2009) 13. Of course there has been a number of serious instances since that publication, most extensively in Syria and Yemen. The latest figures are available from Cluster Munition Coalition, *Cluster Munition Monitor 2018* (2018) pp. 15–20.

[15] The figure comes from Human Rights Watch, *Ticking Time Bombs* (1999), available at www.hrw.org/reports/1999/nato2/, which relies on data from the US General Accounting Office, reporting that during Operation Desert Storm over a three-month period January–March 1991, 47,167 cluster bombs were dropped by US aircraft, resulting in the release of over 13 million submunitions; see also Bonnie Docherty and Human Rights Watch, *Fatally Flawed: Cluster Bombs and Their Use by the United States in Afghanistan* (New York: Human Rights Watch, 2002) p. 2 (stating that 61,000 cluster munitions were used in the Gulf War, releasing 12 million submunitions); Wiebe, 'Cluster Bombs as Indiscriminate Weapons', above n. 9; Breitegger, *Cluster Munitions and International Law*, above n. 9, p. 21; King, 'The Evolution of Cluster Munitions', above n. 12, p. 21.

[16] Human Rights Watch, *Ticking Time Bombs*, above n. 15.

[17] Docherty and Human Rights Watch, *Fatally Flawed*, above n. 15, p. 1; Human Rights Watch, *Ticking Time Bombs*, above n. 15, p. 54.

[18] Handicap International, *Fatal Footprint: The Global Human Impact of Cluster Munitions* (Preliminary Report, 2006), available at www.regjeringen.no/globalassets/upload/kilde/ud/rap/2006/0155/ddd/pdfv/295996-footprint.pdf. Compare the detailed defence of the US operations regarding use of cluster munitions in that conflict by Michael N. Schmitt, 'The Conduct of Hostilities during Operation Iraqi Freedom: An International Humanitarian Law Assessment' (2003) 6 *Yearbook of International Humanitarian Law* 73, pp. 97–9.

[19] See for example, Breitegger, *Cluster Munitions and International Law*, above n. 9, who describes it as a 'triggering moment': p. 26. But note the more cautious assessment by Borrie, *Unacceptable Harm*, above n. 5, p. 64.

they do not use cluster munitions in civilian areas or in places where there is a concentration of civilians,[20] the fact remains that in all contemporary use, civilians have been predominantly affected and this is in great part attributable to the large footprint of cluster munitions.[21]

The second humanitarian concern about cluster munitions relates to the problem of unexploded submunitions – the 'dud rate' or failure rate. Although designed to detonate on impact, in practice a certain number of submunitions fail to explode at the time of initial impact, in essence leaving them as de facto landmines. The fact that a submunition has failed to explode at the time of dispersal does not mean it is not dangerous – in fact, many are extremely sensitive to the presence of humans and can, and do, subsequently detonate. Thus, they present a major continuing hazard to civilians and combatants alike even after the conflict has ended.[22] As an example, from the approximately 300 million cluster munitions dropped in Laos between 1965 and 1975, approximately ninety million remained as unexploded submunitions after that conflict.[23] While extensive clearance operations had been ongoing for several decades, even by 2007, the contamination continued to be a hazard to civilians, and constrained development and agriculture.[24]

There have been radically different accounts of the actual failure rate of cluster submunitions. Initially, cluster bomb manufacturers claimed that the failure rate was 5 per cent or less.[25] As the use of the weapon was subjected to increasing scrutiny, manufacturers argued that they had

[20] See for example the statement by the United Kingdom to the Working Group on Explosive Remnants of War that no cluster munitions were released in an 'urban area' during the Iraq War 2003: United Kingdom, *Military Utility of Cluster Munitions* (CCW/GGE/X/WG.1/WP.1, 21 February 2005), and explaining that in its operations in Iraq cluster munitions were 'the most appropriate air-delivered weapons in many situations because of their ability to destroy enemy assets dispersed over an area' (para. 6).

[21] The footprint of a particular cluster munition will depend on its design and where and how it is used. In the 1970s, it was generally asserted that the footprint of a single cluster munition attack was 100m x 100m: Breitegger, *Cluster Munitions and International Law*, above n. 9, p. 21. By 2005, it was accepted by user states that a footprint might extend to an area 100m x 200m (for example, see the statement by the United Kingdom, 'Military Utility of Cluster Munitions', above n. 20, paras 4 and 5). A 'cluster munitions attack' will usually involve the use of many cluster munitions, so the total footprint could be several square kilometres. My thanks to Bob Mathews for clarifying these points.

[22] Boothby, *Weapons and The Law of Armed Conflict*, above n. 8, p. 253.

[23] United Nations Development Programme (UNDP) 'Assessment of Development Results: Evaluation of UNDP's Contribution' (2007) 44.

[24] Ibid., section 3.5.

[25] See discussion by Borrie, *Unacceptable Harm*, above n. 5, p. 170.

developed the technology sufficiently to reduce the failure rate to 1 percent.[26] However from a humanitarian point of view, even a 1 per cent failure rate represents an unacceptable level of risk. Take the thirteen million submunitions said to have been released in Operation Desert Storm:[27] an 'acceptable' 1 per cent failure rate means that 130,000 munitions lie in wait for post-conflict detonation. Further, it became increasingly clear that there was a significant difference between the failure rate claimed by the manufacturer under test conditions and the failure rate in actual conflict conditions. For example, in the Falklands conflict in 1982, the actual failure rate of the BL755 cluster munition was determined to be 9.6 per cent.[28] Similarly, the failure rate of submunitions in the conflict in Lebanon in 2006 was widely understood to be at least 10 per cent, and some estimates suggest an average of 25 per cent.[29] However, under earlier test conditions in Norway, the same munition had revealed a failure rate of only 1 per - cent.[30] A 10 per cent failure rate applied to Operation Desert Storm, would mean 1.3 million unexploded munitions remaining, not the 'acceptable' 130,000.

The ever-escalating use of cluster munitions, their extremely large footprints leading to indiscriminate effects at the time of the attack, along with unacceptably high failure rates leaving a post-conflict continuing hazard to civilians, have all underpinned the humanitarian concerns about cluster munitions. However, as I will show in the following

[26] Discussed by Gro Nystuen, 'CCW Draft Protocol VI on Cluster Munitions – A Step Backwards' FICHL Policy Brief Series No. 5 (2011) 3.

[27] Simon Conway, 'Cluster Munitions: Historical Overview of Use and Human Impacts', in ICRC, *Humanitarian, Military, Technical and Legal Challenges of Cluster Munitions*, above n. 12, pp. 13, 14.

[28] Rae McGrath, *Cluster Bombs: The Military Effectiveness and Impact on Civilians of Cluster Munitions* (London: UK Working Group on Landmines, 2000), p. 6. McGrath draws this conclusion from the details provided in a written response by the Minister of State for Defence, John Spellar MP to a Parliamentary Question on 28 May 2000 (to the effect that 1492 submunitions were cleared from the Falkland Islands post-conflict and that either 106 or 107 BL755 cluster bombs had been dropped).

[29] The 10 per cent figure comes from Simon Conway, 'Cluster Munitions: Historical Overview of Use and Human Impacts', above n. 27, p. 15. Human Rights Watch, in its comprehensive report and relying on clearance information from UN Mine Action Coordination Center South Lebanon calculates that there could be an average of 25 per cent failure rate. See Human Rights Watch, *Flooding South Lebanon: Israel's Use of Cluster Munitions in Lebanon in July and August 2006* (New York: Human Rights Watch, 2008) pp. 44–8.

[30] Borrie, *Unacceptable Harm*, above n. 5, p. 170.

section, there have been different emphases on each of these concerns at different times.

III The Convention on Cluster Munitions: Consolidating Humanitarian Disarmament

The way in which cluster munitions were framed as a humanitarian problem rather than involving a simple security calculus is perhaps the most immediate and obvious parallel between the CCM and the APLM Convention. However, in this section, I show that the parallels run much deeper than this humanitarian framing and that the CCM is rightly seen as a consolidation of humanitarian disarmament in a number of important respects. As with the APLM Convention before it, the CCM in many ways rests on the campaigns against indiscriminate weapons from the late 1960s through to 1980, and indeed the attempts to regulate cluster munitions in that era faced the same challenges as for APLMs due to the intransigence of the militarily significant states.[31] Both treaty regimes also have roots in the CCW process, although of course those of the CCM developed much later. Both the CCM and the APLM Convention were ultimately negotiated outside the United Nations disarmament architecture, being championed by a coalition of like-minded states and supported by a strong civil society movement. These aspects of how the CCM consolidated the practice of humanitarian disarmament are discussed in turn.

A The Campaigns against Indiscriminate Weapons

As with the APLM Convention, the seeds of the CCM lie in the campaigns against indiscriminate weapons which stretched across the three areas of activity discussed in detail in the previous chapter: the Human Rights in Armed Conflict project which had developed out of the 1968 Tehran Conference; the work of various Expert Group meetings convened by the International Committee of the Red Cross (ICRC) through the 1970s; and finally, the 1977 revisions of international humanitarian law.[32] All of these efforts were concerned with 'certain conventional weapons considered to have indiscriminate effects or cause unnecessary suffering'.[33] The conventional weapons being scrutinised for their

[31] See Chapter 4, Section III and Chapter 5, Section II.

[32] See Chapter 4, Sections III.A and B.

[33] See Chapter 4, Section III.A.

indiscriminate effects or the way in which they caused unnecessary suffering initially fell into four categories: small calibre single projectiles; explosive blast and fragmentation weapons; time-delay weapons such as mines and booby-traps; and incendiary weapons.[34] Cluster munitions, as they came to be known, fell within the category of 'anti-personnel fragmentation' weapons.[35]

In Chapter 4, I demonstrated the way in which prohibitionists states, and particularly those of the Non-Aligned Movement (NAM), lobbied persistently to get some agreement by militarily significant states (namely the USA, the USSR and their respective allies) on restrictions on or even prohibitions against these conventional weapons.[36] The campaigns against cluster munitions were part of those overall campaigns, but as I will show in this chapter, cluster munitions fared even worse than APLMs, in that no progress was made at all during the 1970s in the lead-up to the CCW 1980.

Initially (that is, the late 1960s onwards), debates focused on the first humanitarian concern raised by cluster munitions, that is, their indiscriminate effect at the time of the attack due to the way in which the submunitions are released and spread across a large area. As such, in substantive terms, the humanitarian concern about cluster munitions was initially quite different to those being raised in the context of APLMs. For cluster munitions, concerns focused on the increased mortality risk, increased non-fatal incapacitation, degree of pain and the difficulties in providing effective medical treatment arising from multiple wounds in a single victim.[37] Thus, the humanitarian focus was on the immediate indiscriminate effects of cluster munitions at the time of their use, along with the suffering occasioned by the nature and number of the wounds. There was no reference at all to the question of post-conflict contamination – which, at the time, was the dominant concern about APLMs.[38]

[34] International Committee of the Red Cross (ICRC), Report of the Work of the Experts, *Weapons that May Cause Unnecessary Suffering or Have Indiscriminate Effects* (1973) ('Conference of Government Experts, Geneva, 1973'), chs. III–IV.

[35] Hans Blix, 'Current Efforts to Prohibit the Use of Certain Conventional Weapons' (1974) 4(1) *Instant Research on Peace and Violence* 21, 27.

[36] See Chapter 4, Section III.

[37] Conference of Government Experts, Geneva, 1973, above n. 34, paras 147–9. These concerns were repeated again in 1974: ICRC, *Conference of Government Experts on the Use of Certain Conventional Weapons (Lucerne, 24 Sept.–18 Oct. 1974)*, (1975) ('Conference of Government Experts, Lucerne, 1974'), paras 168 and 169–208; and in 1976: ICRC, *Conference of Government Experts on the Use of Certain Conventional Weapons (Second Session Lugano, 28.1–26.2.1976)*, (1976) ('Conference of Government Experts, Lugano, 1976'), 45.

[38] Breitegger, *Cluster Munitions and International Law*, above n. 9, p. 19.

Despite these differences in focus, the early campaigns against indiscriminate weapons encapsulated both cluster munitions and anti-personnel landmines and the same dynamics were at play as have been outlined in the previous chapters in the specific context of APLMs. Indeed, the claims against cluster munitions were initially more forceful. In February 1974, Egypt, Mexico, Norway, Sudan, Sweden, Switzerland and Yugoslavia issued a Working Paper proposing that cluster munitions be prohibited outright.[39] It was the first proposal of its kind. Not surprisingly, in light of the opposition of the military states discussed in the previous chapter to any attempts to further restrict, much less prohibit, the use of weapons, the proposal failed to get traction.

A second ban proposal was presented in 1976 at the ICRC Expert Meeting in Lugano. This time the proposal had the support of thirteen states: Algeria, Austria, Egypt, Lebanon, Mali, Mauritania, Mexico, Norway, Sudan, Sweden, Switzerland, Venezuela and Yugoslavia, and it also called for an outright prohibition on cluster munitions in order to address the growing humanitarian concerns.[40] The proposal canvassed APLMs as well, but did not call for an outright prohibition – rather, it only went so far as to propose a restriction such that APLMs should not be laid by aircraft.[41] Neither proposal was acceptable to the militarily significant states.

Despite this promising start in terms of calls for an outright prohibition, cluster munitions were eventually dropped from the overall campaign against indiscriminate weapons. They disappeared from view in the Human Rights and Armed Conflict initiative as the focus turned there to incendiary weapons and to anti-personnel landmines.[42] Cluster munitions were also dropped from the preparatory work for the revisions of the Geneva Conventions 1949. There had been resistance to any weapons at all being included in the work of the Diplomatic Conference but states were able to agree that an Ad Hoc Committee on Weapons could be constituted.[43] However, at the Ad Hoc Committee's

[39] *Official Records of the Diplomatic Conference on the Reaffirmation and Development of International Humanitarian Law Applicable in Armed Conflicts, Geneva (1974–1977)* vol XVI, Working Paper CDDH/DT/2 and Add 1 (21 February 1974). Sudan later joined the initiative.

[40] Algeria, Austria, Egypt, Lebanon, Mali, Mauritania, Mexico, Norway, Sudan, Sweden, Switzerland, Venezuela, Yugoslavia, 'Working Paper' (CDDH/IV/201) reproduced in Conference of Government Experts, Lugano, 1976, above n. 37, p. 198.

[41] Ibid., para. V.

[42] See Chapter 4, Sections III.A and B.

[43] See Chapter 4, Section IV.

final session, the scope of that discussion narrowed to three categories of weapons only: APLMs, incendiary weapons and weapons containing non-detectable fragments.[44] The justification offered by the militarily significant states was that discussions had not developed sufficiently for the other weapons types, including fragmentation weapons, to be considered at that time.[45] As discussed earlier, ultimately none of the weapons under consideration made it into the 1977 revisions to the Geneva Conventions 1949, but cluster munitions did not even survive to the discussions in the Ad Hoc Committee.

In large part because of the way specific weapons had been excluded from the scope of the 1977 revisions, the Conference on Excessively Injurious or Indiscriminate Weapons convened from 1979–80.[46] The aim of the Conference was to reach agreement on 'prohibitions or restrictions on the use of specific conventional weapons which may be deemed to be excessively injurious or have indiscriminate effects, taking into account humanitarian and military considerations'.[47] But the neglect of cluster munitions continued in this work. At the Conference's first preparatory meeting in 1978, twelve proposals were submitted covering a wide range of weapons including the regulation of incendiary weapons, fuel-air-explosives, small calibre weapons, anti-personnel fragmentation weapons, flechettes, anti-personnel landmines and booby traps, and non-detectable fragments.[48] However, while Working Groups were established to consider APLMs and incendiary weapons, fragmentation weapons were not considered in depth. Tracing precisely how and why the scope narrowed is difficult but the United Nations *Disarmament Yearbook* sheds some light, reporting that during the preparatory meetings:

> Matters concerning fuel-air explosives, anti-personnel fragmentation weapons and flechettes were discussed only in the plenary meetings of the Preparatory Conference owing to the pressure of time and the

44 Official Records of the Diplomatic Conference, vol XVI, paras 46–8 (on the first session); paras 42–5 (second session); and 53–7 (third session).

45 Ibid., para. 4 (fourth session). For discussion, see Howard S. Levie, 'Prohibitions and Restrictions on the Use of Conventional Weapons' (1994) 68 *St John's Law Review* 643, pp. 647–8.

46 See Chapter 4, Section IV.

47 Official Records of the Diplomatic Conference, vol I, Resolution 22 (IV) *Follow up Regarding Prohibition or Restriction of Use of Certain Conventional Weapons*, p. 215.

48 Robert J. Mathews, 'The 1980 Convention on Certain Conventional Weapons: A Useful Framework Despite Earlier Disappointments' (2001) 83(844) *International Review of the Red Cross* 991, 995.

> complexity of the questions involved. It was recommended that those subjects be studied further nationally, so that discussion on them could begin at the main Conference.[49]

Inevitably, then, when the full Conference met, it was not sufficiently prepared to consider cluster munitions. Thus, the *Yearbook* reported that with 'regard to other types of weapons, no conclusions were reached on proposals concerning anti-personnel fragmentation weapons, flechettes, or fuel-air explosive weapons, as they had not been considered in depth'.[50]

And so, at the conclusion of the Conference in 1980, the *Yearbook* reported:

> Concerning the questions of fuel-air explosives, anti-personnel fragmentation weapons and flechettes, the Committee did not have time for their consideration and consequently no agreement could be reached in those areas. Many States felt, however, that those questions could be taken up in due time in the context of the follow-up mechanism provided for in the convention.[51]

As I explored in detail in Chapter 4, the resulting treaty – the CCW 1980 – did regulate APLMs and incendiary weapons.[52] The *Yearbook* reports suggest that the omission of cluster munitions (and other categories of weapons) was due to lack of time, but it is notable that there was the time to ensure that militarily significant states achieved what they wanted: that is, that the Protocols to the CCW 1980 were drafted in such a way as to exclude any possibility that fragmentation weapons could be included within the definitions of APLMs and/or incendiary weapons. APLMs (regulated but not prohibited in Protocol II to the CCW 1980 (Protocol II)[53] were defined as munitions 'designed to be detonated or exploded by the presence, proximity or contact of a person or vehicle'.[54] This specifically excludes cluster munitions, which are not *designed* with this intent – in fact it is the opposite in that cluster munitions are designed to detonate on release. The fact that the unexploded cluster

49 United Nations, *United Nations Disarmament Yearbook* 4 (1979), p. 259.

50 Ibid., p. 268.

51 United Nations, *United Nations Disarmament Yearbook* 5 (1980), p. 309.

52 See Chapter 4, Section IV.

53 Protocol on Prohibitions or Restrictions on the Use of Mines, Booby-Traps and Other Devices (Protocol II) to the Convention on Prohibitions or Restrictions on the Use of Certain Conventional Weapons which May be Deemed to be Excessively Injurious or to Have Indiscriminate Effects, opened for signature 10 April 1981, 1342 UNTS 137 (entered into force 2 December 1983).

54 Protocol II art. 1(1).

submunitions (that is, the failed submunitions) in fact detonate or explode with similar effect to APLMs does not bring them within the definition.

Similarly, Protocol III to the CCW 1980 (Protocol III) dealing with incendiary weapons specifically excludes fragmentation weapons.[55] Article 1(b)(ii) provides that incendiary weapons do not include munitions 'designed to combine penetration, blast or fragmentation effects with an additional incendiary effect, such as armour-piercing projectiles, fragmentation shells, explosive bombs and similar combined-effects munitions . . . '.[56]

And so, cluster munitions and APLMs continued to follow their own trajectories. APLMs had finally been regulated by the CCW 1980, even if those regulations were not as stringent as many states would have wished.[57] Cluster munitions remained unregulated apart from the application of general international humanitarian law principles – that is, precisely the position insisted upon by the militarily significant states.[58] And so from shared beginnings, the two categories of weapons started to travel on different pathways, and it was to take more than two decades before cluster munitions began to be seriously considered again in the context of the CCW 1980.

B The CCW Review Process: Explosive Remnants of War

Article 8(3) CCW 1980 provided that, ten years following entry into force, any High Contracting Party could request a conference 'to review the

[55] Protocol on Prohibitions or Restrictions on the Use of Incendiary Weapons (Protocol III) to the Convention on Prohibitions or Restrictions on the Use of Certain Conventional Weapons which may be Deemed to be Excessively Injurious or to Have Indiscriminate Effects, opened for signature 10 April 1981, 1342 UNTS 137 (entered into force 2 December 1983).

[56] Protocol III art. 1(1)(b)(ii).

[57] See Chapter 4, Section IV.

[58] A number of authors have expressed different views on why this happened the way it did: lack of time (Malcolm Shaw, 'The United Nations Convention on Prohibitions or Restrictions on the Use of Certain Conventional Weapons, 1981' (1983) 9(2) *Review of International Studies* 109, 119); uncertainty amongst delegations as to the arguments (Shaw, p. 119 and Wiebe, 'Cluster Bombs as Indiscriminate Weapons', above n. 9, p. 157); determined opposition by the military states (Mathews, 'The 1980 Convention on Certain Conventional Weapons', above n. 48, p. 995 and Wiebe, 'Cluster Bombs as Indiscriminate Weapons', above n. 9, p. 157); lack of appreciation of the contamination issue (Wiebe, 'Cluster Bombs as Indiscriminate Weapons', above n. 9, p. 153); and simple conference fatigue (Stephanie Carvin, 'Conventional Thinking?: The 1980 Convention on Certain Conventional Weapons and the Politics of Legal Restraints on Weapons During the Cold War' (2017) 19(1) *Journal of Cold War Studies* 38, 56).

scope and operation' of the Convention and the Protocols. The first such Review Conference was convened in 1995, resulting in Protocol II (on APLMs) being amended and strengthened.[59] That first Review Conference also adopted a new Protocol on Blinding Laser Weapons (becoming Protocol IV).[60] The second Review Conference, convened in 2001, extended the scope of the entire APLM Convention to all types of armed conflict.[61] Regular five-yearly review conferences were also set in train.[62]

There still had been no serious consideration of cluster munitions by states parties, but with five-yearly review conferences now in place, the way was open for them to be returned to active consideration. When that happened, the focus turned to the second humanitarian concern about cluster munitions: the contamination occasioned by submunitions which failed to detonate on impact. In part due to the anti-personnel landmines campaign (both in the context of the CCW 1980, and in the subsequent APLM Convention) understanding of, and concern about, so-called 'explosive remnants of war' (ERW) was growing.[63] Consequently, the ICRC and several NGOs started working to raise awareness and provide information on the risks posed and realised by ERW generally. In that context, cluster munitions started to receive increasing attention. While organisations such as the Mennonite Central Committee, and the Stockholm International Peace and Research Institute (SIPRI) had been campaigning against and providing information on the humanitarian impact of cluster munitions for decades, now other organisations started to pay attention.[64] Human Rights Watch, for example, published a detailed report in 1999 in response to the Kosovo War and also covered data on the

[59] See Chapter 5, Sections II and III.

[60] Protocol on Blinding Laser Weapons to the Convention on Prohibitions or Restrictions on the Use of Certain Conventional Weapons which may be deemed to be Excessively Injurious or to have Indiscriminate Effects, adopted 13 October 1995, 1380 UNTS 370 (entered into force 30 July 1998).

[61] Amendment to Article I of the Convention on Prohibitions or Restrictions on the Use of Certain Conventional Weapons which may be deemed to be Excessively Injurious or to have Indiscriminate Effects, adopted 21 December 2001, 2260 UNTS 82 (entered into force 18 May 2004).

[62] Final Report, *Second Review Conference of the States Parties to the Convention on Prohibitions or Restrictions on the Use of Certain Conventional Weapons Which May be Deemed to be Excessively Injurious or to Have Indiscriminate Effect* (CCW/CONF.II/2, Geneva, 2001) 16 ('Report of the Second Review Conference').

[63] Wiebe, 'Cluster Bombs as Indiscriminate Weapons', above n. 9, p. 161; Nystuen and Casey-Maslen, *The Convention on Cluster Munitions*, above n. 11, pp. 12–13.

[64] On the Mennonite Central Committee (MCC), see Borrie, *Unacceptable Harm*, above n. 5, p. 40; Wiebe, 'Cluster Bombs as Indiscriminate Weapons', above n. 9, draws on the MCC's work to support his data. The Stockholm International Peace and Research

unexploded remnants problem from the 1991 Gulf War, and the conflicts in Afghanistan.[65]

From around 1999, states started to consider the broader issue of ERW more seriously. The ICRC sponsored a meeting in Nyon to discuss the issue, with several states participating along with NGOs.[66] Two years later, at the CCW's Second Review Conference in 2001, a Group of Governmental Experts was established with a mandate to work on ERW.[67] As part of this process, cluster munitions returned to the agenda. But there were two important limitations to the mandate: first, the ERW process was to deal with *all* explosive remnants of war, it was not about cluster munitions in particular; second, the process was only aimed at addressing the second humanitarian concern about cluster munitions: that of post-conflict area contamination.

In any event, this work led to a further Protocol being agreed: Protocol V on Explosive Remnants of War (Protocol V) which put in place a series of post-conflict obligations to deal with contamination by unexploded ordnance.[68] Each state party was obliged to clear explosive remnants of war found post-conflict on its territory.[69] Article 4 set out obligations about recording the whereabouts of such remnants and providing information to the territorial state. There were also provisions for international assistance and cooperation regarding clearance and destruction, and assistance for victims.[70]

Protocol V was inadequate to deal effectively with the cluster munitions problem. Not only did it not deal specifically with cluster

Institute (SIPRI) published a number of early works on the topic: Malvern Lumsden, *Anti-personnel Weapons* (London: Taylor and Francis, 1978) and Arthur H. Westing (ed.), *Explosive Remnants of War: Mitigating the Environmental Effects* (London: Taylor and Francis, 1985).

65 Human Rights Watch, *Ticking Time Bombs*, above n. 15 (on Kosovo); Docherty and Human Rights Watch, *Fatally Flawed*, above n. 15 (on Afghanistan); Human Rights Watch, *Off Target: The Conduct of the War and Civilian Casualties in Iraq* (United States of America: Human Rights Watch, 2003) (on Iraq).

66 For discussion, see Borrie, *Unacceptable Harm*, above n. 5, pp. 44–7.

67 Report of the Second Review Conference, above n. 62, p. 12.

68 Protocol on Explosive Remnants of War to the Convention on Prohibitions or Restrictions on the Use of Certain Conventional Weapons which may be deemed to be Excessively Injurious or to have Indiscriminate Effects, adopted 28 November 2003, 2399 UNTS 100 (entered into force 12 November 2006). 'Explosive remnants of war' were defined in art. 2(2) as 'explosive ordnance that has been primed, fused, armed, or otherwise prepared for use and used in an armed conflict. It may have been fired, dropped, launched or projected and should have exploded but failed to do so'.

69 Protocol V art. 3.

70 Protocol V arts 7 and 8.

munitions, but it also was resolutely focused on the contamination problem – not the problem of indiscriminate effect that had been a central feature of the first phase of the campaign in the 1960s. Even on its own terms (dealing with contamination caused by ERW), Protocol V was inadequate. It did not prohibit the use of explosive weapons that may result in ERW, it simply put in place restrictions on the use of such weapons. It did not even require explosive munitions to have a self-destruct mechanism. While Article 9 touched on the question of prevention rather than clean-up, this was couched in very mild terms, encouraging states parties to 'take generic preventative measures aimed at minimising the occurrence of explosive remnants of war', and referring to the Technical Annex for suggestions of best practice which might be considered by states parties 'on a voluntary basis'.[71]

Thus Protocol V was manifestly inadequate to address the growing concerns about cluster munitions. The requirements on post-conflict clearance were not strong enough and it failed entirely to deal with the root cause of the problem: that given the failure rate of the submunitions, the use of cluster munitions would inevitably result in unexploded remnants. Despite these flaws, a Protocol had at last been agreed.

C Leaving the Multilateral Architecture

Even as it was becoming increasingly clear that Protocol V was an incomplete and inadequate response to the problem, the indiscriminate effects and resulting area contamination from cluster munitions use were ever-more apparent with the Balkan Wars through the 1990s, the Kosovo War 1999, the war in Afghanistan (from 2001) and in the conflict in Iraq (from 2003).[72] In particular, a number of detailed reports on the impacts of the weapons were released.[73] As had been the case with the APLMs campaign, solid technical data underpinned and gave credibility to the prohibitionist claims. The technical data (such as on failure rates of

[71] Protocol V art. 9(1).

[72] See Kenki Adachi, 'Resisting the Ban on Cluster Munitions' in Alan Bloomfield and Shirley V. Scott (eds.), *Norm Antipreneurs and the Politics of Resistance to Global Normative Change* (Abingdon: Routledge, 2016), pp. 39, 43–7.

[73] Human Rights Watch, *Ticking Time Bombs*, above n. 15; Docherty and Human Rights Watch, *Fatally Flawed*, above n. 15; Handicap International, *Fatal Footprint*, above n. 18. See also the list of reports set out in Timothy L. H. McCormack and Paramdeep B. Mtharu, 'Cluster Munitions, Proportionality and the Foreseeability of Civilian Damage' in O. Engdahl and P. Wrange (eds.), *Law at War–The Law as it Was and the Law as it Should Be* (Boston: Martinus Nijhoff Publishers, 2008) p. 191, footnote 30.

unexploded submunitions, the extent of contamination and of injuries and the impact on civilians generally) not only assisted with the momentum towards prohibition, but was a more effective response than a simple moralistic plea of humanitarianism, given that the prohibitionist position was so frequently dismissed as naïve.[74] These reports formed an essential foundation as opinion in a number of European states started to coalesce around the idea of prohibition, or at the very least, much more stringent restrictions.[75]

By 2006, the dynamics within the campaign against cluster munitions were strikingly similar to that of the anti-personnel landmines campaign. There were continuing attempts to work within the CCW review process. However, increasingly divergent positions among states, coupled with the shackle of the consensus rule in CCW decision-making, meant that little or no progress could be made in terms of strengthening Protocol V. At the CCW Third Review Conference in 2006, the dynamic shifted when twenty-five states called for an agreement prohibiting outright the use of cluster munitions.[76] Still there was no meaningful response: the final report of the Review Conference only went so far as to say that consideration of the problem would continue.[77] Frustrated by the lack of progress, the Norwegian government announced that it would host an international conference in Oslo in early 2007 to 'start a process towards an international ban on cluster munitions that have unacceptable humanitarian consequences'.[78]

It was a clear echo of Canada's strategy in 1996 in the context of anti-personnel landmines to leave the multi-lateral process. The Oslo Process had begun.

[74] For an early example of a dismissal of the humanitarian concerns, see W. J. Fenrick, 'New Developments in the Law Concerning the Use of Conventional Weapons in Armed Conflict' (1981) *Canadian Yearbook of International Law* 229, 239 ('other states were represented by delegates with an abundance of humanitarian zeal, but unfortunately this zeal was often coupled with an apparent lack of appreciation of the technical and military considerations involved'). At the time, Fenrick was the Director of International Law for the Canadian Department of National Defence.

[75] Borrie, *Unacceptable Harm*, above n. 5, pp. 64 and 132–4.

[76] 'Proposal for a Decision on a Mandate on Cluster Munitions' CCW/CONF.III/WP.14 discussed by Borrie, *Unacceptable Harm*, above n. 5, pp. 137–8.

[77] Final Report, *Third Review Conference of the States Parties to the Convention on Prohibitions or Restrictions on the Use of Certain Conventional Weapons Which May be Deemed to be Excessively Injurious or to Have Indiscriminate Effect* (CCW/CONF.III/11 (Part II), Geneva, 2006) 6 (Decision 1) discussed by Borrie, *Unacceptable Harm*, above n. 5, p. 138.

[78] Ibid.

D The Oslo Process

The Oslo Conference was convened in February 2007 and closed with a Declaration in which the forty-nine participating states committed themselves to concluding a legally binding instrument by 2008 which would prohibit 'cluster munitions that cause unacceptable harm to civilians' and would 'establish a framework for cooperation and assistance to ensure clearance of contaminated areas, destruction of existing stockpiles of weapons and provision of victim assistance'.[79] Thus, the two humanitarian concerns associated with cluster munitions had converged and cluster munitions were finally being considered through a stand-alone treaty.

In many ways, the ensuing Oslo Process closely followed the blueprint created by the Ottawa Process for APLMs.[80] A 'core group' of states emerged to lead the overall process: Austria, the Holy See, Ireland, Mexico, New Zealand, Norway and Peru.[81] A series of meetings was convened to prepare for the Diplomatic Conference: in Lima, Peru from 23–25 May 2007; in Vienna, Austria from 5–7 December 2007; in Wellington, New Zealand from 18–22 February 2008. Interspersed with the political meetings were several technical meetings and regional meetings in order to garner support for the process and elaborate the issues in more detail.

The Diplomatic Conference itself was convened in Dublin from 19–30 May 2008. As with the Oslo Conference, negotiations were open to all states prepared to commit to the aim of banning cluster munitions.[82] Similarly, the Dublin Conference permitted extensive access by civil society.[83] While voting was provided for in the Rules of Procedure,[84] the treaty was ultimately adopted by consensus, with all 107 attending states agreeing to its adoption. Thus, the Convention on

[79] Declaration, Oslo Conference on Cluster Munitions (22–23 February 2007) reproduced in Nystuen and Casey-Maslen (eds.), *The Convention on Cluster Munitions*, above n. 11, Annex 2 (Oslo Declaration).

[80] Gro Nystuen, 'A New Treaty Banning Cluster Munitions: The Interplay between Disarmament Diplomacy and Humanitarian Requirements' in Cecilia M. Bailliet (ed.), *Security: A Multidisciplinary Normative Approach*, (Leiden; Boston: Martinus Nijhoff Publishers, 2009), pp. 137, 145.

[81] Dáithí O'Ceallaigh, 'Ireland the Negotiation of the Convention on Cluster Munitions' (2014) 25 *Irish Studies in International Affairs* 53, 54.

[82] Draft Rules of Procedure, Diplomatic Conference for the Adoption of a Cluster Munitions Convention, CCM/2, 19 May 2008, rule 1.1.

[83] Ibid., rule 1.2.

[84] Ibid., rule 36.

Cluster Munitions finally took its place beside its sister treaty, the APLM Convention.

E The Convention on Cluster Munitions

In terms of its structure and content, the treaty is closely modelled on the APLM Convention. It bans the use, development, production, acquisition, stockpiling, retention or transfer of cluster munitions.[85] It requires states parties to destroy their cluster munitions stockpiles, and to clear and destroy all cluster munition remnants under their jurisdiction or control.[86] Like the APLM Convention, it is a disarmament treaty in that it not only bans the use of a weapon, but it also requires elimination of the weapons themselves.[87]

Articles 4 and 5 are also generally based on the APLM Convention, but as I will show in more detail in the next section, both articles reveal a significant evolution in the humanitarian approach. Article 4 addresses the question of clearance of cluster munitions remnants. While these provisions are generally based on the APLM Convention and on Protocol V in that there are time-bound requirements for marking, clearing and destroying remnants in contaminated areas, a significant difference is that Article 4(4) introduces a provision whereby user states are assigned *some* responsibility for assisting with clearance munitions which were created prior to the entry into force of the treaty.[88] This is discussed in more detail in Section V below.

Another evolution in the humanitarian approach relates to the provisions requiring assistance to be provided to victims of cluster munitions use. Article 5 provides that each state party, with respect to cluster munitions victims in its jurisdiction or control, must 'adequately provide' assistance including not only medical care, rehabilitation and psychological support, but also provide for their 'social and economic inclusion'. 'Cluster munition victim' is a term defined in Article 2 and extends beyond the individual victim to their families and communities. The broadening of the concept of 'victim' in Article 2, combined with the increased obligations in providing assistance to victims in Article 5, has

[85] CCM art. 1.
[86] CCM arts 3 and 4.
[87] CCM art. 4.
[88] Stuart Casey-Maslen, 'Clearance and Destruction of Cluster Munition Remnants and Risk Reduction Education' in Nystuen and Casey-Maslen (eds.), *The Convention on Cluster Munitions*, above n. 11, p. 273, para. 4.86.

significantly strengthened the humanitarian credentials of the treaty beyond the parameters of the APLM Convention – a point I address further in Section V.A below.

Overall then, in a number of respects the CCM represented a consolidation of the APLM Convention: in terms of the original roots of the campaigns; the early phases of the CCW process; the growing humanitarian concerns and belief among increasing number of states that the CCW consensus decision-making practice was wholly inadequate to address the concerns; and the way in which an alternative multilateral process was pursued. Beyond that, the CCM seemed to have even more robust humanitarian credentials in the way victim assistance obligations were articulated. Seen in this way, humanitarian disarmament had not only consolidated with the conclusion of the CCM, it was gaining ground.

However, the treaty is not just a straightforward consolidation of earlier humanitarian disarmament practice and, as I will show, it is not even a wholly progressive move in humanitarian terms. I explore two key issues in the remainder of the chapter: the first is the way that the CCM defines cluster munitions (Section IV) which I argue is an important progressive development; the second examines the user-state responsibility issue (Section V) and here I raise some concerns about how this undermines the interests of *state* victims of the use of cluster munitions (in distinction to individual victims).

IV Defining Cluster Munitions: Advancing Humanitarian Disarmament

The way in which the treaty defines cluster munitions is a significant departure from the approaches taken in earlier disarmament treaties. As I will show, the definition operates on the basis that all cluster munitions are prohibited by the treaty, unless a particular cluster munition is expressly permitted: that is, the treaty adopts a 'prohibited unless expressly permitted' approach. This is in contrast to the more orthodox approach in earlier treaties in which a prohibited weapon is often defined using a 'permitted unless expressly prohibited' approach. In this section, I explain this development and suggest that it has the potential to fundamentally challenge weapons discourse because it contains the seed of what we might see as a complete reversal of where the burden lies in deciding that a particular weapon is unacceptable.

A The Difficulty with Defining Cluster Munitions

Defining the scope of any weapon prohibition has always been difficult and contentious. Typically, there will be a tug of war between those who are campaigning for the strongest possible ban, advocating the most comprehensive and broad definition of the weapon in question and those who resist any curtailment of what is generally perceived to be the right of sovereign states to equip their armed forces with all and any weapons that have military utility and are not expressly prohibited.

In the context of cluster munitions, the definitional issue was especially complex because of the number of different types of cluster munitions which exist.[89] It has been estimated that there are around 210 different types of cluster munitions available.[90] For example, the number of submunitions contained within the 'parent' munition can vary from two to 700.[91] Further, the size, weight and design of those submunitions can vary enormously. Some cluster munitions are designed to be anti-materiel, others anti-personnel and still others are dual purpose. Cluster munitions can be delivered in a variety of ways: artillery, air-dropped, or rockets or missiles.[92] Some cluster munitions have self-destruct mechanisms with a variety of such mechanisms available: mechanical, electronic or pyrotechnical. The most recent technology has allowed for sensor-fused munitions, meaning that the submunitions can be preprogrammed to attack only a predetermined target, for example, an armoured tank.[93]

In light of this broad range of types of cluster munitions, there was a spectrum of positions on what categories of cluster munitions should be prohibited.[94] At one end of the spectrum, some states (and many in civil society) favoured an absolute ban on all cluster munitions. This position

[89] See overview discussion by Borrie, *Unacceptable Harm*, above n. 5, pp. 21–5.

[90] Mark Hiznay, 'Survey of Cluster Munitions Produced and Stockpiled' in ICRC, *Humanitarian, Military, Technical and Legal Challenges of Cluster Munitions*, above n. 12, p. 23. See also Breitegger, *Cluster Munitions and International Law*, above n. 9, p. 14.

[91] The BLU-24 used in Vietnam, Laos and Cambodia in the 1960s contained 700 BLU-26 submunitions, which in turn potentially released thousands of steel fragments on detonation. See Brietteger, *Cluster Munitions and International Law*, above n. 12, p. 20.

[92] See generally, Geneva International Centre for Humanitarian Demining (GICHD) and Implementation Support Unit, Convention on Cluster Munitions (ISU CCM), *A Guide to Cluster Munitions* (2013).

[93] Hiznay, 'Survey of Cluster Munitions Produced and Stockpiled', above n. 90, p. 27; Breitteger, *Cluster Munitions and International Law*, above n. 12, p. 17.

[94] See Bonnie Docherty et al., 'Article 2. Definitions' in Nystuen and Casey-Maslen (eds.), *The Convention on Cluster Munitions*, above n. 11, 2.33–2.138.

had the advantage of conveying a simple message and it rejected the idea that it was possible to have a 'technical fix' to the humanitarian difficulties, that had been such a feature of the debates in the context of APLMs.[95] The technical fix approach was treated with suspicion on the part of other states because the data on the technology was suspect (for example, the unreliability of data on failure rates).[96] Still other states, particularly from the developing world, distrusted the technical fix approach on the basis that it privileges the technologically advanced and wealthy states which can afford to invest in the new permitted technology, leaving the developing world with outdated and prohibited weapons stocks.

B How the Definition Evolved

At Oslo, the debate about how widely drawn any prohibition should be was sidestepped by avoiding defining the term 'cluster munitions' and instead employing the language of 'unacceptable harm'.[97] Thus, in the Oslo Declaration, states committed themselves to:

Conclude by 2008 a legally binding international instrument that will:

> (i) prohibit the use, production, transfer and stockpiling of cluster munitions that cause unacceptable harm to civilians, . . .[98]

Three months later, in Lima in May 2007, a definition was set out in the discussion text prepared in advance of the meeting:

> Air carried dispersal systems or air delivered, surface or sub-surface launched containers, that are designed to disperse explosive submunitions intended to detonate following separation from the container or dispenser, unless they are designed to, manually or automatically, aim, detect and engage point targets, or are meant for smoke or flaring, or unless their use is regulated or prohibited under other treaties.[99]

95 A common example of a technical solution is self-destruct mechanisms.

96 See for example, the positions of Indonesia, Guatemala, Jamaica, Mexico and Venezuela set out in *Summary Record of the First Session of the Committee of the Whole*, Diplomatic Conference for the Adoption of a Convention on Cluster Munitions (CCM/CW/SR/1, 18 June 2008), p. 5.

97 For a detailed discussion about the drafting of the Oslo Declaration, see Borrie, *Unacceptable Harm*, above n. 5, pp. 153–7.

98 Oslo Declaration, above n. 79.

99 *Chairs' Discussion Text on a Legally Binding International Instrument that will Prohibit the Use, Production, Transfer and Stockpiling of Cluster Munitions that Cause Unacceptable Harm to Civilians* (Lima, 23–25 May 2007), reproduced in Nystuen and Casey-Maslen (eds.), *The Convention on Cluster Munitions*, above n. 11, Annex 3 (*Lima Discussion Text*).

This definition would have excluded the uncontentious flares and smoke munitions as well as the more contentious sensor-fused submunitions, that is, submunitions that have the ability to identify particular targets through infra-red or laser technology.

The definition underwent a fundamental change in Vienna. Now, the Chair's text simply read:

> 'Cluster munition' means a munition that is designed to disperse or release explosive sub-munitions, and includes those explosive sub-munitions. It does not mean the following:

a) . . .
b) . . .
c) . . .[100]

It would be difficult to overstate the significance of this change in structure and approach. The first sentence is as widely drawn a definition as it was possible to envisage and it was left to the second (still incomplete) sentence to articulate what would be excluded from the prohibition. The most significant point is that, under this structure, the onus had shifted from requiring prohibitionist states to provide evidence and justify why a particular type or design of cluster munition should be *included* in a list of prohibited weapons, to resting with permissive states having to provide evidence that a particular type or design should be *excluded* from the broadly stated prohibition.

Such an approach – using a broad-based definition but then going on to list weapons that are not covered within that definition – was not entirely novel. For example, Protocol III to the CCW Convention defined incendiary weapons using the same general structure:

1. 'Incendiary weapon' means any weapon or munition which is primarily designed to set fire to objects or to cause burn injury to persons through the action of flame, heat, or combination thereof, produced by a chemical reaction of a substance delivered on the target.
    (a) Incendiary weapons can take the form of, for example, flame throwers, fougasses, shells, rockets, grenades, mines, bombs and other containers of incendiary substances.
    (b) Incendiary weapons do not include:

[100] Dated 14 November 2007, reproduced in Nystuen and Casey-Maslen (eds.), *The Convention on Cluster Munitions*, above n. 11, Annex 4, art. 2 (*Vienna Discussion Text*).

(i) Munitions which may have incidental incendiary effects, such as illuminants, tracers, smoke or signalling systems;
(ii) Munitions designed to combine penetration, blast or fragmentation effects with an additional incendiary effect, such as armour-piercing projectiles, fragmentation shells, explosive bombs and similar combined-effects munitions in which the incendiary effect is not specifically designed to cause burn injury to persons, but to be used against military objectives, such as armoured vehicles, aircraft and installations or facilities.[101]

However, there is a very significant difference between Protocol III to the CCW Convention and the way in which the definition of cluster munitions was being approached in the context of the CCM negotiations. For incendiary weapons, the exclusions listed were not based on the types of weapons that were considered not to raise humanitarian concerns. Rather, the list of exclusions contained the types of incendiary weapons that the militarily significant states insisted on being able to continue to use against enemy targets irrespective of the extent of unnecessary suffering or indiscriminate effects of the weapons. In other words, they were to be excluded from the prohibition irrespective of any humanitarian concerns because of the asserted imperative of military necessity.

Thus, the development of the prohibited-unless-explicitly-excluded definition in the CCM marked a fundamental shift in how cluster munitions were to be discussed. Previously, the humanitarian consequences had to be weighed against military necessity and it was only if the consequences outweighed the military necessity that the weapon in question would be prohibited.[102] Now, the starting presumption in any discussion was that cluster munitions should be prohibited, unless it could be demonstrated conclusively that any specific cluster munition was sufficiently accurate and reliable to avoid excessive harm to civilians.[103]

This approach – prohibited-unless-explicitly-excluded – remained in place throughout the Oslo Process and forms the basis of the definition as finally agreed in Dublin:

> 'Cluster munition' means a conventional munition that is designed to disperse or release explosive submunitions each weighing less than 20

[101] Protocol III art. 1.
[102] Rappert and Moyes, 'The Prohibition of Cluster Munitions', above n. 5, p. 243.
[103] Ibid., p. 244.

kilograms, and includes those explosive submunitions. It does not mean the following:

(a) A munition or submunition designed to dispense flares, smoke, pyrotechnics or chaff; or a munition designed exclusively for an air defence role;
(b) A munition or submunition designed to produce electrical or electronic effects;
(c) A munition that, in order to avoid indiscriminate area effects and the risks posed by unexploded submunitions, has all of the following characteristics:

(i) Each munition contains fewer than ten explosive submunitions;
(ii) Each explosive submunition weighs more than four kilograms;
(iii) Each explosive submunition is designed to detect and engage a single target object;
(iv) Each explosive submunition is equipped with an electronic self-destruction mechanism;
(v) Each explosive submunition is equipped with an electronic self-deactivating feature. . .[104]

On one view, this definition could be seen as a capitulation to the military technology point of view – a concession to the 'technical fix' approach. Certainly, it did not meet the categorical ban starting point of the prohibitionists.[105] However, the way the definition is drafted has ensured that it does capture the vast majority of cluster munitions in circulation, and given that the requirements of sub-paragraph (c) are cumulative, the definition would seem to have caught cluster munitions that cause 'unacceptable harm'.[106]

What is of interest in this discussion is not so much the scope of the definition, but rather the more fundamental shift which occurred in the way in which the definition was agreed. In effect, the structure and rationale of prohibited-unless-expressly-excluded-from-the-prohibition in the CCM

[104] CCM art. 2(2). For a detailed account of the negotiations on the definition, see Borrie, Treaty To Ban Cluster Munitions, above n. 5, pp. 206–8; 268–79; and 316–17; and Docherty et al., 'Article 2. Definitions', above n. 94, paras 2.33–2.38.

[105] For example, while the BLU744 used in Kosovo and the M85 used in Lebanon are prohibited under the treaty (having 200 submunitions in each parent munition), the British and Swiss-made BONUS and SMArt155 are not caught within the treaty's prohibition because they meet all the (cumulative) requirements of (c), including being sensor-fused. See Rae McGrath (on behalf of Handicap International Network), 'Sensor Fuzed Submunitions and Clean Battlefields: Examining the Facts' presentation to delegates at the Dublin Diplomatic Conference, 21 May 2008.

[106] Borrie, *Unacceptable Harm*, above n. 5, pp. 332–3.

definition marks an important instance of a treaty reversing the burden of proof regarding the humanitarian impact of a particular weapon.

C *Why Reversing the Burden of Proof Matters for Humanitarian Disarmament*

The so-called 'Lotus Principle' in international law – the idea that states are sovereign and restrictions on that sovereignty cannot be presumed – epitomises the consensual understanding of international law which has prevailed for several centuries.[107] In other words, any legal challenge to a state's actions must point to a prohibition, and in the absence of such a prohibition – whether in treaty law or in custom – the actions are presumed to be permitted.[108] Under sustained challenge in a variety of contexts for manifesting an extreme positivist school of thought, the fact remains that this orientation (permitted unless prohibited) is still the bedrock of mainstream international legal discourse today.

In weapons discourse too, this approach is pervasive. That is, the working presumption has been that a weapon is lawful unless a specific prohibition can be identified. Such a prohibition might be drawn from general rules of international humanitarian law (rules against indiscriminate attacks for example) or there may be a particular treaty or customary prohibition of a particular category of weapon. This permitted-unless-prohibited starting point is evident not just in diplomatic negotiations, but also in legal reasoning. For example, the International Court of Justice in the *Nicaragua Case* held that 'in international law there are no rules, other than such rules as may be accepted by the State concerned, by treaty or otherwise, whereby the level of armaments of a sovereign State can be limited'.[109] And in the *Legality of Nuclear Weapons Case*, the permitted-unless-prohibited approach was relied upon by the nuclear powers to underpin their argument about the legality of the use of nuclear weapons or the threat of use.[110]

107 *The Case of the S.S. Lotus*, 1927 PCIJ Series A. No. 10.

108 But see the insightful discussion by An Hertogen, 'Letting *Lotus* Bloom' (2016) 26(4) *European Journal of International Law* 901 arguing that this understanding of *Lotus* is inaccurate.

109 *Military and Paramilitary Activities in and against Nicaragua (Nicaragua* v. *United States) (Merits)* [1986] ICJ Rep 14, para. 269.

110 *Legality of the Threat of Use of Nuclear Weapons* (Advisory Opinion) (Judgment) [1996] ICJ Rep 226. See the detailed discussion of the Lotus Principle in the context of the Advisory Opinion: Ole Spiermann, 'Lotus and the Double Structure of International

Operating within this positivist landscape then, disarmament campaigns generally start from a position of needing to demonstrate why a particular weapon is unacceptable, and the onus of challenging a weapon – on ethical or legal grounds – is on those who adopt the prohibitionist stand. The approach is evident whenever new weapons technology emerges, from the atomic bomb through to contemporary debates on autonomous weapons.[111]

It has also been the dynamic at play in the debates around cluster munitions. As discussed in Chapter 4, in the early attempts to challenge the legality of cluster munitions, throughout the series of expert group meetings convened by the ICRC in the 1970s, the onus lay on those states seeking limits or prohibitions to show, either that existing law did in fact prohibit the use of cluster munitions, or to mount an argument that states ought to agree on such limits or prohibitions.[112] This dynamic persisted through the work of the government experts in the context of the CCW, as discussed in Sections III.A and III.B above.

Vienna, then, represented a paradigm shift for humanitarian disarmament negotiations. With the introduction of the Chair's text, a different logic was at play. Now, all cluster munitions were prohibited – unless an argument could be made that a particular type of munition should be exempted from the prohibition. That is, the animating logic now was prohibited-unless-permitted. In essence, the Vienna text reversed the burden of proof.[113] Consequently, the onus shifted onto the permissive states to justify why a particular category of cluster munition should be permitted.

To what extent is it possible to extrapolate from the CCM and apply the approach either to another category of weapons (for example, autonomous weapons), or more ambitiously, to weapons discourse as a whole? Such an approach may seem to resonate with Article 35(1) of the 1977

Legal Argument' in Laurence Boisson de Chazournes and Philippe Sands (eds.), *International Law, the International Court of Justice and Nuclear Weapons* (Cambridge: Cambridge University Press, 1999), p. 131.

111 On atomic weapons: J. L. Kunz, 'The Chaotic Status of the Laws of War' (1951) 45 *American Journal of International Law* 37. On autonomous weapons: Max van Kralingen, 'Use of Weapons: Should We Ban the Development of Autonomous Weapons Systems?' (2016) 18(2) *International Journal of Intelligence, Security, and Public Affairs* 132.

112 See Chapter 4, Section III.

113 John Borrie, *Unacceptable Harm*, above n. 5, pp. 316–17 and Rappert and Moyes, 'The Prohibition of Cluster Munitions', above n. 5.

Additional Protocol I to the Geneva Conventions 1949 (Additional Protocol I), which provides that 'the right of the Parties ... to choose methods or means of warfare is not unlimited'.[114] It may be thought that this provision supports a prohibited-unless-explicitly-permitted approach. However, the Commentary to Article 35 makes it clear that, far from heralding a new paradigm, the intention behind Article 35(1) was simply to reaffirm the law in force, most obviously Article 22 of the Hague Regulations 1907.[115] It was simply a recognition that there were already treaty and customary rules in existence about methods and means of warfare.

One might also argue that the obligation to review new weapons in Article 36 of Additional Protocol I points to a prohibited-unless-expressly-permitted approach. Article 36 provides:

> In the study, development, acquisition or adoption of a new weapon, means or method of warfare, a High Contracting Party is under an obligation to determine whether its employment would, in some or all circumstances, be prohibited by this Protocol or by any other rule of international law applicable to the High Contracting Party.

However, such an argument would not only ignore the intentions of the drafters of that provision but also the subsequent practice of states in relation to Article 36. During the negotiations, states were firmly opposed to there being any form of international oversight of any such weapons reviews. Rather, the prevailing view was a matter for the sovereign state to determine when and how such a review would take place.[116] Further, subsequent state practice shows that states have continued to jealously guard their sovereignty in their modest and inconsistent implementation of this provision.[117]

A more promising train of thought might rely on the developing precautionary principle in international law. This principle captures the

[114] Protocol Additional to the Geneva Conventions of 12 August 1949, and Relating to the Protection of Victims of International Armed Conflicts (Protocol I), opened for signature 8 June 1977, 1125 UNTS 3 (entered into force 7 December 1978).

[115] International Committee of the Red Cross, *Commentary on the Additional Protocols of 8 June 1977 to the Geneva Conventions of 12 August 1949* (Geneva: Martinus Nijhoff Publishers, 1987), para. 1382.

[116] Boothby, *Weapons and The Law of Armed Conflict*, above n. 8, pp. 342–3.

[117] See generally Natalia Jevglevskaja, *States Weapons Review Obligations under Article 36 of the 1977 Additional Protocol I to the Geneva Conventions and Beyond* (PhD, University of Melbourne, 2018). Indeed, Hays Parks in 2005 argues that the word 'new' in Article 36 creates a rebuttable presumption of legality for pre-existing weapons and munitions: W. Hays Parks, 'Conventional Weapons and Weapons Reviews' (2005) 8 *Yearbook of International Humanitarian Law* 55, 114. My thanks to Natalia Jevglevskaja for pointing this out.

idea that states should refrain from activities that may be hazardous, but where there is scientific uncertainty about the nature or scope of that hazard. It evolved in the international legal system in the context of environmental law and the law of the sea.[118] In its *Legality of Nuclear Weapons Case*, the International Court of Justice (ICJ) opined that the precautionary principle 'is now part of the corpus of international law relating to the environment'.[119] More recently, the ICJ stated in *Pulp Mills on the River Paraguay* that a state is 'obliged to use all the means at its disposal in order to avoid activities which take place in its territory, or in any area under its jurisdiction, causing significant damage to the environment of another State'.[120]

However, as the law stands today, the precautionary principle may not reach far enough to underpin an argument that the burden of proof reversal in the CCM should be repeated, much less that there is some legal obligation to reverse the burden of proof. First, the precautionary principle has only developed in the context of environmental law matters to date, and it is therefore a stretch to apply it to either international humanitarian law (the use of a weapon), or to disarmament (the absolute prohibition of a weapon and its subsequent destruction).[121] Second, the precautionary principle has traditionally been couched in such a way as to capture actions of a state taking place on its territory, rather than all actions (such as treaty negotiations). Third, in *Pulp Mills of the River Paraguay*, the ICJ specifically rejected the argument that a precautionary approach reversed the burden of proof in the litigation before the Court.[122] Quite apart from whether the law has developed sufficiently to require a shift in the burden of proof, or to overturn the Lotus Principle where weapons are concerned, the problem with drawing on the precautionary principle to assess any particular weapon is that the calculation of risks might ignore the dangers posed by other weapons that will inevitably be used as a replacement.[123]

[118] Meinhard Schröder, 'Precautionary Approach/Principle' *Max Planck Encyclopedia of Public International Law* (March 2014).

[119] *Legality of the Threat or Use of Nuclear Weapons*, above n. 110, para. 29.

[120] *Pulp Mills on the River Paraguay* (*Argentina* v. *Paraguay*), ICJ Reports [2010], para. 101.

[121] Despite the pronouncements of the ICJ as discussed above, there are also many who dispute the existence of the precautionary principle as a legal principle. See discussion by Lesley Wexler, 'Limiting the Precautionary Principle: Weapons Regulation in the Face of Scientific Uncertainty' (2006) 39(2) *University of California Davis Law Review* 459, 490–4.

[122] *Pulp Mills on the River Paraguay*, above n. 120, para. 164.

[123] Wexler, 'Limiting the Precautionary Principle', above n. 121, p. 497.

Despite all these difficulties, the CCM did mark an important shift in treaty-drafting practice and the long-term legacy could be that we no longer leave entirely unchallenged the *Lotus* presumption when it comes to weapons. That in turn may be the seeds of the precautionary principle emerging in the context of weapons law.[124]

V User State Responsibility in Humanitarian Disarmament

A second complexity to emerge from the CCM's humanitarian credentials relates to the remedial provisions in the treaty, particularly those on victim assistance. The CCM is considered a major advance and innovation in humanitarian disarmament practice because those provisions went well beyond previous practice.[125] However, I suggest that presenting these provisions as unqualified humanitarian successes masks a deeper dynamic that is revealed when the user state responsibility debate is excavated. That dynamic suggests that the humanitarian credentials of the treaty may have come at a considerable cost. More specifically, I suggest that the inclusion of much stronger victim assistance provisions coupled with the failure to adequately address the responsibility of user states, constitutes a missed opportunity to more fruitfully engage with the source of the problem of explosive remnants of war. There is also a danger that these aspects of the CCM may have set some kind of a precedent.[126]

A The Treaty's Provisions on Victim Assistance

The treaty has extensive and far-reaching provisions on victim assistance and remedial provisions. Leaving aside some general references to civilian suffering, victim assistance is specifically mentioned in five preambular paragraphs.[127] This is an early signal of the importance of the issue in the negotiations and lays the groundwork for what comes in the treaty itself.

124 Rappert and Moyes, 'The Prohibition of Cluster Munitions', above n. 5.

125 For general discussion, see Docherty, 'Breaking New Ground', above n. 3; Markus A. Reiterer, 'Assistance to Cluster Munitions Victims: A Major Step Toward Humanitarian Disarmament' (2010) 1 *Disarmament Forum* 25; and Mika Hayashi, 'The Convention on Cluster Munitions and the Clearance of Cluster Munition Remnants: Whose Responsibility, and How to Ensure Effective Implementation?' (2012) 3 *International Humanitarian Legal Studies* 322.

126 For a discussion on how the question played out in the context of the Treaty on the Prohibition of Nuclear Weapons see Chapter 7, Section VI.B.

127 CCM preambular paras 6, 7, 8, 10 and 18.

Turning to the text, 'cluster munition victim' is expansively defined. Article 2(1) defines the phrase as including:

> [A]ll persons who have been killed or suffered physical or psychological injury, economic loss, social marginalisation or substantial impairment of the realisation of their rights caused by the use of cluster munitions. They include those persons directly impacted by cluster munitions as well as their affected families and communities. . .

Thus, the treaty has adopted a greatly expanded understanding of 'victim' including not only direct survivors or those killed by the weapons, but also their families and communities. In addition to physical harm, the term also captures psychological, social, economic or other harms.

This broad understanding of victim takes on particular significance in light of Article 5, which provides:

> Each State Party with respect to cluster munition victims in areas under its jurisdiction or control shall, in accordance with applicable international humanitarian and human rights law, adequately provide age- and gender-sensitive assistance, including medical care, rehabilitation and psychological support, as well as provide for their social and economic inclusion. Each State Party shall make every effort to collect reliable relevant data with respect to cluster munition victims.

Article 5(2) goes on to specify how those obligations might be fulfilled, including assessing the needs of victims, developing relevant laws and policies, mobilising necessary resources and consulting with victims. The broad understanding of who falls within the term 'victim', coupled with extensive binding obligations to provide specified assistance to those victims, creates potentially far-reaching and onerous obligations.

Clearance and destruction obligations, addressed in Article 4, are also an essential part of the remedial aspects of the treaty. The text is based on the APLM Convention, although the CCM is more detailed, more prescriptive and is couched in obligatory language.[128] Thus, the CCM is more victim-oriented than its predecessors.

However, in examining the question of which states parties take on these far-reaching obligations, a more complex picture emerges. Article 5, setting out the obligations owed to victims, is directed not to states which have used cluster munitions, or even to all states parties to the treaty, but rather to states parties with victims under their jurisdiction or

[128] Compare APLM Convention art. 5(2) with CCM art. 4(2).

control.[129] There is an attempt to counterbalance this emphasis on the territorial state's obligations through Article 6, which calls on states parties 'in a position to do so' to provide assistance to states affected by cluster munitions. That assistance involves assistance in clearance and in destruction,[130] as well as directly with victim assistance.[131] However, Article 6 falls well short of imposing an actual obligation to provide assistance, even for user states. For example, while Article 6(1) provides that each state party has 'the right to seek and receive assistance', Article 6(2) only calls on states parties 'in a position to do so' to provide such assistance. Similarly in the specific context of victim assistance, Article 6(7) calls on states parties 'in a position to do so' to provide such assistance to victims and Article 6(8) refers to contributions to the economic and social recovery needed as a result of cluster munition use in affected states.

The situation is slightly different in the context of abandoned cluster munitions used prior to the entry into force of the treaty. In this context, the user state is 'strongly encouraged' to provide information and assistance to facilitate marking, clearance and destruction of the said weapons, but this language still falls short of imposing an obligation.[132]

B *The User State Responsibility Issue*

The exhortatory language of Article 6 and the silence on the user state's responsibility in Article 5 provide a wholly inadequate counterbalance to the extensive obligations imposed on the territorial state. Given that user state responsibility was such a cornerstone of the NAM campaigns in the 1960s and 1970s, how and why did this shift happen and what does this mean for the practice of humanitarian disarmament?

It was an issue from the start of the negotiations. The first discussion text – the Lima Discussion Text – assigned responsibility for clearance and destruction to the territorial state.[133] The locus of responsibility for victim assistance was implicitly with the territorial state.[134] The corresponding international cooperation and assistance provisions were

[129] CCM art. 5(1).
[130] CCM art. 6, sub-paragraphs 3, 4, 5, 6 and 11.
[131] In particular CCM art. 6, sub-paras 7, 8 and 9.
[132] CCM art. 4(4).
[133] *Lima Discussion Text*, above n. 99, art. 4.
[134] Ibid. art. 6(1).

couched in tentative language.[135] Article 5(1) provided that each state party had a right to 'seek and receive assistance' but only 'where feasible' and 'to the extent possible'. In terms of the obligation to provide assistance, that only applied to those states 'in a position to do so'.[136]

In Vienna, the dynamic of territorial state responsibility became entrenched. Although the 'where feasible' and 'to the extent possible' language was deleted from Article 5(1), thus strengthening the right of the territorial state to seek and receive assistance, the corresponding obligations to provide assistance remained qualified by the 'in a position to do so' language.[137] Further, the general obligations to provide assistance were made more specific and here the definition of victim was broadened. All of this increased the burden on the territorial state. The essential balance remained in the treaty text as ultimately adopted.

It was not that this balance was struck without resistance. It is worth recalling that in the early years during the campaign against indiscriminate weapons more generally, the NAM states were very much focused on the need to assign responsibility to the user states.[138] Not surprisingly then, this shift to the territorial state was resisted by several states. In October 2007 (that is, between the Lima and Vienna meetings), the issue was addressed at the Belgrade Conference of States Affected by Cluster Munitions.[139] While that Conference was an important event in terms of the recognition of the survivors of cluster munitions, with twenty-two out of thirty-seven attending states being countries affected by cluster munitions,[140] it also was an opportunity for those states to address the role of user states. The Commentary (written by the facilitator in question) explains what happened:

> In raising this issue some delegations also demanded reparations for injury incurred through the use of cluster munitions by another State. The sensitivity of this issue, however, could have proven detrimental for the way forward on victim assistance. The facilitator of the victim assistance discussions in Belgrade therefore urged participants to focus on the humanitarian aspects of the victim assistance package.[141]

[135] Ibid. art. 5.

[136] Ibid. arts 5(3) and 5(4).

[137] For discussion, see Markus Reiterer and Tirza Leibowitz, 'Article 5. Victim Assistance' in Nystuen and Casey-Maslen, *The Convention on Cluster Munitions*, above n. 11, para. 5.22.

[138] See Chapter 4, Section III.

[139] Borrie, *Unacceptable Harm*, above n. 5, pp. 179–82.

[140] Ibid., p. 180.

[141] Reiterer and Leibowitz, 'Article 5. Victim Assistance', above n 137, para. 5.16.

Thus, state responsibility for the consequences of use of cluster munitions was subordinated to the rights of victims themselves. Not all states were happy. The Philippines, for example, proposed this text:

> When a State Party, before entry into force of the Convention for it, has used or abandoned cluster munitions in areas under the jurisdiction or control of another State Party, the former State Party *shall have the responsibility to help* the latter State Party in addressing the requirements of victim assistance as delineated in Article 5(1).[142]

Other proposals were less forceful, but still were concerned to strengthen the responsibilities on user states. The Cluster Munitions Coalition, for example, proposed an amendment to Article 6(2) that would have added the words 'and particularly user states' to the provision that exhorted all states parties in a position to do so to provide assistance.[143] A number of other participating states supported strengthening the international assistance provisions in favour of the territorial state. For example, Botswana argued:

> The fact that there is no obligation on States Parties to assist others in the form of a fund to meet the obligation to destroy cluster munitions may prove an obstacle to those in the developing world that may not have enough funds to fulfil their obligations. The current draft refers to the provision of assistance by States Parties 'in a position to do so', which lacks obligatory force. Part of the Mine Ban Treaty failure has been a lack of funding. Therefore, the provisions of Article 6 should be strengthened.[144]

Indonesia as well wanted the treaty to recognise the special responsibility of user states.[145] None of these arguments prevailed. The response was couched in the language of the need to ensure that the victim provisions were not compromised. The Facilitator justified this position in the Commentary to Article 6:

> A discussion of user responsibility could have lead to an undue politicization of the debate on a topic that had hitherto profited from its predominantly humanitarian character. The President of the Conference, in

142 Proposal by the Philippines for the Amendment of Article 5, Diplomatic Conference for the Adoption of a Convention on Cluster Munitions (CCM/58, 19 May 2008). Emphasis added.

143 Nystuen and Casey-Maslen, *The Convention on Cluster Munitions*, above n. 11, p. 673.

144 *Summary Record of the Second Session of the Committee of the Whole*, Diplomatic Conference for the Adoption of a Convention on Cluster Munitions (CCM/CW/SR/2, 18 June 2008) p. 8.

145 Ibid., p. 9.

> a move to preserve the humanitarian character of the debate, advised the Committee of the Whole without entering into any substantive discussion of the proposition that 'any issues of international cooperation and assistance' would be dealt with under Article 6. Subsequently, the issue of user responsibility only resurfaced rather briefly during the discussions on victim assistance.[146]

The shift in the locus of responsibility is more understandable when considered in the light of the implementation practice of the APLM Convention. There, over a period of several years, the 'specially affected states' (meaning the victim states) started to be assigned special responsibility for clearance and for victim assistance.[147] This shift in approach was justified in a number of ways: the need for states to have a sense of ownership of the problem; the need to fit assistance programmes for APLM victims in with existing national programmes; a concern about sovereignty and the suggestion that somehow external assistance (if it was indeed an obligation) would be seen as somehow imperialist or interventionist.[148] It was also considered that the growing emphasis on the responsibility of the specially affected states was balanced by the international cooperation and assistance provisions in the APLM Convention.[149]

The shift can also be understood as a compromise necessary to ensure the participation of the majority of states. Nevertheless, it ought to be presented as a *compromise*, rather than as a humanitarian triumph. Absolving user states of responsibility is a significant shift in the practice of humanitarian disarmament and, as I will show in the next chapter, one that is in danger of replicating itself in other contexts.

VI Conclusion

This chapter has shown the ways in which the CCM manifests and consolidates the practice of humanitarian disarmament, and builds on the APLM Convention before it. However, I have argued that the CCM was not only a consolidation, or a progression in the practice of humanitarian disarmament: while in some ways it represents a significant evolution, such as the way in which the weapon is defined, in other

146 Reiterer and Leibowitz, 'Article 5. Victim Assistance', above n 137, para. 5.36.
147 Evident from a reading over the years of the *Landmine Monitor Report*.
148 Reiterer, 'Assistance to Cluster Munitions Victims', above n. 125, p. 29.
149 Reiterer and Leibowitz, 'Article 5. Victim Assistance', above n 137, para. 5.53.

ways, it can be seen as being regressive, such as in relation to its provisions (or lack thereof) on user state responsibility.

In terms of the treaty's impact on the ground, or its normative influence, the evidence is mixed. There are fewer states parties and less buy-in to date from the Asian and African states than for the APLM Convention.[150] More recent years have seen catastrophic levels of use of cluster munitions in the Syrian conflict and in Yemen.[151] In November 2017, the United States reversed its stated policy to use cluster munitions only with a dud rate of less than 1 per cent after 2018.[152] However, there are other promising signs: in August 2016, the sole remaining US-based producer of cluster munitions announced it would stop producing the weapons, explaining that there was dwindling demand.[153] The Meetings of the States Parties continue to be a mechanism of oversight and, at times, condemnation.

More than a decade on from its conclusion, it is still not possible to say that the treaty has been an overwhelming success, either in terms of its contribution to the norm against cluster munitions, to the reality on the ground of ongoing cluster munition use or to the overall progression of humanitarian disarmament. That being said, the treaty is infinitely more relevant than the relatively weak protections offered by Protocol V or the more generally applicable provisions of international humanitarian law. And, as we will see in the next chapter, the treaty also provided guidance for what would become the next treaty in the story of humanitarian disarmament: the Treaty on the Prohibition of Nuclear Weapons.

150 At the time of writing, 107 states parties for the CCM, compared to 164 for the APLM Convention.

151 Cluster Munitions Coalition, Cluster Munition Monitor 2018.

152 Daryl Kimball, 'Cluster Munitions at a Glance' *Arms Control Association* (December 2017).

153 Thomas Gibbons-Neff, 'Why the Last U.S. Company Making Cluster Bombs Won't Produce them Anymore' *The Washington Post* (online), 2 September 2016, www.washingtonpost.com.

7

The Humanitarian Campaigns against Nuclear Weapons

I Introduction

A key insight to emerge from the preceding chapters is that the ultimately successful campaigns to negotiate treaties to ban anti-personnel landmines (APLMs) and cluster munitions in 1997 and 2008 respectively were not simply manifestations of a post–Cold War sense of optimism and renewed humanitarian sensibilities. Rather, those treaties had their roots in decades-long efforts to stigmatise, prohibit and eliminate the weapons in question. The same is true for nuclear weapons. The Treaty on the Prohibition of Nuclear Weapons (TPNW),[1] adopted in July 2017, is best understood, not just as the third instance of a post–Cold War humanitarian disarmament treaty following in the footsteps of the 1997 Anti-Personnel Landmines Convention (APLM Convention)[2] and the Convention on Cluster Munitions (CCM) adopted in 2008,[3] but rather as the culmination of over seventy years of campaigning against nuclear weapons.

The story of the overall 'struggle against the bomb' is so long, so varied and conducted on so many fronts that it would be impossible to capture in one chapter, or indeed in a single project.[4] Thus, my aim in this

[1] Treaty on the Prohibition of Nuclear Weapons, opened for signature 20 September 2017, (not yet in force).

[2] The Convention on the Prohibition of the Use, Stockpiling, Production, and Transfer of Anti-Personnel Mines and on their Destruction, opened for signature 3 December 1997, 2056 UNTS 211 (entered into force 1 March 1999).

[3] Convention on Cluster Munitions, opened for signature 3 December 2008, 2688 UNTS 39 (entered into force 1 August 2010).

[4] The expression 'struggle against the bomb' is taken from Lawrence Wittner's three volume history of the global movement against nuclear weapons: Lawrence S. Wittner, *One World or None: A History of the World Nuclear Disarmament Movement Through 1953* (Stanford: Stanford University Press, 1993); Lawrence S. Wittner, *Resisting the Bomb: A History of the*

chapter is not so much to give a full account of the various campaigns over the decades, but rather to confine my discussion to selected campaigns against nuclear weapons to explore whether and to what extent those campaigns can be seen as fitting within the rubric of 'humanitarian disarmament'. Because of this focus, a number of important issues and initiatives are excluded from consideration here: bilateral arms control initiatives between the Soviet Union (USSR) and the United States (US); the building of the nuclear non-proliferation regime in the form of the Nuclear Non-Proliferation Treaty 1968 (NPT);[5] debates and campaigns about the economic consequences of militarism;[6] attempts to bring a human rights lens to bear to the nuclear weapons debate;[7] and challenges to the authority of executive power.[8]

My focus here is on other campaigns against nuclear weapons which I argue are rightly seen as being exercises in 'humanitarian disarmament' and I suggest that this is so for two key reasons. First, I show how concerns about human health, the environment, the destruction that would be wrought by a nuclear war and the damage being caused by nuclear testing formed the core of the anti-nuclear campaigns. Thus, to a very large extent, the campaigns from the beginning were humanitarian in ethos and challenged the prevailing security discourse, that is, the

World Nuclear Disarmament Movement 1954–1970 (Stanford: Stanford University Press, 1997); and Lawrence S. Wittner, *Toward Nuclear Abolition: A History of the World Nuclear Disarmament Movement 1971 to the Present* (Stanford: Stanford University Press, 2003). See also the abbreviated version of this work in Lawrence Wittner, *Confronting the Bomb: A Short History of the World Nuclear Disarmament Movement* (Stanford: Stanford University Press, 2009).

5 Treaty on the Non-Proliferation of Nuclear Weapons, opened for signature 1 July 1968, 729 UNTS 161 (entered into force 5 March 1970).

6 See for example, Bertrand Russell, *Common Sense and Nuclear Warfare* (London: George Allen and Unwin Ltd, 1959).

7 See for example, Thomas G. Weiss and John Burroughs, 'Weapons of Mass Destruction and Human Rights' (2004) *Disarmament Forum* 3; Tim Wright, 'Do Nuclear Weapons Violate the Right to Life Under International Law?' (2008) 3 *Australian Journal of Peace Studies* 99; Louise Doswald-Beck, 'Human Rights Law and Nuclear Weapons' in Gro Nystuen, Stuart Casey-Maslen and Annie Golden Bersagel (eds.), *Nuclear Weapons Under International Law* (Cambridge: Cambridge University Press, 2014), p. 435.

8 See for example, Peter Quint, *Civil Disobedience and the German Courts: The Pershing Missile Protests in Comparative Perspective* (London: Routledge-Cavendish, 2008); Robert Surbrug, 'The Nuclear Weapons Freeze Movement in Massachusetts: 1980–1985' in Robert Surbrug (ed.), *Beyond Vietnam: The Politics of Protest in Massachusetts* (Amherst, Boston: University of Massachusetts Press, 2009); Jane Hickman, 'Greenham Women Against Cruise Missiles and others v Ronald Reagan and others', in John Dewar, Abdul Paliwala, Sol Picciotto and Matthias Ruete (eds.), *Nuclear Weapons, The Peace Movement and the Law* (Basingstoke: The Macmillan Press Ltd, 1986).

orthodoxy that nuclear weapons were essential for national security. This is despite the fact that those campaigns were not explicitly framed in humanitarian terms until relatively recently when they were repackaged under the humanitarian umbrella in the wake of the successful negotiations for the APLM Convention and the CCM.

The second basis on which I argue that from the beginning these campaigns constitute exercises in humanitarian disarmament is that civil society played a key part over the long history of the campaigns against nuclear weapons and was engaged from the immediate aftermath of the atomic bombings of Hiroshima and Nagasaki, forming key partnerships at different times with states in order to advance their anti-nuclear campaigns.

The chapter is structured chronologically with Section II analysing the period 1945–74, that is, the period from the first use of nuclear weapons through to the conclusion in the early 1970s of the *Nuclear Tests Cases* in the International Court of Justice (ICJ).[9] A central feature of the opposition to nuclear weapons in these decades was fear: fear of annihilation in the event of nuclear war; fear of radiation poisoning from the ongoing and escalating testing; and fear of environmental disaster from both use and testing. These concerns would endure beyond the 1970s, initially presented in the language of human health and (later) environmental protection; and ultimately relabelled within the 'Humanitarian Initiative' which emerged from 2010.

Section III explores two campaigns from the 1990s (both of which originated in the 1980s): the World Court Project (WCP), which led to an Advisory Opinion from the ICJ on the threat or use of nuclear weapons,[10] and the campaign to conclude the Comprehensive Test Ban Treaty 1996 (CTBT). In different ways, both these campaigns manifested significant instances of humanitarian disarmament practice and discourse. The WCP was a vivid example of civil society engagement with groups of states within the General Assembly and the World Health Organisation Assembly, and in preparing pleadings before the Court. Quite apart from the substance of the pleadings or the ultimate reasoning of the Court, that engagement marks the WCP as a key 'humanitarian disarmament' moment. The CTBT is an important milestone in humanitarian disarmament in that when its adoption stalled in the Conference on Disarmament

[9] *Nuclear Tests (New Zealand* v. *France) (Judgment)* [1974] ICJ Rep 457; *Nuclear Tests (Australia* v. *France) (Judgment)* [1974] ICJ Rep 253.

[10] *Legality of the Threat or Use of Nuclear Weapons (Advisory Opinion)* [1996] ICJ Rep 226.

(CD), the decision-making was moved to the General Assembly to sidestep that deadlock. This signalled a willingness by many states to step outside the orthodox disarmament architecture where necessary, a dynamic that we saw repeated again with the APLM Convention and the CCM.

The most recent humanitarian disarmament campaign, which culminated in the TPNW in 2017, is explored in Section IV. While this most recent phase was squarely modelled on the campaigns against APLMs and cluster munitions, there were some important nuances in the context of nuclear weapons (perhaps in part due to the differences in the weapons themselves). I focus on two important points: first, I argue that the victim assistance provisions in the TPNW evolved in important respects from the CCM; second, I suggest that perhaps the most important legacy of this treaty may be the way in which it has allowed the General Assembly to formally (re)carve out a role for itself in pursuing the cause of nuclear disarmament.

II 1945–74: from Hiroshima to the Hague

On 6 August 1945, as the Second World War was coming to an end, the United States launched an atomic bomb attack against the Japanese city of Hiroshima. Three days later, a second attack was launched against Nagasaki – a port city some 300 kilometres to the south. In the two attacks, over 100,000 people were killed instantly, and hundreds of thousands of people subsequently died of their injuries or of radiation sickness.[11]

The bombings heralded the nuclear age. Within twenty years, five states had successfully tested a nuclear weapon and weapons stockpiles are estimated to have reached 37,320.[12] By 1986 (just over forty years later), six states possessed nuclear weapons with an estimated total of 64,099 nuclear warheads worldwide.[13] The 1945 attacks remain as the only hostile use of nuclear weapons. However, as the number of nuclear weapons and the number of states possessing such nuclear weapons have grown, so too has the existential threat of a global nuclear war.

[11] Paul Ham, *Hiroshima Nagasaki* (Sydney: HarperCollins Publishers, 2011), pp. 408–13.

[12] In chronological order of successful testing, with estimated stockpile numbers as at 1965 following in brackets: the United States (US) (31,139), the Soviet Union (USSR) (6,144), the United Kingdom (UK) (271), France (32) and China (5). Source is the Bulletin of the Atomic Scientists available at https://thebulletin.org/nuclear-notebook-multimedia.

[13] US (23,317); USSR (40,159); UK (350); France (355); China (224) and Israel (44). Source is the Bulletin of the Atomic Scientists available at https://thebulletin.org/nuclear-notebook-multimedia.

With the dawn of the nuclear age, so began the campaigns against nuclear weapons. This section of the chapter examines the first thirty years of those campaigns – from the lead-up to the Hiroshima and Nagasaki bombings in 1945 up to and including the attempt in 1974 by New Zealand, Australia and a number of Pacific states to challenge the legality of French nuclear testing in the Pacific before the ICJ. In these decades, opposition was variously framed as concern about the destructive force of the weapons, about the human health implications in terms of radiation release from testing, and, as time went on, about the impact of testing on the environment. Humanitarianism was not explicitly articulated in the campaigns, but the campaigns contained the seeds of what would become, in time, an explicitly humanitarian discourse.

A The Early Responses: Concerns about Destructive Capacity

The first concerns about the atomic bomb came from a group of scientists working within the atomic development programme in the United States – the Manhattan Project – whereby some of those involved started to question the bomb on moral grounds.[14] For example, eight weeks before the bombings, a group of seven scientists – the so-called Franck Committee – proposed that the Japanese should be warned about the bomb before using it, perhaps by means of a demonstration nuclear explosion in an unpopulated area.[15] Another petition was presented by Leo Szilard, a Hungarian nuclear physicist working on the programme on behalf of sixty-nine scientists urging the United States to first present a warning to Japan.[16] The petitions went unheeded.

[14] Josef Rotblat serves as a good example of the change of heart experienced by the scientists. See Alice Kimball Smith, *A Peril and a Hope: The Scientists' Movement in America: 1945–47* (Chicago: University of Chicago Press, 1965). See also discussion by Coit D. Blacker and Gloria Duffy, *International Arms Control: Issues and Agreements* (Stanford: Stanford University Press, 1984), pp. 29–32 examining the reaction of scientists, physicians and religious leaders; David Cortright, *Peace: A History of Movements and Ideas* (Cambridge: Cambridge University Press, 2008), ch. 7; and Wittner, *Confronting the Bomb*, above n. 4, p. 3.

[15] Joseph Rotblat, 'Movements of Scientists Against the Arms Race' in Joseph Rotblat (ed.), *Scientists, the Arms Race and Disarmament* (London/Paris: Taylor and Francis/UNESCO, 1982), p. 116. See also Cortright, *Peace: A History of Movements and Ideas*, above n. 14, p. 129.

[16] Wittner, *Confronting the Bomb*, above n. 4, pp. 4–5. See also Nina Tannenwald, *The Nuclear Taboo: The United States and the Non-Use of Nuclear Weapons since 1945* (New York: Cambridge University Press, 2007), p. 85.

While the bombings caused a massive civilian toll, they were far from unique in terms of their destructive force in the context of the war as a whole. For example, the US firebombing of Tokyo in the previous March had resulted in over 87,000 deaths, with 40,918 injured and over a million people rendered homeless.[17] This perhaps explains the general lack of concern about the atomic bomb from the general population in the United States, despite the concerns expressed by some scientists.[18] In fact, after the bombings of Hiroshima and Nagasaki, the mood in the United States was generally triumphant and proud, rather than remorseful or reflective about the scale of the destruction.[19]

Outside of the scientific community, there were some early attempts to bring to light the human suffering caused by the atomic bombs. One striking example was an article simply entitled 'Hiroshima' published in the *New Yorker* in 1946 by John Hersey.[20] He traced the experiences of six survivors from their routines earlier that morning, to their experience of the bomb itself and its immediate aftermath, and on to the days and weeks following the bombing. The article closes a year on from the bombing. With that deeply personalised account, a human face emerged from the catastrophe. Each survivor in their own way behaved with kindness and dignity, from the young clerk who had risen early that day in order to prepare food for her family; to the widowed mother, exhausted from yet another broken night of trudging to the air-raid shelter with her three children; to the junior doctor, one of only a handful of surviving doctors in the Red Cross hospital, doing what he could to bring some ease to the thousands dying around him. The accounts in the article are sometimes gruesome, all the more so for their quiet, understated delivery:

> Mr. Tanimoto found about twenty men and women on the sandspit. He drove the boat onto the bank and urged them to get aboard. They did not move and he realized that they were too weak to lift themselves. He reached down and took a woman by the hands, but her skin slipped off

[17] Mark Seldon 'Bombs Bursting in Air: State and Citizen Responses to the US Firebombing and Atomic Bombing of Japan' in K. Yau Shuk-ting (ed.), *Natural Disaster and Reconstruction in Asian Economies* (New York, Basingstoke: Palgrave Macmillan, 2013).

[18] See Chapter 3, Section III.A.

[19] Paul S. Boyer, *By the Bomb's Early Light: American Thought and Culture at the Dawn of the Atomic Age* (Chapel Hill: University of North Carolina Press, 1994), pp. 10–12.

[20] John Hersey, 'Hiroshima' (31 August 1946) *New Yorker*. Also published in book form as John Hersey, *Hiroshima* (New York: Alfred A. Knopf Inc., 1946). A number of Japanese works also recounted the suffering, but those publications were censored by the Occupation Authorities in Japan. See Wittner, *One World or None*, above n. 4, pp. 47–8.

> in huge, glove-like pieces. He was so sickened by this that he had to sit down for a moment.[21]

The article was considered a landmark in journalism and met with wide acclaim at the time.[22] However, for all its power and truth, it failed to effect government policy or to have any meaningful impact on public opinion.[23]

In any event it seems that state policy, particularly within the US and the USSR, in these early years was entirely impervious to any calls for restraint in using or further developing nuclear weapons. As the only nuclear weapon possessor state within the newly formed United Nations, almost immediately the US tabled what came to be known as the Baruch Plan – essentially a proposal that an international atomic development authority be established to control and inspect all nuclear projects. Once it was established, the proposal was that all existing nuclear weapons would be destroyed and there would be no further weapons development.[24] The USSR, still three years away from successfully testing a nuclear weapon, immediately objected, arguing that elimination of weapons ought to precede an international control system, rather than follow it.[25]

Leaving the merits or otherwise of the Baruch Plan aside, the relevant point for present purposes is that these debates could not have been more removed from the emerging moral and humanitarian concerns. The overwhelming focus was on relative military power, with both the US and the USSR steadfastly pursuing development of their own arsenals. Thus, even as the Baruch Plan was being tabled at the UN in July 1946, the United States was carrying out two further nuclear tests in what was then the Trust Territory of the Pacific Islands – today's Marshall Islands. The United States was not alone in its gap between rhetorical commitment to banning or even regulating the weapons and actual practice. In 1949, the USSR, still stonewalling the US proposal to develop an international system of regulation, and insisting on including provisions on extermination of the civilian population (as code for including a prohibition against

[21] Hersey, *Hiroshima*, above n. 20, 60.

[22] Kathy Roberts Forde, 'Profit and Public Interest: A Publication History of John Hersey's "Hiroshima"' (2011) 88(3) *Journalism and Mass Communication Quarterly* 562, 563.

[23] See Wittner, *One World or None*, above n. 4, p. 58. The US authorities refused to allow publication of the article in Japan until 1949: at p. 47.

[24] See Chapter 3, Section IV.

[25] Tannenwald, *The Nuclear Taboo*, above n. 16 pp. 101–2; Wittner, *One World or None*, above n. 4, pp. 251–4.

nuclear weapons) at the negotiations for what would become the Geneva Conventions 1949, went on to detonate its first successful nuclear test a few weeks later and so become the second state in what was becoming the 'nuclear club'.[26]

Less than two years after the attacks on Hiroshima and Nagasaki, the US arsenal of nuclear weapons had risen to thirteen. By late 1949, as the USSR had joined the nuclear club, the United States had 171 nuclear weapons.[27] Whatever concerns there may have been in some sectors of the public and scientific community in the language of humanitarianism or otherwise, the nuclear arms race was progressing at full pace and being justified on the basis of the imperative of protecting international peace and security (including in the United States, protection from communism): deterrence theory had emerged. For some states, that was the humanitarian imperative.

B Health and Environmental Concerns

Whereas the initial concerns by groups of scientists within the Manhattan Project had rested on the sheer destructive power of the bomb and the inevitable consequential impact on civilians, public and scientific attention increasingly turned to concerns about the radiation released by the bomb. While nuclear weapons have not been used since then in conflict, from the end of the Second World War nuclear weapons testing began in earnest and on a much wider scale than within the Manhattan Project – first by the United States, and then extending to (in order of successful testing) the USSR (1949), the United Kingdom (1952), France (1960) and China (1964).[28] The damage caused by atmospheric testing, in particular the release of radiation, became an increasing focus of opposition as it was an ongoing concrete manifestation of the dangers posed by nuclear weapons.[29]

Testing increased both in terms of actual number of tests as well as the yield, or power, of those explosions. The number of tests in the early part

[26] See Geoffrey Best, *War and Law Since 1945* (Oxford: Oxford University Press, 1997), pp. 110–14.

[27] See Bulletin of the Atomic Scientists: www.thebulletin.org.

[28] It is not certain when North Korea and Israel, understood to possess nuclear arsenals, started to conduct their tests. India and Pakistan did not develop their arsenals until the 1990s, although India did conduct a 'peaceful nuclear explosion' test in 1974.

[29] In this sense, the opposition campaigns were very different to earlier campaigns against conventional weapons, in that those campaigns were focused on the impact of *use* of the weapons.

of the 1950s remained reasonably constant,[30] but increased from the middle of the decade rising from 24 in 1955 to 33 (1956), 55 (1957) and 116 in 1958.[31] A short moratorium on testing meant there were no tests in 1959, but testing resumed again in 1961 and the number of tests continued to rise.[32]

The yield of these explosions rose exponentially with the development of the hydrogen bomb. Again, the United States was the first to progress, but by 1961, all five nuclear powers were testing the much more destructive technology.[33] To give a sense of the increased yield, in 1961, one of the USSR's tests was equivalent to fifty million tons of TNT, compared to the 15,000 tons of TNT equivalent for Hiroshima – over 3000 times more powerful.

All five of the testing states positioned their test sites away from their own large metropolitan centres, and indeed, the United States, France and the UK did so by testing outside their own territories: France in Algeria and, following Algerian independence, in its Pacific colonial territories; the UK in Australia and in the Pacific; and the United States (in addition to its extensive testing in continental US) in what is today the Marshall Islands in the northern Pacific.[34] These attempts to keep the tests and resulting radioactive fallout away from (their) population centres and so dampen opposition and fear of radioactivity failed spectacularly in light of the catastrophic Castle Bravo test carried out by the United States on 1 March 1954. That single test would become one of the major catalysts for rising opposition to nuclear testing. The explosion's yield was equivalent to fifteen million tons of TNT, that is, it was 1000 times the size of the Hiroshima bomb. It destroyed an entire atoll (Bikini Atoll), causing massive illness, burning and death of islanders including those who had been 'relocated' from the atoll in advance of the test. A number of Japanese

30 The number of tests each year were: 1951 (18); 1952 (11); 1953 (18); 1954 (16).

31 Daryl Kimball, 'The Nuclear Testing Tally' Factsheet (September 2017) available at www.armscontrol.org.

32 In a report tracking the testing of eight states, the Arms Control Association calculates that there have been 2,056 tests since 1945: USA (1030); USSR/RF (715); France (210); UK (45); China (45); North Korea (6); India (3) and Pakistan (2). See, Kimball, ibid. There is no mention of Israel, the ninth nuclear weapons possessor state, in that listing. The testing record is unknown, but there are suggestions of a test in 1979 with the co-operation of South Africa: see Leonard Weiss, 'Flash from the Past: Why an Apparent Israeli Nuclear Test in 1979 Matters Today' *Bulletin of the Atomic Scientists* (8 September 2015).

33 In order of testing: UK (1957); France (1960); USSR (1961); China (1967).

34 The United States had started its test programme within the continental US, but from 1946, it moved the site of its tests to its trust territory in the Pacific Ocean. From 1946–58 the US conducted sixty-seven tests in the territory of what is now the Marshall Islands.

fishermen on a fishing vessel (the ill-named Lucky Dragon) well away from the blast area were also impacted, one dying shortly afterwards.[35]

Fears that the ensuing radiation had spread as far as the continental US generated concern there about atmospheric pollution and particularly in relation to the presence of strontium-90 and caesium-137, both of which were known to enter the food chain.[36] In Europe as well, fear of radiation poisoning escalated.

At the same time, dangers posed by the resulting radioactivity were steadily becoming more apparent from the scientific literature.[37] In 1956 and again in 1960, the UK Medical Research Council reported on the medical and genetic aspects of nuclear radiation.[38] In January 1958, with the support of 9,235 scientists from forty-nine countries, scientist Linus Pauling petitioned UN Secretary-General Hammarskjold to consider the damage caused by nuclear testing to the genetic health and welfare of all human beings.[39] Three years later, in 1961, Physicians for Social Responsibility (PSN) was created to focus on the threat posed by nuclear weapons and the threat to health posed by radioactive fallout.[40]

Thus, by the early 1960s, nuclear testing and the resulting radioactive fallout had become a major public concern.[41] This, along with the Cuban Missile Crisis, provided the impetus for what would become the 1963

35 Holger Nehring, 'Cold War, Apocalypse and Peaceful Atoms. Interpretations of Nuclear Energy in the British and West German Anti-Nuclear Weapons Movements, 1955–1964' (2004) 29(3) *Historical Social Research* 150, 155.

36 *Report of the United Nations Scientific Committee on the Effects of Atomic Radiation* UN GOAR, 13th sess, Supp No 17 (A/3838) (1958) p. 12.

37 For one account, see Christopher Jolly, 'Linus Pauling and the Scientific Debate over Fallout Hazards' (December 2002) 26(4) *Endeavour* 149.

38 Medical Research Council, *The Hazards to Man of Nuclear and Allied Radiations* (June 1956) Cmnd. 9780 and Medical Research Council, *The Hazards to Man of Nuclear and Allied Radiations: A Second Report to the Medical Research Council* (December 1960) Cmnd. 1225.

39 Linus Pauling, *No More War* (London: V. Gollancz, 1958), pp. 11–12.

40 Physicians for Social Responsibility, 'The Medical Consequences of Thermonuclear War' (1962) 266 *New England Journal of Medicine* 1126. See John Humphrey, 'The Development of the Physicians' Peace Movements' (1985) 1(2)*Medicine and War* 87.

41 Rebecca Johnson, *Unfinished Business: The Negotiation of the CTBT and the End of Nuclear Testing* (Geneva: UNIDIR, 2009) p. 11. It should be noted that European and American fears of radiation poisoning were focused on their own health, rather than the lives, health and livelihood of those people living in the testing areas. For example, an attempt led by India to petition the Trusteeship Council challenging the US about its testing in the Marshall Islands was unsuccessful. India, then a champion (in reality, not only rhetorically) against nuclear weapons, also called for an immediate 'standstill agreement' on nuclear testing – a proposal which was submitted to the UN Disarmament Commission on 29 July 1954, without success.

Partial Test Ban Treaty (PTBT).[42] The treaty fell far short of the hopes of civil society and of the growing number of non-nuclear states in that it was not a comprehensive ban on testing (that would take another thirty-three years in the form of the 1996 Comprehensive Test Ban Treaty (CTBT), a treaty that is still not in force).[43] However, the PTBT was still an important achievement in that with the US, the USSR and the UK becoming states parties, and ceasing atmospheric testing, the treaty resulted in substantially reduced atmospheric testing and therefore radiation contamination.[44] It is also an important example of how health concerns were at least part of the dynamic in concluding the treaty. The background to the treaty also shows the potential for civil society engagement. Norman Cousins, a long-time disarmament advocate, played a significant role in not only generating public support for the treaty, but also acting as an intermediary between USSR Premier Khrushchev and US President Kennedy, in a time when direct diplomatic outreach was difficult.[45]

Environmental concerns also became an important feature of opposition to nuclear weapons albeit developing later than the human health concerns. As with the health concerns, this line of opposition would endure to form a central thread of the humanitarian initiative in later decades. Its evolution can be traced to the 1972 Conference on the Human Environment held in Stockholm, an event which is generally accepted as the birth of the modern international environmental movement.[46] Principle 26 of the Final Declaration of the Conference addressed nuclear weapons stating that 'Man and his environment must be spared the effects of nuclear weapons and all other means of mass destruction. States must strive to reach prompt agreement, in the relevant international organs, on the elimination and complete destruction of such weapons'.[47] Environmental concerns formed an important part of

[42] Treaty Banning Nuclear Weapon Tests in the Atmosphere, in Outer Space and under Water, opened for signature 5 August 1963, 480 UNTS 43 (entered into force 10 October 1963).

[43] *Comprehensive Nuclear-Test-Ban Treaty*, opened for signature 24 September 1996, 35 ILM 1439 (not yet in force).

[44] China and France continued to conduct atmospheric testing for at least another decade.

[45] Lawrence S. Wittner, 'Norman Cousins and the Limited Test Ban Treaty of 1963' (December 2012) 42(10) *Arms Control Today* 34.

[46] P. H. Sand, 'The Evolution of International Environmental Law' in D. Bodansky, J. Brunnée and E. Hey (eds.), *The Oxford Handbook of International Environmental Law* (Oxford: Oxford University Press, 2007), pp. 29–43.

[47] Stockholm Declaration of the United Nations Conference on the Human Environment, Report of the UN Conference on the Human Environment, 5–16 June 1972, UN Doc A/Conf./48/14.

the legal challenges against the French nuclear test programme which had moved from Algeria (as it became independent) to French territories in the Pacific in 1966.[48] Between 1966 and 1974, France conducted twenty-five atmospheric nuclear test explosions on Mururoa and Fangata'ufa Atolls.[49] While France was not a party to the PTBT, and thus as a matter of international treaty law was not prohibited from atmospheric testing, the tide of public opinion had coalesced against atmospheric testing, particularly in New Zealand, Australia and in the Pacific. This eventually left the governments concerned with little choice but to respond to the ongoing tests.

From the initial diplomatic correspondence through to the eventual filing of proceedings before the ICJ in 1973, environmental concerns were central.[50] The applications to the Court by Australia, New Zealand and Fiji (as intervenor) all stress the health and environmental impacts of the radioactive fallout caused by nuclear testing, including mental stress.[51] Environmental law was still in its infancy at the time and the 'precautionary principle' was some decades away from being explicitly formulated. Nevertheless, there is a precautionary sense from the pleadings – an idea that even if there was a lack of consensus about the nature or scale of the damage, testing should not proceed.[52] In 1974, before the case could proceed to the merits, France unilaterally declared that it would cease all further atmospheric tests and so the litigation came to an end, because the Court determined that the claims against France no longer had any object.[53] As such, ultimately the humanitarian (health and environment) claims were not tested.

[48] J. Stephen Kós, 'Interim Relief in the International Court: New Zealand and the Nuclear Test Cases' (1984) 14 *Victoria University of Wellington Law Review* 357, 361.

[49] Catherine F. Dewes, 'The World Court Project: The Evolution and Impact of an Effective Citizens Movement', PhD thesis, University of New England (October 1998), ch. 7.

[50] *Nuclear Tests Cases*, above n. 9. The correspondence is available as Annexes in the proceedings. Discussed by Kós, 'Interim Relief in the International Court', above n. 48, p. 361.

[51] 'Request for the Indication of Provisional Measures of Protection Submitted by the Government of New Zealand', *Nuclear Tests Cases (New Zealand* v. *France)* above n. 9, pp. 49–50; 'Application for Permission to Intervene Submitted by the Government of Fiji', *Nuclear Tests Cases (New Zealand* v. *France)* above n. 9, pp. 89–90; 'Request for the Indication of Provisional Measures of Protection Submitted by the Government of Australia', *Nuclear Tests Cases (Australia* v. *France)* above n. 9, paras 8 and 40.

[52] William K. Ris Jr, 'French Nuclear Testing: A Crisis for International Law' (1974) 4 *Denver Journal of International Law and Policy* 111, 115–17.

[53] 'Judgment', *Nuclear Tests Cases (New Zealand* v. *France)*, above n. 9, 457, p. 475. The same reasoning and result applied to the Australian proceedings.

Importantly, there are indications that the humanitarian campaigns may have helped to prevent any further hostile use of nuclear weapons. They were not used in either the Korean or Vietnam conflicts and indeed, opinion polls never went above a 20 per cent approval rate to use nuclear weapons in Korea.[54] Tannenwald argues that the emerging taboo and revulsion against nuclear weapons were at least part of the explanation why they were not used, citing in support of this contention the statement of US Secretary of State and Foreign Policy Spokesman that 'in the present state of world opinion we could not use an A-bomb, we should make every effort to dissipate this feeling, especially since we have been spending such vast sums on the production of weapons we cannot use'.[55]

III The Ending of the Cold War: Two Humanitarian Disarmament Initiatives

The sense of urgency about the health and environmental consequences of nuclear testing dissipated as testing went underground in the wake of the PTBT and the French undertaking following the *Nuclear Tests Cases*. However, in the early 1980s, the world re-entered an era of heightened international instability. The number of nuclear weapons in existence peaked in 1986 with an estimated 64,099 nuclear warheads stockpiled globally.[56] That alone was cause for real concern, but nuclear accidents such as that which occurred at Three Mile Island in the United States in 1979 and the Chernobyl nuclear station in the USSR in 1986 also highlighted the very real and serious dangers and consequences of a major release of radiation.[57]

Increasingly, public concerns started to refocus on the risk of an actual nuclear war, rather than simply the human health and environmental consequences of testing the weapons. For example, the 'Nuclear Winter' campaign, triggered by the publication of Carl Sagan's article entitled 'Would Nuclear War be the End of the World?' in *Parade* magazine in October 1983, reignited popular debate and concern about the consequences of a nuclear war.[58]

[54] Tannenwald, *Nuclear Taboo*, above n. 16, p. 151, n. 144.

[55] Ibid., p. 150.

[56] Numbers are: USSR (40,159), USA (23,317), France (355), UK (350), China (244), Israel (44), North Korea (<10). Source is *Nuclear Notebook, Bulletin of the Atomic Scientists*.

[57] For an account of near-misses, see Eric Schlosser, *Command and Control: Nuclear Weapons, the Damascus Accident, and the Illusion of Safety* (New York: Penguin Press, 2013).

[58] See generally Lawrence Badash, *A Nuclear Winter's Tale: Science and Politics in the 1980s* (Massachusetts: MIT Press, 2009).

In 1987, the USSR and the US negotiated and adopted the Intermediate Nuclear Forces Treaty (INF Treaty).[59] The treaty committed the two states to eliminating all nuclear and conventional ground-launched ballistic and cruise missiles with ranges of 500–5,500 kilometres.[60] On-site inspections and monitoring to verify the destruction processes began in 1988 and within three years, all missiles, related support equipment and support structures had been eliminated. Partly as a result of the treaty, partly on account of the transformed international dynamic, fears of a catastrophic nuclear war receded and the US and USSR nuclear weapons stockpiles shrank significantly.[61] It was the beginning of the end of the Cold War.

There were two important anti-nuclear initiatives which took place against this backdrop which I see as falling within the rubric of 'humanitarian disarmament': the World Court Project, which led to an Advisory Opinion on the legality of nuclear weapons at the ICJ; and the successful adoption of the CTBT. In different ways, the two initiatives can be seen as exercises in humanitarian disarmament: the World Court Project because of the way in which civil society led the way, both in lobbying to bring the case before the ICJ, and in the way the campaigns consolidated the language of human health, environment, international humanitarian law and human rights in the arguments being presented to the Court. The CTBT is significant in this context because it marked the first occasion when diplomats retreated from the traditional multilateral disarmament architecture of the CD, and resorted to the more inclusive and non-consensus-bound General Assembly to adopt a nuclear weapons related treaty.

A The World Court Project

The aim of the World Court Project (WCP) was to challenge the legality of nuclear weapons before the ICJ – to take the hitherto political

[59] Treaty Between the United States of America and the Union of Soviet Socialist Republics on the Elimination of their Intermediate-Range and Shorter-Range Missiles 1987 signed 8 December 1987 (entered into force 1 June 1988). This treaty came to an end on 1 February 2019, with the formal withdrawal of the United States six months earlier due to concerns about Russian (non)compliance with the treaty.

[60] INF Treaty arts IV and V.

[61] Overall stockpiles dropped by almost a third between 1986 and 1991. From its height in 1986, when there was an estimated total of 64,099 stockpiled nuclear warheads (23,317 USA; 40,159 Russia; 350 UK; 355 France; 224 China; 44 Israel; less than 10 held by North Korea), by 1991 the number was falling rapidly, having dropped to 48,992. Source is *Nuclear Notebook* from *Bulletin of the Atomic Scientists.*

campaigns against nuclear weapons to a legal forum.[62] The campaign had germinated within civil society in the 1980s, garnering support over time from within the NAM, and in particular from Pacific Island states which had borne the brunt of nuclear testing over the years.[63] Two routes to the Court were explored: through the World Health Organization (WHO) and through the General Assembly, the former on the basis that the use of nuclear weapons would be catastrophic in terms of human health and the environment. The Court declined to render the WHO request on the basis that the question fell outside the scope of the WHO's powers, despite its careful reference to health and environmental effects of nuclear weapons.[64]

However, the Court did render an Advisory Opinion in response to the UN General Assembly, which had asked whether the threat or use of nuclear weapons in any circumstances was permitted under international law.[65] By a narrow majority, the Court found that the threat or use of nuclear weapons 'would generally be contrary to the rules of international law applicable in armed conflict' but also stated that it could not 'conclude definitely whether the threat or use of nuclear weapons would be lawful or unlawful in an extreme circumstance of self-defence, in which the very survival of a state would be at stake'.[66] Despite the slightly ambiguous phrasing, it was a remarkable outcome and marks the first time that the Court engaged substantively with the question of nuclear weapons.[67]

[62] See generally, Dewes, *The World Court Project*, above n. 49; Kate Dewes and Robert Green, 'The World Court Project: How a Citizen Network can Influence the United Nations' (1995) 7(2) *Pacifica Review: Peace, Security and Global Change* 17.

[63] The idea of an Advisory Opinion had been mentioned some decades before: Andrew Martin, *Legal Aspects of Nuclear Disarmament* (London: British Institute of International and Comparative Law, 1963) discussing the Accra Assembly: p. 20.

[64] *Legality of the Use by a State of Nuclear Weapons in Armed Conflict (Advisory Opinion) (Judgment)* [1996] ICJ Rep 66. For discussion see Dino Kritsiotis, 'The Fate of Nuclear Weapons after the 1996 Advisory Opinions of the World Court' (1996) 1(2) *Journal of Conflict and Security Law* 95, 95–8.

[65] *Request for an Advisory Opinion from the International Court of Justice on the Legality of the Threat or Use of Nuclear Weapons*, GA Res 49/75K, UN GAOR, 49th sess, 90th plen mtg, UN Doc A/RES/49/75K (15 December 1994). For a detailed discussion, see Dewes, *The World Court Project*, above n. 49, pp. 283–307.

[66] *Legality of the Threat or Use of Nuclear Weapons (Advisory Opinion)*, above n. 10, para. (2)E of the *Dispositif*.

[67] The *Nuclear Tests Cases* in 1974 had ended before any substantive outcome due to the French declaration that it would discontinue its testing programme, see above Section II. B. There had been persistent attempts to bring nuclear weapons before *domestic* courts. See Peter Weiss, 'Nuclear War in the Courts' in John Dewar, Abdul Paliwala, Sol Picciotto and Matthias Ruete (eds.), *Nuclear Weapons, The Peace Movement and*

The Advisory Opinion stands as an important part of the humanitarian disarmament campaign against nuclear weapons in a number of respects. First, the case is significant for the role of civil society in bringing the two requests to the Court.[68] There is little doubt that if it were not for NGO activism in terms of generating the requests and in assisting states taking part in the proceedings, the case would not have proceeded.[69] Considerable civil society lobbying lay behind persuading the non-aligned and Pacific Island states to push for the referral in the General Assembly.[70] Even during the proceedings, while not granted the right to address the Court directly, civil society continued to be actively engaged, assisting a number of less-resourced states with their submissions before the Court.[71]

A second aspect of the Advisory Opinion that is significant in terms of its 'humanitarian disarmament' credentials was that the proceedings canvassed the legality question not just in terms of state security, but also in terms of health and environmental consequences, international humanitarian law and human rights law. Thus, these discourses, which for decades had underpinned campaigns against nuclear weapons, were now squarely before, and discussed by, the Court.

The third humanitarian disarmament aspect was the result itself. The Court not only concluded that the use or threat of nuclear weapons would generally be unlawful but also underscored the responsibility of all states to engage in disarmament negotiations in good faith. In its closing *dispositif*, all fifteen judges expressed the view, based on article VI of the NPT, that there exists an 'obligation to pursue in good faith and

the Law (Basingstoke: The Macmillan Press Ltd, 1986), p. 178 and Abdul Paliwala 'Peace Protest, State and Law' in the same publication, p. 139.

68 For an account, see Wittner, *Towards Nuclear Abolition*, above n. 4, pp. 454–5. Richard Falk considers the Advisory Opinion as an instance of a 'new jurisprudence': Richard Falk, 'Nuclear Weapons Advisory Opinion and the New Jurisprudence of Global Civil Society' (1997) 7 *Transnational Law and Contemporary Problems* 333, 337–8.

69 Michael N. Schmitt, 'Book Review: *Nuclear Weapons and the World Court*' (1998–9) 9 *United States Air Force Academic Journal of Legal Studies* 179, 181. See as well the discussion by Yaël Ronen, 'Participation of Non-State Actors in ICJ Proceedings' (2012) *The Law and Practice of International Courts and Tribunals* 77, 107.

70 Not all the judges were impressed. Compare *Legality of the Threat or Use of Nuclear Weapons (Advisory Opinion)*, above n. 10, pp. 438 and 533–4 (Judge Weeramantry) and pp. 285–7 (Judge Guillaume).

71 Dewes, *The World Court Project*, above n. 49, ch. 12.

bring to a conclusion negotiations leading to nuclear disarmament in all its aspects under strict and effective international control'.[72]

This would turn out to be the seed of the TPNW that was still two decades away.

B *The CTBT: Leaving the Conference on Disarmament*

The second important development in the post–Cold War era for nuclear weapons campaigns came with the adoption of the CTBT in 1996 by the General Assembly.[73] The treaty banned all nuclear explosions, wherever conducted, thus closing a crucial gap in the PTBT which had not captured underground testing.[74] It put in place a global network of monitoring stations which detect nuclear test explosions whether carried out in the atmosphere, underground or in the oceans.[75]

Of significance for present purposes is the way in which the CTBT was adopted. Originally proposed by India in 1954, the idea of a comprehensive ban on testing had been on the agenda of the CD for decades, and while there was almost complete agreement on its substantive provisions by most members, it proved impossible to adopt a treaty, in large part due to the consensus-based decision-making process within the CD.[76] Ultimately Australia, supported by 127 co-sponsors, introduced the treaty text as a draft Resolution to the General Assembly in September 1996 where it was adopted and opened for signature.[77] Although there are 183 signatory states, 166 of which have also ratified the treaty, it has not yet entered into force.[78] However, despite its lack of formal status, nuclear tests have stopped since the treaty was adopted, except for by North Korea, Pakistan and India.[79]

[72] *Legality of the Threat or Use of Nuclear Weapons (Advisory Opinion)*, above n. 10, para. 105(2)(f).

[73] It was overwhelmingly (but not universally) adopted: 158 votes in favour, 3 against (Bhutan, India and Libya) with 5 states abstaining (Cuba, Lebanon, Mauritius, Syria and Tanzania).

[74] CTBT art. I (1).

[75] Ibid., art. IV.

[76] Keith A. Hansen, *The Comprehensive Nuclear Test Ban Treaty: An Insider's Perspective* (Stanford: Stanford University Press, 2006), pp. 5–13; Johnson, *Unfinished Business*, n. 41, chs. 2 and 3.

[77] *Comprehensive Nuclear-Test-Ban Treaty*, GA Res 50/245, UN GAOR, 50th sess, 125th plen mtg, UN Doc A/RES/50/245 (10 September 1996).

[78] CTBT art. XIV requires that all forty-four 'nuclear capable' states listed in Annex 2 ratify the treaty for it to enter into force.

[79] Leading to a debate about whether there is now a customary prohibition on nuclear testing. Compare Masahiko Asada, 'CTBT: Legal Questions Arising from Its Non-Entry-

Both the WCP and the CTBT signalled a willingness by states to step outside the orthodox disarmament architecture to make progress on disarmament and thus, in different ways, both projects can be seen as part of a 'humanitarian campaign' against nuclear weapons. The WCP in particular was fostered by civil society and maintained by civil society. Behind the CTBT as well, despite its long gestation in the shuttered Conference on Disarmament, was a long and hard-fought campaign by civil society which stretched back for decades.[80] For these reasons, both projects are rightly seen as part of the humanitarian disarmament story in the context of nuclear weapons.

Following the adoption of the CTBT in 1996, anti-nuclear campaigns weakened again whether couched in the language of humanitarianism or otherwise. However, as I will show in the next section, a new momentum was about to emerge.

IV The Humanitarian Initiative Emerges

With the Advisory Opinion and adoption of the CTBT by the General Assembly, 1996 had been a year of renewed optimism for anti-nuclear activists and states, particularly in light of the fact that the NPT had now been extended indefinitely.[81]

However, the years following were less encouraging.[82] A new generation of civil society activists turned their attention more firmly to conventional weapons, starting with APLMs, and moving on in the following decade to cluster munitions. The war on terror, unleashed following the attacks in the United States in September 2001, dominated public attention and changed risk perception, shifting the focus from threats from states to non-state actors. By the mid-2000s, climate change was seen as the foremost existential threat. Civil society based anti-nuclear campaigns had lost momentum.

Into-Force' (2002) *Journal of Conflict and Security Law* 85, 93–4 and Lisa Tabassi, 'The Nuclear Test Ban: *Lex Lata* or *Lege Ferenda*' (2009) *Journal of Conflict and Security Law* 309, 333–5.

[80] For a comprehensive account of the CTBT negotiations and background, see Johnson, *Unfinished Business*, above n. 41.

[81] Review and Extension Conference of the Parties to the Treaty on the Non-Proliferation of Nuclear Weapons 1995, *Extension of the Treaty on the Non-Proliferation of Nuclear Weapons*, Final Document, NPT/CONF.1995/32, Part I, Annex, Decision 3. Art X.2 NPT provided that states parties to the treaty would convene after twenty-five years to decide whether the treaty would be continued indefinitely, or extended for some other fixed period of time.

[82] See generally, Wittner, *Toward Nuclear Abolition*, above n. 4, pp. 474–83.

At a state level, matters had also stalled. The rancour within the CD caused (at least in part) by the CTBT end-game endorsement had left a bitter legacy and the CD essentially became defunct. The failure of the US Senate in 1999 to vote in favour of ratifying the CTBT effectively destroyed any serious prospect that the treaty could enter into force any-time soon. With the CD in deadlock, there was no meaningful avenue for discussions about nuclear disarmament.

Nevertheless, a number of anti-nuclear states persisted with their efforts within the First Committee of the General Assembly as well as through the Review Conference mechanisms of the NPT. In the UN in 1997, Costa Rica and Malaysia tabled a draft Nuclear Weapons Convention which had been prepared by several civil society groups including the International Association of Lawyers against Nuclear Arms, International Physicians for the Prevention of Nuclear War and the International Network of Engineers and Scientists Against Proliferation.[83] In 1998, a group of states formed the New Agenda Coalition (NAC) to work collectively to put pressure on the NWS to take meaningful steps towards fulfilling the commitments made as part of the agreement to indefinitely extend the NPT in 1995.[84] Civil society organisations persisted in their demands for meaningful progress in nuclear disarmament. However, for all the persistence, no meaningful process was made towards nuclear disarmament and momentum was difficult to maintain.

A *Stirrings*

It is always difficult to pinpoint the start of a movement – the moment when change starts.[85] In terms of the start of the momentum which would eventually lead to the Humanitarian Initiative and from there to the TPNW in 2017, one such moment might be the publication of an article in 2007 in the *Wall Street Journal*, written by four former American states-men – George Schultz, William Perry, Henry Kissinger and Sam Nunn.[86]

83 Chargé d'affaires of the Permanent Mission of Costa Rica, Letter dated 31 October 1997 to the United Nations addressed to the Secretary-General, UN Doc. A/C.1/52/7 (17 November 1997).

84 'A nuclear-weapons-free world: the need for a new agenda' Joint Declaration by Brazil, Egypt, Ireland, Mexico, New Zealand, Slovenia, South Africa and Sweden (9 June 1998).

85 See the more detailed account by John Borrie, Michael Spies and Wilfred Wan, 'Obstacles to Understanding the Emergency and Significance of the Treaty on the Prohibition of Nuclear Weapons' (2018) *Global Change, Peace and Security* 1, 4–13.

86 George P. Schultz, William J. Perry, Henry A. Kissinger and Sam Nunn, 'A World Free of Nuclear Weapons', *Wall Street Journal*, 4 January 2007.

They argued that the end of the Cold War had rendered the doctrine of deterrence obsolete, and that with the rise of non-state terrorist groups, the most serious threats now lay outside the state paradigm and thus beyond deterrence. They called on the possessor states to engage in a 'joint enterprise' to work towards a world free of nuclear weapons.

This constituted a direct challenge to deterrence theory, which from the very start of the nuclear arms race, had been deployed as a counterweight to humanitarian concerns about using or testing nuclear weapons. That is, deterrence theory rests on the assertion that nuclear weapons ensure, not threaten, safety and well-being of human beings. By arguing that deterrence was now obsolete, the article provided a little more space for the humanitarian concerns about nuclear weapons to be examined. The article was also important because it placed the responsibility for the next steps squarely at the door of the possessor states.

Another 'moment' often considered to have been the trigger point was the speech by then US President Barack Obama in April 2009.[87] Characteristically stirring and inspiring, President Obama addressed the dangers of nuclear weapons in his speech to an expectant Czech public. Noting the 'moral responsibility' of the United States, he went on to say:

> So today, I state clearly and with conviction America's commitment to seek the peace and security of a world without nuclear weapons. I'm not naive. This goal will not be reached quickly – perhaps not in my lifetime. It will take patience and persistence. But now we, too, must ignore the voices who tell us that the world cannot change. We have to insist, 'Yes, we can.'

While the Wall Street Journal article and the Prague speech are both important moments and certainly contributed to the stirring of energy, neither could reasonably be considered to fall within anything like a 'humanitarian' discourse. Certainly the *Wall Street Journal* article challenged deterrence orthodoxy and called upon the nuclear weapons states to take responsibility, but it did so squarely in the language of state sovereignty and security. Similarly, President Obama's speech while lamenting the dangers of nuclear weapons, in no way suggested an alternative framing of the problem. A full reading of his speech reveals that nuclear weapons were

[87] Office of the Press Secretary, The White House, Remarks by President Barack Obama, Hradcany Square, Prague, Czech Republic, 5 April 2009.

still being framed as providing safety and security rather than being a threat to peace, health and environmental safety.[88]

B A Turning Point

The Final Declaration of the 2010 NPT Review Conference expressed 'deep concern at the catastrophic humanitarian consequences of any use of nuclear weapons'.[89] This Declaration marked the first occasion on which an official NPT Review Conference document used the expression 'catastrophic humanitarian consequences' and, in hindsight, it does seem to have marked a paradigm shift. In accounts of the Review Conference (RevCon) there are hints of the transformation that was already underway. Participating civil society were pushing hard to reframe the debate on nuclear disarmament and were attempting to generate discussion based on democracy, human security, medical consequences and health and environment. In doing so, they were picking up on strands from earlier campaigns.[90] In statements to the RevCon, Switzerland, Liechtenstein, Norway and the Holy See all referred to the need to consider the question of nuclear disarmament in the light of the catastrophic humanitarian consequences of those weapons being used.[91]

Momentum started to gather quickly following the RevCon. In 2011, the Council of Delegates of the International Red Cross and Red Crescent Movement adopted a resolution expressing deep concern about the 'unspeakable human suffering' caused by nuclear weapons and appealing to states to pursue negotiations for a binding agreement prohibiting nuclear weapons.[92] In 2012, during the first session of the Preparatory Committee working towards the 2015 NPT RevCon, sixteen states joined in a statement solely focused on the humanitarian consequences issue,

[88] 'Make no mistake: As long as these weapons exist, the United States will maintain a safe, secure and effective arsenal to deter any adversary, and guarantee that defense to our allies . . . '.

[89] 2010 Review Conference of the Parties to the Treaty on the Non-Proliferation of Nuclear Weapons, *Final Document*, document NPT/CONF.2010/50 (Vol. 1)*, 2010, part 1, 19.

[90] See the collection of papers in United Nations Office for Disarmament Affairs, *Non-Governmental Organization Presentations at the 2010 Nuclear Non-Proliferation Treaty Review Conference* (UNODA, 2010).

[91] See the 'NPT News in Review' published throughout the RevCon by Reaching Critical Will, available at www.reachingcriticalwill.org/disarmament-fora/npt/2010.

[92] Council of Delegates of the International Red Cross and Red Crescent Movement, *Working Towards the Elimination of Nuclear Weapons* (Resolution 1, 26 November 2011).

concluding that '[f]or this review cycle, it is essential that the humanitarian consequences of nuclear weapons are thoroughly addressed'.[93]

Later in 2012, in the First Committee and in the General Assembly, the humanitarian framing of the issue was also emphasised. Switzerland delivered a statement expressing concern about the humanitarian consequences of any use of nuclear weapons, now with thirty-four states joining.[94] Norway announced that it would host a conference early in 2013 to consider the humanitarian consequences aspect. The General Assembly voted to convene an Open-Ended Working Group to 'develop proposals to take forward multilateral nuclear disarmament negotiations'.[95]

A new energy was seizing the civil society community as well. The formation of the International Campaign to Abolish Nuclear Weapons (ICAN) in 2007 was a crucial development. Modelled on the earlier civil society campaigns against APLM and cluster munitions, ICAN brought together a coalition of NGOs already working in the area, seeking to mobilise and re-energise existing campaigns and work more effectively in a coalition.[96] It sought to reorientate the discourse away from an orthodox security paradigm towards humanitarian concerns.[97] Reaching Critical Will, the disarmament branch of Women's International League for Peace and Freedom published a collection of papers on the humanitarian impact of nuclear weapons, drawing together earlier strands of the discourse but explicitly framing them under the umbrella term 'humanitarian consequences'.[98] UNIDIR published a series of pieces considering the

[93] 'Joint Statement on the Humanitarian Dimension of Nuclear Disarmament' delivered by HE Ambassador Benno Laggner of Switzerland on behalf of Austria, Chile, Costa Rica, Denmark, Holy See, Egypt, Indonesia, Ireland, Malaysia, Mexico, New Zealand, Nigeria, Norway, Philippines, South Africa, Switzerland to the First Session of the Preparatory Committee for the 2015 Review Conference of the Parties to the Treaty on the Non-Proliferation of Nuclear Weapons (2 May 2012) 2.

[94] 'Joint Statement on the Humanitarian Dimension of Nuclear Disarmament' to the First Committee, UNGA, delivered by Switzerland (Ambassador Lagger), 22 October 2012.

[95] *Taking Forward Multilateral Nuclear Disarmament Negotiations*, GA Res 67/56, UN GAOR, 67th sess, 48th plen mtg, UN Doc A/RES/67/56 (4 January 2013). 147 states voted for the Resolution; 4 voted against (France, Russian Federation, the United Kingdom and the United States); 31 states abstained from voting including China, India, Israel and Pakistan.

[96] See www.icanw.org.

[97] See generally Matthew Bolton and Elizabeth Minor, 'The Discursive Turn Arrives in Turtle Bay: The International Campaign to Abolish Nuclear Weapons' Operationalization of Critical IR Theories' (2016) 7(3) *Global Policy* 385.

[98] Reaching Critical Will, *Unspeakable Suffering: The Humanitarian Impact of Nuclear Weapons* (Geneva: Reaching Critical Will, January 2013).

implications of a humanitarian framing.[99] These, and other similar publications, provided crucial factual information on the impacts of nuclear weapons.

The momentum continued in the following years with increasing numbers of states joining statements on the humanitarian impact of nuclear weapons in the preparatory meetings for the NPT RevCon, in the First Committee and in the plenary meeting of the General Assembly.[100]

A series of three conferences examining the humanitarian impact of nuclear weapons was convened – by Norway in 2013, and by Mexico and Austria in 2014.[101] The aim of the conferences was to provide a forum for facts-based analysis and discussions on the humanitarian consequences of nuclear weapons. Three key points emerged from those discussions. First, there was agreement that no state or international body could address the immediate humanitarian emergency caused by a nuclear weapon detonation in an adequate manner and provide sufficient assistance to those affected. Second, the historical experience from the use and testing of nuclear weapons was accepted as having demonstrated the devastating immediate and long-term effects of nuclear weapons. Third, it was clear that the effects of a nuclear weapon detonation, irrespective of cause, could not be constrained by national borders, and would affect states and people in significant ways, regionally as well as

[99] Tim Caughley, *Humanitarian Impacts of Nuclear Weapons: Tracing Notions about Catastrophic Humanitarian Consequences*, Humanitarian Impact of Nuclear Weapons project papers, no. 1 (Geneva: UNIDIR, 2013); John Borrie, *Viewing Nuclear Weapons through a Humanitarian Lens: Context and Implications*, Humanitarian Impact of Nuclear Weapons project papers, no. 2 (Geneva: UNIDIR, 2013). Although note that UNIDIR had first explored the idea of disarmament as explicitly humanitarian action as early as 2005: J. Borrie and V. Martin Randin (eds.), *Alternative Approaches in Multilateral Decision Making: Disarmament as Humanitarian Action* (Geneva: UNIDIR, 2005); in particular, see J. Borrie, 'Rethinking Multilateral Negotiations: Disarmament as Humanitarian Action' in that collection.

[100] See for example, 'Joint Statement on the Humanitarian Impact of Nuclear Weapons' delivered by Ambassador Abdul Samad Minty, Permanent Representative of South Africa to the Second Session of the Preparatory Committee for the 2015 Review Conference of the Parties to the Treaty on the Non-Proliferation of Nuclear Weapons, 24 April 2013 (Geneva, 24 April 2013) (80 states joining); 'Joint Statement on the Humanitarian Impact of Nuclear Weapons' delivered by Ambassador Dell Higgie of New Zealand, to the First Committee of the United Nations General Assembly, 21 October 2013 (125 states joining); 'Joint Statement on the Humanitarian Consequences of Nuclear Weapons delivered by Ambassador Dell Higgie of New Zealand, to the First Committee of the United Nations General Assembly, 20 October 2014 (155 states joining).

[101] See Elizabeth Minor, 'Changing the Discourse on Nuclear Weapons: the Humanitarian Initiative' (2015) 97(899) *International Review of the Red Cross* 711, 717–21.

globally. Looking at the detail of the conferences, in fact, there was not much in the way of new information but what was significant was that the information had been updated on the basis of new scientific understandings: it was absolutely clear now that there could not be an adequate humanitarian response to any nuclear war, even a very limited nuclear weapons war, for example between India and Pakistan.[102]

There had been some who hoped that the Humanitarian Impact conferences might have led to an ad hoc negotiating forum in the way that had happened both with cluster munitions and with anti-personnel landmines. While no such ad hoc forum was created, a Pledge emerged from the final conference. Presented by Austria, it urged all states 'to identify and pursue effective measures to fill the legal gap for the prohibition and elimination of nuclear weapons'.[103] The Pledge was subsequently circulated at the First Committee in October 2015, now rebranded from the Austrian Pledge to the Humanitarian Pledge, and was adopted by the First Committee, and subsequently by the plenary General Assembly, passing by an overwhelming majority.[104] The humanitarian discourse was firmly entrenched now and had, for an increasing number of states, replaced the deterrence-security narrative.

Progress was being attempted on another front as well, through the mechanisms of two Open-Ended Working Groups established by the General Assembly. The first, in 2013, had been tasked by the General Assembly to 'develop proposals to take forward multilateral nuclear disarmament negotiations'.[105] While it was useful that this inaugural working group allowed for discussion of the issues outside of the Conference on

[102] Reaching Critical Will issued reports of the three conferences: Reaching Critical Will, *Conference Report on the Humanitarian Impact of Nuclear Weapons, Oslo, Norway, 4–5 March 2013* (2013); Ray Acheson, Beatrice Fihn and Katherine Harrison, *Report from the Nayarit Conference* (2014); Reaching Critical Will, *Filling the Gap: Report on the Third Conference on the Humanitarian Impact of Nuclear Weapons, Vienna, Austria, 8–9 December 2014* (2014) all available from www.reachingcriticalwill.org.

[103] Michael Linhart, Secretary-General of Foreign Ministry 'Austrian Pledge' delivered to the Third International Conference on the Humanitarian Impacts of Nuclear Weapons (Vienna, 9 December 2014).

[104] *Humanitarian Pledge for the Prohibition and Elimination of Nuclear Weapons*, GA Res 70/48, UN GAOR, 70th sess, 67th plen mtg, UN Doc A/RES/70/48 (11 December 2015). A total of 139 states voted in favour, 17 states voted against and 29 states abstained from voting.

[105] *Report of the Open-ended Working Group to Develop Proposals to Take Forward Multilateral Nuclear Disarmament Negotiations for the Achievement and Maintenance of a World Without Nuclear Weapons*, attached to the *Note by the Secretary-General*, A/ 68/514, 9 October 2013 (*OEWG Report 2013*).

Disarmament or the more formal strictures of the General Assembly, including greater engagement with civil society, the Working Group was not as action-oriented as many states and civil society desired.[106]

In 2016, a second Open Ended Working Group (OEWG) was convened – there had been some concerns that this could be a delaying tactic as the Group did not have the mandate to engage in any negotiations, but rather was to 'substantively address concrete effective legal measures, legal provisions and norms that will need to be concluded to attain and maintain a world without nuclear weapons'.[107] However, exceeding the expectations of many, the OEWG completed its work by recommending that a United Nations conference be convened in 2017 to negotiate a legally binding instrument to prohibit nuclear weapons, leading to their total elimination.[108]

The reframing agenda had borne fruit.

V The Treaty on the Prohibition of Nuclear Weapons

As mandated, the Conference convened during 2017, and on 7 July 2017, the Treaty on the Prohibition of Nuclear Weapons (TPNW) was adopted.[109] While its roots reach back to the very first resolution of the General Assembly,[110] the treaty's immediate context had been the humanitarian campaign which had been gaining momentum since 2010. The following sections explore the ways in which the TPNW can be seen as fitting within the evolving practice of humanitarian disarmament, starting with an overview of the treaty's core provisions, showing that the treaty is an important milestone despite the lack of universal support.

[106] See the reports by Reaching Critical Will, at www.reachingcriticalwill.org/disarmament-fora/oewg/2013/reports.

[107] *Taking Forward Multilateral Nuclear Disarmament Negotiations*, GA Res 70/33, UN GAOR, 70th sess, 67th plen mtg, UN Doc A/RES/70/33 (11 December 2015).

[108] *Report of the Open-Ended Working Group Taking Forward Multilateral Nuclear Disarmament Negotiations*, GA Res 71/371, UN GAOR, 71st sess, UN Doc A/RES/71/371 (1 September 2016), para. 67; *Taking Forward Multilateral Nuclear Disarmament Negotiations*, GA Res 71/258, UN GAOR, 71st sess, 68th plen mtg, UN Doc A/RES/71/258 (23 December 2016).

[109] Treaty on the Prohibition of Nuclear Weapons, A/Conf.229/2017/8, 7 July 2017. The treaty was adopted by vote with 122 voting in favour of adoption, one state (the Netherlands) voting against adoption, and one state (Singapore) abstaining from the vote.

[110] See Chapter 3, Section IV.

A An Important Milestone, despite Lack of Universal Support

It is impossible to predict whether this treaty, in time, will lead to actual nuclear disarmament, particularly in light of the opposition of the nuclear weapons possessor states.[111] Nevertheless, it is undoubtedly an important milestone in the evolution of nuclear weapons law, in that it is the first multilateral treaty to ban nuclear weapons.[112]

States parties are prohibited from using, threatening to use, developing, producing, manufacturing, acquiring, possessing, stockpiling, transferring, stationing or installing nuclear weapons or assisting with any prohibited activities.[113] Article 2 requires each state party to declare whether it owns or possesses any nuclear weapons, whether it has eliminated a past nuclear weapons programme or stockpile, and whether it has another state's weapons stationed on its territory. Those declarations are to be made to the United Nations and will be transmitted by the Secretary-General to all states parties to the treaty. Further, states parties must maintain their existing safeguards agreements with the International Atomic Energy Agency (IAEA) and states parties that have not yet concluded such an agreement must, at a minimum, conclude a comprehensive safeguards agreement.[114]

None of the states possessing nuclear weapons participated in the negotiations, and several have made categorical statements that they will never join.[115] Nevertheless, the negotiating states were of the view that the treaty had to make some provision for any possible future participation by nuclear weapons possessor states. Thus, Article 4, entitled 'Towards the total elimination of nuclear weapons', sets out two possible pathways. First, a nuclear possessor state could destroy its arsenals and then join the treaty – the destroy-then-join option.[116] A second pathway would be for a possessor state to join the treaty and then subsequently destroy its arsenals – the join-then-destroy option.[117] In very general terms, Article 4 articulates the ensuing obligations,

[111] See generally Ramesh Thakur, 'The Nuclear Ban Treaty: Recasting a Normative Framework for Nuclear Disarmament' (2017) 40(4) *The Washington Quarterly* 71.

[112] Of course, the web of Nuclear Weapons Free Zones treaties had long since banned nuclear weapons in their respective zones, but this treaty is a global expression of the norm.

[113] TPNW art. 1.

[114] TPNW art. 3.

[115] See for example, *Joint Press Statement from the Permanent Representatives to the United Nations of the United States, United Kingdom and France on the Adoption of a Treaty Banning Nuclear Weapons*, New York City, 7 July 2017.

[116] TPNW art. 4.1.

[117] TPNW art. 4.2.

including that joining states conclude safeguards agreements with the IAEA, that all weapons be removed from operational status and that reports be provided to the Meeting of the States Parties of the TPNW. It also anticipates a future 'competent international authority' to deal with the disarmament process (in the join-then-destroy path) or verification of destruction (in the destroy-then-join path).

In line with earlier humanitarian disarmament treaties, the TPNW includes positive obligations, including the obligation to provide victim assistance and environmental remediation of contaminated areas.[118]

Regardless of when (or whether) the treaty enters into force, it stands as an important exercise in the practice of humanitarian disarmament. Two aspects of the treaty in particular are analysed here in order to more fully examine the humanitarian disarmament credentials of the treaty and to determine how the practice of humanitarian disarmament might be evolving. First are the provisions on victim assistance, which I argue shifted considerably from the CCM. Second, I consider the significance of the forum in which the treaty was negotiated, that is, in the General Assembly, and suggest that this might represent an important shift in the overall discourse about nuclear weapons and perhaps even disarmament practice more generally.

B Victim Assistance

Earlier chapters discussing the APLM Convention and the CCM have shown the way in which victim assistance provisions are an important part of humanitarian disarmament practice.[119] However, as I argued in the context of the CCM, the broad definition of 'victim' coupled with the imposition of extensive assistance obligations on states parties on the one hand, with an emphasis on the responsibility of the territorial state on the other, is problematic in that it essentially places the burden of victim assistance on the 'victim state', not on the user state.[120] My argument here is that this (im)balance has been redressed, at least to a certain extent, in the TPNW.

Victim assistance was always going to be an important concern in the negotiations given the emphasis throughout the campaigns on the humanitarian impact of nuclear testing and use of nuclear weapons, particularly

118 TPNW. arts 6 and 7.

119 See Chapter 5, Section IV.D and Chapter 6, Section V.A.

120 See Chapter 6, Section V.A.

in the Humanitarian Impact conferences. A significant difference between the earlier treaties and the TPNW is that here, all of the 'user states' – those states which had tested or actually used nuclear weapons – had absented themselves from the negotiations.[121] Thus, none of the states negotiating the text were themselves facing potential responsibility if responsibility was assigned on the basis of having caused the damage. In fact, many of the negotiating states were victims of nuclear testing.[122]

Even so, the balance between reconciling the needs and rights of victims with the imperative to fairly assign responsibility for redress proved difficult. The first draft of the victim assistance provisions in the treaty was modelled on the CCM and placed responsibility for victim assistance on territorial states.[123] Further, reflecting the text of CCM, draft Article 6(2) provided that contaminated states had the right to request and receive assistance. Draft Article 6(3) went on to specify that '[s]uch assistance may be provided, inter alia, through the United Nations system, international, regional or national organizations or institutions, non-governmental organizations or institutions, or on a bilateral basis'.

A number of states took the position that the provisions were an encouraging starting point, and that a victim focus was appropriate from a human rights perspective, such that the obligations would be owed towards the victims by the territorial or jurisdictional state, regardless of the origins of the harm.[124] However, a significant number of states opposed the draft, and instead proposed that the treaty ought to provide for user or testing state responsibility.[125] Yet others called for a balance between the human rights obligations of the territorial state on the one hand and an acknowledgement of the damage caused by the user/testing states on the other.[126] Some delegations expressed concern that however

[121] Being China, France, India, Israel, North Korea, Pakistan, the Russian Federation, the United Kingdom and the United States.

[122] Japan, the only state to be a victim of an actual nuclear weapons attack, did not attend the main negotiations in June/July, but did attend the preparatory March session.

[123] Draft Convention on the Prohibition of Nuclear Weapons Submitted by the President of the Conference, A/CONF.229/2017/CRP.1, 22 May 2017, art. 6(1).

[124] This was also the position of many in civil society. See, Article 36 (co-authored with the International Human Rights Clinic, Human Rights Program at Harvard Law School), Victim Assistance in the Nuclear Weapon Ban Treaty: A Comprehensive and Detailed Approach, A/CONF.229/2017/NGO/WP.32, 9 June 2017.

[125] Plenary session 20 June 2017, notes on file with the author. Egypt, Vietnam, Brazil, Ecuador, Ghana, Nigeria, Cuba, Iran, Malaysia and Marshall Islands.

[126] Plenary session 20 June 2017, notes on file with the author. Ecuador.

compelling the call to hold users and testers to account, the 'chilling effect' on future potential ratifications by possessor states of adopting strong responsibility language should be carefully considered.[127]

Despite the varying views being expressed, there was little change in the Chair's second draft issued on 27 June 2017.[128] Due to the reordering of provisions, victim assistance was now in draft Article 7, renamed to more properly reflect its content as 'Victim assistance and environmental remediation'. The assistance provision that had been in original draft Article 6(3) was moved to draft Article 8 and strengthened in that the treaty text now recognised a 'right to seek and receive assistance'.[129] Regardless, the fundamental problem remained in that responsibility for assistance lay with the territorial (victim) state.

From there, discussions moved into informal consultations, chaired by the Facilitator from Chile. On 30 June 2017, the Facilitator reported back to the plenary that, while disagreement persisted about how to express the nature of the responsibility of a user/testing state, there was agreement in principle that some such provision should be included.[130] Two significant amendments to the text were proposed to reflect this. First, there would be an additional sub-paragraph (at the time, draft Article 7), to include the following:

> The obligations under (1) and (2) shall be without prejudice to the duties and obligations of any other States under international law or bilateral agreements.

The second addition was even more far-reaching, coming at the end of the international cooperation and assistance article (at the time, draft Article 8), in sub-paragraph (6):

> Without prejudice to any other duty or obligation that it may have under international law, a State Party that has used or tested nuclear weapons or any other nuclear explosive devices shall have a primary/the fundamental responsibility to provide adequate assistance to affected States Parties, for the purpose of victim assistance and environmental remediation.

Despite the Facilitator's advice that there had been agreement in principle to this approach of shifting some way towards user state

[127] For example, Ireland and New Zealand. Notes on file with the author.

[128] Draft Treaty on the Prohibition of Nuclear Weapons A/CONF.229/2017/CRP.1/Rev.1, 27 June 2017 (Draft Treaty, 27 June).

[129] Draft Treaty, 27 June art. 8(2).

[130] Plenary session 30 June, notes on file with the author.

responsibility, when the Chair's third draft was circulated, the second addition (being draft Article 8(6)) was not included.[131] The omission was quickly corrected in light of the repeated concerns by many states.[132] Eventually, the reinstated text was refined to refer to 'a responsibility' thus avoiding the choice between 'primary' or 'fundamental', which the Facilitator had been unable to resolve earlier.[133]

The treaty as finally adopted retained strong, human rights focused victim assistance and environmental remediation provisions – with those obligations resting with the territorial state. In this respect, it very much built on the CCM. However, the TPNW contains stronger provisions addressing the responsibility of user/testing states. The concerns raised by some states as to 'ratification-chill' could well be borne out in time, but the relevant point in the context of this discussion is that the provision stands as an important evolution in the practice of humanitarian disarmament – that the human rights focus does not have to preclude user state responsibility entirely.

While the particular balance struck here was made possible in part because of the absence of user/testing states from the negotiations, victim assistance provisions, however calibrated, have clearly now become an indelible aspect of the humanitarian disarmament landscape.

C *Nuclear Disarmament Comes Home*

The locus of negotiations has always been a fraught issue in disarmament. In the League of Nations, the contest was between the Council and the Assembly, with similar dynamics playing out in the early years of the United Nations.[134] The campaign to ban APLMs moved back and forth between the ICRC and UN structures, with many states calling for the Conference on Disarmament as the appropriate negotiating body.[135] For both cluster munitions and APLMs, the eventual route was an ad hoc process independent of existing structures, but still avowedly multilateral in scope.

In the case of nuclear weapons, once the momentum towards some kind of a prohibition treaty had rekindled, at least four possible

131 Draft Treaty on the Prohibition of Nuclear Weapons A/CONF.229/2017/L.X.

132 Substantive Revisions to A/CONF.229/2017/L.X. Submitted by the President of the Conference, A/CONF.229/2017/CRP.3, 6 July 2017.

133 Plenary session 5 July, notes on file with the author. See the statements by Ireland and New Zealand.

134 See Chapter 2, Section IV.B and Chapter 3, Section IV.

135 Chapter 4, Sections III and IV.

institutional avenues presented themselves. The first was the CD.[136] Nuclear disarmament had been a permanent feature of the CD's agenda from the beginning and in that sense then, it was a natural home. However, while there had been some achievements over the decades, by the mid-1990s, it was clear that no progress could be made on nuclear disarmament (or any other disarmament negotiations) in that forum. In fact, even the United Nations has acknowledged this in the 2018 *Agenda for Disarmament*, stating that the CD has 'not lived up to [its] promise for quite some time'.[137]

The difficulties within the Conference were complex but two points stand out making it an inappropriate avenue to take forward the multilateral negotiations called for by the Open-Ended Working Group. First, only sixty-five states are members of the Conference, less than one-third of the states in the world. Given the repeated insistence that nuclear disarmament was the responsibility of all states, a less than universal forum was inappropriate as a negotiation forum. Second, the CD continued to be mired in a consensus-based decision-making framework, which essentially meant that it would have been impossible to move forward on nuclear disarmament in that framework.

The second possible framework was the NPT Review Conference process. This possibility made sense given that the NPT contained within it a reference to nuclear disarmament providing that:

> Each of the Parties to the Treaty undertakes to pursue negotiations in good faith on effective measures relating to cessation of the nuclear arms race at an early date and to nuclear disarmament, and on a treaty on general and complete disarmament under strict and effective international control.[138]

However, it is not clear whether the Review Conferences have the power to convene a negotiation for a text which would go beyond the terms of the NPT itself. Article VIII(3) NPT states that the purpose of the review

[136] UNIDIR has published a number of papers analysing the Conference on Disarmament, often neglected in the academic literature, including: Tim Caughley, *Breaking the Ice in the Conference on Disarmament: A Wrap-up* (Geneva: UNIDIR, 2011); John H. King, *Transforming the Conference on Disarmament: Multilateral Arms Control and Disarmament for a Pluralistic World* (Geneva: UNIDIR, 2011); Tim Caughley, *The Conference on Disarmament: Issues and Insights* (New York, Geneva: UNIDIR, 2012); and Ignacio Cartagena, *Mandate and Working Methods in the Conference on Disarmament* (New York: UNIDIR, 2019).

[137] *Securing Our Common Future: An Agenda for Disarmament* (New York: United Nations Office for Disarmament Affairs, 2018), p. 62.

[138] NPT art. VI.

conferences are 'to review the operation of this Treaty with a view to assuring that the purposes of the Preamble and the provisions of the Treaty are being realised'. Responding to this, there were proposals that an amendment conference could be convened, perhaps with the idea of negotiating a Protocol to the NPT.[139]

Even if there had been agreement on this course of action, it would not have solved the issue of how to include the nuclear weapons possessor non-states parties to the NPT (India, Pakistan, Israel and North Korea), allowing them rights to participate in negotiations.[140] More fundamentally though, the NPT process was (and remains) mired in the consensus rule. Rule 28.1 of the Rules of Procedure 2015 provides that every effort should be made to reach agreement by consensus, and that there should be no voting until all other avenues have been exhausted. In fact, this has meant that the NPT Review Conference process has been hampered over time and given the stalemate there too in terms of the divisions between the nuclear weapons states on the one hand and the non-nuclear weapons states, the NPT was not a promising option for treaty prohibition negotiations.

The third option was that a state, or group of states, from within the ever-increasing group of like-minded states would decide to launch a process modelled on the Ottawa or the Oslo process for APLMs and cluster munitions respectively. Indeed, such a pathway might have been seen as a natural evolution from the three Humanitarian Impact conferences. While attractive in that such an ad hoc approach can easily avoid the consensus rule and yet is multilateral and open to all states, some states may have been concerned that such an approach would destabilise the existing architecture. Working within an established multilateral forum is important in this context because of the need to provide legitimacy to any outcome. Politically as well, this option would be more difficult given the implacable opposition to any negotiations taking place.[141] Any ad hoc process would require a single state to take the lead in hosting a negotiating conference and this might be a step too far in defying those states which were implacably opposed to any negotiations taking place.

It was the fourth option that was ultimately favoured – that of the General Assembly. From the beginning of the United Nations, the

[139] Annika Thunborg, 'Statement on Pathways' to Panel V of the Open-Ended Working Group, 11 May 2016.

[140] Although all of those states chose not to participate in the General Assembly-based negotiations.

[141] Somini Sengupta and Rick Gladstone 'United States and Allies Protest UN Talks to Ban Nuclear Weapons', *The New York Times*, 28 March 2017, A10.

General Assembly had dealt with issues of nuclear disarmament. The very first resolution of the General Assembly addressed the question of nuclear disarmament, establishing a commission of the Security Council 'to ensure the elimination from national armaments of atomic weapons and all other major weapons adaptable to mass destruction'.[142] Many key developments over the years have emanated from the General Assembly: the request for the Advisory Opinion, which was to be a core plank in the building humanitarian platform, and the adoption of the CTBT in 1996 as a workaround to the deadlocked CD. Even in the years when nuclear disarmament seemed a distant and unrealistic goal, there was never a year when the General Assembly did not adopt a resolution calling for progress on nuclear disarmament. As such, the General Assembly was the natural home for the negotiations.

There were several advantages to taking this route. Working within the General Assembly of the United Nations, or a subsidiary body of the Assembly, allowed for universal participation in negotiations. Compared to the CD, it had the advantage of having a much wider representation of states. The forum was also advantageous in that it avoided consensus decision-making. Finally, it allowed for much greater engagement by civil society.

The fact that the TPNW was negotiated in the General Assembly is significant for the practice of humanitarian disarmament because it ensured that nuclear disarmament had the legitimacy of working within the traditional disarmament architecture but also providing for the possibility of universalised engagement with the process. Importantly as well, the ongoing implementation of the treaty, whereby states parties will meet to discuss the implementation of the treaty and 'further measures for nuclear disarmament',[143] will keep the issue within this institutional setting. This may prove to be one of the most important consequences of this treaty.

VI Conclusion

My argument in this chapter has been that many of the campaigns against nuclear weapons since 1945 should be understood as falling within the rubric of 'humanitarian disarmament' both because of the way in which

[142] *Establishment of a Commission to Deal with the Problems Raised by the Discovery of Atomic Energy*, GA Res 1(1), UN GAOR, 1st sess, 17th plen mtg, UN Doc A/RES/1/1 (24 January 1946).

[143] TPNW art. 8.

civil society (or just 'the public') has always campaigned against the weapons and because a humanitarian impulse (a concern about human suffering) has always underpinned that opposition even if the explicit language of humanitarianism was not used until much more recently.

The history traversed here also allows a number of observations to be made about these particular campaigns, many of which can be extrapolated to other humanitarian disarmament campaigns.

First, accurate and clear information about the dangers posed by nuclear weapons was an essential underpinning to the campaigns: from the early work of scientists involved, to explanations of the risk of a 'nuclear winter' in the 1980s, to the work of the Humanitarian Impact conferences in more recent years. This need for objective, accurate information about the impact of a particular weapon type was also evident in the campaigns against APLM and cluster munitions and is a key feature of 'humanitarian disarmament' and one to which civil society is well placed to contribute.

A second observation is the way in which the campaigns and their successes (or otherwise) ebbed and flowed across the decades, and how that complex trajectory shows us that this history does matter. Specifically, it allows us to see more clearly how contingent success (and failure) can be. There was not a steady, building momentum to prohibition of nuclear weapons – rather the movement against them, both from states and from civil society, rose and fell with the times. The failures, or what appeared as failures at the time, are part of the process.[144] This was also the case when the longer histories of the campaigns against APLMs and cluster munitions were considered in earlier chapters.

Finally, while the TPNW falls firmly within the rubric of humanitarian disarmament, the process by which it came about, and its precise content, show how 'humanitarian disarmament' is not a fixed, stable concept, but rather how its practice continues to evolve and develop.

[144] As discussed in Chapter 1, Section II. For an exposition of this idea, see Blair L. M. Kelley, 'What Civil Rights History Can Teach Kavanaugh's Critics' *New York Times*, OpEd, 13 October 2018 available at: www.nytimes.com/2018/10/13/opinion/kavanaugh-activism-civil-rights.html.

8

Rethinking Humanitarian Disarmament

I Introduction

This thesis has shown that a sensibility of humanitarianism, both as a stand-alone ideal, but also in the context of disarmament and the regulation of armaments, has a long and rich history. Far from being an invention of the post–Cold War era, a humanitarian sensibility has been a feature of disarmament discourse since at least 1868.[1] That is not to say that a plea for humanitarian ideals has always succeeded in banning or even curtailing the use of a particular weapon. Far from it. As earlier chapters have shown, the history of disarmament attempts has had many setbacks and failures, but also some important successes.

In this chapter, I engage with humanitarian disarmament as a concept rather than examining its practice in any particular context. Despite its growing rhetorical importance, only a sparse literature attempts to engage critically with the concept of humanitarian disarmament. In contrast, a rich literature from a range of disciplines considers humanitarianism generally – its history, meaning, complexities and consequences. The aim here is to advance the literature on humanitarian disarmament by distilling general critiques of humanitarianism and exploring whether, and if so how or to what extent, they might apply in considering humanitarian disarmament. That is, I want to determine whether critiques of humanitarianism have traction when applied to the more specific instance of humanitarian disarmament.

[1] See the discussion of a series of much earlier examples (the use of crossbows, use of poison, the submarine, even the use of the gun in seventeenth and eighteenth century Japan) in Neil Cooper, 'Humanitarian Arms Control and Processes of Securitization: Moving Weapons Along the Security Continuum' (2011) 32(1) *Contemporary Security Policy* 134, 141.

Surprisingly, given its pervasive presence in military intervention debates, international lawyers have paid relatively little attention to the concept of humanitarianism. David Kennedy's *The Dark Side of Virtue* contains some relevant discussion, but his concern is more about the 'saviour mentality' of humanitarians (and indeed, international lawyers generally), and it does not go so far as to critically analyse the general concept of 'humanitarianism'.[2] Ruti Teitel and Martti Koskenniemi have had an exchange about 'humanity's law' – presumably a close relation of 'humanitarianism' (although the point is not explicitly discussed).[3] Teitel's book, *Humanity's Law*, presents an account of the rise of human-centred discourse in international law, blending together international criminal law, international human rights law and international humanitarian law. She argues that this language of humanity has spread.[4] Koskenniemi, reviewing the book, agrees with Teitel as a matter of fact, but criticises her for simply mapping and surveying instances of that language, and being apparently unconcerned with its political implications.[5] Unfortunately, but perhaps unsurprisingly in book review form, Koskenniemi himself does not go on to elaborate a critique of humanitarianism, or 'humanity's law', other than to point out that the language of universality implicit in 'humanity' lifts the speaker's values to an exalted position.[6]

Thus, given the paucity of engagement by legal scholars, by necessity this chapter draws on a range of different disciplines to interrogate the idea of 'humanitarianism'. This lays the groundwork to critically evaluate the ideas and ideals underpinning 'humanitarian disarmament' as a concept.

The chapter is structured around four broad critiques of humanitarianism. The first (Section II) takes as its starting point the way in which discourses based on humanitarianism purport to be apolitical. Claims

[2] David Kennedy, *The Dark Sides of Virtue: Reassessing International Humanitarianism* (Princeton: Princeton University Press, 2004).

[3] Ruti Teitel, *Humanity's Law* (Oxford: Oxford University Press, 2011), reviewed by Martti Koskenniemi, 'Review of *Humanity's Law*' (2012) 26 *Ethics and International Affairs* 295. And see her response to the review: Ruti Teitel, 'Author's Response to Martti Koskenniemi's Review of *Humanity's Law*' (2013) 27 *Ethics and International Affairs* 233. See as well, Robert Howse and Ruti Teitel, 'Does Humanity-Law Require (or Imply) a Progressive Theory of History? (and Other Questions for Martti Koskenniemi)' (2013) 27(2) *Temple International and Comparative Law Journal* 377.

[4] Teitel, *Humanity's Law*, above n. 3, p. 216.

[5] Koskenniemi, 'Review of *Humanity's Law*', above n. 3, p. 395.

[6] Ibid. Such a critique is well made by Makau Mutua, 'Savages, Victims, and Saviors: The Metaphor of Human Rights' (2001) 42(1) *Harvard International Law Journal* 201.

based on a humanitarian sensibility are couched in moralistic, universalistic terms, appealing to a sense of global kinship. Even as they lay claim to a moral universalism, humanitarianism is presented as a form of expertise, or a technical problem. This positioning is an integral part of an explicitly apolitical posture. I show this posturing in Section II.A and I argue that, far from being a technical problem above politics, humanitarianism is deeply political. It is not above politics – it *is* an expression of politics. I go on to argue that the apolitical positioning of humanitarianism is problematic because it renders invisible structural injustice (Section II.B). I then explore how this concern has resonance in the context of a humanitarian disarmament discourse: that is, a focus on suffering caused by one particular weapon type obscures structural violence and a culture of militarism (Section II.C).

The second broad critique of humanitarianism is canvassed in Section III, that is, its complicity with militarism. There is a prevailing sense that humanitarianism exists in opposition or as a challenge to militarism, but in fact, I argue that humanitarianism is often complicit with militarism. In Section III.B, I explore the way in which humanitarian concerns often complement a security discourse and I use the example of the bombing of Afghanistan in 2001 to illustrate the way in which humanitarianism and security are easily intertwined. I then examine the extent to which this complicity critique might apply to humanitarian disarmament and, using the Iraq War 2003 as an example, I show that alleged possession of certain types of weapons by certain states becomes the basis (or at least justification) for military intervention (Section III.C).

The third critique of humanitarianism – what I call the 'imperative of action', drawing on the work of Anne Orford – is explored in Section IV.[7] The idea here is that a humanitarian crisis frequently impels a response, and that response is often military in nature. Thus, this critique is concerned, not so much with the concept of humanitarianism itself, but with the ways in which humanitarian discourses are deployed in particular circumstances and the consequences of those shifts in discourse (Section IV.B). I conclude this Section by showing how the responses to the use of chemical weapons in the Syrian conflict illustrate how the critique applies to a humanitarian disarmament discourse (Section IV.C).

In Section V, I examine the way in which a humanitarian discourse inevitably and unavoidably sets up a 'hierarchy of humanity' (Section V.A)

[7] Anne Orford, *Reading Humanitarian Intervention: Human Rights and the Use of Force in International Law* (Cambridge: Cambridge University Press, 2003), pp. 162–5.

and I show how this dynamic is replicated in the discussions of humanitarian disarmament (Section V.B).

While this chapter draws on a series of critiques about humanitarianism, and shows how those critiques have traction in the specific context of humanitarian disarmament, this does not lead me to reject a humanitarian discourse in the context of disarmament. Instead, those critiques lead to the conclusion that humanitarianism should not be held out as a holy grail, as the untouchable answer to all disarmament issues. My conclusion is that humanitarianism is one of several possible discourses that can, and does, illuminate disarmament, but that it has its own complexities, political context and difficulties.

II The Politics of Humanitarian Practice and Discourse

A The Apolitical Posture

In Chapter 2, drawing on the work of Professor Barnett, I traced the emergence of what I termed 'modern humanitarianism' being the concern for suffering for 'strangers in distant lands' that emerged as part of the Enlightenment project.[8] I showed how, even at that early point, humanitarianism purported to be apolitical, epitomising a shared universal humanity and therefore situating itself above and beyond the political. I explored how the two great humanitarian movements of this early period – the abolitionist campaign and what would become the Red Cross Movement – both explicitly espoused apolitical mandates.

Of course, this was an entirely flawed self-understanding. Think of Henri Dunant, the 'sacred' founding father of international humanitarian law: he himself was a coloniser and in fact, he was on his way to obtain concessions in Algeria when he stumbled across the (in)famous Battle of Solferino.[9] Yet, this fact is erased in the dominant progressive humanitarian story told of the founding of the Red Cross Movement. In fact, the idea that there is (or should be) an apolitical humanitarian space has always been open to question.[10] Even Florence Nightingale, a quintessential

[8] See Chapter 2, Section II.

[9] Frédéric Mégret, 'From "Savages" to "Unlawful Combatants": A Postcolonial Look at International Humanitarian Law's "Other"' in Anne Orford (ed.), *International Law and its Others* (Cambridge: Cambridge University Press, 2009), pp. 265, 272.

[10] There is a vast literature on this point. For some examples, see: Peter Gill, *Today We Drop Bombs, Tomorrow We Build Bridges* (London: ZED Books Ltd, 2016); Monika Krause, *The Good Project: Humanitarian Relief NGOs and the Fragmentation of Reason* (Chicago: University of Chicago Press, 2014); Maggie Black, *A Cause for our Times: Oxfam the First*

humanitarian, thought the idea that there could be, or should be, impartiality and neutrality in the delivery of humanitarian aid was absurd.[11] Further, looking at the campaign against slavery – another great 'humanitarian movement' – while many historians subscribe to the view that the humanitarian impulse was determinative to its success, many others suggest that there were other, complex motivations involved, including particularly that the campaign against slavery was in part a critique of Empire, that it was driven at least in part by a sense of evangelicalism; and that economic self-interest was also involved in curtailing American economic advantage.[12]

Nevertheless, the apolitical positioning of humanitarianism persisted. The relief agencies established following the First World War transformed humanitarianism in terms of its scale and its professionalism.[13] However, studies of the key relief agencies show that, with some notable exceptions, even as they espoused a universal humanitarianism, they generally provided aid to the citizens of US allies, neglecting for example the needs of the German population.[14] Thus, far from being impartial, the patterns of relief, and the practice of post-War humanitarianism in large part reflected the politics of wartime.

As discussed in Chapter 3, things were no different following the Second World War.[15] Once again, the scale and institutionalisation of the humanitarian relief effort was unprecedented, this time in the form of the United Nations Relief and Rehabilitation Agency (UNRRA). And once again, despite its insistence in impartiality and political neutrality, UNRRA was neither.[16] In terms of its establishment, the overall plan to create a relief agency played not only to humanitarianism but also to economic self-interest and as a means to redress American isolationism.[17] In terms of its implementation, while its mandate was to

Fifty Years (Oxford: Oxford University Press, 1992); Linda Polman, *War Games: The Story of Aid and War in Modern Times* (London: Viking Press, 2010).

11 Polman, *War Games*, above n. 10, p. 8.

12 Discussed by Michael N. Barnett, *The Empire of Humanity: A History of Humanitarianism* (Ithaca, London: Cornell University Press, 2011), pp. 59–60.

13 Bruno Cabanes, *The Great War and the Origins of Humanitarianism 1918–1924* (Cambridge: Cambridge University Press, 2014), p. 4.

14 Ibid., p. 5. See also Barnett, *Empire of Humanity*, above n. 12, p. 83.

15 See Chapter 3, Section III.

16 'UNRAA is to be as politically neutral as clearly as possible': Philipp Weintraub, 'UNRRA: An Experiment in International Welfare Planning' (1945) 7(1) *Journal of Politics* 1, 14.

17 Jessica Reinisch, 'Internationalism in Relief: The Birth (and Death) of UNRRA' (2011) Supplement 6, *Past and Present* 258, 261–72.

provide relief to all peoples, including those in the former enemy territories of Germany, Japan, Italy and Finland, in fact its allocation of relief was not impartial, with increasing challenges from its recipient (and non-recipient) states.[18]

Claims to impartiality and separation from politics proved increasingly difficult for humanitarian agencies as the Cold War wore on.[19] This was particularly true because states became key sources of funding, as the shift away from private philanthropy continued, and as the emphasis shifted from relief in times of disaster to aid with the aim of development. And yet, the claimed apolitical stance persisted.

With the move to the age of what Barnett calls 'liberal humanitarianism' (that is, the period since the end of the Cold War), these debates have persisted and indeed come to the fore with the explosion of the humanitarian sector in the decades since 1990.[20] No-one working in the field of humanitarian assistance today would deny that there are politics at play in any provision of aid, whether it is delivery of emergency assistance, or for long-term developmental projects.[21]

While those facing the complexities of humanitarian practice on the ground may be mindful of the politics of their work, it is often a 'thin' politics that is acknowledged. That is, politics are recognised in the sense that a particular crisis might receive funding for reasons other than pure altruism – due to strategic security concerns, for example. There is still very little consideration of the deep, structural politics at play. Outside of the aid sector, there appears to be little reflection at all on the concept of 'humanitarianism' and its politics, 'thin' or structural. Rather there

[18] Weintraub, 'UNRRA', above n. 16, p. 8 discusses who received the relief. See Emily Haslam, 'United Nations Relief and Rehabilitation Administration (UNRRA)' in Rüdiger Wolfrum et al. (eds.), *The Max Planck Encyclopedia of Public International Law* (Oxford: Oxford University Press), at [13], referring to a resolution of the Council making relief for enemy and ex-enemy areas subject to a number of other conditions. It seems as though CARE (Cooperative for American Remittances to Europe) might have been an exception to this partiality: see the discussion by Barnett, *Empire of Humanity*, above n. 12, pp. 114–18.

[19] See Chapter 3, Section III.

[20] Barnett, *Empire of Humanity*, above n. 12, p. 167. See generally, Gill, *Today We Drop Bombs*, above n. 10.

[21] Gradually through the 1990s, to be 'apolitical' was seen as being complicit, thus we see statements such as: 'Humanitarianism should not be used as a substitute for political action' as discussed by David Chandler, 'The Road to Military Humanitarianism: How the Human Rights NGOs Shaped a New Humanitarian Agenda' (2001) 23 *Human Rights Quarterly* 678, 696.

remains an enduring assumption that to be humanitarian is to be apolitical.

B Obscuring Structural Injustice

If apolitical positioning (whether conscious or not) is what it takes to get results on the ground, does the lack of reflection on political implications really matter? Many commentators in a wide range of disciplines consider that it does because they say the humanitarian framing of an issue obscures deeper, structural, political issues.

Articulated forcefully by Didier Fassin, this concern highlights how the humanitarian framing of an issue shifts a discourse from one of rights to one of pity.[22] Across his body of work, his argument is that this approach invokes the trauma of the individual or victim community rather than recognising structural violence by directing our attention to the suffering individual or community. Thus, while the practice of presenting an individual suffering (the starving child, the anti-personnel landmine victim) purports to epitomise the suffering, in fact it obscures structural problems. In this way, the discourse shifts from one of rights, to one of pity. Fassin argues that humanitarianism, by explicitly ignoring structural problems embeds itself *in* politics rather than existing distinct from politics.[23]

Lilie Chouliaraki makes a comparable point from the discipline of media and communication studies.[24] She argues that the moral emphasis on pity in humanitarian discourse and practice displaces the politics needed to look at structural problems that are causing or at least contributing to the suffering.

In anthropology, Miriam Ticktin uses the example of famine relief to show this dynamic in practice.[25] She shows how such relief is structured

[22] Didier Fassin, *Humanitarian Reason: A Moral History of the Present* (Berkeley: University of California Press, 2012); Didier Fassin, '*Noli me Tangere*: The Moral Untouchability of Humanitarianism' in Erica Bornstein and Peter Redfield (eds.), *Forces of Compassion: Humanitarianism between Ethics and Politics* (Santa Fe: School for Advanced Research Press, 2011); Didier Fassin and Richard Rechtman, *The Empire of Trauma: An Inquiry into the Condition of Victimhood* (Princeton: Princeton University Press, 2009); Didier Fassin, 'The Predicament of Humanitarianism' (2013) 22(1) *Qui Parle: Critical Humanities and Social Sciences* 33.

[23] Fassin, 'The Predicament of Humanitarianism', above n. 22, p. 39.

[24] Lilie Chouliaraki, 'Post-humanitarianism: Humanitarian Communication Beyond a Politics of Pity' (2010) 13(2) *International Journal of Cultural Studies* 107, 108.

[25] Miriam Ticktin, 'Transnational Humanitarianism' (2014) 43 *Annual Review of Anthropology* 273, 278.

as a medical, technical intervention, not as a political intervention. The focus on the technical rather than the structural, she argues, epitomises the anti-politics of the disaster relief industry.[26] Another anthropologist, Müller, explores this idea in the context of the Ethiopian famine in 1983/84, which triggered one of the largest humanitarian responses of the contemporary era.[27] Müller shows how there were complex causes for the famine in Ethiopia, in particular a war with rebels in the north, who were opposed to the famine-inducing politics of the government.[28] Framed as an issue about the absence of food, the famine was viewed as a natural disaster. But in reality, there was sufficient food in the country for the entire population and it was a devastating combination of politics and warfare that stopped that food being available and/or distributed effectively.[29] Thus, far from being a natural disaster, or a technical problem, the famine was a complex political emergency. If a humanitarian organisation were to make a comment on that, it would be to wade into the politics of the situation directly, which in turn could have jeopardised their access. In failing to recognise the complex structural problems, attention is only paid to the 'suffering bodies'.[30] This in turn brings a focus on the benevolent giver, and in that shift, an inequality emerges whereby charity is emphasised over obligation, and structural problems are left untouched.[31]

C Humanitarian Disarmament Discourses

Even in the early manifestations of humanitarian disarmament in the League of Nations era and before, I traced how the various disarmament campaigns pitted themselves against the prevailing politics of the time.[32]

Apolitical posturing was also evident in all three of the humanitarian disarmament campaigns which arose in the period since the United Nations: anti-personnel landmines (APLMs), cluster munitions and nuclear weapons. Taking APLMs as an example, the focus on the suffering of victims was presented in opposition to the insistence of some states

[26] Ibid.
[27] Tanja R. Müller, '"The Ethiopian Famine" Revisited: Band Aid and the Antipolitics of Celebrity Humanitarian Action' (2013) 37(1) *Disasters* 61.
[28] Ibid., p. 68.
[29] Ibid., p. 69.
[30] Ibid., p. 74.
[31] Ibid., p. 75.
[32] See Chapter 2, Section II and Section IV.A.

that all landmines, including anti-personnel mines, were necessary for their security.[33] Thus, in the early phase of opposition to APLMs, during the 'human rights in armed conflict' campaigns of the 1970s, the UN Secretary-General noted his understanding 'that the purpose of the General Assembly in examining the question of respect for human rights in armed conflicts is a humanitarian one, independent of any political considerations which may relate to specific conflicts . . . '.[34] The humanitarian campaigns against cluster munitions and nuclear weapons as well were often presented as an apolitical appeal to focus on the suffering caused by those weapons and was juxtaposed against the politics of national security (for cluster munitions) and deterrence (for nuclear weapons).[35]

However, the question to be considered in this section is whether the apolitical posturing of disarmament campaigns is vulnerable to the same critiques that have been made in the context of humanitarianism generally.

Writings from critical security studies suggest that the general critique is indeed relevant. Mirroring Fassin's critique of humanitarianism that it obscures structural violence, Neil Cooper suggests that the focus on individual suffering in humanitarian disarmament campaigns obscures the broader more permissive framework of militarism, which remains unchallenged.[36] Thus, he says that while the contemporary movement of humanitarian arms control can be seen as a form of arms control 'from below' in light of the direct engagement with civil society, in fact, the humanitarian campaigns are articulated 'within the logic of militarism from above'.[37] Ostensibly attempting to shift from the world of politics, Cooper argues that the humanitarian disarmament discourse, in socially constructing pariah weapons, reinforces power structures.[38]

This argument is also made in the context of the APLM campaign specifically. For example, Beier suggests that however progressive the humanitarian disarmament discourse might seem, such campaigns may unwittingly become implicated in legitimising the rhetoric of military

[33] See Chapter 4, Section III.
[34] Warren E. Hewitt, 'Respect for Human Rights in Armed Conflicts' (1971) 4 *New York University Journal of International Law and Politics* 41, 41.
[35] See Chapters 6 and 7.
[36] Cooper, 'Humanitarian Arms Control', above n. 1, p. 141.
[37] Neil Cooper, 'The Post-Cold War Arms Trade Paradox' in Jackie Smith and Ernesto Verdeja (eds.), *Globalization, Social Movements and Peacebuilding* (Baltimore: Syracuse University Press, 2013), pp. 21, 45.
[38] Ibid., p. 22.

action.[39] This is because the focus on the use of a particular weapon leaves the broader questions about the resort to military force unchallenged.

As discussed above, the framing of an issue as a technical problem is a common depoliticising technique in the general humanitarian discourse. In the context of disarmament, opponents of bans or restrictions on weapons frequently adopt the approach of reducing the question of increased regulation of weapons to a technical problem. That is, the human impact of a weapon becomes reduced to a technical problem of the need to distinguish between a combatant and a non-combatant, suggesting that with 'better' technology the problem of (civilian) human suffering would be eliminated.[40] It is easy to see how this approach is similar in dynamic to reducing famine to a technical issue of lack of food.

Brier argues that a consequence of this type of technical framing is that a campaign becomes less a demand to resist violence and more about 'managing' weapons, which itself is a form of depoliticisation.[41] He argues that the fascination with weapons technology, particularly since the 1991 Gulf War, renders the human invisible and thus profoundly depoliticises war.[42] Looking specifically at the campaign against anti-personnel landmines, Beier shows that the movement consciously strove to put the human back into the frame by showing clearly the devastating human consequences of the weapons use. However, to do that, the campaign had to frame the weapon as inherently indiscriminate. That is, the campaign had to show that better human behaviour could not redeem this weapon.[43] Thus, in this way the weapon becomes the problem, not the human agent, and it becomes possible to denounce the weapon without denouncing organised violence. While this is essential to a clear and successful campaign – that is, there must be an unambiguous message that anti-personnel landmines are inherently indiscriminate and must be banned, not further regulated – it inevitably results in a resounding silence about the broader issues of violence and conflict.[44]

39 J. Marshall Beier, 'Dangerous Terrain: Re-reading the Landmines Ban through the Social Worlds of the RMA' (2011) 32(1) *Contemporary Security Policy* 159, 161.

40 Ibid.

41 Ibid.

42 Ibid., 162–3.

43 Ibid., 168–9.

44 And see as well, Ritu Mathur, 'Humanitarian Practices of Arms Control and Disarmament' (2011) 32(1) *Contemporary Security Policy* 176.

III Humanitarianism's Complicity with Militarism

A Introduction

The second broad critique of humanitarianism considered in this chapter is its complicity with militarism. The classic image of the humanitarian in conflict is captured by the International Committee of the Red Cross (ICRC) tending to those caught up in a conflict, and caring for the wounded and the sick. We imagine NGOs delivering aid in the form of food, water and medical supplies and the United Nations working to house the displaced. In these images, humanitarianism is assumed to be a counter to militarism. It is trying to mitigate the suffering inflicted because of armed conflict.

However, some critiques suggest that in taking this approach, humanitarianism might be complicit with militarism. There are increasing concerns around the blurring of the lines between humanitarian action in armed conflict and military action. Think about, for example, the situation where peacekeepers deliver aid, or where humanitarian actors are actively protected by military personnel. However, the point being considered here is different. That is, the concern is not so much problems arising because of a blurred boundary between militarism and humanitarianism, but rather the idea that humanitarianism might (sometimes) function as a *complement* to militarism, rather than in *opposition* to it.[45]

B Counter or Complicity?

The way in which humanitarianism might be seen as a complement to militarism rather than in opposition to it is evident in the way in which the 'humanitarian intervention' debates are conducted in international law.

There is a long history of debate on the legality or otherwise of humanitarian intervention: that is, the question of whether it is legally permissible in international law to carry out a military intervention to save the lives of, or to prevent atrocities against, people in another state.[46]

[45] Vasuki Nesiah, 'From Berlin to Bonn to Baghdad: A Space for Infinite Justice' (2004) 17 *Harvard Human Rights Journal* 75, 76.

[46] The debate is not new and stretches back at least to the Christian just war tradition (ideas of right authority, just cause and right intention) of Thomas Aquinas and later Hugo Grotius. For an overview discussion, see: Christine Gray, *International Law and the Use of Force, 4th ed.* (New York: Oxford University Press, 2018); Yoram Dinstein, *War, Aggression and Self Defence, 4th ed.* (Cambridge: Cambridge University Press, 2005).

In contemporary discourse, much of the debate is carried out in doctrinal terms: whether the prohibition on the use of force in the United Nations Charter (Charter) can be interpreted as to allow use of force for the protection of human rights.[47] Another strong thread of doctrinal debate explores whether customary international law has evolved, alongside the Charter, allowing for a military intervention on humanitarian grounds.[48] In addition to these doctrinal debates, there are commentators considering the issue from a systemic perspective. Thus, some international lawyers hold the view that allowing for a right of humanitarian intervention will undermine the rule of law and thereby weaken the overall system.[49] Others take the position that it is preferable to breach the narrow positive law rule to better preserve the underlying values of the international legal system.[50]

Of greater interest in the present context are the scholars who attempt to critically interrogate the ideas underlying humanitarian intervention. For example, reflecting on the war in Afghanistan from 2001 onwards, Vasuki Nesiah explores what she calls the discourses of humanitarian cosmopolitanism.[51] Examining the reactions to the intervention in Afghanistan, she shows how the concept of humanitarianism functioned not in opposition to militarism, but rather as a complement to it.[52] The war in Afghanistan started out as an exercise of self-defence: the United States taking military action against the Taliban, which, in the view of the United States, was refusing to cooperate fully in containing Al Qaeda

[47] Art. 2(4) of the Charter prohibits 'the threat or use of force against the territorial integrity or political independence of any state, or in any other manner inconsistent with the Purposes of the United Nations'. The debate here is whether use of force aimed at protecting the slaughter of civilians is a 'use of force' against the 'territorial integrity or political independence' of that state.

[48] See Orford, *Reading Humanitarian Intervention*, above n. 7, pp. 40–7 for a concise but thorough overview of the different schools of thought both in terms of the end result (is force permitted or not?) and the route taken to get to that conclusion (doctrinal or 'for the sake of the system'). See also Thomas M. Franck, *Recourse to Force: State Action Against Threats and Armed* Attacks (Cambridge: Cambridge University Press, 2002), p. 136; Christine Gray, 'The Principles of Non-use of Force' in Vaughan Lowe and Colin Warbrick (eds.), *The United Nations and the Principles of International Law* (Abingdon: Routledge, 1994), p. 33; Dino Kritisiotis, 'Reappraising Policy Objections to Humanitarian Intervention' (1998) 19 *Michigan Journal of International Law* 1005; Fernando R. Teson, *Humanitarian Intervention: An Inquiry into Law and Morality, 2nd ed.* (New York: Transnational Publishers, 1997) p. 270.

[49] As discussed by Orford, *Reading Humanitarian Intervention*, above n. 7, p. 45.

[50] Ibid.

[51] Nesiah, 'From Berlin to Bonn to Baghdad', above n. 45, p. 77.

[52] Ibid., p. 76.

following the attacks in the United States in September 2001. However, even before the military campaign started, ideas of humanitarianism were called on in order to bolster the narrower claims of self-defence. This was particularly easy to do because for many years, there had been repeated and persistent concerns raised about human rights standards in Afghanistan under Taliban rule. The statement by then UK Prime Minister Tony Blair, some days before the war started, illustrates this interweaving of the security argument with human rights. He said:

> Our stated aim, as you know, is to bring to justice those responsible for the attacks of a fortnight ago, which killed several thousand people, including many, many British people. The Taliban regime stands in the way of that. But I also want to add this: our fight is with that regime, not with the people of Afghanistan. These people have also suffered for years: their rights abused, women's rights non-existent, poverty and illness ignored, a regime without respect or justice for its own people. A regime founded on fear, and funded largely by drugs and crime.[53]

Laura Bush, then United States First Lady, was able to declare that the war in Afghanistan was about the rights of women.[54] President George Bush's 'axis of evil' statement in January 2002 weaves together terrorism/security issues with the language of human rights repression. He said:

> Our second goal is to prevent regimes that sponsor terror from threatening America or our friends and allies with weapons of mass destruction. Some of these regimes have been pretty quiet since September the 11th. But we know their true nature. North Korea is a regime arming with missiles and weapons of mass destruction, *while starving its citizens.*
>
> Iran aggressively pursues these weapons and exports terror, while an unelected few *repress the Iranian people's hope for freedom.*
>
> Iraq continues to flaunt its hostility toward America and to support terror. The Iraqi regime has plotted to develop anthrax, and nerve gas, and nuclear weapons for over a decade. This is a regime that has *already used poison gas to murder thousands of its own citizens – leaving the bodies of mothers huddled over their dead children.* This is a regime that agreed to international inspections – then kicked out the inspectors. This is a regime that has something to hide from the civilized world.
>
> States like these, and their terrorist allies, constitute an axis of evil . . .[55]

[53] Tony Blair, Statement delivered at 10 Downing Street, 25 September 2001.

[54] Laura Bush, Radio Address to the Nation, 16 November 2001, available at www.whitehouse.gov/new/releases/2001/11/20011117.html.

[55] George W. Bush, State of the Union Address, 29 January 2002, available at https://georgewbush-whitehouse.archives.gov/news/releases/2002/01/20020129-11.html. Emphasis added.

This weaving together of security imperatives along with humanitarian concerns is not just a rhetorical move by the states involved (in particular the United States and the United Kingdom), but by key non-state actors as well. Human Rights Watch, for example, called repeatedly for a larger military role by the United States in order to protect human rights in Afghanistan.[56] During the Bosnian War, Human Rights Watch shifted its stance towards favouring the use of force to ensure delivery of humanitarian aid.[57] Within Amnesty International as well, there was a shift in approach as it drafted Guidelines for the use of force, with the Guidelines becoming more receptive to the use of military force to respond to humanitarian atrocities.[58] This shift by the humanitarian organisations towards approving (more or less explicitly) military intervention was probably inevitable given their earlier shift from simply providing assistance to wanting long term solutions.[59] Once a long-term solution is sought, it is only a short further step towards advocating for what Chandler terms as 'rights based interventions'.[60]

Whatever the reason for the shift within some agencies and some sectors of civil society, through these examples we see that humanitarianism can be, and is, co-opted by the military agenda and is not always, or perhaps ever, entirely separate from the impulse to military action.

C Application to Humanitarian Disarmament Campaigns

Does humanitarianism's complicity with militarism have any traction when humanitarianism migrates into the world of disarmament? On first blush, the answer would seem to be 'no'. It is not immediately apparent how disarmament could be seen as anything other than anti-military. Weapons are, after all, the tools of the military and therefore eliminating entire categories of weapons seems to be difficult to fit within a 'complicity-with-militarism' paradigm. However, even allowing for its overblown rhetoric, a re-reading of the extract above from the 2002 State of the Union address above allows us to see clearly how *weapons* are the

[56] Discussed by Nesiah, 'From Berlin to Bonn to Baghdad', above n. 45, p. 94.

[57] Karen Engle, '"Calling in the Troops": The Uneasy Relationship Among Women's Rights, Human Rights, and Humanitarian Intervention' (2007) 20 *Harvard Human Rights Journal* 189, 202.

[58] Ibid., p. 203.

[59] Chandler, 'The Road to Military Humanitarianism', above n. 21, p. 683.

[60] Ibid., p. 689.

centrepiece of the perceived threat from North Korea, Iran and Iraq.[61] It seems that one of the triggers to becoming a pariah state is the possession of pariah weapons and that can, and does, trigger a militaristic response. Part of that dynamic is an assessment that the pariah state is in some way anti-humanitarian in the way it treats its own citizens.

While the diplomatic exchanges and academic discussions around all three situations (Iraq, North Korea and Iran) show the link between possession of weapons or the alleged failure to disarm on the one hand and a threat of military intervention on the other, the clearest example of this dynamic playing out was the Iraq War 2003. That experience shows us the way in which disarmament and militarism can be intertwined.

The alleged possession of nuclear, chemical and biological weapons by Iraq was the basis on which the United States, the United Kingdom and Australia claimed to be acting lawfully in launching Operation Freedom in March 2003, and subsequently removed Saddam Hussein's government from power. As with humanitarian intervention discussed above, the literature on the Iraq War 2003 is replete with debates about whether and to what extent the self-defence exception was applicable (the so-called pre-emptive self defence argument), how Security Council resolutions should be interpreted and applied, and indeed whether there was a new exception emerging to the ban on use of force triggered by the possession of weapons of mass destruction.[62] There was also extensive debate about the reliability and accuracy of the allegations of continued weapons-possession by Iraq, due to the fact that there had been international inspectors in Iraq for much of the 1990s.[63]

My interest here is not in the merits or otherwise of those doctrinal debates, or even the debate about the facts, but rather I want to pay attention to the way in which alleged possession of certain categories of weapons became the basis for military intervention and that is made easier by a claim of some type of humanitarianism. For example, the British Government released a paper on Iraq's weapons programme in September 2002.[64] The final chapter of that report is devoted to the

[61] State of the Union Address, above n. 55.

[62] See generally the collection of essays in (2003) 97(3) *American Journal of International Law* 553.

[63] See generally, Hans Blix, *Disarming Iraq* (New York: Pantheon Books, 2004); Report of a Committee of Privy Counsellors *The Report of the Iraq Inquiry* (6 July 2016) (*Chilcott Report*).

[64] Iraq's Weapons of Mass Destruction: The Assessment of the British Government (September 2002).

human rights abuses by the Iraqi government (although note that the purpose of the paper was to provide an assessment of the intelligence around the weapons issue). Paragraph 9 of the Executive Summary explicitly links the disarmament and the rights issue by saying: 'But the threat from Iraq does not depend solely on the capabilities we have described. It arises also because of the violent and aggressive nature of Saddam Hussein's regime. His record of internal repression and external aggression gives rise to unique concerns about the threat he poses'.[65] This linkage is significant because in retrospect, the discourse around the weapons clearly laid the basis for the idea of 'rogue' weapons, although in fact the discourse at the time was framed around the idea of 'rogue states'. The fact that the USA, the UK and Australia used the alleged possession of a category of weapon in order to justify their invasion of Iraq suggests that, at least in the minds of some political leaders, there is a link between a humanitarian ideal and military intervention. Thus we see that humanitarianism and militarism are not necessarily in opposition and can be complementary, even in the context of disarmament.[66]

IV Humanitarianism's Imperative of Action

A Introduction

The third critique of humanitarianism, related to the concern about complicity discussed in Section III, is that framing a situation as a humanitarian crisis sets up an imperative to act, and frequently that imperative is closely tied to a military response. This section explains that critique and then examines how it applies in the context of humanitarian disarmament by means of an analysis of the responses to the use of chemical weapons in the Syrian War.

B The Imperative of Action

Anne Orford wrote *Reading Humanitarian Intervention* in the wake of the Kosovo intervention in 1999 and as the East Timor

[65] Ibid.

[66] For another example of how arms control might actually support militarism, see the thoughtful discussion about how some aspects of international nuclear law, while apparently constituting resistance against nuclear weapons, in fact serve to enhance the value of those weapons: Anna Hood, 'Questioning International Nuclear Weapons Law as a Field of Resistance' in Jonathan L. Black-Branch and Dieter Fleck (eds.), *Nuclear Non-Proliferation under International Law - Volume V* (The Hague: TMC Asser Press, 2020), 11.

intervention was unfolding.[67] The book explores her concern that all voices in the humanitarian intervention debates (for or against, and whether doctrinal or systemic in orientation) tend to share an implicit assumption that international law is somehow emancipatory, and that humanitarian intervention (whether 'lawful' or not) is a manifestation of that emancipation. One of Orford's key concerns is what might be described as the 'humanitarian imperative' – the way in which humanitarian crises are constructed and thus trigger a reaction of 'we must do *something*!' That 'something' is locked into a binary of military force or standing back and allowing atrocity to happen.[68] She argues that while humanitarian intervention appears to be a commitment to emancipatory ideals of freedom from oppression, responsibility for human dignity and valuing human life, in fact, rights undergo a significant shift when they are turned from a 'discourse of rebellion and dissent into that of state legitimacy'.[69] Thus, the core of Orford's critique is the way in which a humanitarian discourse locks us into an imperative of (military) action, as it becomes unacceptable in the face of a humanitarian crisis to 'do nothing'. The problem is that often (or perhaps, usually) this is a false binary that obscures other choices for action.

C The Imperative of (Military) Action and Humanitarian Disarmament

I turn now to consider this 'imperative of action' critique of humanitarian intervention and its possible relevance to the idea of humanitarian disarmament. A clear link between humanitarianism and militarism can be seen in the context of the use of chemical weapons in the Syrian War. Although of course there have been many attacks in the course of the war using chemical weapons, three episodes in particular are considered here: the sarin attacks in Ghouta, a suburb of Damascus in August 2013 resulting in approximately 1400 deaths; the sarin attacks in Khan

[67] Orford, *Reading Humanitarian Intervention*, above n. 7.

[68] See as well Hilary Charlesworth, 'International Law: A Discipline of Crisis' (2002) 65(3) *Modern Law Review* 377 for this line of thinking in the context of the Kosovo intervention; Hilary Charlesworth, 'Saddam Hussein: My Part in His Downfall' (2005) 23 *Wisconsin International Law Journal* 127 for her reflections on the Iraq War in a similar vein; and Hilary Charlesworth, 'Feminist Reflections on the Responsibility to Protect' (2010) 2 *Global Responsibility to Protect* 232.

[69] Orford, *Reading Humanitarian Intervention*, above n. 7, p. 35.

Sheikhoun in April 2017, in which approximately eighty people died; and the chlorine gas attacks in Douma in April 2018.[70]

My argument is that in both 2013 and 2018, an emphasis on the particular suffering wrought by chemical weapons (in other words, a humanitarian discourse of suffering) was an important part of the justification by the United States and its allies towards a military response in Syria. Although hundreds of thousands of Syrians had been subjected to horrendous suffering and deaths through the use of conventional weapons for many years, with the use of chemical weapons, a 'shared universal' norm against a certain weapon type (here chemical weapons) was exploited in order to provide justification for military invention. Thus, we see an 'imperative of action' being generated with the assertion that use of chemical weapons in and of itself justifies military intervention.[71]

In fact, even before chemical weapons were actually used in the conflict, the 'imperative of action' became evident when, in August 2012, then US President Obama stated that any use of chemical weapons in the Syrian war would be a 'game changer' and would constitute a 'red line' in terms of how the United States would approach the conflict.[72] This statement was in response to repeated allegations by various rebel groups that government troops either were, or were preparing to, use chemical weapons. The concerns were not without foundation. Syria had remained steadfastly outside of the Chemical Weapons Convention, the centrepiece of international law's contemporary prohibition on these weapons, one of only seven states in the world at the time to do so.[73] In the arms

[70] Many other instances of chemical weapons use are also alleged or documented, see for example: René Pita and Juan Domingo, 'The Use of Chemical Weapons in the Syrian Conflict' (2014) 2 *Toxics* 391; further, the Joint Investigative Mechanism confirmed at least three instances of the use of chlorine in October 2016; for a media investigation, see Bashar Al-Assad, 'A year after Khan Sheikhoun, Syria chemical weapons "still used"' *Al Jazeera*, 9 April 2018 available at www.aljazeera.com/indepth/features/year-khan-sheikhoun-syria-chemical-weapons-180404120132586.html. See as well Tim McCormack, 'Chemical Weapons and Other Atrocities: Contrasting Responses to the Syrian Crisis' (2016) 92 *International Legal Studies* 512. For an overview of chemical weapons use in the Syrian War, see Arms Control Association, *Timeline of Syrian Chemical Weapons Activity, 2012–2018*, June 2018.

[71] Now asserted by some as customary international law: see Michael P. Scharf, 'Striking a Grotian Moment: How the Syria Airstrikes Changed International Law Relating to Humanitarian Interventions' (2019) 19(2) *Chicago Journal of International Law* 586.

[72] See Mark Landler, 'Obama Threatens Force against Syria' *New York Times* (20 August 2012) A 7.

[73] Convention on the Prohibition of the Development, Production, Stockpiling and Use of Chemical Weapons and on their Destruction, opened for signature 13 January 1993, 1975

control community, both at state level, and among NGO commentators, it was generally understood that Syria had stockpiles of mustard gas (a blistering agent) as well as the more lethal sarin (a nerve agent) and VX, another nerve agent, many times more lethal than sarin. Therefore, the idea that chemical weapons might be deployed in the conflict was not fanciful, and indeed was borne out by subsequent events.

Despite the warning from the United States, chemical weapons were indeed used and President Obama's 'red line' was well and truly crossed. While a military response was not ultimately forthcoming following the 21 August attack, of interest here is the way in which the various responses evinced a clear momentum towards the possibility of a military response because of the particular weapon used.

This was particularly clear from the UK response. On 29 August 2013, the UK Government issued a legal opinion on the question of the legality of any use of force in Syria in response to the Ghouta attacks.[74] The document is a clear example of the melding of the humanitarian discourse with the use of a particular category of weapon.[75] Paragraph 2 states:

> The use of chemical weapons by the Syrian regime is a serious crime of international concern, as a breach of the customary international law prohibition on use of chemical weapons, and amounts to a war crime and a crime against humanity. However, while the legal basis for military action would be humanitarian intervention; *the aim is to relieve humanitarian suffering by deterring or disrupting the further use of chemical weapons.*[76]

UNTS 45 (entered into force 29 April 1997). At the time, in addition to Syria, the non-parties were: Angola, Democratic Peoples' Republic of Korea, Egypt and Somalia, with Israel and Myanmar which had signed the treaty but not taken the step of becoming states parties. Since then, along with Syria, Myanmar, Angola and Somalia have all become states parties, leaving DPRK and Egypt entirely outside the treaty and Israel remaining as a signatory state.

[74] Prime Minister's Office, Chemical Weapon Use by Syrian Regime: UK Government Legal Position (Policy Paper, 29 August) available at www.gov.uk/government/publications/chemical-weapon-use-by-syrian-regime-uk-government-legal-position/chemical-weapon-use-by-syrian-regime-uk-government-legal-position-html-version (UK Government Legal Position).

[75] For a discussion of how this document is considered by some to contribute to an emerging right of humanitarian intervention, see the discussion by Christian Henderson, 'The UK Government's Legal Opinion on Forcible Measures in Response to the Use of Chemical Weapons by the Syrian Government' (2015) 64(1) *International and Comparative Law Quarterly* 179, 182. See also Scharf, 'Striking a Grotian Moment', above n. 71, pp. 607–8.

[76] Emphasis added.

Thus, the United Kingdom was justifying the idea of military action as a means of averting a humanitarian catastrophe being the further use of chemical weapons. Echoing the Guidelines proposed following the Kosovo intervention in 1999, the opinion went on to assert that even if the Security Council was unable to act due to the exercise of a veto power by one of the permanent members, the United Kingdom would still have the legal authority: 'to take exceptional measures in order to alleviate the scale of the overwhelming humanitarian catastrophe in Syria by deterring and disrupting the further use of chemical weapons by the Syrian regime'.[77] The three conditions echo the Guidelines proposed following the Kosovo intervention in 1999, that is:

> (i) there is convincing evidence, generally accepted by the international community as a whole, of extreme humanitarian distress on a large scale, requiring immediate and urgent relief;
> (ii) it must be objectively clear that there is no practicable alternative to the use of force if lives are to be saved; and
> (iii) the proposed use of force must be necessary and proportionate to the aim of relief of humanitarian need and must be strictly limited in time and scope to this aim (i.e. the minimum necessary to achieve that end and for no other purpose).[78]

Addressing the first of those conditions, the Opinion went on:

> The Syrian regime has been killing its people for two years, with reported deaths now over 100,000 and refugees at nearly 2 million. The large-scale use of chemical weapons by the regime in a heavily populated area on 21 August 2013 is a war crime and perhaps the most egregious single incident of the conflict. Given the Syrian regime's pattern of use of chemical weapons over several months, it is likely that the regime will seek to use such weapons again. It is also likely to continue frustrating the efforts of the United Nations to establish exactly what has happened. Renewed attacks using chemical weapons by the Syrian regime would cause further suffering and loss of civilian lives, and would lead to displacement of the civilian population on a large scale and in hostile conditions.[79]

The point to note in this context is that while the first sentence of this paragraph refers to the overall death count and how many people had been displaced, the remainder of the paragraph deals with the chemical

[77] UK Government Legal Position, above n. 74, para. 4.

[78] Ibid., reflecting the 'guidelines' discussed in House of Commons Select Committee on Foreign Affairs, Fourth Report on Kosovo (2000).

[79] UK Government Legal Position, above n. 74, para. 5(i).

weapons attack. Even by its most 'generous' estimates at the time of approximately 1300 deaths, that would represent a tiny fraction of the casualties in the overall conflict. So despite the language of 'large-scale' use of the weapons, it is clearly the *type* of weapon that is claimed to be of concern, not the *number* of casualties. It is the use of chemical weapons, not the number of casualties, that triggers the humanitarian concern.

In the United States, although there was a much greater emphasis on the threat to security of the United States, there were still a number of references to the moral disgust at the use of chemical weapons. On 31 August 2013, President Obama appealed to a sense of a universal moral community, and stressed the imperative of action when he simply stated that 'if we really do want to turn away from taking appropriate action in the face of such an unspeakable outrage, then we must acknowledge the costs of doing nothing'.[80]

The following month, again referring to the Ghouta attack, President Obama said that 'the world watched in horror as men, women and children were massacred in Syria'.[81] He closed the statement with a call to military action, by saying 'our security and our values demand that we cannot turn away from the massacre of countless civilians with chemical weapons'.[82]

The French as well were appalled by the attacks, with 50 per cent in favour of sanctioning (read: 'intervening against') President Assad. The language of the President was focused on avenging the massacre of civilians.[83] The language of universal condemnation, universal community was notable: a French journalist wrote 'Aleppo belongs not to Syria, but to the world'.[84]

[80] Statement by United States President Barak Obama, 31 August 2013, www.whitehouse.gov/the-press-office/2013/08/31/statement-president-syria.

[81] The White House, Remarks by the President in Address to the Nation on Syria (10 September 2013), www.whitehouse.gov/the-press-office/2013/09/10/remarkspresident-address-nation-syria.

[82] Ibid. And see the discussion by Michelle Bentley, 'The Problem with the Chemical Weapons Taboo' (2015) 27(2) *Peace Review* 228 and Michelle Bentley, 'Strategic Taboos: Chemical Weapons and US Foreign Policy' (2014) 90(5) *International Affairs* 1033, 1034: 'US policy with regard to Syria cannot be comprehended purely as a direct reaction to the use of chemical weapons, but should be seen in the light of its exploitation as a rhetorical tool for shaping international response'.

[83] John Gaffney, 'Political Leadership and the Politics of Performance: France, Syria and the Chemical Weapons Crisis of 2013' (2014) 12 *French Politics* 218.

[84] Bernard-Henri Lévy, 'Save Aleppo!' 19 June 2013 from www.thedailybeast.com/save-aleppo (writing in the context of the overall destruction of Aleppo).

As matters played out, there was no military response to the 21 August 2013 attack in Ghouta as a result of the sarin attacks. Rather, the United States and Russia worked together to broker a deal with Syria, whereby Syria joined the Chemical Weapons Convention, and agreed to an expedited process to declare its chemical weapons stockpiles and have those stockpiles destroyed under international verification.[85] My argument though is to observe the manner in which the use of a particular weapon garnered momentum towards military action.

The second major chemical weapons attack, in Khan Sheikhoun, Idlib Province on 4 April 2017, in which eighty people died, did in fact elicit an immediate military response. On 7 April 2017, the United States launched fifty-nine missiles against an airfield understood to have been used to store chemical weapons and to have housed the aircraft involved in the sarin attacks.[86]

There is again some evidence linking humanitarian concerns to a military imperative. For example, US President Donald Trump described the attack as 'intolerable' and 'reprehensible', warning that it could not be ignored by 'the civilized world'.[87] At an emergency session of the Security Council, the US Ambassador to the United Nations took the humanitarian discourse to a whole new level standing in the Council Chamber, holding photographs of victims of the chemical weapons attacks during the ensuing debate, as she advocated for military response.[88]

As Michelle Bentley argues however, to use this example as the basis for evidence of a shift of US policy to a moral compass, or in humanitarian solidarity with Syrians would be an error.[89] Rather she suggests factors such as President Trump's own personal strategic interests or a show of strength.[90] While she concedes that aspects of his rhetoric at the

[85] McCormack, 'Chemical Weapons and other Atrocities', above n. 70, pp. 518–26. He suggests that their shared bilateral commitment to preventing the re-emergence of chemical weapons lies behind their willingness to set aside their differences at that point and work together to bring Syria 'into the fold' of the CWC community.

[86] Scharf, 'Striking a Grotian Moment', above n. 71, p. 591.

[87] The White House, Statement from President Donald J Trump (4 April 2017) www.whitehouse.gov.

[88] Somini Sengupta and Rick Gladstone, 'US May Act Alone Over Syria' *New York Times* (6 April 2017) A10.

[89] Michelle Bentley, 'Instability and Incoherence: Trump, Syria, and Chemical Weapons' (2017) 5(2) *Critical Studies on Security* 168, 169.

[90] Ibid., p. 170.

time did chime with the taboo against chemical weapons, there was little evidence that he had, in fact, considered the taboo.[91]

The third attack in April 2018, which took place in Douma, another suburb of Damascus and resulted in forty deaths,[92] not only elicited a military response but, as had been the case for the 2013 attack, the rhetoric immediately tuned into the suffering brought on by use of this particular weapon. The statement of the United Kingdom at the ensuing Security Council debate not only melded together humanitarian sensibilities and an imperative of (military) action, but also attempted to position itself above and beyond the politics of the situation.[93] Ambassador Karen Pierce said this:

> The use of chemical weapons is an escalatory and a diabolical act. What Russia is trying to do, it strikes me, Mr President, is to turn the debate in this Council away from a discussion of the use of chemical weapons into a dispute between East and West, presenting itself as the victim. It is far too important, Mr President, to play games with the politics between East and West in respect of chemical weapons. Russia's crocodile tears for the people of Eastern Ghouta has an easy answer. It is to join us in a non-political attempt to get in humanitarian and protection workers from the UN to do their job of looking after and mitigating the risk to civilians.[94]

The French Ambassador's statement appealed to a sense of shared victimhood, explicitly linking the 'devastating effects' of the weapon with the need for a military response: 'My country, which knew at first hand the devastating effects of chemical weapons during the First World War, will never again allow impunity for their use. . . . [L]ast night's strikes are a necessary response to the chemical massacres in Syria. They are a response in the service of law . . .'.[95] I am not concerned with the

[91] Ibid., p. 169. See as well Jasmine Gani, 'Why Trump's Syria Strike May Have Been a Positive Step', blog, 11 April 2017, available at https://blogs.lse.ac.uk/usappblog/2017/04/11/why-trumps-syria-strike-may-have-been-a-positive-step/, suggesting that the response did not represent a new moral policy for the US Administration.

[92] Various media sources reported the number as forty. The Arms Control Association put the deaths at 'several dozen': Arms Control Association, *Timeline*, above n. 70.

[93] By this point, the relationship between the UK and the Russian Federation was particularly fraught. Not only had the Russians supported President Al Assad throughout the Syrian War, including providing military support, but Russia stood accused of being behind an attack against a former Russian officer, Sergei Skripal in the UK, using a chemical agent, Novichok.

[94] Ambassador Karen Pierce, United Kingdom Permanent Representative to the United Nations, Statement to Security Council Session on the use of chemical weapons by Syria in Douma (9 April 2018).

[95] Comments of François Delattre in UNSCOR, 73rd sess, 8233rd mtg, UN Doc S/PV.8233 (14 April 2018).

doctrinal debate here (does the use of chemical weapons trigger an exception to the prohibition on the use of force?). Rather, examining the responses to the use of chemical weapons in Syria allows us to see the way in which the debates turned on the notion of an 'unacceptable' or 'barbaric' weapon. A key point to note is the way in which the debate collapses two different lines of thinking into one. There is no question that use of chemical weapons is, and was at that time, unlawful as a matter of international law. This is the case both in terms of state responsibility at customary international law, and as well, it is accepted that the use of chemical weapons is an international crime.[96] Even accepting the fact that chemical weapons had been used, and even accepting that such use constituted an international crime, that does not mean that we leap from breach of a rule to (military) enforcement by a select coalition of states. This is a question of enforcement, and that needs to take account of other fundamental rules of the system – namely in this instance, the rule of non-intervention.[97]

That leap from breach of a norm to some kind of selective enforcement by self-appointed 'international law sheriffs' depends on a wholescale acceptance of an imperative to action based on the 'humanitarian' crisis caused by chemical weapons. If the conflict is reduced to this one (manageable) question, then if we do something about this, we have done something about the conflict. It creates the illusion that we have 'done something'.

V Hierarchies of Suffering and the Construction of 'Pariah Weapons'

A Introduction

The final critique of humanitarianism is concerned with the way in which humanitarianism, inadvertently but inevitably, creates hierarchies of humanity. This is a question about whose suffering is accorded value. I explain why creating such a hierarchy is problematic and explore whether the criticism has any traction in the context of humanitarian disarmament.

[96] Rome Statute of the International Criminal Court, opened for signature 17 July 1998, 2187 UNTS 90 (entered into force 1 July 2002) art. 8(2)(b)(xviii); UN Doc S/Res/2118 (27 September 2013). See generally, Carsten Stahn, 'Syria and the Semantics of Intervention, Aggression and Punishment: On "Red Lines" and "Blurred Lines"' (2013) 11(5) *Journal of International Criminal Justice* 955.

[97] Stahn, 'Syria and the Semantics of Intervention', above n. 96, p. 958.

B Hierarchies of Humanity

Returning again to the work of Didier Fassin, he argues that humanitarianism is most often concerned about the suffering of what he calls 'distant others' rather than the destitute at our doorstep, and how that leads us to create hierarchies of humanity – some are deserving of compassion and the rest are the undeserving.[98]

But even within the world of 'distant others', hierarchies form. A combination of constant social and traditional media, along with the international lawyer's addiction to the cortisol triggered by a crisis,[99] means that attention lurches from those left destitute from tsunamis, to those traumatised and rendered homeless by earthquakes, to victims of ISIS beheadings, to displaced communities trudging to ill-equipped camps. All of these humanitarian crises grab our attention (for a day), before moving on to the next sensationalist deadline. In fact, we have even seen precisely that phenomenon in the Syrian context – with whole-scale outrage to the sarin attacks in August 2013, much less attention paid to the two subsequent attacks in April 2017 and April 2018, even though these last two actually did result in military responses, and almost utter indifference to repeated chlorine attacks in between.

Generally speaking, slow burning, less dramatic human tragedies are neglected and ignored. Take, for example, the problem of slow starvation. The FAO estimates that in 2017, there were 821 million people suffering from undernourishment in the world, that is, around one person in every nine (the figure is one in five in Africa).[100] That undernourishment is so severe in places that data from 2013 shows that 875,000 children under the age of five died as a result.[101] Despite some improvement between 2005–14, the overall figures have started to rise again.[102] The failure to respond to this could well be the ill-defined 'lack of political will', or the fact that the disaster is too slow-moving to interest a relentless twenty-four-hour-a-day international media and thus garner public pressure. The relevant point here, though, is that the humanitarian reliance on the 'shock factor' is complicit in legitimising this lack of attention and in

[98] Fassin, *Humanitarian Reason*, above n. 22, p. 223.

[99] The term is borrowed from Charlesworth, 'A Discipline of Crisis', above n. 68.

[100] Food and Agriculture Organization of the United Nations, *State of Food Security and Nutrition in the World: Building Climate Resilience for Food Security and Nutrition* (2018) p. 8.

[101] Ibid., p. 19.

[102] Ibid., p. 3, Figure 1.

doing so, sustains the hierarchy, where fast-moving human tragedy is privileged over slow-burning forms of suffering.

One reasonable response to this criticism is that it is not possible to fix every crisis, and it is better to attempt to contribute to one crisis in a small way – something is better than nothing.[103] However, the simple point for this discussion is that in 'doing something', a hierarchy of suffering has become inescapable, but is generally unacknowledged.

It is difficult to reconcile the hierarchy with the espoused ideal of a shared humanity (recall the claim that 'Aleppo belongs to us all').[104] That is, even as humanitarianism brings focus to an individual's suffering, that trauma is presented as having a universal quality and is therefore presented as a 'suffering without borders'.[105] Writing in the context of international law, Martti Koskenniemi expresses concerns about the language of universal humanity, which he argues is now pervasive in international legal discourse. This 'shared humanity' discourse, he argues, renders invisible the reality of political choices and lifts the speaker's values to an exalted position.[106] This is particularly evident when it comes to celebrity humanitarianism – the Bob Geldof/Band Aid phenomenon – again in the context of the Ethiopian famine.[107] Humanitarianism becomes a lifestyle choice rather than being centred on the victim, let alone providing space for a serious (or any) consideration of the structural injustices lying beneath a particular crisis.[108]

C Hierarchies of Weapons?

The regulation of weapons (that is, limitations on the ways or circumstances in which weapons can be deployed) as well as disarmament (that is, elimination of the weapons themselves) has always privileged some weapons and demonised others. Within the body of the law of armed conflict, we can see that the law prohibits or regulates certain weapons explicitly and prohibits or regulates some weapons implicitly. As discussed in Chapter 2, examples of explicit prohibitions can be seen as early as the St Petersburg Declaration in 1868 outlawing the use of explosive

[103] This feeds into the imperative of action point discussed in the preceding section.
[104] Lévy, 'Save Allepo!', above n. 84.
[105] Fassin and Rechtman, *The Empire of Trauma*, above n. 22.
[106] Koskenniemi, 'Review of *Humanity's Law*', above n. 3, p. 395.
[107] See generally, Müller, '"The Ethiopian Famine" Revisited', above n. 27.
[108] This point is an echo of some of the thinking of Mutua, 'Savages, Victims and Saviors', above n. 6.

projectiles and the Hague Declaration IV in 1899 prohibiting the use of expanding bullets.[109] Implicit prohibitions came later and can be seen in provisions such as Article 35 of the Additional Protocol I in 1977, which provides that 'the right to choose means and methods of warfare is not unlimited'.[110] Thus, some weapons are prohibited if they result in indiscriminate casualties (that is, cannot differentiate between civilians and combatants, the latter constituting lawful targets in war). The relevant point is that international humanitarian law does not prohibit *all* attacks, or *all* weapons, in fact it has as its basic assumption that there will be attacks (and therefore weapons) and that some attacks are excused by the law.[111] By necessity then, it can only prohibit or regulate *some* weapons. It is inherently hierarchical.

It is not surprising then that the closely related area of disarmament has also been partial in its approach. To cite one simple example: chemical and biological weapons have been prohibited, with almost all states in the world under a legal obligation to eliminate their stockpiles of these two categories of weapons.[112] However, until very recently there has been no equivalent ban on nuclear weapons, but the Treaty on the Prohibition of Nuclear Weapons (TPNW) concluded in 2017 is not yet in force and in any event the nuclear weapons possessor states have clearly indicated

[109] Declaration Renouncing the Use, in Time of War, of Explosive Projectiles under 400 Grammes Weight, opened for signature 29 November 1868, [1901] ATS 125 (entered into force 11 December 1868); Declaration (IV, 3) Concerning Expanding Bullets 1899, reproduced in James Brown Scott (ed.), *Hague Conventions and Declarations of 1899 and 1907: Accompanied by Tables of Signatures, Ratifications and Adhesions of the Various Powers, and Texts of Reservations, 2nd ed.* (New York: Oxford University Press, 1915); see discussion in Chapter 2. The Declaration stands as a vivid example of hierarchies of humanity in that the prohibition only applied as between 'civilized nations' on the justification that the natives in the Empire would simply not desist in their attacks faced only with ordinary weaponry.

[110] Protocol Additional to the Geneva Conventions of 12 August 1949, and relating to the Protection of Victims of International Armed Conflicts, opened for signature 12 December 1977, 1125 UNTS 3 (entered into force 7 December 1978) art. 35(1).

[111] Leading Jeanne Woods to argue that therefore international humanitarian law is actually permissive of violence: Jeanne Woods, 'Theorizing Peace as a Human Right' (2013) 7 *Human Rights and International Legal Discourse* 178.

[112] Convention on the Prohibition of the Development, Production and Stockpiling of Bacteriological (Biological) and Toxin Weapons and on their Destruction, opened for signature 10 April 1972, 1015 UNTS 163 (entered into force 26 March 1975) (172 states parties) and Convention on the Prohibition of the Development, Production, Stockpiling and Use of Chemical Weapons and on their Destruction, opened for signature 13 January 1993, 1975 UNTS 45 (entered into force 29 April 1997) (193 states parties).

that they will not participate in the regime.[113] There are, of course, well-known political reasons why this situation prevails, but my point here is to demonstrate that there have always been hierarchies in terms of both weapons regulation and elimination.

The fact that a humanitarian discourse is being used to garner support for additional weapons prohibitions does not eliminate the hierarchy dynamic – it simply reflects it. That is not to say that we should not attempt to ban anti-personnel landmines, cluster munitions and so on, but in doing so, we should acknowledge that we are engaging in the construction of a hierarchy of suffering. Even as we create a category of 'pariah' weapons, we implicitly accept the use of other weapons. In this way, we arrive at the Syrian war where the international community so clearly privileged the deaths arising from chemical weapons, but has refrained from expending anything like this same outrage on lives lost due to 'ordinary' weapons, even when those weapons have been deployed unlawfully (being deliberately targeted at civilians, or deliberately used in densely populated residential areas).[114]

This last point closes our circle. In 1899, with the opening of the Hague Peace Conference, the modern era of disarmament began.[115] It was a *peace* conference, not a *disarmament* conference. It did not achieve peace, but did achieve some modest gains in disarmament. It raised, squarely, the question of which comes first: peace or disarmament? That question persists. Peace is seen as utopian and hopeless: the 'peace movement' routinely derided as foolishly following a naïve, and some say, dangerous, agenda. Disarmament of particular categories of weapons was the fall-back position – better than nothing. A pragmatic response to the reality of a world awash in weapons. But in choosing the incremental road since 1899, we have implicitly endorsed some weapons and some killing. Applying a humanitarian discourse to our disarmament campaigns has not changed that.

VI Conclusion

My aim in the chapter has been to step away from the practice of humanitarian disarmament and instead critique it as a concept. In

[113] Treaty on the Prohibition of Nuclear Weapons, opened for signature 20 September 2017 (not yet in force). See Chapter 7, Section VI.A.

[114] And see Bentley, 'Instability and Incoherence', above n. 89.

[115] Andrew Webster, 'Hague Conventions (1899, 1907)' in Gordon Martel (ed.), *The Encyclopedia of War* (Oxford: Blackwell, 2012), p. 1.

doing so, I have shown how critiques of humanitarianism generally have traction in the context of humanitarian disarmament. Specifically, I have argued that humanitarian disarmament is vulnerable to four critiques: it purports to be apolitical and thus somehow beyond reproach; it is often complicit with militarism as seen through the experience of the Iraq War 2003; it can impel a military response as witnessed in the Syrian War; and it unavoidably sets up hierarchies of suffering even as it purports to establish a universally shared morality.

These critiques do not lead me to reject the humanitarian discourse entirely in the context of disarmament: it has been clear in earlier chapters that a key factor in the successes of the various humanitarian disarmament campaigns has been the way in which the real, human impacts of weapons have been brought to the fore and used to challenge the orthodox security paradigm. However, the discussion in this chapter should stand as a caution about the limitations and complexities of a humanitarian discourse in relation to weapons.

9

Conclusion

My core argument in this book has been that, far from being an invention of the post–Cold War era, humanitarian disarmament has had a long and complex history dating back at least 150 years to the St Petersburg Declaration in 1868.[1] My aim in drawing out that history (or at least some of it) has been to expose humanitarian disarmament's failures as well as successes, ebbs as well as flows, limitations as well as potential. I have shown that humanitarian disarmament, both in practice and in theory, is a complex and politicised concept, and one which is still evolving today. Thus, in Chapter 2 examining key moments which I have presented as constituting the origins of humanitarian disarmament, I have shown how the humanitarian appeals in the nineteenth century, as well as in the era of the League of Nations, were offered as a way to transcend the politics of the time, but that contemporary humanitarian discourses were themselves imbued with a particular politics. Similarly, in Chapters 4, 5 and 6, as the Non-Aligned Movement took form, the humanitarian concerns being raised about indiscriminate weapons were themselves – at least in part – motivated by political interests. The longer story of the humanitarian campaigns against nuclear weapons drawn out in Chapter 7 reveals, as well, the way in which those campaigns can be seen as highly political, rather than espousing a 'pure' humanitarian sensibility.

One of my key aims in the book as a whole has been to question what I see as the over-reliance on humanitarian discourse in contemporary disarmament campaigns. To that end, in Chapter 8, I considered four key critiques of 'humanitarianism' and I explored how those critiques have traction in the specific context of humanitarian disarmament. However, in adopting such a critical approach, it is not my intention to completely dismiss the idea of a humanitarian framing of disarmament because to do

[1] Declaration Renouncing the Use, in Time of War, of Explosive Projectiles under 400 Grammes Weight, opened for signature 29 November 1868, [1901] ATS 125 (entered into force 11 December 1868).

so would be to fail to acknowledge the continuous human suffering wrought by weapons of all kinds during the period I have studied here. It would also be blind to the impact that public opinion can, and at times does, play in how states formulate their disarmament (or armament) policies. Rather, I have adopted a critical approach in order to better understand and evaluate the practice and theory of humanitarian disarmament, while avoiding the 'celebratory commentary' and 'heroic' narrative of civil society victories on the one hand, and the increasingly moribund cynicism of the realists on the other.[2]

As signalled in Chapter 1, humanitarian disarmament is not simply a framing strategy – it is also a question of process, of engagement with a wider group of stakeholders beyond states.[3] In the longer story of humanitarian disarmament told in this book, those stakeholders – from the peace societies of the late nineteenth and early twentieth centuries to the social-media savvy umbrella civil society organisations of today – undoubtedly play an important part in disarmament processes. However, my explorations have revealed some complexities about this ever-closer relationship between states and civil society. In particular, I have shown in Chapters 5 (on anti-personnel landmines) and 6 (on cluster munitions) that the ever-closer cooperation between civil society and 'like-minded' states has resulted in a gap opening up where critical reflection ought to be. More specifically, I suggested in Chapter 5 that the work of ICBL in the post-EIF verification processes of the APLM Convention might risk co-option.[4] It seems that the increasingly close relationships between states and civil society raise important questions of accountability and transparency. Again, little work has been done on this aspect of humanitarian disarmament.

There is a great deal that I have not considered here, and much else that has been passed over in a perfunctory way that warrants much closer attention in future projects. While historians have engaged with

[2] Nik Hynek, 'Re-Visioning Morality and Progress in the Security Domain: Insights from Humanitarian Prohibition Politics' (2018) 55 *International Politics* 421, 422. See also the detailed and useful discussion calling for a more nuanced and up-to-date theory of engagement by transnational advocacy networks by John Borrie, Michael Spies and Wilfred Wan, 'Obstacles to Understanding the Emergency and Significance of the Treaty on the Prohibition of Nuclear Weapons' (2018) *Global Change, Peace and Security* 1, 18–23.

[3] Chapter 1, Section IV.C.

[4] Convention on the Prohibition of the Use, Stockpiling, Production and Transfer of Anti-Personnel Mines and on their Destruction, opened for signature 3 December 1997, 2056 UNTS 211, entered into force 1 March 1999.

disarmament efforts in the League era and before, international lawyers have been slower on the uptake. There is much more to explore about the humanitarian sensibilities of the time and the disarmament work of the League. The same is true for the period after 1945 into the Cold War era. Indeed, the relative silence of international lawyers in relation to disarmament during these decades is in itself a topic for study.[5] I omitted a number of multilateral disarmament treaties from the contemporary period from the discussion here, such as the Biological Weapons Convention 1972 and the Chemical Weapons Convention 1993, on the basis that in many respects they epitomise not so much humanitarian sensibilities but rather state security ideals. However, as I alluded to briefly in Chapter 5, there may be important similarities between those disarmament treaties and the more recent treaties, the point being that a closer consideration of a broader field of treaties might be illuminating. It is also the case that a great deal of actual disarmament has taken place in the context of bilateral treaties, in particular between the United States and the (now) Russian Federation. Might these be useful legal models for lawyers to consider in other contexts?

One of my key conclusions – that humanitarianism is not the only possible alternative to a security framing of disarmament – brings us to further unexplored parts of the disarmament landscape. What other discourses might be employed? A human rights lens was attempted in the 1980s, without significant success.[6] More recently, there are signs of what might be a new generation of human rights campaigns, with a focus on the right to life. The Human Rights Committee has recently adopted a new General Comment on the Right to Life, in which it states that the use of nuclear weapons would be incompatible with respect for the right to life, and may amount to a crime under international law.[7] Civil society

[5] For an attempt in this direction, see Treasa Dunworth, 'Disarmament Law: A Call to Arms' in Treasa Dunworth and Anna Hood (eds.), *Recovering Disarmament Law* (Routledge, forthcoming 2020).

[6] See for example, Stephen Marks, 'Emerging Human Rights' (1980–1) 33 *Rutgers Law Review* 435; Philip Alston, 'Peace as a Human Right' (1980) 11 *Security Dialogue* 319; Ved Nanda, 'Nuclear Weapons and the Right to Peace under International Law' (1983) 9 (2) *Brooklyn Journal of International Law* 283; and Saul Mendlovitz, 'Filling out the Right to Peace' (1983) 9(2) *Brooklyn Journal of International Law* 297. See the overview of attempted litigation in Tim Wright, 'Do Nuclear Weapons Violate the Right to Life under International Law?' (2008) 3 *Australian Journal of Peace Studies* 99.

[7] Human Rights Committee, *General Comment No. 36 (2018) on Article 6 of the International Covenant on Civil and Political Rights, and on the Right to Life*, 124th sess, UN Doc CCPR/C/GC/36 (30 October 2018).

worked hard to promote the General Comment, making detailed submissions supporting the inclusion of nuclear weapons in the Comment.[8] With the increasing challenges to state authority in the context of war-making powers, might the next frontier be a challenge to states' decision-making authority about the weapons of war?[9] What other ways of talking about disarmament might be available to us?

These questions, and many others besides, provide a rich research agenda for future scholarship. For now, it is my hope that the accounts set out here might help to open up a space for further enquiry and critique.

[8] My thanks to John Burroughs for our discussion on this point and for sharing his reflections. For submissions see Daniel Rietiker, 'The incompatibility of WMDs with the right to life (Article 6 ICCPR) – a submission to the UN Human Rights Committee' Association of Swiss Lawyers for Nuclear Disarmament, 8 September 2016; International Association of Lawyers against Nuclear Arms (IALANA) and Swiss Lawyers for Nuclear Disarmament (SLND), 'Threat or Use of Weapons of Mass Destruction and the Right to Life: Follow-up Submissions to the UN Human Rights Committee on draft General Comment no. 36', 5 October 2017. And on contemporary thinking on the right to peace, see Carolos Villán Durán, 'The Human Right to Peace: A Legislative Initiative from the Spanish Civil Society' (2009) 15(1) *Spanish Yearbook of International Law* 143.

[9] On war-making powers see, for example, Wolfgang Wagner et al., 'The Party Politics of Legislative-Executive Relations in Security and Defence Policy' (2017) 40(1) *West European Politics* 20. On the question of executive authority over use of nuclear weapons, see: Elaine Scarry, *Thermonuclear Monarchy: Choosing between Democracy and Doom* (New York: W. W. Norton and Co, 2014).

INDEX

CAMBRIDGE STUDIES IN INTERNATIONAL AND COMPARATIVE LAW

Books in the Series

151 *Marketing Global Justice: The Political Economy of International Criminal Law*
Christine Schwöbel-Patel

150 *International Status in the Shadow of Empire*
Cait Storr

149 *Treaties in Motion: The Evolution of Treaties from Formation to Termination*
Edited by Malgosia Fitzmaurice and Panos Merkouris

148 *Humanitarian Disarmament: An Historical Enquiry*
Treasa Dunworth

147 *Complementarity, Catalysts, Compliance: The International Criminal Court in Uganda, Kenya, and the Democratic Republic of Congo*
Christian M. De Vos

146 *Cyber Operations and International Law* François Delerue

145 *Comparative Reasoning in International Courts and Tribunals*
Daniel Peat

144 *Maritime Delimitation as a Judicial Process* Massimo Lando

143 *Prosecuting Sexual and Gender-Based Crimes at the International Criminal Court: Practice, Progress and Potential*
Rosemary Grey

142 *Capitalism as Civilisation: A History of International Law*
Ntina Tzouvala

141 *Sovereignty in China: A Genealogy of a Concept Since 1840*
Adele Carrai

140 *Narratives of Hunger in International Law: Feeding the World in Times of Climate Change*
Anne Saab

139 *Victim Reparation under the Ius Post Bellum: An Historical and Normative Perspective*
Shavana Musa

138 *The Analogy between States and International Organizations*
Fernando Lusa Bordin

137 *The Process of International Legal Reproduction: Inequality, Historiography, Resistance*
Rose Parfitt

136 *State Responsibility for Breaches of Investment Contracts*
Jean Ho

135 *Coalitions of the Willing and International Law: The Interplay between Formality and Informality*
Alejandro Rodiles

134 *Self-Determination in Disputed Colonial Territories*
Jamie Trinidad

133 *International Law as a Belief System*
Jean d'Aspremont

132 *Legal Consequences of Peremptory Norms in International Law*
Daniel Costelloe

131 *Third-Party Countermeasures in International Law*
Martin Dawidowicz

130 *Justification and Excuse in International Law: Concept and Theory of General Defences*
Federica Paddeu

129 *Exclusion from Public Space: A Comparative Constitutional Analysis*
Daniel Moeckli

128 *Provisional Measures before International Courts and Tribunals*
Cameron A. Miles

127 *Humanity at Sea: Maritime Migration and the Foundations of International Law*
Itamar Mann

126 *Beyond Human Rights: The Legal Status of the Individual in International Law*
Anne Peters

125 *The Doctrine of Odious Debt in International Law: A Restatement*
Jeff King

124 *Static and Evolutive Treaty Interpretation: A Functional Reconstruction*
Christian Djeffal

123 *Civil Liability in Europe for Terrorism-Related Risk*
Lucas Bergkamp, Michael Faure, Monika Hinteregger and Niels Philipsen

122 *Proportionality and Deference in Investor-State Arbitration: Balancing Investment Protection and Regulatory Autonomy*
Caroline Henckels

121 *International Law and Governance of Natural Resources in Conflict and Post-Conflict Situations*
Daniëlla Dam-de Jong

120 *Proof of Causation in Tort Law*
Sandy Steel

119 *The Formation and Identification of Rules of Customary International Law in International Investment Law*
Patrick Dumberry

118 *Religious Hatred and International Law: The Prohibition of Incitement to Violence or Discrimination*
Jeroen Temperman

117 *Taking Economic, Social and Cultural Rights Seriously in International Criminal Law*
Evelyne Schmid

116 *Climate Change Litigation: Regulatory Pathways to Cleaner Energy*
Jacqueline Peel and Hari M. Osofsky

115 *Mestizo International Law: A Global Intellectual History 1842–1933*
Arnulf Becker Lorca

114 *Sugar and the Making of International Trade Law*
Michael Fakhri

113 *Strategically Created Treaty Conflicts and the Politics of International Law*
Surabhi Ranganathan

112 *Investment Treaty Arbitration As Public International Law: Procedural Aspects and Implications*
Eric De Brabandere

111 *The New Entrants Problem in International Fisheries Law*
Andrew Serdy

110 *Substantive Protection under Investment Treaties: A Legal and Economic Analysis*
Jonathan Bonnitcha

109 *Popular Governance of Post-Conflict Reconstruction: The Role of International Law*
Matthew Saul

108 *Evolution of International Environmental Regimes: The Case of Climate Change*
Simone Schiele

107 *Judges, Law and War: The Judicial Development of International Humanitarian Law*
Shane Darcy

106 *Religious Offence and Human Rights: The Implications of Defamation of Religions*
Lorenz Langer

105 *Forum Shopping in International Adjudication: The Role of Preliminary Objections*
Luiz Eduardo Salles

104 *Domestic Politics and International Human Rights Tribunals: The Problem of Compliance*
Courtney Hillebrecht

103 *International Law and the Arctic*
Michael Byers

102 *Cooperation in the Law of Transboundary Water Resources*
Christina Leb

101 *Underwater Cultural Heritage and International Law*
Sarah Dromgoole

100 *State Responsibility: The General Part*
James Crawford

99 *The Origins of International Investment Law: Empire, Environment and the Safeguarding of Capital*
Kate Miles

98 *The Crime of Aggression under the Rome Statute of the International Criminal Court*
Carrie McDougall

97 *'Crimes against Peace' and International Law*
Kirsten Sellars

96 *Non-Legality in International Law: Unruly Law*
Fleur Johns

95 *Armed Conflict and Displacement: The Protection of Refugees and Displaced Persons under International Humanitarian Law*
Mélanie Jacques

94 *Foreign Investment and the Environment in International Law*
Jorge E. Viñuales

93 *The Human Rights Treaty Obligations of Peacekeepers*
Kjetil Mujezinović Larsen

92 *Cyber Warfare and the Laws of War*
Heather Harrison Dinniss

91 *The Right to Reparation in International Law for Victims of Armed Conflict*
Christine Evans

90 *Global Public Interest in International Investment Law*
Andreas Kulick

89 *State Immunity in International Law*
Xiaodong Yang

88 *Reparations and Victim Support in the International Criminal Court*
Conor McCarthy

87 *Reducing Genocide to Law: Definition, Meaning, and the Ultimate Crime*
Payam Akhavan

86 *Decolonising International Law: Development, Economic Growth and the Politics of Universality*
Sundhya Pahuja

85 *Complicity and the Law of State Responsibility*
Helmut Philipp Aust

84 *State Control over Private Military and Security Companies in Armed Conflict*
Hannah Tonkin

83 *'Fair and Equitable Treatment' in International Investment Law*
Roland Kläger

82 *The UN and Human Rights: Who Guards the Guardians?*
Guglielmo Verdirame

81 *Sovereign Defaults before International Courts and Tribunals*
Michael Waibel

80 *Making the Law of the Sea: A Study in the Development of International Law*
James Harrison

79 *Science and the Precautionary Principle in International Courts and Tribunals: Expert Evidence, Burden of Proof and Finality*
Caroline E. Foster

78 *Transition from Illegal Regimes under International Law*
Yaël Ronen

77 *Access to Asylum: International Refugee Law and the Globalisation of Migration Control*
Thomas Gammeltoft-Hansen

76 *Trading Fish, Saving Fish: The Interaction between Regimes in International Law*
Margaret A. Young

75 *The Individual in the International Legal System: Continuity and Change in International Law*
Kate Parlett

74 *'Armed Attack' and Article 51 of the UN Charter: Evolutions in Customary Law and Practice*
Tom Ruys

73 *Theatre of the Rule of Law: Transnational Legal Intervention in Theory and Practice*
Stephen Humphreys

72 *Science and Risk Regulation in International Law*
Jacqueline Peel

71 *The Participation of States in International Organisations: The Role of Human Rights and Democracy*
Alison Duxbury

70 *Legal Personality in International Law*
Roland Portmann

69 *Vicarious Liability in Tort: A Comparative Perspective*
Paula Giliker

68 *The Public International Law Theory of Hans Kelsen: Believing in Universal Law*
Jochen von Bernstorff

67 *Legitimacy and Legality in International Law: An Interactional Account*
Jutta Brunnée and Stephen J. Toope

66 *The Concept of Non-International Armed Conflict in International Humanitarian Law*
Anthony Cullen

65 *The Principle of Legality in International and Comparative Criminal Law*
Kenneth S. Gallant

64 *The Challenge of Child Labour in International Law*
Franziska Humbert

63 *Shipping Interdiction and the Law of the Sea*
Douglas Guilfoyle

62 *International Courts and Environmental Protection*
Tim Stephens

61 *Legal Principles in WTO Disputes*
Andrew D. Mitchell

60 *War Crimes in Internal Armed Conflicts*
Eve La Haye

59 *Humanitarian Occupation*
Gregory H. Fox

58 *The International Law of Environmental Impact Assessment: Process, Substance and Integration*
Neil Craik

57 *The Law and Practice of International Territorial Administration: Versailles to Iraq and Beyond*
Carsten Stahn

56 *United Nations Sanctions and the Rule of Law*
Jeremy Matam Farrall

55 *National Law in WTO Law: Effectiveness and Good Governance in the World Trading System*
Sharif Bhuiyan

54 *Cultural Products and the World Trade Organization*
Tania Voon

53 *The Threat of Force in International Law*
Nikolas Stürchler

52 *Indigenous Rights and United Nations Standards: Self-Determination, Culture and Land*
Alexandra Xanthaki

51 *International Refugee Law and Socio-Economic Rights: Refuge from Deprivation*
Michelle Foster

50 *The Protection of Cultural Property in Armed Conflict*
Roger O'Keefe

49 *Interpretation and Revision of International Boundary Decisions*
Kaiyan Homi Kaikobad

48 *Multinationals and Corporate Social Responsibility: Limitations and Opportunities in International Law*
Jennifer A. Zerk

47 *Judiciaries within Europe: A Comparative Review*
John Bell

46 *Law in Times of Crisis: Emergency Powers in Theory and Practice*
Oren Gross and Fionnuala Ní Aoláin

45 *Vessel-Source Marine Pollution: The Law and Politics of International Regulation*
Alan Khee-Jin Tan

44 *Enforcing Obligations* Erga Omnes *in International Law*
Christian J. Tams

43 *Non-Governmental Organisations in International Law*
Anna-Karin Lindblom

42 *Democracy, Minorities and International Law*
Steven Wheatley

41 *Prosecuting International Crimes: Selectivity and the International Criminal Law Regime*
Robert Cryer

40 *Compensation for Personal Injury in English, German and Italian Law: A Comparative Outline*
Basil Markesinis, Michael Coester, Guido Alpa and Augustus Ullstein

39 *Dispute Settlement in the UN Convention on the Law of the Sea*
Natalie Klein

38 *The International Protection of Internally Displaced Persons*
Catherine Phuong

37 *Imperialism, Sovereignty and the Making of International Law*
Antony Anghie

35 *Necessity, Proportionality and the Use of Force by States*
Judith Gardam

34 *International Legal Argument in the Permanent Court of International Justice: The Rise of the International Judiciary*
Ole Spiermann

32 *Great Powers and Outlaw States: Unequal Sovereigns in the International Legal Order*
Gerry Simpson

31 *Local Remedies in International Law* (second edition)
Chittharanjan Felix Amerasinghe

30 *Reading Humanitarian Intervention: Human Rights and the Use of Force in International Law*
Anne Orford

29 *Conflict of Norms in Public International Law: How WTO Law Relates to Other Rules of International Law*
Joost Pauwelyn

27 *Transboundary Damage in International Law*
Hanqin Xue

25 *European Criminal Procedures*
Edited by Mireille Delmas-Marty and J. R. Spencer

24 *Accountability of Armed Opposition Groups in International Law*
Liesbeth Zegveld

23 *Sharing Transboundary Resources: International Law and Optimal Resource Use*
Eyal Benvenisti

22 *International Human Rights and Humanitarian Law*
René Provost

21 *Remedies against International Organisations*
Karel Wellens

20 *Diversity and Self-Determination in International Law*
Karen Knop

19 *The Law of Internal Armed Conflict*
Lindsay Moir

18 *International Commercial Arbitration and African States: Practice, Participation and Institutional Development*
Amazu A. Asouzu

17 *The Enforceability of Promises in European Contract Law*
James Gordley

16 *International Law in Antiquity*
David J. Bederman

15 *Money Laundering: A New International Law Enforcement Model*
Guy Stessens

14 *Good Faith in European Contract Law*
Reinhard Zimmermann and Simon Whittaker

13 *On Civil Procedure*
J. A. Jolowicz

12 *Trusts: A Comparative Study*
Maurizio Lupoi and Simon Dix

11 *The Right to Property in Commonwealth Constitutions*
Tom Allen

10 *International Organizations before National Courts*
August Reinisch

9 *The Changing International Law of High Seas Fisheries*
Francisco Orrego Vicuña

8 *Trade and the Environment: A Comparative Study of EC and US Law*
Damien Geradin

7 *Unjust Enrichment: A Study of Private Law and Public Values*
Hanoch Dagan

6 *Religious Liberty and International Law in Europe*
Malcolm D. Evans

5 *Ethics and Authority in International Law*
Alfred P. Rubin

4 *Sovereignty over Natural Resources: Balancing Rights and Duties*
Nico Schrijver

3 *The Polar Regions and the Development of International Law*
Donald R. Rothwell

2 *Fragmentation and the International Relations of Micro-States: Self-Determination and Statehood*
Jorri C. Duursma

1 *Principles of the Institutional Law of International Organizations*
C. F. Amerasinghe